Jumbos and Jumping Devils

Jumbos and Jumping Devils

A Social History of Indian Circus

Nisha P R

OXFORD

UNIVERSITY PRESS

OXFORD
UNIVERSITY PRESS

Oxford University Press is a department of the University of Oxford.
It furthers the University's objective of excellence in research, scholarship,
and education by publishing worldwide. Oxford is a registered trademark of
Oxford University Press in the UK and in certain other countries.

Published in India by
Oxford University Press
22 Workspace, 2nd Floor, 1/22 Asaf Ali Road, New Delhi 110002, India

© Oxford University Press, 2020

The moral rights of the author have been asserted.

First Edition published in 2020

ISBN-13 (print edition): 978-0-19-949670-9
ISBN-10 (print edition): 0-19-949670-6

ISBN-13 (eBook): 978-0-19-099207-1
ISBN-10 (eBook): 0-19-099207-7

Typeset in ITC Giovanni Std 9.5/13
by Tranistics Data Technologies, Kolkata 700 091
Printed in India by Rakmo Press, New Delhi 110 020

Disclaimer: Every effort has been made to trace the copyright holders of Figures 2.3, 2.4, 3.1, 3.2, 4.1, 4.2, and C.1. The publisher would be pleased to hear from the copyright owner so that proper acknowledgement can be made in future editions.

Contents

Images

Images

Acknowledgements

This book grew out of many tents; both in circus and the academia.

Late Biswamoy Pati, Dilip Menon, and Mahesh Rangarajan, supervisors of my doctoral research, have always made sure that the show goes on.

Dr Pati, I sincerely wish and pray that you are holding this book wherever you are. Dr Dilip taught me the *art* of researching. I am very grateful for the support and interest you have shown in my work over the years. I will always cherish my days in South Africa as a 'Witsie'. Dr Mahesh, thank you for broadening my outlook and perspective, for the warmth and concern, for the critiques that shaped this work, and for being a treasure of resources.

My gratitude to the circus community is beyond words.

In Kerala: late Prabhakarettan, Ramaniyechi, Raviyettan, Sukumarettan and late Sunitiyechi, Kausuechi (Chirakkuni), Kausuechi (Melur), Raghavettan, K. K. Sreedhrettan, P. Sreedharettan, M. Sridharettan, Karimkka, Reejechi and Babuettan, Vasanthechi, Anithechi, Pushpechi, Nazeerkka, Rajettan, Narayanan master, Yamunechi, Kiran, Stephettan and Daisiechi, late Springnet Naranettan and Umadeviyechi, Saraswathiyechi and Bhaskarettan, all those who interacted with me in Galaxy, Gemini, Jumbo, Royal, and Rambo circuses, circus union leaders C. C. Asok Kumar and late K. V. Raghavan, trainers, wardens, and children of the Kerala Circus Academy, C. M. Ramachandran, circus owners Chandran, Gemini Sankaran, Asok Sankar and Ajay Sankar, Dilipnath, Prakashan, Kamala amma and late Mukundettan at Kamalalayam, Edward Williams (Keeleri uncle) and family, and Radha Kannan.

In Maharashtra: late Parasuram Maliji and family in Sangli; Rajendra Deval and family in Miraj; Umesh Akashe bhayya, Janaki More and family, Amul bhayya, Rahulji, Dilip and Sujit Dilip in Pune; and Bhagwantrao D. More in Mumbai.

Many thanks to B. Priyaranjanlal for the cover design, Pooja Jain for the cover image, and Agoston of Rambo Circus for the majestic pose for Pooja's work.

Staff and teachers at the Department of History, University of Delhi—Ankita, Sanjeev bhayya, Shahid Amin, Raizuddin Aquil, Prabhu Mohapatra, Yasser Arafath, Aparna Balachandran, Sunil Kumar, Upinder Singh, and Amar Farooqui.

I am grateful to the Centre for Studies in Social Sciences Calcutta (CSSSC), Kolkata, and Purnujjal Trust for selecting me as the first recipient of the Papiya Ghosh Memorial Fellowship; and to Tuktuk Kumar, the late Anjan Ghosh, Partha Chatterjee, Gautam Bhadra, Tapati Guha Takurta, and Ranjana Dasgupta for being the amazing people they are.

The Indian Council of Historical Research (ICHR) fellowship has always been a boon for research scholars in Indian universities.

The Swedish South Asian Studies Network (SASNET) short-term postdoctoral fellowship gave me the opportunity to explore Scandinavia and the European academia. My thanks to Professor Anna Lindberg, Lars Eklund, Bubu-di, Pernille Gooch, Andreas Johansson, Andreas Mattson, Jacco Visser, and Ravinder Kaur.

The Charles Wallace Grant opened for me the door to the vast collections of the British Library and the National Fairground Archives, Sheffield. Thanks to Richard Alford and the CWT, Professor Venessa Toulmin, and Professor Rosie Thomas.

The Social Science Research Council (SSRC) Transregional Fellowship was a great bonus to the historian and to the wanderlust in me. My transnational research in Uganda, Kenya, Tanzania, Ethiopia, and Nepal, as well as my stint at the international conference on 'Circus Histories and Theories' at the Centre for Indian Studies in Africa, Johannesburg, could not have been realized without the enormous monetary and academic support from SSRC. The inter-Asia workshops in Delhi and Chiang Mai provided me with a whole lot of connections and networking opportunities.

The 2020 Writing Fellowship with Johannesburg Institute for Advanced Study was an honour and boost for my ongoing research in Africa.

Udaya Kumar, Janaki Nair, Gunnel Cederlof, Indrani Chatterjee, Isabel Hofmeyer, Vivek Dhareswar, Nizar Ahammed, late R. Viswanathan, late M. S. S. Pandian, Artist Marar Mash, R. Nandakumar, E. V. Ramakrishnan, Janaki Sreedharan, and Vineetha Menon are warmly remembered for their love, kindness, and help.

To all the librarians and archivists who made me undergo the pain and pleasure that only historical research can bring, thanks to:

Department libraries, Central Library, and Ratan Tata Library at the University of Delhi, Nehru Memorial Museum and Library, Jawaharlal Nehru University Library, Indira Gandhi National Centre for the Arts (IGNCA) Library, V. V. Giri National Labor Institute, National Archives, American Institute of Indian Studies, Sahitya Academy Library, ICHR Library, Central Secretariat Library, and Ajoy Bhavan Library in Delhi; University of Kannur Library, Victoria Memorial and Sporting Youth libraries, Government Brennen College Library, and Melur and Chirakkuni libraries at Thalassery; Anveshi and Public Library at Kozhikode; Bombay University Library, Maharashtra State Archives, Centre for Education Documentation (CED) in Mumbai; CSSSCAL, Kolkata; Indo-American Centre for International Studies, Hyderabad; Centre for Development Studies, Sri Chithira Thirunal Library, Public Library, Natural History Museum Library, University of Kerala Library, AKG Centre Library, and CPI State Office Library in Thiruvananthapuram; Centre for the Study of Culture and Society (CSCS) Library, Bangalore; Lund University and Malmo University Library, Sweden; The British Library, United Kingdom; Hebrew University of Jerusalem, Israel; and University of Johannesburg Library and William Cullen Library, South Africa.

Without the help and passion for research of K. P. Abdul Majeed, archivist at Kozhikode Archives, I would not have been able to find many things. I am also immensely grateful to Champa-di (NMML), Anil (Thiruvananthapuram Museum Library), Vijayalakshmi chechi (Delhi University History Department Library), Ruksana and Rajani (Kerala University Library), Matthew Neill (National Fairground Archives, UK), and Robert Cline (Circus Historical Society, USA).

Over the years, this research has been presented at various academic conferences and universities. I am grateful to all those who listened and responded to it at Indian Institute of Sciences, Bangalore; English and Foreign Languages University, Shillong; Indian Institute of Advanced Study, Shimla; CSSSC; Nehru Memorial Museum and Library NMML, Jamia Millia Islamia University, Jawaharlal Nehru University, and Ambedkar University, Delhi, India; University of Witwatersrand and University of Johannesburg, South Africa; Lund University and Linnaeus University, Sweden; Rutgers University, USA; The Hebrew University of Jerusalem, Israel; Aarhus University, Denmark; University of Kelaniya, Sri Lanka; University of Zagreb, Croatia; the 10th International Convention of Asian Scholars in Thailand, European Conference on South Asian Studies in Paris, France, the Association for Asian Studies (AAS)-in-Asia Conference in Delhi, India, and the Japanese Association of South Asia Studies Conference in Tokyo, Japan.

I express my gratitude to the members of 3 X Rien, the French circus company; SAI, Thalassery; CVN Kalari, Thiruvangad and Thiruvananthapuram; Dr Charles Chandra, Shivadasapillai, and S. Abu at Thiruvananthapuram Zoo; and Yesoda Bai IFS, Tirupati Zoo.

I thank Manuprasad, the best friend I ever had; Shibani, for a 'home' in Delhi; Noushad, for trusting me always; Sasi, for the foody food-filled JNU evenings; Meera, my missing friend; Sreebitha, for all the laughter we shared together; Chitra, for the still-cherished childhood memories; Latifa Mrisho, for our red-wine moments; Laone Tsimakoko, my most beautiful guest; Sonia, for all the songs she sang for me; Jana, for the spontaneous friendship; Yosef Sintayehu, for being a brother-friend.

I am also grateful to Gustav, Jeremy, Ambika, Pedro, Lee, Malcom, Asma, Tim, Anna, Diana, Lyn Ossome, Tosin, Jake, Liz Gunner, Nazime and family, Paul Keil, Gabriele Ciampini, Soren Hoyner, Jayashree, Bash, Bikki, Brena, Monalisa, Kageso, Freda Mama, Senayon, Sajiyettan, Abbas, Mussa, Prasun Chatterjee, Moutushi Mukherjee, Ravinder Kaur, Anjali and Jayshankar, Blessy, Vinita, Vishal, Lathika, Shaji, Shimna, Suleesh, Ratheesh and, Sameena, Tshimangadzo Mugwena, Roy, Robert Batra, Shilpi Rajpal, Jiji, Amith, Shimna, Bindu Menon, Aravind Menon, Jugoslav Paser, Tal Dranitzki, Professor Gideon Shelach-Lavi, Bindu KC, Vibodh Parthasarathi, Rosmin Mathew, Reshma Bharadwaj, Aryan, Arathy, Minto, Sachin and, Divya, Praveen, Father Felix and,

Sister Elise, Manu and, Rose, Deepa, Vinod, Priyaranjanlal, Aadithyan, Amrith, Vidya Ravindranath, Sreevasudeva and Narayana Bhattathiris, Gyothir Ghosh, Dhiraj Kumar, Jonathan Sojohanson Andrew, Bhuvan Ribhu, Harikrishnan, Dr Bongani Ngqulunga, Professor Paul Bouissac, Dr Brenda Assael, Dr C. S. Venkiteswaran, Dr J. Devika, Dr Indrani Sen, Professor R. C. Thakran, Dr G. Balachandran, Professor Rita, Dr Chitra Joshi, Priya Konthoujam, Angira Mukherjee, Sana Fathima, Kaveri, Reshmi, Sonia, Ajayan chettan and Megha, Salam, Suniti, Clive, Rohan Deb Roy, Moa Peterson, Sujeewa, Sudarshini, Abid, the hostel warden Rosamma, Chandanji at the Board of Research Studies in Delhi University, and also the tea vendor Gopalji and the chole-kulche vendor Bhanti bhayya.

Thanks also to:

Late Thampi Valliachan and Kamala Valiyamma for the love and affection.

My niece, Akshara, who accompanied me to many circus tents and her younger sister, Nakshatra, who always wanted to come along but was too young; hugs and kisses to both.

My late father, A. C. Gopalakrishnan, who would have found so many 'mistakes' in the following pages and would have said proudly that 'she is the first doctoral degree holder in the family'. I miss having those bread toasts and too-sugary tea at midnight with him when I lost sleep while writing.

Jack, the dog, and the cats of Thalassery, Thiruvananthapuram, and the Johannesburg homes, especially, Muthus and Kunjammo.

My late mother-in-law, K. G. Vijayamma, for sharing her space, stories, recipes, and love; Jayan chettan whom I have never met and never will.

I am grateful to those invisible hands that held me and always gifted new surprises. Just as I have been trying to fill the gaps in my writing, this book has also been shaping me. There were times in my life when this work was my only pleasure.

This book is dedicated to the memory of my mother P. R. Komalam, to my life partner S. Sanjeev, and to all those in circus.

Introduction

One Step inside the Ring

In 1955, a group of friends who were famous writers, journalists, and actors from the erstwhile princely state of Travancore in the south made a trip to the northern state of Malabar. The times were chaotic. The new territorial unit, Kerala, would come into being the next year as part of the Indian Union, merging three regions—Travancore, Cochin, and Malabar.

Although common culture and language were being upheld as the integrating agents, they were highly contentious terrains.[1] In this context, the trip made by the southern luminaries could definitely be read as a prominent instance of treading into the 'unknown'. The travelogue 'Malabaarilekku oru Ethinottam' (A peep into Malabar) written by K. Balakrishnan, a renowned writer and editor amongst them, and published in his *Kaumudi Weekly* in 1955 lay bare such anxieties and predicaments. Let us take up one such defining dilemma from Balakrishnan's interesting text. The following incident happened while the group was staying at the home of the eminent short-story

---

[1] S. Sanjeev, 'On Castes, Malayalams and Translations', in *Translation in Asia: Theories, Histories, Practices*, eds Ronit Ricci and Jan van der Putten (Oxon and New York: Routledge, 2014), 168.

writer Pattathuvila Karunakaran in Kozhikode, one of the major towns in Malabar:

> The next morning, we saw a strange figure at the veranda of the neighbouring house. A beautiful girl of about eighteen years in a bright green skirt and blouse stretching forward with her hands held high, with a firm grip on the block above the door. She slowly lifted from the ground, hanging on to the hands and then came down bending backwards, like a ballerina. She must have not seen us. For us, such a performance on the veranda was weird and we right away came to the conclusion that the house is 'indecent' and the girl is 'licentious'.
>
> 'Watching the circus?' we heard our host asking. Then only we realized it was a circus camp. That girl was reminding us that Malabar tops the circus rings in India; as if the dynamism in the circus arena follows her everywhere in life.[2]

The angst about the feminine other in this masculine tourist 'peep' is strikingly obvious. But what is equally striking is that a popular and overriding narrative comes in handy for conflict resolution: circus and Malabar.

Unlike the other two regions that went into the making of Kerala, Malabar had been under direct British rule. The town of Thalassery[3] in north Malabar was a major trade point and also the judicial centre of the British administration. Thalassery still figures in the postcolonial imaginary as a showpiece of the colonial heritage. For instance, the official website of Kerala State Tourism Department brags that '[i]t [Thalassery] is often called the city of "three Cs" in the state—cricket, cake, and circus. It is the place where the British first played cricket, the first cakes introduced by the British were baked here in the Mambally's Royal Biscuit Factory, and Indian circus had its origins in this town as well.'[4]

---

[2] K. Balakrishnan, 'Malabaarilekku oru Ethinottam' [A peep into Malabar], *Kaumudi Weekly*, Malayalam Era 1131 Midhunam 4–Karkidakam 15 (7 issues), reprinted in *Kaumudi Special Edition* (July–September, 2009): 27; all translations from Malayalam are mine, unless specified.

[3] 'Tellicherry' in colonial parlance and records; I will be following the Malayalam 'Thalassery'.

[4] Available at http://www.keralatourism.org/kerala-article/212/historic-thalassery.php, last accessed on 14 November 2012.

Sreedharan Champad, a retired circus artiste and writer who has penned half a dozen novels and quite a few articles and books on circus in Malayalam, notes in his web blog *The Big Top* that 'the great master of circus Keeleri Kunhikannan teacher belongs to Thalassery, Kerala, so Thalassery is known as the maternity [*sic*] home of Indian circus art.'[5] M. T. Vasudevan Nair, one of the most renowned Malayalam writers in the country, goes overboard claiming that 'circus is a universal physical art like *kalaripayatt* or *kathakali* which Keralam can rightly claim as its own; Keralam's gift to the universe'.[6] The walls of many restaurants in Thalassery proudly display images of the 'three Cs' and the bearers would be more than happy to enlighten the visitors about this glorious past. Popular representations and common sense have always let this imaginary flourish. Generations have grown up amidst this fable and I am no exception. In fact, it brought me into this research when I started knowing and understanding lives from the other side of the circus fable.

The Circus Town

My student life at the Department of Studies in English at Kannur University's Palayad campus in Thalassery has a lot to do with my interest in circus. I used to reach the campus early—my home is about 15 kilometres away—during my MPhil coursework, which began at 10:30 in the morning. Sweeper women were the only people around and I naturally struck up friendships with them. One of them was a retired circus artiste, Anitha. One day she stopped coming and I came to know that she had been dismissed from the job. She lived near the campus and when I went to meet her, she told me that a new order of the Government Employment Exchange stipulated 8th standard school education as the minimum qualification for university sweepers. She had only gone to school for two or three years and then joined the circus. Anithechy[7] informed me that many of the circus artistes have no

---

[5] Available at http://sreedharanchampad.blogspot.in/search?q=home%, last accessed on 20 November 2012.

[6] M. T. Vasudevan Nair, *Ramaneeyam Oru Kalam* [Beautiful times] (Thiruvananthapuram: Maluben, 1998), 149.

[7] 'Elder sister' in Malayalam; often appended to a name to express respect and intimacy.

more than primary education. I realized that this meant that once they left the circus ring they would not be eligible even for menial jobs in the public sector. This made me think and, with the help of Anithechy, I met some other women in the neighbouring area who were also in the circus.[8] I started realizing that the town and especially the places around the campus were mostly populated by circus people, far from the mythical tales about the 'origin of circus'—Melur, Andalur, Kavumbhagam, Dharmadam, Chirakkuni, Vadakkumbad, and Kathirur. For decades, hundreds of men and women had been joining the circuses around the country in various capacities—as artistes, ring boys, trainers, technicians, and entrepreneurs.[9]

The project I had in mind at the time was to study the women and the configurations of gender in circus. We may recall the nervousness of the southern celebrities when they saw the 'strange figure' doing 'weird' things with her body on the veranda of a house. In no time they had reached the conclusion that 'the house is indecent and the girl is licentious'. If the performance of the female body on the verandah of a house could stir up such repugnance, one can only imagine what would have been the reaction of a society in the first half of the twentieth century deeply entrenched in Brahminical patriarchy towards the women who roamed around the subcontinent performing amazing feats with their bodies in skimpy attire. But as I moved along, I recognized the need to place circus in a broader framework of history, addressing other crucial questions such as physical cultures, animal life, and technologies. I will not be pondering over the linear and sequential order of 'firsts' or 'origins' or 'fathers' (originators), not only because of a critical understanding of conventional historiographies but also because I have arrived at the arena via the aforesaid course.

My attempt would obviously have cracks and fissures as I have gone through many moments of uncertainties and ambiguities throughout

---

[8] Nisha P R, 'Vishamam Kondum, Ishtam Kondum: Stree Circus Kalakarikalude Athmakathanangal' [Out of misery, out of love: autobiographical narrations of women circus artists], *Pachakuthira* 2 (10) (2006): 5–7.

[9] A 1968 think-piece notes that there are 48 circus companies owned by Keralites and approximately 95 per cent acrobats from the subcontinent are Malayalis; Balachandran, 'Viswavijnanam 2000 Chodyangalil' [Global knowledge in 2000 questions], *Janayugam* 37 (xi) (1968): 16.

the research. What I have tried to do is to explore some key moments and aspects in different spaces of circus in this part of the world, spanning over 150 years. I have no inclination for establishing 'centres' and 'fathers'. An accidental rendezvous and chat with an old scholar in his late seventies at The Nehru Memorial Museum and Library in Delhi might well sum up the dilemmas I am trying to put forth. The veteran scholar began the chat with some criticisms of Nehru as a statesman and then enquired about my topic. He said that circus is a very good subject and an area that definitely needs research. He also believed the problems of the circus community should be brought into the mainstream. Then, he shot the crucial query: In what ways would research on circus enrich 'knowledge'? How will it benefit the society at large?

For me, these reservations were not at all unfamiliar. Many a time I have received responses from outside the academic community such as 'why don't you choose something serious for a doctoral study?' accompanied by a wry grin. From the peers, the responses have mostly been: 'A wonderful subject! But is there any circus left now?' Many of them expressed doubts regarding the extent of its past, conveniently forgetting that cinema has also only that much history. Responses from the circus community on the other hand are entirely different. The majority of them—both retired and active—were happy to share their memories and memorabilia with me. Even when they did not quite understand the kind of work I have undertaken (some thought I was a journalist, some others believed I was a representative of a government survey), they trusted me and believed that something 'good' will come to the community with my work, such as a raise in their pensions/salaries or better labour laws and working conditions. At the same time, my fieldwork had caused blood-pressure variations in some owners and managers. With recent legislations and bans on using wild animals and employing children, they reasonably misread the 'researcher' as a guise for some law enforcement body or non-governmental organization.

Circus in the subcontinent is deeply embedded with the arrival of the modern, the remaking of caste and gender hierarchies, the transformation of physical cultures, bodies, and performances, the expansion of itinerant entertainment, the emergence of new trans-regional and transnational spaces, the interventions of the colonial and the postcolonial states on nature, humans, and animals, and the development of various technologies. I am sure the idea of the production of knowledge around these fields should have satisfied the sceptic in that old scholar. But the stumbling block before anyone working on the vocation and life of beings on the margin is the glaring absence and invisibility of them in conventional archives.

Shahid Amin, eminent historian and one of the founders of *Subaltern Studies*, points out in his lecture 'Walking in and out of Archives' that if subalterns do not figure in the official archives, it could only mean that those archives exist outside the official spaces.[10] But while attempting a history of circus in this part of the world, the major challenge one faces is not only the absence of state archival sources but also non-statist sources, such as personal histories, memoirs, or diaries. It might be interesting to note here that numerous life stories, biographies, historical studies, and literary works have been published on circuses in Australia, Europe, and the United States of America. While some works are available on the circus in East Asia, South-East Asia, South Asia, and Africa are yet to be explored.[11] In the Indian subcontinent, Kerala and Maharashtra have a rich past in circus acrobatics, animal training, and entrepreneurship. But books on circus are rare, even though Kerala boasts of being one of the most vibrant print cultures supplemented by a 100 per cent literacy rate.

Circus in the Academia

Most of us must have been to circus at one point in life or another. But while popular culture, body, performance, and marginal communities

---

[10] Shahid Amin, 'Walking In and Out of Archives', inaugural address of the workshop 'Reckoning with the Past: History in the Classroom' at Khalsa College, University of Delhi, 12 November 2010.

[11] It seems that the world circus itself has faced this neglect to some extent. Marius Kwint observes about the English circus: 'Until recently, the circus has both provided plentiful stereotypes and has been the subject of detailed specialist scholarship, but it has been surprisingly neglected by more mainstream social and cultural historians.' See Kwint Marius, 'Circus and Nature in Late Georgian England', in *Histories of Leisure*, ed. Rudy Koshar (New York: Oxford University Press, 2002), 75.

are being widely studied in university departments and films are, in fact, being written about in 'excess', circus remains a totally unexplored area in South Asia. On the other hand, circus figures prominently in the common sense as an awful and exploitative space with abused women and children, crudely and cruelly treated animals, primitive labour relations, and extremely dangerous working conditions. We shall bear in mind here that the majority of circus people are from 'lower' classes and castes.

We have noted earlier the fear and anxiety about the women who perform with their body in public. During my fieldwork, many of the female artistes were reluctant to share their photos. Their grown children thought those 'half naked' photos of their mothers disgraced the family. It is a past they want to leave behind. A major Malayalam film producer and distributor, N. G. John, narrates an interesting story in his autobiography about his father's decision to not distribute Gemini Vasan's magnum opus *Chandralekha* (1948) in Kerala because of the 'indecent exposure' of the heroine's body in some scenes depicting the circus: '[in] the low angle shots in the circus scenes in which T R Rajakumary is performing on the trapeze, the thighs were visible. [Father said] they were provocative shots and should be deleted.' Vasan refused and said they were meant to be provocative and his company Gemini distributed the film in Kerala and it was a huge hit.[12]

The stigma of the profession haunts the other gender too. A Nepali male artiste in Jumbo Circus told me that circus artistes are not respected in his land, while a Bengali artiste told me that he was finding it difficult to get a suitable proposal for his daughter because of his vocation. The attitude of other cultures also seems to be compatible with this information. Paul Bouissac notes in his semiotic study of the circus how 'some people think of the circus as a meaningless remnant of an ancient tradition' and that circus seems to be both '"within" and "outside" culture'.[13] As we all know, the word 'circus' is commonly

[12] N. G. John, *Cinemayum Njanum: 70 Varshangal* [Cinema and me: 70 years] (Kottayam: D. C. Books, 2012), 25.

[13] Paul Bouissac, *Circus and Culture: A Semiotic Approach* (Bloomington: Indiana University Press, 1976), 6–7.

deployed for many a preposterous thing; 'political circus' to cite the
most common of these.[14]

Circus has figured occasionally in literature and cinema. The aforementioned perceptions must have definitely fired the imagination of
those who conceived of these representations.[15] There are a few literary
works in Assamese, Bengali, Kannada, Hindi, Malayalam, and Marathi
based on Indian circus. But hardly any of these have been translated into
other languages. They do not seem to appear in the mainstream literary
world either. A glaring instance is the half a dozen novels representing
the circus world published in Malayalam by circus-artiste-turned-writer
Sreedharan Champad. To most Malayali readers, Champad is still a
marginal writer. For that matter, a reader here will have to look at an
American novel such as *The Son of Circus* by John Irving for a portrayal
of Indian circus. Interestingly, the autobiography *Wild Animal Man*
(1961) of the internationally renowned circus-animal trainer from
Pune, Damoo Dhotre—the only autobiography of its kind in all
probability—had also been published in English in the United States
of America. *Wild Animal Man* was translated into Dhotre's mother

---

[14] For instance, 'With elections around the corner, AAP circus back in town;
Kejriwal spends night in Tihar' (*Hindustan Times*, 21 May 2014); 'The surreal
world of Pakistan's "political circus"' (BBC News, 5 September 2014); 'Republic
Circus' (Cartoon), 'Jeevitha Circus [Life circus]' (Story) (*Mathrubhumi Illustrated
Weekly*, 22 January 1956 and 27 May 1956).

[15] *Naayaru Pidicha Pulivalu* (Malayalam, 1958, Dir: P. Bhaskaran), *Thambu*
(Malayalam, 1978, Dir: G. Aravindan), *Mera Naam Joker* (Hindi, 1970, Dir:
Raj Kapoor), *Mela* (Malayalam, 1980, Dir: K. G. George), *Valarthu Mrugangal*
(Malayalam, 1981, Dir: Hariharan), *Apoorva Sagodharargal* (Tamil, 1989, Dir:
Singeetam Srinivasa Rao), *Kabuliwalah* (Malayalam, 1993, Dir: Siddique-Lal),
Joker (Malayalam, 2000, Dir: A. K. Lohithadas), and *Ee Pattanathil Bhootham*
(Malayalam, 2009, Dir: Johny Antony) are the major films that have come out
over the past 50 years, almost entirely based on circus life. It should be noted
that not only 'popular' films but also 'art/parallel' cinema—*Thambu* (Malayalam,
1978), *Mela* (Malayalam, 1980), *Valarthu Mrugangal* (Malayalam)—has represented the lives in tents. In drama, some of the notable attempts are Sundaran
Kallayi's *Trapezium* of the 1980s and the recent *Clowns and Clouds* (2013) by
Abhilash Pillai. The TV series on Doordarshan called *Circus* (1989–90), directed
by Aziz Mirza and Kundan Shah, with the debut appearance of the Bollywood
superstar Shahrukh Khan, was very popular.

tongue, Marathi, years later. This extraordinary autobiographical endeavour must have been realized only because Damoo Dhotre worked with the American circus empire, the Ringling Brothers. Interestingly, Dhotre had attempted to write a history of the Indian circus. In his letter to K. P. Kesava Menon, the chief editor of *Mathrubhumi Illustrated Weekly*, dated 28 July 1962, he writes,

> I feel sure you will be interested to know that at present I am writing a very important book on Indian Circus History. I am enclosing 10 copies of my circular with a request to you to pass on [to] each one of those people who could be helpful to furnish me needed materials and information that I could use in writing Indian circus history.

He further adds, 'I wish to get full particular life history of Keeleri Kunhikannan Teacher (Circus Guru) of Tellicherry, Kerala. Also, full history of Gull mhomed [*sic*] circus, the first and oldest circus of Kerala.'[16]

It is worthwhile noting here that *Mathrubhumi Illustrated Weekly*, the most respected and popular Malayalam periodical at the time, regularly published articles and photographs on circus, including cover images, during the 1950s and 1960s. We can reasonably assume that this was due to the affection that its editor Krishna Warrier had for circus. He edited the magazine from 1952 to 1968. Krishna Warrier's love for circus comes across in a biography very warmly written by N. V. Rama Warrier, his young brother. N. V. Rama Warrier quotes a letter written by Krishna Warrier in response to the strong dislike for circus expressed by him:

> Circus is a harmless expression of adventurous action. It demonstrates certain possibilities of the human body. Circus accidents are rarer than car accidents. We don't loathe cars for that, do we? So there is no reason to detest circus. And besides, circus in India is a Keralite art and industry. So we have the responsibility to see as much as circus as possible and praise and encourage the performers.[17]

The two notable biographies of Indian circus in Malayalam had been undertaken by persons from within the circus community: Kandambulli Balan in *Circus* (1961) and Sreedharan Champad in *Circusinte Lokam*

[16] Private collection, late Shyamala Shirolker, Pune, Maharashtra.
[17] N. V. Rama Warrier, *Njangalude Kunjettan* [*Our Brother*] (Kottayam: Current books, 2000), 103–4.

(The world of circus) (2008).[18] Understandably, both endeavours have dealt in detail with the 'origins' and 'fathers', tracing and in turn constructing fabulous chronologies. Two Malayalam autobiographies, co-authored with professional writers, have been published in recent times while my doctoral project was underway; *Thamb Paranja Jeevitham* (Life told by tent) of Sreedharan Champad, and *Malakkam Mariyunna Jeevitham* (Somersaulting life), the life story of the circus owner Gemini Sankaran in 2012, and an English biography of Gemini Sankaran by Sreehari Nair, titled *Gemini Shankaran & the Legacy of Indian Circus*, as well as an English edition of Champad's *Circusinte Lokam* (The world of circus), titled *An Album of Indian Big Tops: History of Indian Circus* in 2013.

There have been some earlier attempts, such as Abanindrakrishna Basu's *Bangalir Circus* (Bengali circus) (1936), in Bengali.[19] There have also been a couple of autobiographical endeavours in Marathi, such as *Circusichya Jagaat* (The world of circus) (1961) and *Grand Circus* (1964) by S. S. Karlekar, and Bandopant Deval's *Circus Barobal Chaleez* (Along with circus for forty years) (1982). Parasuram Mali told me that he is working on a brief history of the Indian circus in Marathi.[20]

---

[18] Kandambulli Balan (1915–1971) was working as a journalist in Ceylone (Sri Lanka) when he entered the circus sphere in the late 1940s as 'organizing manager' of the tour of Kamala Circus in South East Asia. He has worked as circus manager in various circus companies, such as Bharath, Gemini, and the Great Gemini. His work, *Circus*, won him the Kerala Sahitya Academy award in 1966. V. K. Sreeraman, 'Kandambulli Balan', *Bhashaposhini* (September, 2014): 44; Sreedharan Champad was a flying trapeze artiste. Some of his novels based on circus are *Koodaram* [The tent] (2007), *Komali* [The clown] (1979), *Ring* (1987), and *Antharam* [The difference] (2004). He has acted in the film *Thampu* (1978) and collaborated with the film script for *Mela* (1980).

[19] Scholars have pointed out that Priyanath Bose, who established the Great Bengal circus, popularized the Bengali circus during the early twentieth century; Mimasha Pandit, 'Circus, Performance, and Building of National "Self"', *Feeling National: Swadeshi Circus, Performance, and Building of National Self*, July 2013. Available http://theinclusive.org/posts/2013-01-spart-03.html, last accessed on 7 December 2019; John Rosselli, 'The Self-Image of Effeteness: Physical Education and Nationalism in Nineteenth-Century Bengal', *Past & Present* 86 (February, 1980): 121–48.

[20] Interview, Parasuram Mali, Tasgaon, 25 December 2012. Mr Mali passed away in 2017.

Kandambulli Balan's *Circus* published in 1961, probably the earliest and definitely the most comprehensive book on circus in Malayalam, narrates the story of the 'origin' of circus. He points out, notably, that each country has its own claims to 'prove' the origin. He also traces back the origin of the word 'circus' to Rome. According to him, although Thomas Cook established the first circus company in 1750, it was Philip Astley who could claim 'fatherhood' of the modern circus. The narrative could be summarized thus: In 1769, Philip Astley left home to join the army. His adventures on horseback pleased the higher officials. During his wanderings he met a girl who was an expert in horse-riding and they got married. Astley found some acrobats, clowns, tightrope walkers, and knife throwers to perform for him. Thus, the modern circus came into existence.[21]

Sreedharan Champad's narrative in *Circusinte Lokam* (The world of circus) traces the origin back to Roman hippodromes and amphitheaters of the British circus by Philip Astley.[22] Some of the headings of his descriptions go on as follows: 'The Early Fathers of Circus', 'The

---

[21] Kandambulli Balan, *Circus* (Kottayam: NBS, 1961), 1–36.

[22] Sreedharan Champad, *Circusinte Lokam* [The world of circus] (Kozhikode: Mathrubhumi, 2008), 20–5; see the narrative in Charles Ricketts's book, *The Boswells: The Story of a South African Circus* (2003):

> The origins of the Circus are lost in the mists of time, and whether it evolved from the gladiatorial spectacles of Ancient Rome, or from the more refined Greek gymnasium, is largely a matter of conjecture. What is certain, however, is that Phillip Astley, an ex-Sergeant Major of the British Army conceived the circus more or less as we know it today. The year was 1768 and the place was London. He laid out a circular arena on a piece of wasteland in Lambeth between Black friars and Westminster bridges in an area known as Halfpenny Hatch. Here he established a riding school and gave demonstrations of trick riding ... to these displays of trick riding, he later added gymnastics and clowning and so formulated the beginnings of the modern circus. One of his protégés was George Hughes, who became a rider of great distinction, and through his pupils, was instrumental in the rapid spread of the Circus throughout Europe and the Americas.

Available at http://www.circusfederation.org/uploads/circus_culture/about/southafrica_boswells.pdf, last accessed on 19 November 2012.

Birth and Growth of Modern Circus', and 'The King of Modern Circus'. Writings on circus concerned with its origin mostly hang on to this Rome to Astley to 'us' route.

In a similar vein, Kandambulli Balan charts the arrival of circus in India under the title 'The Blackman's Arrogance' spread over 10 pages. The story goes like this: On 8 December 1879, the Italian circus company of William Chirni disembarked on the Bombay port. On 25 December, the Kurundvad Raja, Balasaheb, visited the circus along with his horse trainer, Vishnupanth Vinayak Chatre. A white man performed on the high trapeze and a thin metal rod and the animal trainer in a black suit made the lion and the tiger perform. Then, the owner, Chirni, came to the arena with his horses and proclaimed that nobody could excel him in training the horses and the items they performed. He challenged that he would give a thousand sovereigns and one of his horses to anyone who could outdo him. On a particular strike of the whip, the horses turned on their hind legs with forelegs lifting high up on the ground. Vishnupanth Chatre, a native of Bijapur, took up the challenge and stated that he could not only make his horse perform these items but also make them walk forward and backward on their hind legs. Besides, he put forward a counter-challenge that if he could not do what he claimed, he would give the Italian circus owner one thousand sovereigns and ten horses with the help of his patron, the Raja of Kurundvad. Within sixty days, Chatre's horse began to perform the items he promised, and on 20 March those acrobatics were performed in public before an invited audience. Later, Chatre bought the equipment and animals of Chirni's circus, which was running at a loss in Calcutta. He assembled the acrobats who performed in markets and temple festivals and formed the first circus in India during the Christmas season in 1880. He taught his wife, Avdabai, to perform on the trapeze and train animals. Thus, she became the 'first' woman in Indian circus. With the interest of the rajas of Kurundvad and Bijapur, the governor of Bombay inaugurated 'Chatre's New Indian' circus.[23]

Bhagwantrao D. More, a retired IPS officer from Maharashtra, claims that the 'Grand Indian More' circus established by his great-grandfather,

---

[23] Balan, *Circus*, 36–45.

Yeshwantrao Gangaram More, was the 'first' circus company. He preserves an old ragged letter pad with 1881 as the establishment year. His ancestral house near Sangamner in Vadgaonpan village is surrounded with circus artistes, animal trainers, and other circus labourers of a bygone era.[24] A press report on this circus narrates a tale similar to that of the customary Chatre story:

> One day, he [Yashwantrao Gangaram More] visited Mumbai, then Bombay, to see something called circus, a term completely alien to him. The show was put up by a Russian circus company. After watching the show, a gutsy Yashwantrao walked up to the circus owner and told him that anyone could perform the mediocre acts of his artists. The owner laughed and retorted, if you feel so why don't you do it? The owner's taunt haunted Yashwantrao on his way back to the village. … Finally, at the age of 23, in the year 1881, Yashwantrao launched Grand Indian More Circus.[25]

Kandambulli Balan then attempts a chronological progression of circus from the Marathis to the Malayalis: 'Keeleri Kunhikannan Gurukkal who was a physical education trainer in the Thalassery Mission School happened to visit the Chatre circus in 1888; a significant turning point in the history of Indian circus.'[26] But Champad argues that Keeleri saw a European circus first in 1884 and then visited the Chatre circus in 1887. This meeting, he writes, paved the way for the idea of the circus *kalari*[27] and the Malabar Circus.[28]

Shyamala Shirolker traces the origin of circus acrobatics to ancient 'India' and cites examples from the Mahabharata to substantiate her

---

[24] Interview, Bhagwantrao D. More, Mumbai, 27 December 2012.

[25] Available at http://indianexpress.com/article/news-archive/web/show-and-tell-7/, last accessed on 16 October 2014.

[26] Balan, *Circus*, 49.

[27] Circus training centre, see Chapter 1.

[28] Champad, *Circusinte Lokam*, 129. Elsewhere in 'Circussinte Eettillam [The birthplace of circus]', Champad mentions that it was the Hippodrome Circus that Keeleri first attended. 'Circussinte Eettillam [The birthplace of circus]', in *Smrithichitra: Thalassery Vidyabhyasa Jilla*, ed. Raju Kaattupanam (Thalassery: Vidyarangam and Subject Council of Thalassery Educational District, 2004–5), 129.

arguments. She also provides a chronological list of circus companies.[29] Her desire to pen a history of the circus is evident in the questionnaires and letters she sent around to various circus proprietors all over India during the 1970s: 'I am attempting to put a focus on the history of Indian Circus and to find out to what extend each old and existing circus has contributed to the development of Circus Art in general which will be a matter of Great Interest to readers of all ages.' She further states the reason for undertaking such a project: 'No attempt has been made to emphasize the contribution of Indian Circus throughout the ages and through these recent centuries, though the art of circus or to be more correct the art of exhibition of physical culture has, an undercurrent since the oldest civilization of the world- i.e., civilization of India had begun.'[30] It is interesting to note here that K. Damodaran also refers to the 'Vedic Origin of Circus' saying, '[T]he Plastic act, Frog act, and Contortionist Trapeze of today are but based on the Sutras of Patanjali.'[31]

One can reasonably assume that most of the 'historical accounts' related to the origin of circus rely on the same narratives which are invariably reproduced.[32] In an official *Gazeteer* of the district in which Thalassery is situated, the author, well-known Kerala historian A. Sreedhara Menon, notes: 'The Indian circus as a show business came into existence only in 1880 with the inauguration of Vishnupanth

---

[29] Shyamala Shirolker, *Circus! Circus!* (Pune: Sri Iswaryaganesh Publications, 2004); I am grateful to Janaki More, daughter of late Shyamala Shirolker, for providing me with the translations of essential sections of her mother's work. M. N. Vijayan—writer, orator, and academic—notes the acrobatics performed by legendary warriors in the Mahabharata and also cites examples of the acrobatic performances during sixth century CE mentioned in *Chilappathikaram*. *Nammude Sahityam Nammude Samooham*, 453.

[30] Private collection, late Shyamala Shirolker, Pune.

[31] K. Damodaran, 'Vedic Origin of Circus', *Big Top* 1 (1) (1965): 7.

[32] M. N. Vijayan reproduces the same story of circus in *Nammude Sahityam Nammude Samooham 1901–2000*, Vol. 2 [Our literature, our society 1901–2000, vol. 2] (Thrissur: Kerala Sahitya Academy, 2000). Contemporary historical explorations also, alas, reiterate the same narrative. For instance, K. Sreejith, 'Leisure in Colonial Malabar', *Exploring History: A Journal of Indian and Asian History* 3–4 (1–2) (January–June, 2013): 1–19.

Chatre's "New Indian Circus". Thus Maharashtrians were the pioneers of Circus in India. But Maharashtrian circus was dominated by animal shows such as horse riding, elephants, etc., and was lacking in the human field.'[33] While Kandambulli Balan and Sreedhara Menon referred to Chatre's circus as the 'New Indian' circus, the name given to it in Sreedharan Champad's *Circusinte Lokam* is 'Great Indian' circus and in Shirolker's book, the 'Grand Indian' circus.[34]

An Archive of Their Own

As stated earlier, the trajectory of my enquiry would be how indigenous structures and traditions confronted and negotiated with colonial modernity; the transnational and transregional movement of people, animals, and technologies; the intermingling of castes, genders, languages, and cultures with body and performance as axis points; and the characteristics of an industry that is almost 150 years old.

The sources one uses has a lot to do with the kind of history being written. Likewise, the way of reading these sources determines the ways in which the narratives are weaved from those source materials. Whether we read along the lines of the authorial intent or against the grain, looking for the small voices and silences beneath the surface makes all the difference. In the face of the dearth of conventional archives, one needs to look for those archives that exist outside. Memories and memorabilia of the circus community have been such rich sources for me. Photographs, notices, posters, letters, labour union memorandums, and diaries aided by pulsating memories constitute many archives hitherto unexplored. It is worthwhile noting here that in the United States of America, circuses such as the Ringling Brothers have museums showcasing their spectacular past. Also worth mentioning is the establishment of institutions such as the Circus Historical Society. In Britain as well magnificent archival collections on circus have been set up, such as the National Fairground Archives. These institutions

---

[33] A. Sreedhara Menon, *Kerala District Gazeteers: Canannore* (Trivandrum: Government Press, 1972), 244–5.

[34] Balan, *Circus*, 49; Sreedhara Menon, *Kerala District Gazeteers*, 245; Shyamala Shirolker, *Circus! Circus!*, 25; Champad, *Circusinte Lokam*, 124.

naturally inspire, support, and make possible historical explorations and research work on circus.[35]

Oral narrations and personal collections of artistes form the crux of my primary sources. News items and articles in newspapers and magazines, and available materials in various public archives supplement them as other primary sources. I have made field trips to small and big circuses: Galaxy (small), Gemini, Jumbo, Royal, Rambo, and Rajkamal (big).[36] I have interviewed performers, animal trainers, acrobatic trainers, musicians, managers, owners, tent masters, ring boys, labour contractors, contract labourers, publicity departments, security guards, ticket staff, drivers, electricians, welders, carpenters, painters, ironsmiths, and cooks. It should be mentioned here that these include Russian, Belgian, African, and Nepalese artistes. Members of the Indian Circus Employees Union and Circus Labour Union have been regular interlocutors. My fieldwork has also covered the retired circus artistes of Melur, Mahe, and Panoor in the Thalassery sub-district and also Kannur, Payyannur, and Thrissur in Kerala; Thasgaon, Pune, Miraj, Sangli, and Mumbai in Maharashtra; and Bangalore, Karnataka. Family members of circus practitioners of the early twentieth century, such as the legendary master, Keeleri Kunhikannan, have also been of immense help in sharing memories and materials. My current work explores the transnational history of Indian circus in the context of performers from African countries. My stint with the Centre for Indian Studies in Africa (CISA), University of the Witwatersrand, supported by a Social Science Research Council (SSRC) Transregional Research Fellowship, enabled me to conduct fieldwork at circus schools in South Africa, Uganda, Ethiopia, Kenya, and Tanzania and meet performers and trainers.

[35] For instance, 'The Circus and Respectable Society in Victorian Britain' by Brenda Assael (1997); 'Family and Economics in an English Circus: 1975–9' by Yoram Carmeli (1985); and Jessica Kendall's doctoral work, '"African Fever": The Politics of Race in the International Circus Arena' (School of Oriental and African Studies) looks at how circus performers strategize in the process of international careers.

[36] The size of the company depends on the number of king poles used. Big companies in India are mainly four pole circuses while the small ones are double poled. See Chapter 3.

With the support of SSRC and the Mellon Foundation, on 21–2 June 2018, I organized an international conference, 'Circus Histories and Theories', for CISA at the University of the Witwatersrand. Both veteran and young research scholars from around the world presented their works on diverse themes related to circus, ranging from the representations of Africans in the nineteenth-century American Wild West shows to the contemporary social circus. In recent years, the few scholars working on this marginal area, the circus, have made initial but remarkable attempts in organizing conferences, and the anthology *Routledge Circus Studies Reader (2016)*, which came out in 2016, is a breakthrough in introducing circus studies. Unfortunately, however, Africa and South Asia remained outside the research considerations of this volume. The conference explored an array of ideas such as subalternity, body and performance, spectatorship, itinerant entertainments, animal subjectivity, representations, children, various indigenous and contemporary technologies, emotion, legality, ethics of human–animal relations, transnational migration, global economy, and the structural power of race, gender, and caste.

While I was in the final stages of my doctoral research and thesis writing, a few exciting academic research on the Indian circus were going on and commencing in the universities of Munich, Chicago, and Jawaharlal Nehru University, Delhi: Anirban Ghosh's doctoral work titled 'The Tropic Trapeze: Circus in Colonial India' (2014), Eleonore Rimbault's ongoing work tentatively titled 'On the Circus Ground: Stigma and Innocence in South Indian Circuses', and Aastha Gandhi's ongoing research titled 'A Critical History of Indian Circus: Negotiations with Popularity, State and Laws (1947–2015)'. Rimbault and Gandhi have presented their research in the CISA conference.

The 161st birth anniversary of Keeleri Kunhikannan Teacher was celebrated by the Kerala Sangeetha Nataka Akademi in his hometown on 11 August 2016.[37] This official celebration, supported by the State Sports Ministry, was initiated following a proposal submitted by this author. During my research, I realized the painful truth that the great teacher has no memorial in his hometown and lives only in the memories of the circus community. I had a hard time finding the master's

[37] Nisha P R, 'The Circus Man Who Knew Too Much', *Economic and Political Weekly* 52 (34): 18–19.

home when I first went there about 10 years ago. Last year, as part of the anniversary celebration, the road that leads to this home was named after Keeleri by the Thalassery Municipality.

At the 2015 Keeleri anniversary celebration, 21 Malayali circus artistes and labourers, both retired and working, were honoured with a citation and a cash award of INR 10,000. This was the first time in the history of Kerala Sangeetha Nataka Akademi that circus artistes were recognized as performing artists and honoured. The awardees included the 103-year-old Thattari Lakshmi and the paralysed trapeze artiste Ajith Kumar, who has been bedridden for the last 20 years after an accident in the circus ring. Subsequently, the Akademi incorporated all Malayali artistes presently working in companies around India into their health insurance scheme. The Akademi Chairman Soorya Krishnmoorthy had promised to expand this scheme to include the retired artistes too, even though the celebrations much awaited by the circus did not happen in the following years when the next government was elected.

I have collected approximately 2,000 photographs from various artistes, labourers, and owners dating from the early twentieth century.[38] This collection made possible the photo exhibition on Indian circus I curated at Nehru Memorial Museum and Library, New Delhi, in January 2013. One will definitely find some images of tent life with almost all the persons from the circus community. It is as if they have been creating 'an archive of one's own'. These images are wonderful visual records of not only performances of women, children, men, and animals but also of ceremonies and celebrations in the tent, such as marriages and birthdays. I have also photographed artistes, animals, tents, rings, and labourers in their work places and the ruins of circus *kalari*s in Thalassery.[39]

Personal correspondences such as letters not only tell of intimacy and bonding but also the ideas the subjects shared. The bundle of letters from the collection of E. Ravindran, trainer and programme manager from Thalassery, has been a rich source of information regarding the birth and growth of the circus labour union. Diaries are even

---

[38] See Nisha P R, 'India Circus Images', *The Circus Historical Society Newsletter* 4 (3) (June, 2013): 3–4.

[39] As part of my study on circus *kalari*s, I have also interviewed *kalaripayatt* practitioners and photographed their exercises.

more personal. But the diaries of P. K. Balakrishnan and Sreedharan, retired artistes from Thalassery, are more of account books of wages and give us a fair idea regarding the wage structure. The diary of the late Balakrishnan, Kausu's husband, also tells us about the births of their children and the deaths of some of their colleagues. Many of the circus people have also religiously saved newspaper cuttings of circus related news, but unfortunately most of these cuttings do not have dates or other relevant details. Much to my delight, manuscripts of programme lists prepared by programme managers had luckily found a place in the personal collection of Radha Kannan, a retired artiste and proprietor from Thalassery, now based in Bangalore. I have also collected printed programme books meant for spectators and booking agents.

Publicity posters and notices printed by circus companies over the years, dating back to the 1940s, are other valuable sources. Bouissac notes, 'It is the modern technological expression of a traditional phenomenon organically linked to the circus itself.'[40] They represent different animals, jokers, jugglers, and artistes in their costumes and with the various equipment used for performance. I have interviewed the staffs of different companies who are in charge of posters and notices. I have also collected notices of circus *kalaris* dating back to an earlier era.

I am also lucky to have got hold of the few surviving issues of the *Circus Worker* magazine of the 1980s, published by the Indian Circus Employees Union; some of the publications by Akhil Bharath Circus Karmachari Sangh, an extinct labour union of the 1960s; and another valuable source material, a 1965 issue of the *Big Top* magazine published by the Indian Circus Federation of circus owners, all from personal collections. The archival collections in the British Library and the National Fairground Archives in Sheffield were of immense importance to this research.

I have interviewed both working and retired administrators of the zoos in Tirupati and Thiruvananthapuram, the latter being one of the oldest zoological parks in the subcontinent, established in the mid-nineteenth century. The records there have helped me trace the history

---

[40] Bouissac, *Circus and Culture: A Semiotic Approach*, 177.

of trade and exchange of wild and other animals between them and the circus companies.[41]

The archival sources mainly constitute the revenue files of Malabar and Bombay, the Tellicherry sub-collector's records and the census reports of Malabar, Madras, and the Bombay Presidencies. I have also examined the Napier Museum cover files in the Kerala State Archives, Thiruvananthapuram. I have also looked at the parliamentary debates at the Central Secretariat Library and revenue files in the National Archives, Delhi.

The articles, pictures, and advertisements from newspapers circulated in the first half of the twentieth century are the best existing archival materials regarding early circus history. Malayalam newspapers such as *Mitavadi* and *Mathrubhumi* published from Kozhikode, *Malayala Manorama* (hereafter 'MM') from Kottayam, and The *Hindu*, *Bombay Chronicle* (hereafter 'BC'), and *Times of India* (hereafter 'TOI') published from Madras and Bombay respectively helped me gather information about circus companies, artistes, animals, tents, publicity, zoos, accidents and mishaps, methods of body maintenance, and various physical cultures. Newspapers from the online digital archives of Australian National University, Australia, such as *Cairns Post, Gippsland Times, Morwell Advertiser*, and *The North Eastern Ensign*, have been of immense use to me with their reports on visiting circuses. I was also able to use materials from the British News Paper Archive digital library and the digital British Library.

The principal secondary sources are books, articles, research papers, and doctoral dissertations on circuses in the United States of America and Britain. Textual resources such as books and articles, periodicals in local libraries, photographs, and internet sources also form part of the secondary sources. Historical works on oral narratives, entertainment, and leisure in general have also helped shape my arguments. It should be said here that I have always cautioned myself that there is only a thin line between the categorizations of 'secondary' and 'primary'. Both sources can be primary and vice versa.

---

[41] I have interviewed the present zoo officials as well as the retired ones. The information and photographs provided by Dr Charles Chandra, a retired veterinary surgeon who had served in the Thiruvananthapuram Zoo for more than 35 years, have been of immense value regarding the exchanges between the zoo and the circus.

The Wanderer–Performer

Before moving on to the outline of the chapters, let me briefly explain what would come under the tent of the term 'circus' here; or to put it in the negative, what would not. A variety of people and communities with physical performances and/or animal acts as their vocation have always existed in places and times we are discussing. We know one cannot miss such feats and actions in our everyday life at present—in street corners, in rail coaches, or at one's doorstep. I have neither attempted to place them in a grand lineage of 'pre-circus' or assimilate them into an expansive category of circus with prefixes such as 'street' circus. Same is the case with the various items exhibited at both permanent and itinerant carnivals or touring exhibitions. Instances of items such as the 'exhibition of the abnormal' are abundant in the news reports of early-twentieth-century colonial presidencies such as Bombay.

Jugglers, acrobatic performers, conjurers, buffoons, animal dealers, and many other such groups which we see as 'circus' now were present in the historical era we will be looking at. Census of the Bombay Presidency, 1872, mentions the presence of 'jugglers'.[42] The Imperial Census of 1881 mentions males and females engaged in 'Exhibition and Show Service' and such groups as 'conjurer, performer' and 'tumblers and rope dancers'.[43] There were many caste and tribal groups performing various kinds of acrobatic performances and animal acts around the subcontinent. Indigenous groups with such vocations are ubiquitous in the early-twentieth-century Malabar and neighbouring South Canara. Kanipayoor Sankaran Namboodiripad in his three-volume autobiography, which attempts to 'write history in autobiographical form', lists a variety of such communities and acts common

[42] The Census of the Bombay Presidency, 1872, mentions the total number of 'Actors, Dancers, Jugglers' under 'Fine Arts' in the presidency as 1,382 (Census of the Bombay Presidency, 1872, General Report and Tables of the Population, Houses, & C., Enumerated in the Bombay Presidency on 21 February 1872, Part II [Bombay: Government Central Press, 1875], 167); The Census of India, 1971, Series-9, Kerala, Part II, Report and Tables on Establishments mentions 'jugglers' too on page 26.

[43] Imperial Census of 1881, Digest of the Results in the Presidency of Bombay including Sind by Order of Government (Bombay: Government Press, 1881), ixx, ixxvi, ixxviii.

during his childhood in the early twentieth century: *Maappilakkali* (Mappila act),[44] *Njaninmelkali*, *Kambamkoothaadichikal*, *Kuravanmaar*. The *Maappilakkali* performers were excellent acrobats who roamed around with *chenda* (tom-tom), wires, coir ropes, and bamboo poles. *Njaninmelkali* refers to rope-walking and *Kambamkoothaadichikal* is pole acrobatics.[45] Pannikkotta Karunakara Menon makes note of such tribes as Urali, Karimbalan, Kuruvikaran, and Valayan in south India whose occupations are described as hunting, poaching, and catching birds and snakes, and also such tribes as Dummer who perform on the rope and do some magic tricks.[46] *The Mysore Tribes and Castes* mentions a wandering tribe called Dombars in the Karnataka state who are acrobats and tumblers by profession. In the Vizagapatam district of the Madras Presidency they are known as Itevallu. The book further elaborates, 'They are described as people who exhibit different shows, such as wrestling, ascending high poles, and walking on ropes. The women act as common prostitutes.'[47]

However, the census reports that mention circus supposedly distinct from other occupational forms or caste occupations mentioned above seem to be deceptive, typical of massive population-enumeration endeavours. While the Census of India, 1901, documents 497 'circus managers' and 28 'circus owners' in the Bombay Presidency,[48] the

---

[44] Mappilas are Malabar Muslims whose ancestry is often traced to the Arab traders/settlers; M. T. Ansari, *In the Interstices of India: Islam and the Processes of Narration*, PhD dissertation, Central Institute of English and Foreign Languages, Hyderabad, 2002, 141.

[45] Kanippayyur Sankaran Namboodiripad, *Ente Smaranakal II* [My reminiscences] (Kunnamkulam: Panchangam, 2005), 263–92.

[46] Pannikkotta Karunakara Menon, *Dakshinendyayile Jaathikal* [Castes in south India] (Calicut: Vidya Vilasam, 1915), 16, 35, 54, 243.

[47] L. K. Ananthakrishna Iyer, *The Mysore Tribes and Castes*, Vol. III (Mysore: Mysore University Press, 1930), 139.

[48] The Census of India, 1901, also records that there were 496 exhibitors of trained animals and 35 animal catchers in the presidency. It also mentions the presence of 'tumblers, acrobats, wrestlers', elephant catchers, camel owners, drivers, breeders, dealers, and attendants. It also mentions elephant and horse trainers. *The Census of India*, Vol. XIA, Bombay (Towns and Island), Part VI, Tables by S. M. Edwades, ICS (Bombay: Times of India Press, 1901), 132–74.

census report of 1951 has 13 people, 10 men, and 3 women in the Malabar district whose occupation has been entered as circus.[49]

Rosie Thomas has argued,

> Since the mid-eighteenth century the circus had been gradually intro-
> duced alongside this [street] culture; by the start of the twentieth century
> Indian circuses, incorporating Indian traditional martial arts, acrobatics,
> magic and lion-taming acts, were travelling India's entertainment circuits
> alongside circuses from Europe, Russia, Japan and elsewhere, inviting
> audiences to wonder at apparently impossible feats that confounded the
> rules of the ordinary world. All such shows celebrated bodies pushed
> to their extremes and wild beasts subdued by men's—and women's—
> remarkable powers. An underclass of artistes from European, middle-
> Eastern, Indian and Anglo-Indian backgrounds provided the bodies that
> peopled these extravaganzas, which were, in many senses, transcultural
> shows, seen as ambiguously both modern and traditional. European
> and Asian traditions merged to present hybrid fantasies of exotic other-
> ness. Anecdotal accounts suggest circus images were almost as popular as
> Hindu gods and goddesses in the turn-of-century magic lantern as shows
> that toured India.[50]

Newspapers published from Bombay have several news articles about acrobatic groups in the first decades of the twentieth century. But it seems the performers were mainly foreigners. These performances were part of drama and silent film shows. Sometimes band music also formed part of these performances. These shows included acrobatic feats, magical illusions,[51] dances, and comic jokes. *BC* (12 March 1913) has numerous advertisements on these shows conducted mainly at the Excelsior, Olympia Picture Palace, and America–India Cinema; to

---

[49] *1951 Census Handbook of Malabar*, Kozhikode Regional Archives, 25. This is the only census report concerning Malabar in the Kozhikode Regional Archives which mentions the circus people.

[50] Rosie Thomas, 'Still Magic: An Aladdin's Cave of 1950s B-Movie Fantasy', *Tasveer Ghar: A Digital Archive of South Asian Popular Visual Culture*, 2010. Available at http://tasveerghar.net/cmsdesk/essay/103/index.html, last accessed on 17 October 2014.

[51] Vaikkam Chitrabhanu notes that many of the magical and hypnotic tricks in use were performed in circus rings as well. Chitrabhanu, *Magikkinte Lokam* [The world of magic] (Kottayam: NBS, 1974), 35. Also see P. C. Sorcar, *History of Magic* (Calcutta: Indrajal, 1970).

cite an example, 'Mazdie, King of Magicians in New Illusions' and the 'Bothwick Party of Comedians'. 'Leo Montagne, the quaint comedian, Gardner Brown's globe-trotters' along with comic performances by both male and female performers figure in the advertisements. Another advertisement is about 'the amazing Riedel Brothers in their startling acrobatic performance including the greatest somersault feat ever performed [BC, 15 April 1913]. These men are kings of the air, must be seen to be believed'. The news entitled 'The Viswabharath Exhibition: Variety Entertainment' from TOI (16 January 1926) published from Bombay is interesting:

> The variety entertainment at the Viswa Bharath Laxmi Exhibition at the Colaba Cotton Green which opened on Wednesday night is different from the usual run of entertainments in Bombay and is worth a visit. Included in the program is a thrilling event by Dare Devil George, who drives from a height of forty feet into a canvas chute; a tiny boy of six years of age who performs stunts on a trapeze high up in the air and who is one of the best turns on the whole program; there's a lady who dances barefooted on broken bottles and eats fire, another who entertains with some original dancing, while the living statuary act is an artistic turn. Last but not least is Funniman, the famous Calcutta Society entertainer, who amused the audience with some humorous skits on the Calcutta Bar.

An advertisement by the same group published in the same newspaper four days later reads thus:

> Wonderful Baby With Four Hands. Four Legs, Two Backs And One Head.
> The Three Headed Man, The Human Spider, The Floating Girl And Many Other Worth Seeing
> Don't Miss, From 20th January 1926:-
> Eighth Wonder Of The World Competes The Horned Man
> Living Boy And Girl
> (combined in one human form)
> & The Living Six-Legged Monkey. (TOI, 20 January 1926)

Interestingly, in the early twentieth century we can see 'breaking an iron bar' or 'letting an elephant stand on his chest' performed in circus as well as the Strong Man, Professor Ramamurthy Naidu,[52] well

---

[52] 'Professor Ramamurti Naidu from Madras, "India's Strongest Man" and another circus leader, gave a lecture and demonstration in Calcutta in 1909 to

known as the Indian Sandow, for his individual shows (*Mitavadi*, April 1919).

A historiography which is anxious about 'origins' and 'roots' would obviously label the above as some sort of precursor of 'circus'. But we must understand that many performers neither call their act 'circus' nor themselves as 'circus performers' even today when it is supposed to have become a generic term. In fact, some of them define their art as beyond circus.[53] Sreedhara Menon argues, 'the Bounding Rope Acrobatics, commonly known as Rope Dance which had its origin in Kerala ages ago and was performed by the Kuruva tribe (snake charmers) was another item of Indian circus developed by Kerala artistes'.[54] But even when one is preoccupied with concerns regarding a linear history of progression, one might stumble upon other possibilities of understanding the past. Sasikumar notes how Keeleri *combined* the nomads' tight-rope walking and the play on the thick rope into rope dance in his circus *kalari*.[55] Here, one must bear in mind that the circus *kalaris* established at Thalassery during the beginning of the twentieth century where training in circus acrobatics was given had also emerged

---

advance the cause of National Education.' John Rosselli, 'The Self-Image of Effeteness: Physical Education and Nationalism in Nineteenth-Century Bengal', 146; Ramamurthy is taught in the school syllabi in Andhra Pradesh along with other prominent Telugu nationalists. Carey Watt also mentions the nationalist aspect of Ramamurthy in his paper 'The Meaning and Legacy of Physical Culturist Eugene Sandow's Visit to India in 1904–5', presented at the international conference 'Physical Cultures: Bengal and Beyond', Jadavpur University, 21–2 February 2014. It is said Ramamurthy also owned a circus company by the name 'Hindu Hercules'; see Champad, *Circussinte Lokam*.

[53] For instance, Sajeevan, a street performer, says that to many of his spectators what he does—eating glass pieces, florescent tubes, and fragments of soda bottles—is circus. But for him his art is much higher than that. As he proudly states to the onlookers, 'You have seen what a magician or a circus performer cannot do.' Interview, Sajeevan, Thalassery, 13 January 2010.

[54] Sreedhara Menon, *Kerala District Gazeteers*, 244–5.

[55] Sasikumar Kallidumbil, 'Kalaripayattum Circussum' [Kalaripayatt and circus], in *Gnanodayayogam Sathabdi Charithra Smaranika 2005*, ed. Champadan Vijayan (Thalassery: Sree Gnanodayayogam Centinary Committee for History Preparation, October 2005), 205.

out of such drastically new ideas and processes. The spatial economy and culture of a rigid caste-based physical culture such as *kalaripayatt* were radically reimagined and refashioned, to accommodate a 'modern' form, and the circus *kalari* became a social space for different castes, communities, and genders. Sreedharan Champad argues, while discussing Chatre, that he *found out* the nomads and *brought them* to Kurundvad and *modified* their acrobatic feats, such as knife-throwing, tight-rope walking, somersaulting, and jumping through the ring *to fit the circus ring*.[56] Acrobatic performances and animal acts have existed in many forms among various communities. New groups, 'modern' ones, must have also emerged over time. Many of them might have joined the circus. As I have been reiterating, my concern in this research would be to look at certain key moments from the lives of the forms, spaces, and beings that in some way or other tagged them *as* 'circus'; for instance, the establishment of circus *kalaris* or state interventions, such as the ban on the performance of wild animals that turned the world of the circus community upside down or the emergence of a labour union furtively in the closing decades of the twentieth century.

Chapter Outline

Acrobatic performances are the most important and striking in a circus ring. The first chapter examines in detail the various aspects of these human performers. The focal point would be the circus *kalaris* established at Thalassery during the beginning of the twentieth century where a 'new' and 'modern' physical culture was shaped. It was undoubtedly an absolutely radical refashioning of the space of *kalaripayatt* that emerged out of the caste system and was sanctioned by its tradition. Circus *kalaris* were training centres where women and men from different communities got trained and went on to become renowned artistes in various companies around the subcontinent in the first half of the last century. The chapter tries to look at how *kalaripayatt*, the 'traditional' physical culture, Indian wrestling, and the European acrobatic practices such as gymnastics and the Sandow system have contributed to the making of an acrobatic culture of Indian circus. It is a transcultural and transnational

---

[56] Champad, *Circusinte Lokam*, 124; emphasis added.

form. I have also discussed the influences of different indigenous medicinal systems such as Ayurveda and dietary practices. This will be supplemented by brief biographies of a number of great performers from the early era who broke barriers and borders with the art of their bodies, literally and figuratively.

Wild animals have always been an indispensable part of circus around the world. Indian circus is no exception. The second chapter traces their trajectory from the 'wild' to the 'submissive'. In relation to this, I would also be looking at the attitudes of colonial and post-colonial states towards animals in general and the changes over time in relation to circus animals. Wild animals have been killed, stuffed, and each and every part of them has been exported from colonies for exhibitions and scientific purposes. Zoos all over the world are institutions engaged in the breeding and trading of wild animals. Although the circus community argues that it is also a similar establishment, it obviously lacks the indubitable tags of 'scientific' and 'public'. The acquisition of animals for circus is deeply implicated in the history of hunting, wildlife management, and forest policies of colonial and post-colonial governments. This chapter examines such statist double standards focusing at the ban of wild animals in Indian circus by the environment ministry that proved to be fatal for both circus people and the animals. I have also tried to look at how the present 'conservation' ideas exclude and thus jeopardize certain historical practices of animal taming, training, and performance.

One cannot imagine the circus without a tent. The itinerant character of the circus is best exemplified by the tents. The life and work in the circus happens in and around various tents. The disasters related to circus also inevitably bring in the imagery of tents. In a sense, they have twin facets of both the *carnivalesque* and the dangerous. The third chapter looks at the spatial economies and the shifting technologies of the circus tent over the decades. Tents have been ubiquitous from the nineteenth century and were indispensable for a colonial state that was desperate to spread its tentacles.

Circus has always figured in the common sense as a place of extreme exploitation with dangerous working conditions, wretched living conditions, miserable wages, irregular working hours, physical and mental harassments, and insecure employment and life. Strangely, however, if we look at the history of trade unions in India we would hardly find a circus workers' union. We may bear in mind here that circus flourished in Malabar along with communist movements and trade union movements in the early decades of the twentieth century. In the fourth chapter, I try to look at this structure of hierarchy with both its vertical and horizontal moments. The chapter examines the efforts to organize and even start a company of the labourers' own: the Akhil Bharath Circus Karmachari Sangh organized under the communist party in the late 1960s had attempted and indeed succeeded to an extent to establish a workers' circus—owned, worked, and managed by the workers. Another key organization, which is the only existing circus workers' union in India now, the Indian Circus Employees Union, was established at Thalassery under the leadership of Indian National Trade Union Congress (INTUC) in as recent as the 1980s. Major companies are also discussed contextually.

In the concluding part, I will be discussing the 2011 ban on child performers in Indian circus. I critically examine how 'cruelty' becomes a dominant parameter when it comes to circus, while in other traditional forms such as *kalaripayatt* or *kathakali* the rigorous training imparted to children is seen as part of mastering the form. I will also examine the various attempts made within the community and government institutions to establish circus training centres at various points of time.

1 Performing Bodies and Physical Cultures

In 1959, a report on Indian circus in the *King Pole* magazine published by the Circus Friends Association in Britain wondered: 'To-day there are several really large Indian circuses whose artists are predominantly young girls, most of whom hail from a place called KERALA. Who are these girls and where do they get their training?' The anonymous author then added, 'Well they are mainly working class girls mostly from rural families—there are many young boys too and they are apprenticed to the circus at the age of five or six years.'[1] Kerala has provided acrobats, gymnasts, and performers to Indian circuses for the better part of the twentieth century. Yet, in South Asia, a comprehensive study has not been made of circus acrobatics and the various physical cultures that shaped it. How could one forget the legendary teacher-artistes such as Keeleri Kunhikannan or Mannan who could sense the temperament of a body and moulded it accordingly? How could one overlook the significant history of the training spaces—the circus *kalaris*—they had established for women and men from all walks of life in early twentieth-century Malabar, rife with caste untouchability and gender discrimination?

This chapter aims to explore a history of circus acrobatics in Malabar, locating the ways in which colonial modernity and indigenous

---

[1] Circus Friends Association, 'The Circus in India', *King Pole* 2, no. 15 (1959): 21.

traditions constitute the structure of circus acrobatics. We shall see how different physical cultures come together in this process by looking at the circus *kalari*s and the individuals who had established them. I argue that these circus *kalari*s, training centres for circus acrobatics, established at the beginning of the twentieth century had emerged out of radically new ideas and processes. The space and culture of a rigid caste-based physical culture such as *kalaripayatt* was reimagined and refashioned as to accommodate a 'modern' form, and the circus *kalari* became a social space for different castes, communities, and genders. This could also show how transcultural and transnational histories shape the configuration of circus in this part of the world.

Circus *Kalari*s

Circus *kalari*s[2] undeniably played a role in laying the ground for circus acrobatics in India, training the early circus acrobats in north Malabar. These training institutes housed in permanent structures, unlike a circus, open up key questions regarding culture, body, gender, and caste. Though training institutes of circus acrobatics were initiated later on, we do not have much information regarding the existence of similar endeavours in other parts of the subcontinent during this time.

---

[2] The term 'circus *kalari*' is popularly used among circus artistes. The magazine *Circus Worker* also refers to it as 'circus *kalari*', while historians such as Sreedhara Menon and Murkoth Ramunny refer to it as either 'circus training school' or 'circus training institute'. This could be because circus *kalari*s are less known to people outside it or because the word '*kalari*' in itself has become equivalent to *kalaripayatt* by now; A. Sreedhara Menon, *Kerala District Gazeteers: Canannore* (Trivandrum: Government Press, 1972), 245; Interview, late Murkoth Ramunny, Dharmadam, 31 January 2009.

It is interesting to note that in Britain, where the first unified circus company of its kind was organized, Astley, the man behind it, opened a 'riding school' before he started a company. Another interesting factor is that several of them learned their extraordinary gymnastic skills while being trained in the British army for the Seven Years' War and 'sought to turn their skills to profit by performing stunts ... at pleasure gardens and fairgrounds across Britain'; Marius Kwint, 'Circus and Nature in Late Georgian England', in *Histories of Leisure*, ed. Rudy Koshar (New York: Oxford University Press, 2002), 45.

Anyone interested in the culture and history of Kerala will be famil-iar with the martial art called *kalaripayatt*. Along with other 'traditional' forms such as *kathakali* and *theyyam*, *kalaripayatt* has been written about extensively within and outside academia, in India and abroad. Some prominent writers have mentioned in passing about the obvi-ous links between *kalaripayatt* and the development of circus acrobatics in Malabar. In the introduction of his celebrated book on *Kalaripayatt*, Philip B. Zarrilli points to the influence of it in training the early generations of circus artistes in the region.[3] Marxist historian K. K. N. Kurup notes that *kalaripayatt* was influential in the growth of *theyyam*, *poorakkali*, *mutiyett*, and circus.[4] Interestingly, however, neither of them mentions the few circus *kalaris* (circus training centres) that came into being in the Thalassery and Kannur regions in late nineteenth and early twentieth centuries. It could be because the circus *kalaris* are not seen as integral to 'tradition' as the other arts and physical cultures mentioned above.[5] So, despite it being an amazing space of physical strength, skill,

---

[3] Zarrilli, having pointed out the long history of martial arts being adapted for different practices and presentations in various contexts, directs our atten-tion to the uses of *kalaripayatt* in training other arts such as *kathakali* or *teyyam*, and stresses on 'its use in training the first Indian (Malayali) circus performers in the late nineteenth century'; Philip. B. Zarrilli, *When Body Becomes All Eyes: Paradigms, Discourses, Practices of Power in Kalaripayattu, a South Indian Martial Art* (New Delhi: Oxford University Press, 1998), 3. It should be noted here that just as early *kalaripayatt* practitioners joined the circus, many of them had entered the cinema industry as stunt masters (I am grateful to Prof. Partha Chatterjee for pointing this out to me). One of the doyens in the southern industry, stunt master Thyagarajan, who had mastered *kambuvati* and *kalar-ipayatt* as a child, says, 'One who does not have suppleness of body cannot do this job' (*Mathrubhumi Weekend Edition*, 29 March 2009). Gyan Prakash also notes that 'Indian stunt films drew on deeply rooted traditions of physi-cal culture and performance'; Gyan Prakash, *Mumbai Fables* (Delhi: Harper Collins, 2010), 108.

[4] K. K. N. Kurup, *Samooham, Charithram, Samskaram* [Society, history, culture] (Kozhikode: Poorna Publications, 1990), 96–112.

[5] It is interesting to note that the circus *kalaris* are cherished by the local memory. For instance, the area where M. K. Raman's circus *kalari* had been established is still known among the people of the locality and auto-rickshaw drivers in the town of Thalassery as 'Chirakkara *Kalari*'.

and display, the *kalaripayatt* admirers seem to have paid no attention to the circus *kalari*s that produced most of the renowned circus acrobats from Malabar who ruled the tents across borders in the first part of the twentieth century.

Those from within the circus community who had ventured into writing the history of their vocation do refer to circus *kalari*s. Regrettably, however, they do not go deeper into exploring the significant role these centres had in shaping this particular physical culture. In his book *Circus*, Kandambulli Balan writes about Keeleri Kunhikannan's circus *kalari*, but fails to mention the other two major centres. Sreedharan Champad's *Circusinte Lokam* mentions the circus *kalari*s established by Keeleri Kunhikannan and M. K. Raman but hardly speaks about their characteristics or what brought about such an endeavour. Likewise, he rarely mentions the circus *kalari* training systems in his other two books. Circus artiste and entrepreneur Gemini Sankaran also mentions Keeleri Kunhikannan's *kalari* briefly in his reminiscences from where he started his career. While Sankaran refers mostly to Keeleri's disciples who went on to work in various circus companies, Sreehari Nair's biography of Gemini Sankaran in English is totally silent about these *kalari*s.[6]

Others who have written about the links between *kalaripayatt* and circus fail to consider circus *kalari* as a distinct site and the sociocultural significance of its transformation. For instance, Sasikumar Kallidumbil's article about circus and *kalaripayatt* contributed to *Gnanodayayogam*[7] *Sathabdi Charithra Smaranika* mentions Keeleri's circus *kalari* but does not talk about the *kalari*s of M. K. Raman and M. Mannan.[8]

---

[6] Gemini Sankaran and Thaha Madayi, *Malakkam Mariyunna Jeevitham* [Somersaulting life] (Kottayam: DC Books, 2012); Sreehari Nair, *Gemini Shankaran & the Legacy of Indian Circus* (Thalassery: Gayathri Designs and Promotions, 2013).

[7] *Gnanodaya Yogam* was a Thiyya organization founded in 1905 in North Malabar; Dilip M. Menon, *Caste, Nationalism and Communism in South India: Malabar, 1900–48* (Cambridge: Cambridge University Press, 1994), 67.

[8] Sasikumar Kallidumbil, 'Kalaripayattum Circussum' [Kalaripayatt and circus], in *Gnanodayayogam Sathabdi Charithra Smaranika 2005* (Thalassery: Sree Gnanodayayogam Centinary Committee for History Preparation, October 2005), 195–205.

Etymology and Meaning

The combination of the words 'circus *kalari*' perhaps refers to the combination of various cultures too. 'Circus' is a Latin word which comes from the Greek word 'kirkos', meaning 'circle', 'oval', or 'ring',[9] while the word *kalari*, as Zarrilli explains, originates from the Tamil word *kalam*. He says, 'It derives from the Tamil *kalam* meaning "arena, area for dramatic, gladiatorial, or gymnastic exhibitions, assembly, place of work or business". In Malayalam *kalari* (also) idiomatically refers to the special place where martial exercises are taught.'[10] But the Malayalam word also refers to any site of learning, especially writing.[11] Probably, the compound word contains elements of performance, exhibition, and acrobatics, and also the obvious merging of the colonial 'modern' and the indigenous 'tradition'. The particular arrangement of the word, that is, the word 'circus' as the adjective qualifying the noun '*kalari*' can be interpreted in terms of the emergence of the *kalari*, originally meant for *payatt*, as a site for circus training.

---

[9] *The New Encyclopedia Britannica*, Vol. 16 (Chicago: Encyclopedia Britannica, 1998), 1768–71; 'The word [circus] has the same root as "circle" and "circumference" and therefore also recalls the distinctive environment in which such entertainment is presented—the ring, a circular performance area, usually bounded with a short fence (or "curb") and surrounded by tiers of seats for spectators, which may itself be enclosed in a circular building or tent ... the term "circus" was first used when a rival horseman and former employee named Charles Hughes opened the Royal Circus a few hundred yards south of Astley's Amphitheatre.' The Circus Historical Society in the USA notes on its website message board: 'Most circus histories will note the connection to the Latin word circus meaning circle, which, in turn, comes from the Greek kirkos meaning circle or ring. From it we get a whole group of English words related to circle or ring such as circuit, circular, circulate, circumference, circumscribe, and so on.' Available at http://www.circushistory.org/Query/Query 06g.htm, last accessed on 1 February 2014.

[10] Zarrilli, *When Body Becomes All Eyes*, 25.

[11] Sreekanteswaram Padmanabhapillai G., *Sabdataravali* (Kottayam: NBS, 1983 [1923]), 525–6; Rosmin Mathew, *Kalaripayattu: Ankathattum Rangavediyum* [Kalaripayatt: combat space and performing stage] (Thiruvananthapuram: The State Language Institute, 2009), 8.

The 'High' and the 'Low'

Malabar of the nineteenth and early twentieth centuries was notorious for its brutal caste discrimination. Stringent spatial and physical distance—even to the extent of keeping the 'lower' castes out of sight—was practised to maintain the 'purity' of caste Hindus. The distancing was enforced according to the position each caste had been ascribed in the hierarchy. Udaya Kumar notes about the system prevalent in the provinces including Malabar, 'The movement of the body in public spaces was regulated through a system of distance pollution—the sacredness of the space and the purity of the body being dependent on restrictions of access to other bodies in terms of visibility, touch, hearing and clearly specified distances'.[12] For instance, while a Thiyya could not go near a Nambudiri household, a Cheraman could not set foot in the vicinity of a Thiyya house.[13] According to F. Fawcett:

> The mere approach anywhere near his [Nair's] vicinity of a Cheruman, a Pulayan or any inferior being, even a Tiyan … is pollution, and he must turn and bathe again ere he can enter his house and eat. Buchanan tells us that in his time, about 99 years ago, a man of inferior caste thus approaching the Nayar would be cut down instantly with a sword: there would be no words. Now that the people of India are inconvenienced with an Arms Act which inhibits sword play of this kind, and with a law-system under which high and low are rated alike, the Nayar has to contend himself with an imperious grunt-like shout for the way to be cleared for him as he stalks on unperturbed. His arrogance is not diminished, but he cannot now show it in quite the same way.[14]

The tension and the struggle for power and authority existed especially between the immediate 'upper' and its 'lower' castes. The practice of *kalaripayatt* was seen as an ancestral and a community occupation of

---

[12] Udaya Kumar, 'Self, Body and Inner Sense: Some Reflections on Sree Narayana Guru and Kumaran Asan', in *The Indian Postcolonial*, ed. Elleke Boehmer and Rosinka Chaudhari (London and New York: Routledge, 2011), 215.

[13] P. Bhaskaranunni, *Keralam Irupatham Noottandinte Aaarambhathil* [Kerala at the beginning of twentieth century] (Thrissur: Kerala Sahitya Academy, 2000), 356.

[14] F. Fawcett, *Nayars of Malabar* (Madras: Government Press, 1915), 254–5.

the Nairs.[15] Nairs were established as soldiers and chieftains of kings and royal families.[16] Jacob Canter Visscher's *Letters from Malabar* says, 'They may be justly entitled born soldiers, as by virtue of their descent they must always bear arms.'[17] In spite of the fact that Thiyyas were also supreme practitioners of *payatt* and had an unavoidable presence in the militia of the ruler, they were not allowed in the military services.[18] It should be noted here that like the popular Nair Brigade of Travancore, there were Thiyya regiments formed by the French and the British governments in Mahe and Thalassery, though less known.[19] But this 'claim' over this physical culture by the Nairs was unquestionable since the caste occupation of the Thiyyas was supposed to be toddy-tapping. On the other hand, exceptionally talented Thiyya *kalaripayatt* practitioners were given the title *chekavan/chekon*, and each local ruler had his

---

[15] P. Bhaskaranunni, *Keralam Irupatham Noottandinte Aaarambhathil*, 397.

[16] Zarrilli wrote:

Although by birth Sudra, royal lineages developed among the Nairs such as the Zamorins of Kozhikode or chieftains of smaller localized districts who functioned as kshatriyas; however the numerical majority of the lower-ranking Nayars provided military, personal or managerial services for Namboodiri Brahmans, kshatriyas, or higher-ranking Nayars. Some served as district chieftains and soldiers in service to a ruler, military trainers for royal families or at the village level, managers and/or supervisors of estates, palanquin bearers, oil extractors, washermen or barbers. Although between the twelfth century and the beginning of the British rule in 1792 Nayar males constituted the largest group possessing the right to bear arms in service to a leader, as noted earlier Cattar (or Yatra) brahmans, as well as significant numbers of Christians, Muslims and a special sub-group among the Illava (Tiyya) community also learned, taught and practised all aspects of Kalarippayattu.

Zarrilli, *When Body Becomes All Eyes*, 35–6; also see K. Vijayakumar, *Kalaripayatt: Keralathinte Sakthiyum Soundaryavum* [Kalaripayatt: strength and beauty of Kerala] (Trivandrum: Department of Cultural Publications, 2000), 72.

[17] Jacob Canter Visscher, *Letters from Malabar* (Madras: Adelphi Press, 1862), 122.

[18] P. Bhaskaranunni, *Keralam Irupatham Noottandinte Aaarambhathil*, 359; Mathew, *Kalaripayattu*, 43.

[19] K. Vijayakumar, *Kalaripayatt*, 70–1.

own militia of *chekons*.[20] Despite all this, the *chekons* were lined up for combats and duels, representing the dominant in disputes.[21] In short, they were mercenaries who fought and died for the dominant, protecting their life and property.[22] The caste discrimination and belittlement towards these practitioners cannot be more pronounced.

Vadakkanpattukal, the orally transmitted folk ballads of the north Malabar region which date back to the fourteenth century, also sing stories of Thiyya heroes, Aromal Chekavar and Arinhodan—who was the owner of eighteen *kalaris* in Kolathnad—and also the daring Thiyya heroine, Unniyarcha.[23] Kambil Ananthan, a Thiyya reformer and writer, says, '[I]t is said that about 100–150 years back there were a lot of *kalaris* owned by *avarnas* ["low" castes] in Kerala.'[24] He also describes the story of the Nair *kalaripayatt* warrior–hero Thacholi Othenan who created troubles in Andalur *Kavu*, a Thiyya dominant *Kavu*[25] at Thalassery, and how the Thiyyas punished and brought him to his knees. The story not only unravels the heroism and the practice of *kalaripayatt* among the Thiyyas but also the occasional triumph they had over the 'claim' of their immediate 'upper' caste, the Nairs. Yet, over the decades, as represented and reiterated by films, comics, and television soaps, all these Thiyya heroes and their world of *kalaripayatt* have been rendered as 'Nair'. Murkoth Kumaran, a social reformer and thinker, in his unfinished autobiography written in the form of a letter addressed to

[20] Kambil Ananthan, 'Pracheena Acharanahalum Viswasanhalum [Ancient observations and beliefs]', in *Gnanodayayogam Sathabdi Charithra Smaranika 2005*, 85.

[21] K. Vijayakumar, *Kalaripayatt*, 70–1.

[22] Zarrilli points out that this was a safe method adopted by the ruler to protect the life and property of the Nairs in his service and for the *chekons*, they could not reject those who came for *ankam* as that was a question of his honour; *When Body Becomes All Eyes*, 42.

[23] Kambil Ananthan, 'Pracheena Acharanahalum Viswasanhalum', 82–3; Thikkurissi Gangadharan, *Puthariyankam* [The first battle] (Thiruvananthapuram: The State Language Institute, 1984), 22.

[24] Ananthan adds, 'Till recently, those Nairs having the statuesque of *kalaris* had been seen rendering their offerings in many of the old Thiyya ancestral households that makes clear where the base of their practice lies.' 'Pracheena Acharanahalum Viswasanhalum', 82.

[25] A place of worship which was caste specific.

his eldest son Murkoth Kunhappa, is definitely displeased at this cock-and-bull story that must have started cropping up during that time. He wrote, 'The recent notion that *Kalaripayatt* is exclusively for Hindus in general and Nairs in particular, is wrong. Let us not forget that there were great *payatt* practitioners among Mappilahs and Thiyyas. You must know that even today, the great guru of *Kalaripayatt* in North Malabar is the very old, respected (Kottaykal) Kanaran Gurukkal, a Thiyya.'[26]

Decades later, the son Murkoth Kunhappa, writing on the occasion of the 75th-year celebrations of the Sri Narayana Guru Dharma Paripalana Yogam (SNDP) Movement, shares the paternal sentiment in a sarcastic tone: 'Nairs were martial superheroes, agreed. But to say, they were the only brave hearts would be a blatant lie. There is substantial evidence that Thiyyas and Nairs were on close footing in *kalaripayatt*.'[27]

Though almost all caste groups performed *kalaripayatt*, there were certain criteria to be followed in the case of lower castes.[28] There were *kalari*s for different caste groups, such as Nair *kalari*s, Thiyya *kalari*s, Pulaya *kalari*s, and Kaniyan *kalari*s, as well as Muslim and Christian *kalari*s.[29]

The vicious peculiarity of caste system also ensured that the Brahmins stayed away from such physical activities. For instance,

[26] Murkoth Kumaran, 'An Unfinished Autobiography', *Kaumudi: Murkoth Kumaran Special Edition* (January–March 2009) [1937]: 13.

[27] Murkoth Kunhappa, 'Thiyyarude Charithram: Oru Vihaga Veekshanam [History of Thiyyas: an elaborate perspective]', in *Gnanodayayogam Sathabdi Charithra Smaranika 2005*, 108–9.

[28] Zarrilli, though he does not mention much about the caste-distinct bodies in *Kalaripayatt*, recognizes the practice of *kalaripayatt* among different caste groups for different purposes. But he hardly speaks of the 'lower' bodies in the *kalari*, whether the *kalari* provided an equal space for 'all' castes has not been mentioned with details. At one point, he mentions citing Zacharia (who records Gouvea) in one of his footnotes that in areas where the Christians and Nairs practised, they practised together under the same master whoever he may be, which, in fact, throws light on the exceptionality of the practice. That he treats them as footnote shows he took the caste and body easily and did not probably recognize the complications associated with it; *When Body Becomes All Eyes*, 259.

[29] K. Vijayakumar, *Kalaripayatt*, 61–2, 71; Zarrilli, *When Body Becomes All Eyes*, 36.

Poomulli Neelakandan Namboodiripad, popularly known as Aram Thampuran (Sixth Lord), had interest in *kalaripayatt* and *kusti* (Indian wrestling) and even built a *kalari* on his property. His childhood friend Nayathil Narayanan Nambuthiri mentions that Brahmins could not engage in any activity involving arms and that it was a grave sin which could result in ostracism from one's caste.[30]

Thottampattu mentions that the Pulayas did not have a right to learn *payatt*.[31] Fawcett also remembers having seen a 'lower' caste Paravan instructor in a *kalari* at Payyoli during 1895. He makes clear that since this instructor had the honorific 'kurup', given to the teachers of *kalaripayatt*, suffixed to his name, it took him some time to recognize that he was a Paravan.[32] Murkoth Kunhappa states, 'In fact, *payatt* is a martial art without caste and religious differences.'[33] But the very mention of such instances shows that they must be exceptions. Sivadasan, the *kalaripayatt* instructor at CVN Kalari, Thiruvanhad, told me that during his father's (who was also a *kalari gurukkal* [*kalari* teacher]) time, people from other castes could not enter the Nair *payatt kalari*. They could only stand away and take a peep.[34] Dilip Menon points out that often there were spaces where the 'lower' castes could subvert the 'higher' castes' dominance.[35] But popular rituals performed by 'low' castes, such as *Theyyam* in Malabar, have been read as a scheme to undermine real subversion. In his seminal work *Elementary Aspects of Peasant Insurgency in Colonial India* Ranajit Guha notes that *Theyyam* could be seen as a safety-valve device of the caste system. He argues that such simulated inversions mediated by religion at regular calendric intervals were

---

[30]   V. K. Sriraman (ed.), *Pumulli Aaram Thamburan* [The sixth lord of Pumulli] (Kozhikode: Mathrubhumi, 2013), 91–2.

[31]   Mathew, *Kalaripayattu*, 35.

[32]   Fawcett, *Nayars of Malabar*, 290.

[33]   Kunhappa, 'Thiyyarude Charithram', 107.

[34]   Interview, Sivadasan, Thiruvanhad, 14 February 2009; 'Most of the *kalari*s were built as family *kalari*s or adjacent to their house. Therefore, during the high castes' dominance and untouchability, they obviously did not let the lower castes enter their *kalari* spaces.' Interview, K. G. Muraleedharan, Kottayam, 7 March 2014; A. K. B. Pillai states in the glossary that 'kalari' is 'a military training school attached to chieftain and wealthy families'. A. K. B. Pillai, *The Culture of Social Stratification/Sexism: The Nayars* (Massachusetts: Copley, 2005), 221.

[35]   Dilip M. Menon, *Caste, Nationalism and Communism in South India*, 58–9.

designed to prevent real insurrections from happening.[36] So, at that time, a space where all castes were welcome and caste-distinct bodies could interact freely and intimately must have been somewhat impossible to imagine. But Keeleri Kunhikannan, a *kalaripayatt gurukkal* himself, did exactly that. Therefore, Keeleri's conversion of the traditional *payatt kalari*—where caste and its embedded social status dominated in many ways—into a circus *kalari* that undermined that system of exclusion by recasting the body with a new physical culture was definitely one of the most significant moments of the era.

That this does not figure in any colonial, nationalist, or subaltern historical narratives of 'resistance' or 'reform' in Malabar or Kerala goes without saying. Nettoor P. Damodaran notes sharply in his memoirs that Keeleri 'selected his pupils from underprivileged families stigmatized as untouchables by the upper castes'.[37] Ramanathan, who is from the Mukkuva (fishing) community, proudly told me that 'his people' were the favourite of Keeleri.[38] Edward Keeleri said that his grandfather trained Mukkuvas from Thalayi, a coastal region in Thalassery, in large numbers, including the renowned Parammel Keshavan, the acrobat turned animal trainer.[39] Along with Thiyyas and Mukkuvas, other 'low' caste members of Saliya, Vannan, and Asari communities also joined the early circuses to become acrobats.[40]

Keeleri Kunhikannan, the 'Teacher'

'When any circus company pitches a tent in Tellicherry and starts a show, you can always see a tall, hefty yet supple bodied "strong men"

[36] Ranajit Guha, *Elementary Aspects of Peasant Insurgency in Colonial India* (New Delhi: Oxford University Press, 1999), 30–1.

[37] Nettoor P. Damodaran, *Anubhavachurulukal* [Folds of memory] (Kottayam: NBS, 1987), 11.

[38] Interview, Ramanathan, Thalassery, 18 June 2013.

[39] Interview, Edward Williams, Chirakkara, 26 March 2010.

[40] Rosselli notes that members of early Bengali circus were 'a mixture of odd members of the upper castes or the educated category and people of unclear but probably humble social origin'; 'The Self-Image of Effeteness: Physical Education and Nationalism in Nineteenth-Century Bengal', *Past & Present* 86 (February 1980): 144.

[*sic*] sitting in the reserved seat. The artistes and acrobats are all his students or students of his students,' Murkoth Kunhappa quotes his father, Murkoth Kumaran, describing Keeleri Kunhikannan.[41] The same writer states elsewhere that at that time in Malabar, 'teacher' meant nobody else but Keeleri Kunhikannan.[42] Quoting Murkoth Kumaran, S. Narayanan says that only the famous elephant of Chengannoor could contest Keeleri Kunhikannan in prowess.[43] The circus community in Kerala respects him as the 'Guru' and 'Father' of circus acrobatics in this part of the world. Many of the artistes trained by him went on to perform and teach circus feats to subsequent generations, establishing a lineage of teachers, students, owners, and performers.

Keeleri Kunhikannan joined the BEMP School[44] in Thalassery as a gymnastics teacher in 1884. He also taught horizontal and parallel bars and the Swedish Drill.[45] In his autobiography, C. H. Kunjappa, writer and editor of *Mathrubhumi*, warmly remembers the affectionate but strict teacher while recounting his student days at Basel Mission School.[46] Nettoor P. Damodaran, another alumnus of Basel Mission School, who represented the Thalassery parliamentary constituency in the first Lok Sabha, also has loving memories about his 'iron fisted' drill teacher.[47]

Keeleri was born on 12 August 1855 in Thalassery. At an early age, he started learning *kalaripayatt*, wrestling, gymnastics, and weight lifting.

[41] Murkoth Kunhappa, 'Circus in Malabar: Keeleri Kunhikannan Teacher', *Malabar Mahotsav 1993 Souvenir*, ed. M. G. S. Narayanan (1993): 124.

[42] Murkoth Kunhappa, 'Circus: Malayalikalude Sambhavana' [Circus: contribution of Malayalis], *Mathrubhumi Illustrated Weekly* 51, no. 28 (1951): 35.

[43] S. Narayanan, 'Prof. Keeleri Kunhikannan', *Circus Worker* 1, no. 4 (1980): 5.

[44] In 1856, the Basel German Mission began the first school in North Malabar in Thalassery. Later on, it became the Basel Evangelical Mission; Raghavan Mangalatt, 'Thalassery', *Mathrubhumi Illustrated Weekly* 38, no. 25 (1960): 33.

[45] A. Sreedhara Menon, *Kerala District Gazeteers*, 245; Murkoth Kunhappa, 'Circussilude Arogya Sambadanam' [Gaining health through circus], *Circus Worker* 1, no. 3 (1980): 23.

[46] C. H. Kunhappa, *Smaranakal Maatram* [Memories only] (Thrissur: Current Books, 2000), 74–7.

[47] Damodaran, *Anubhavachurulukal*, 10–12.

He was also into games such as cricket, which had been popular in that colonial town. He underwent gymnastics training in Madras for a year under the Field Games Association and learnt *kalaripayatt* under Maroli Ramunni Gurukkal, and later on under Unni Kurup.[48] *Mitavadi* (January 1914) also notes that after gaining expertise in indigenous physical sports such as *muchaan*, *otta*, *kettuvari*, *thotti*, *maravu*, *kunthapayatt*, he travelled to Madras, Mysore, Trichi, and Madhura and found teachers there to fulfill his learning: 'He has also become skilled at Punjabi wrestling and foreign practices such as the *cheti*, *baana*, *lejj* and *shankilipothu*. He has been teaching all these to people in his native land.'

Keeleri's rendezvous with circus must have been an ordinary happening in Tellicherry, a colonial hub. But there are different narratives regarding his 'first' encounter and the subsequent mastering of the art. Balan writes,

> Keeleri Kunhikannan Gurukkal who was a physical education teacher at Thalassery Mission School happened to see India's first circus, Chatre Circus, in 1888 at Thalassery. This was a turning point in the history of Indian circus. Gurukkal, who had not seen an organized circus till then, decided to try whether the breathtaking items of Chatre's circus could be taught to Malayali youngsters. He was optimistic about this experimentation because he believed that the land of North Malabar, where the daring heroes and heroines of *Vadakkanpattukal* were born and brought up, was fertile for physical arts to flourish.[49]

Champad writes, 'The first circus Keeleri saw was the European Hippodrome and later on Chatre's circus at Thalassery.'[50] Elsewhere he notes, '1884—it was in Madras that Keeleri saw a circus, some European circus. ... In 1887 Chatre's circus came to Thalassery and Keeleri and Chatre met. The rendezvous of two physical art masters.'[51] Gemini Sankaran writes, 'Circus patriarch, Vishnupanth Chatre visited Keeleri Kunhikannan at Thalassery having heard about his fame. Chatre recognized Kunhikannan Gurukkal's body skill and invited him

---

[48] *Mitavadi*, January 1914; S. Narayanan, 'Prof. Keeleri Kunhikannan', 5, 8; Sasikumar Kallidumbil, 'Kalaripayattum Circussum', 205; Sreedharan Chambad, 'Circussinte Eettillam', 149.

[49] Balan, *Circus*, 49.

[50] Champad, 'Circussinte Eettillam', 149.

[51] Champad, *Circusinte Lokam*, 129.

Image 1.1 Keeleri Kunhikannan, circa 1938
Source: Private collection of Edward Williams.

to circus.'[52] Nettoor Damodaran says that Keeleri had a keen interest in both *kalaripayatt* and circus acrobatics and spent his youth learning them. He also notes that circus was most popular in Maharashtra at that time and Keeleri travelled all around India.[53]

Whatever knowledge and training Keeleri had gained in the field of circus acrobatics had the flavours of many cultures and styles. Circus acrobatics in the Indian subcontinent is a complex and hybrid form where different sorts of bodily acts and performances, different regions and cultures come together. And Keeleri's passion for the form and his decision to establish a training centre to disseminate it might have

[52] Sankaran and Madayi, *Malakkam Mariyunna Jeevitham*, 26.
[53] Damodaran, *Anubhavachurulukal*, 11.

a more radical reckoning to it. He must have found in this 'modern' and 'assorted' physical culture the possibility to imagine an egalitarian space of the bodies, of different castes and genders. The daring choices he made in his private life stand testimony to his constant seeking out for a better and equal world.

Keeleri was born into Thiyya caste. But he did not believe in the caste system and married from a 'lower' caste and joined the Brahma Samaj.[54] *MM* (29 April and 17 June 1903) reported that a meeting had been called by significant personalities from the Thiyya community and had decided that the Thiyyas who joined the Brahma Samaj will be declared outcastes by the Thiyya Sabha. But the brutal caste masters could not subdue the spirit of a being like Keeleri. He converted to Christianity and remained so until his death on 22 September 1939 at the age of 81.[55]

[54] M. Madhavan notes,

Brahma Samaj made its entry into Malabar in 1898 with the establishment of its branch at Calicut. They gave more attention to the depressed castes. Brahma Samaj warned the people not to send their children to mission schools. The Theosophists and the nationalists propagated the concept of national education. Annie Besant called upon the Hindus to establish their own schools, as in Mission schools their religion was blasphemed. They opposed the domination of religious ideals in the educational activities of the Basel Mission. They also attacked the prevailing caste system, untouchability and other evils in the society.

M. Madhavan, *Social Reform Movements in Malabar*, PhD dissertation, University of Calicut, Kerala, 2010, 79–80.

[55] I have gleaned this life history from C. H. Kunhappa's *Smaranakal Maatram*, Nettoor Damodaran's *Anubhavachurulukal*, Sreedharan Champad's 'Circussinte Eettillam', and personal interviews with Keeleri's grandson, Edward Williams. Keeleri Kunhikannan Teacher was buried at CSI Gundert Church Cemetery, Illykkunnu, Thalassery. The epitaph says: 'Keeleri Karunakaran (Prof. Keeleri Kunhikannan Teacher) Father of Circus who Spent his Life Time in the Service of the Poor and Needy Died on 22-9-1939 - Aged 81. He died as He Lived Every One's Friend Till God Called Him Home'. After converting to Christianity, he changed his name to 'Keeleri Karunakaran'; Interview, Edward Williams. It is interesting to note that he adopted a 'Hindu' name rather than an explicit 'Christian' name even after conversion.

The Teacher's *Kalari*

C. H. Kunjappa recounts poignantly that in the circus *kalari* established by Keeleri 'anyone [could] learn any of the circus items': 'When teacher is nearby no one needs to be afraid of anything. Those two hands would be always there to hold you. Any broken bone would be massaged and straightened by those hands. Whether it was 'trapeze' or 'bar', a child would fall only into those hands.'[56] The circus *kalari* was built at Chirakkara, in Thalassery, adjoining his home.[57] A notice published as part of the endeavour to revive this *kalari* in 1949 states the year of establishment as 1888.[58] While Kandambulli Balan, Keezhanthi Gopalan Teacher, and Sreedhara Menon are of the opinion that it was built in 1901, Sreedharan Champad says that it was built as a 'temporary shed' in 1888.[59]

Mitavadi (January 1914) notes that Keeleri established a 'kalari for modern circus acrobatics' where both men and women got trained. It also mentions the visit of Sandow Ramamurthy to this *kalari* the previous year and his donation of 100 rupees to Keeleri in the former's circus tent. However, although Zarrilli, K. K. N. Kurup, and Sasikumar refer to the influence of *kalaripayatt* in circus acrobatics, they seem to have missed the key aspect that it was a *payatt kalari* that Keeleri transformed into a circus *kalari*.[60] In the *Circus Worker*, Thayath Raghavan describes it as the 'first circus *kalari* in India, or even Asia'.[61] Murkoth Ramunny recounts thus:

> He [Kunhikannan Teacher] had a *payattkalari* on his own property near his house before he started the circus school [circus *kalari*].

[56] Kunhappa, *Smaranakal Maatram*, 75.

[57] Interview, Edward Williams.

[58] Notice dated August 1949: 'Late Prof. Keeleri Kunhikannan Teacher's All India Circus Training Hall, Cherakkara, Tellicherry (N. Malabar)'.

[59] Kandambulli Balan, 'Maharashtrathil ninnu Malayalathilekk' [From Maharashtra to Malayalam], *Circus Worker* 1, no. 1 (1980); Keezhanthi Gopalan Teacher, 'M K Raman', *Mathrubhumi Illustrated Weekly* 29, no. 52 (1960): 22; A. Sreedhara Menon, *Kerala District Gazeteers*, 245; Sreedharan Champad, *Circusinte Lokam*, 129.

[60] Zarrilli, *When Body Becomes All Eyes*; Kurup, *Samooham, Charithram, Samskaram*; Sasikumar, 'Kalaripayattum Circussum'.

[61] Thayath Raghavan, 'Kalakeralathinte Romancham' [The thrill of Kerala art scene], *Circus Worker* 1, no. 3 (1980): 9.

He was the instructor of *kalaripayatt* and my father, Murkoth Kumaran was his pupil there. There were many *kalaripayatt* instructors at that time, but he was the most well-known. … He saw the British camp at Canannore in 1800 or so. … I've seen it [circus *kalari*] only as a passerby. It was this pit like thing of *kalaripayatt* [pit *kalari*], that he modified, brought this and that [what Keeleri Kunhikannan saw in the British camp] together, I don't know how he did it, but the circus *kalari* was built. … To train artistes here was easy for him, because he already had a *payatt kalari*.[62]

This circus *kalari* was built at the ground level. Both the length and breadth of it was different from the *payatt kalaris*. The length of the practice *kalari* meant for *payatt* is 42 feet and the dwell *kalari* is that of 64 feet. The traditional *kalari* is always built according to the *Taccusastra*.[63] The approximate height of this circus *kalari* was 20 feet and the length was about three times more. The roof and walls were thatched with coconut leaves and was open on the four sides. The ground was leveled and smoothened with a heavy layer of sand.[64] From the descriptions of Murkoth Kunhappa, it could be assumed that at BEMP the building for gymnastics exercising also had similar features.[65]

Zarrilli and Vasudevagurukkal point out that women of certain castes such as the Nair and Ezhava were given training in *payatt* from early

[62] Interview, Murkoth Ramunny, Dharmadam, 31 January 2009.

[63] Zarrilli, *When Body Becomes All Eyes*, 62; *Taccusastra* is a traditional architectural science.

[64] Interview, Raman, Melur, 29 March 2008; Murkoth Ramunny also remembers that 'there was a beautiful drill ground [at BEMP School] smoothened over with sand. The parallel bar and rings were built there. He considered each of us individually, what one could do and could not. He allowed me to try on the parallel bar, but when it came to rings or something else, he would say, *"mone inikk venda"* [no son, not for you].' Interview, Murkoth Ramunny.

[65] Kunhappa, 'Circussilude Arogya Sambadanam', 22; the grandson of C. V. Narayanan Nair, Sathyanarayanan, a *kalaripayatt* and *kalari* medicine practitioner, said that the Thulu *kalaris* of South Canara regions were mainly ground *kalaris*, longer in size compared to the pit *kalaris* and Thulu *kalari* exercises consisted of a wide range of somersaults and jumping. There were pits dug (with rice hull filled to the brim) inside the *kalari*, especially for practicing these somersaulting exercises; Interview, Sathyanarayanan, CVN Kalari, Thiruvananthapuram, 12 November 2014.

times.[66] In the folk ballads of *Vadakkanpattukal*, there are prominent female warrior figures. So the considerable presence of women in the circus *kalari* could be deemed as quite customary, but the significant aspect was that they came from all castes and communities. Edward Williams said that his grandfather, Keeleri Kunhikannan, trained men and women and placed them in the circus companies owned by Marathis, and later in Malayali companies.[67] Almost all the items, such as 'horizontal bar', 'varmachattam' (frog), 'trapeze', 'rope dance', 'weight lifting', 'rings', 'foot juggling', 'pole', and 'wire', performed in the circus companies used to be taught in the circus *kalaris*, except 'cycling', 'clowning', and items with animals.[68] After the completion of training, the acrobat could suggest the name of the company s/he wanted to join and the Teacher helped them out by arranging a bond of four to five years with the company. At times, the companies sent agents to him for acrobats talented in some particular item.[69] A torn fragment of a letter in the personal collection of Edward Williams is an instance of the warm relationship that existed between the master and his disciples touring all over the world with various companies. The letter dated '06/04/1936' from 'Nellore' is written on the letterhead of the famous Russian company 'F. Isako's Circus & Menagerie', which was 'Touring the East' with '110 European Artists' and 'Menagerie Consisting of 300 Rare Specimens'. With his meticulous blending of different physical cultures in circus acrobatics, Keeleri was, in fact, reconstructing the very structure of acrobatics in the world circus arena. This could be one of the reasons why his disciples got almost instantaneous recognition with their distinguishing feats not only in Indian circus companies but also all over the world.

Kunhiraman, who is 90 now, joined the Teacher's *kalari* at the age of 8 and got trained for a year before going on to join the Whiteway Circus. There were about 10 big circus companies run by Malayalis at that time. He remembers that there were about 30 students, also children and

---

[66] Zarrilli, *When Body Becomes All Eyes*, 73; E. P. Kadathuruthi Vasudevagurukkal, *Kalaripayatt: Keralathinte Thanathu Ayodhanakala* [Kalaripayatt: the original martial art of Kerala] (Kottayam: DC Books, 2000), 233.

[67] Interview, Edward Williams.

[68] Interview, Gemini Sankaran, Kannur, 29 October 2012; Kunhiraman, Melur, 24 January 2009; Sreedharan Champad, *Circusinte Lokam*, 131.

[69] Interview, Kunhiraman.

women, who came to the *kalari* and did physical exercises such as *vala-chil, othiram, dand* (push-ups), and *bethak* (sit-ups).[70] Teacher usually trained in the morning and evening, before and after his duty in the BEMP School. When Teacher was not there, the senior students were in charge of the circus *kalari*. There were some students from very poor families whom he supported. Kannan Bombayo (Teacher's nephew, who was supposedly referred to as 'the jumping devil of India' by Adolf Hitler), Poovadan Kunjamboo, Paremmal Keshavan, Kunnath Yesoda, T. K. Krishnan, Gopalan Nambiar, Keeleri Kunhikannan (later the owner of Whiteway Circus), Ambu Master (later the owner of Grand Fairy Circus), and Kallan Gopalan (later the owner of Rayman Circus) were some of his disciples.[71] The *Mitavadi* (January 1914) report notes:

> More than sixty people belonging to different castes, from the Brahmins, and religions trained in [Keeleri's] *kalari* have been getting salaries of more than hundred rupees from various circus companies. There are some girls among them as well. The leading fifteen performers of the famous Chatre's circus are the disciples of Mr. Keeleri Kunhikannan. The best of the lot is M K Raman who performs with bars on the bar. He has received lots of rewards from kings and nobles. M. Yesoda of the same circus company, and M Madhavi and O Devaki from National circus are also his disciples. The ten year old boy, Chandu, who enthralls the specta-tors with his tight-rope items, is also one of his foremost disciples. Many Malayalis must have seen the performances of P Kunhambu, P Govindan, Parayali Kannan and K Kanari, the main players of Karlekar[72] circus.

[70] Interview, Kunhiraman; these exercises are discussed in detail in the fol-lowing section.

[71] Interview, Kunhiraman; *Balarama Digest*, ed. Bina Mathew (Kottayam: MM, 2005), 33; Surendran, 'Koodara Smaranakalude Thanalil' [In the shade of tent memories], *Kalakaumudi* (280) (1981): 18.

[72] Karlekar, Walavalkar, and Shelar, who later became known as the Marathi circus owners, were leading performers in the Royal Maratha circus owned by Bhimrao Patil; Praveen Prabhakar Walimbe, *The World of Circus* (Pune: Tanaya-Esha, 2003), 17; 'In 1912 Sadashiv Rao N. Karlekar of "Karlekar's Grand Circus" died. He had given equal partnership to two of his employees, Shankar Rao Lahaane and Thukkarm Ganpath Shellar, when he was in financial crisis in the beginning of twentieth century.' Sreedharan Champad, *An Album of Indian Big Tops* (Houston: Strategic Books, 2013), 18.

There are also other renowned acrobats such as Keeryatt Kunhikannan, P R Krishnayyar, Govindan Nair, Appa Nair and M Mannan.

Kandambulli Balan quotes Kasinath Vinayak Chatre, the second owner of Chatre's Circus, who introduced his Malayali acrobats to the nationalist, Bal Gangadhar Tilak—'these are the lion cubs of my company; compared to them, the Maratha acrobats are simple lambs'—and further adds that such expert performers as Keezhanti Gopalan, Mannan, M. K. Raman, Keeleri Kunhikannan Junior, and Padikkal Kunjananthan worked in this company together.[73]

All India Circus Training Hall

A noteworthy effort was made to re-establish Keeleri's circus *kalari* a decade after the master's death by Keeleri's son, Devadas,[74] and his brother-in-law, O. K. Victor (mentioned in the notice about the endeavour as O. K. Kutty), along with his disciples and some public personalities.[75] The committee was constituted with his disciple Nettur P. Damodaran as the secretary, K. Kelappan (who headed the Indian National Congress in the region at the time) as the president, and M. P. Damodaran, M. L. A., and T. K. Narayanan as the vice presidents. The objective of the committee was to collect an estimated fund of INR 18,000 to construct a large hall for the circus *kalari* at Thalassery. The committee planned to collect this amount from the donations of circus artistes, owners, and other interested parties.

The notice,[76] published in both Malayalam and English, is addressed to 'the generous public and lovers of physical culture'. It is interesting to note that while the English notice describes the training centre as 'All India Circus Training Hall', catering to the 'national' mood of the

[73] Kandambulli Balan, *Circus*, 44.

[74] He had served during the 1950s as a manager in some of the circuses run by Keeleri's disciples Ambu Master, the owner of 'Grand Fairy', and Kallan Gopalan, the owner of 'Rayman' circus; Interview, Edward Williams.

[75] Interview, Edward Williams.

[76] Notice dated August 1949: 'Late Prof. Keeleri Kunhikannan Teacher's All India Circus Training Hall, Cherakkara, Tellicherry (N. Malabar)', private collection, Edward Williams, Thalassery, Kerala.

times most probably, the Malayalam version retains the original *kalari*. This translation of the 'regional' into 'national' in English is definitely interesting. The notice claims that 'the All India Circus Training Hall has been incepted by late Professor Keeleri Kunhikannan some 60 years ago' and in the logo states the year of establishment as 1888. As pointed out earlier, this is a contentious issue.

The notice further adds that 'this organisation had fashioned innumerable young men in the marvellous feats displayed in circuses all over India, in the Far East and in Europe'. The Malayalam version mentions that Keeleri's son has been running the circus *kalari* after his father's death. Edward remembers the disciples and *ustads*[77] assembling in the front yard of his house early in the morning for practice on the land which they called *kalari paramb* (*kalari* land). They fixed the horizontal bar on the northern side adjacent to their house, the trapeze on the nearby coconut tree, and also practised cycling. There were two main *ustads*, among whom Basara Achu, another known *ustad* from the Mukkuva community, used to teach the bunch of disciples.[78] Now let us move on to the circus *kalari* built by one of Keeleri's illustrious disciples M. Mannan in the 1930s.

M. Mannan

M. Mannan was also a drill teacher like his master. He taught *Roman rings* and *parallel bars* at the Municipal High School in Kannur. There is hardly any literature on Mannan's circus *kalari*, probably because he ran it as a family enterprise. The only source is Sreedharan, the son of Mannan. Sreedharan, who is 94 now, remembers that his father's circus *kalari* was built circa 1937 at Thalap, Kannur.[79] It was built on

---

[77] The Urdu word '*ustad*', meaning teacher, is a common usage for trainers in the circus community. But interestingly, the first-generation trainers such as Keeleri, M. K. Raman, and Mannan are still referred to as 'teacher'.

[78] Interview, Edward Williams.

[79] Interviews with Sreedharan conducted in Thalassery over the years 2006–9; Sreedharan was a very popular artiste during 1940s and 1950s. Popularly known as 'seven bar Sreedharan' for his spectacular act on the seven bars, Sreedharan has performed this item in S. S. Vasan's magnum opus *Chandralekha* (1948). The 'bar' used to be one of the most adventurous and strenuous items

the land of Mannan's second wife, Devi. It should be noted here that his other two wives—O. K. Narayani, Sreedharan's mother who was from Kannur, and Yesoda from Thalassery—were famous women circus artistes. Mannan and his brother Kumaran, who were both drill teachers, were among those early 'bar' players. Both of them had been taught by Krishnan Teacher, who was also a drill teacher. Mannan saw the performance of Ramamurthy on the triple bar at Patwardhan Circus and practised on the five bar with the help of Krishnan Teacher, after which he joined the Patwardhan and the Chatre Circuses with a troupe. Sreedharan remembers that it was after his return from the Patwardhan Circus that his father, Mannan, started a circus *kalari* at Kannur.

It was a provisional structure with a cloth roof, which was later thatched with coconut leaves. According to Sreedharan, all four sides were left open. It was more than 50 feet in length and 20 feet in height and width. The exterior space was also utilized for training items such as 'loose wire', 'knife-throw', 'rings', 'rope dance', and 'balancing on and shaking the ladder'. But the equipment for the 'bar' and the 'trapeze' were installed inside. He told me that almost all items performed in the circus company were taught there. In the circus *kalaris*, although the women exercised on the single parallel bar, they rarely performed any 'bar' items. Before he settled down in Kannur teaching his disciples, he owned a circus company named 'Great Indian', which he had started after leaving his job at the school. According to Sreedharan's memory, his father 'donated' the company to his guru, Krishnan Teacher, who

---

that are no longer played in Indian circus. There were three, five, and seven 'bar' items, all of which were played on the horizontal bar. Five and triple 'bars' were common items. But the 'seven bar' was considered the most dangerous and spectacular of all; Nisha P R, 'Jeevitham Kondoru Reality Show' [A reality show with life], *Mathrubhumi Illustrated Weekly* 86, no. 9 (May 2008): 22–6.

Sreedharan told me that it is played without any safety net and the performer will be at a height of 15 feet, higher than the trapeze. He says he was one of those premier expert players in the 'seven bar' and has received gold and silver medals from luminaries. He adds, 'Girls won't play "bar" in India. Girls do all other items, they can't do the "bar". No girl in India has ever done the "bar", but in Russia, China, and Japan, women perform all the items, including the "bar",' which is probably a glaring instance of the gender bias in the Indian circus arena.

was going through a severe financial crisis at the time. Under Krishnan Teacher's proprietorship, this company went through some makeovers and had different names, such as 'South Indian Ladies' Circus and 'Malabar Ladies' Circus. Finally, it became 'Kamala Three Ring' Circus, the largest circus in Asia and the second largest in the world, under his son Damodaran's management. Mannan then started another company called the 'International'.

Sreedharan recounts that the primary objective of his father in establishing the *kalari* was to train his own children, numbering around 30, from the three wives:

> I and my mother stayed at Cantonment in Kannur. I would go to the *kalari* at Kakkad from here on a bicycle at 4 o'clock in the morning. There was practice from 6 to 12. From there I would again be back home when the alarm whistles from the machine shop nearby. Again at 2 o'clock I would move. There would be practice from 3 o'clock till 6. When it was over I would go back home. That was how my father taught me the *bar*.

However, approximately 15 students from outside the family were also trained at this *kalari*. Kumaran assisted Mannan in teaching the students. The teaching of exercises began at the ages of 10 to 12. Belgium Nanu is one disciple of his father whom he remembers. Nanu, after his retirement from circus, used to play tricks and small single feats in his later years in schools and colleges. Unlike M. K. Raman's *kalari*, which was more popular, there were no girl students whom his father trained. Sreedharan remembers that his father's desire was to train him in 'seven bar' and outshine his peer 'five bar' players.

> Sankaran and Narayanan, nephews of Moosari Ramettan, were excellent *bar* players in the Marathi 'G.I' circus. There was a tiff going on between Marathis and Malayalis in the circus. The tents and food of Malayalis were on the one side and the Marathis at the opposite. No Marathi manager or proprietor should pass through the Malayali area, that was the order of the brothers, Sankaran–Narayanan. Malayalis did not have much power in the circus then. But the brothers stopped playing and punched the Marathi ringmaster. The owner, Abbas Babu,[80] was tired of them.

---

[80] *Babu* (probably adopted from Bengali) is an affix often used by circus people after the names of circus owners to show their respect and complaisance. See Chapter 3 for more discussion on the circus vernacular.

He approached Moosari Ramettan for a *bar* player who could excel them. He said he had none and told him there was Mannan Teacher's son. That is how I joined my first circus company as per the agreement my father made with the owner.

This interesting narration shows the power the circus *kalari*–trained artistes had in a company. This also throws light on the turbulent relationship that existed between Marathis and Malayalis during a time when the former held the ownership and management of circuses.[81]

Narayani, Devi, and Yesoda

Among the land-owning castes such as Nairs and Thiyyas in Malabar, the kinship system and property rights were channelized through women. Devi, Mannan's wife, must have wielded some power as the land on which the *kalari* was built belonged to her. Even though there were few girls in the circus *kalaris* in the beginning phases, by the 1930s they outnumbered their male counterparts in circus companies.[82] O. K. Narayani (also known as Nani) joined circus as an artiste after marrying Mannan. They were at the Patwardhan Circus together where she played the *cycle*, *wire*, and *ladder* acts. They had eight sons, all of whom found their living in the circus tents. Sreedharan believes that his mother's long and healthy life—she died at the age of 105—was because of the circus life with its proper exercises and diet.[83] *Mitavadi* (April 1916), while reporting about Lady Sandow, Tarabai, states that two young girls, Yesoda and Nani, from Malabar are coming up as expert circus acrobats.

---

[81] Nisha P R, 'Performing Bodies, Physical Cultures: Looking at the Circus Kalaris in Malabar', *Social Science Probings* 22, no. 1 (June 2010): 87.

[82] Sreedharan Champad, 'Circussinte Eettillam', 150.

[83] The health and youthful spirit of many of the old circus artistes—some over eighty—is an interesting factor I have observed during my fieldwork. Kamala, a circus artiste from Thalayi, and Gemini Sankaran, the artiste-turned-company-owner, told me that they still practise the exercises they learnt in their circus life every morning. Interview, Kamala, Thalayi, 24 September 2010; Interview, Gemini Sankaran.

Champad describes Kunnath Yesoda as the 'first' Malayali woman to join circus, while the first Indian artiste, he says, is Avdabai Parulelkar, the second wife of Vishnupanth Chatre.[84] *MM* (29 April 1908) mentions the presence of 'a single girl among some Thiyyas' in the Malabar Grand Circus, the first circus company from Malabar.[85] Raghavan says that Yesoda 'left the first standard in school before learning the compound letters in Malayalam and walked out with the known acrobat and native from Kannur, Poovadan Kunhambu, to step on the significant ladder of the circus world. She, who joined Keeleri Kunhikannan teacher's circus *kalari*, is the first Malayali woman who performed in various circus companies'.[86] Raghavan also mentions that there was another girl called Velandi Madhavi who practised along with Yesoda. According to Raghavan's account, Yesoda stayed with a relative of Keeleri to learn from the *kalari*. She joined Chatre's circus when it performed in Thalassery. She spent 18 years in Chatre's circus and the owner treated her like his own daughter. She introduced the item of performing the 'ladder on the rope' but met with an accident in Tanjore. Raghavan concludes his article lamenting her abject condition in a rented house with no one for any help during her old age.

M. K. Raman

Keezhanthi Gopalan Teacher, a renowned 'bar' player, recounts the fame and reputation of M. K. Raman (1885–1959) among the circus

---

[84] Sreedharan Champad, *Circusinte Lokam*, 132.

[85] During 1898, the Parayali Kannan's troupe played as a side show to a European bioscope company. The troupe included Poovadan Kunjambu, M. K. Raman, and his brother, apart from Parayali. They played items such as the 'bar', 'somersaulting', and 'balancing the ladder' and drew a salary of Rs 150 monthly. After one-and-a-half years, they decided to start a circus company of their own. Keezhanthi Gopalan Teacher, 'M K Raman', 22; in Parayalis' Malabar Grand Circus, the first circus company by Malayalis which was inaugurated by Keeleri in 4 February 1904. There were no animals but only human acrobatic feats. Balan, *Circus*, 52; *Mitavadi* (January 1914) also notes 1904 as its founding year.

[86] Thayath Raghavan, 'Kalakeralathinte Romancham', 11.

lovers in Bengal thus: 'There was an admirer in Calcutta who came to the show a dozen times just to see Raman performing [on the bar]. ... There was no need for any other publicity if the name M K Raman was there.'[87] *Mitavadi* (January 1914) says, 'Of the fifteen of Keeleri's disciples in the Chatre circus, M. K. Raman who plays with bar on the bar, is the most adept.' He played on five bars when it was not common even in the European circus companies, and it earned him the name 'Indian Champion'.[88] In a single swing he played on the three bars and did back somersaults.[89] Raghavan further narrates the great guru–disciple relationship: 'The owner of Parasuram lion circus approached Keeleri Kunhikannan Teacher to employ Raman. ... The Chatre's had promised him a salary equivalent to his weight, but he left them just to keep the word that his teacher had given.'[90]

Raman was an artiste in the Malabar Circus, the first circus company from Malabar, Indian Wonderful Circus, New India Circus, Parasuram Circus,[91] and Padvardhan Circus,[92] and later owned a circus company called Star of India.[93] He was an expert in 'double somersaulting', 'trapeze' acts, 'bar', 'wire walking', 'juggling', and 'clowning'. Kings and Lords bestowed him with titles and certificates. It was after his company

[87] Keezhanthi Gopalan Teacher, 'M K Raman', 22; Many circus artistes told me that in many parts of North India, people stayed for two to three days sleeping on a simple sack to watch even a small circus. These instances raise larger questions such as how was circus received and who were its spectators.

[88] Thayath Raghavan, 'Kalakeralathinte Romancham', 10.

[89] Keezhanthi Gopalan Teacher, 'M K Raman', 22.

[90] Thayath Raghavan, 'Kalakeralathinte Romancham', 10.

[91] Notice from the collection of Parasuram Mali shows that Parasuram Circus was started in 1897. Parasuram Mali's grandfather, Parasuram Yallappa Mali, was the owner of this company. He was born in Tasgaon and began his career as an animal trainer in Chatre's circus; interview, Parasuram Mali.

[92] Padvardhan circus was owned by Dathathreya Padvardhan who started his company in 1911. He was an advocate and an animal trainer by profession; Sreedharan Champad, *Circusinte Lokam*, 130.

[93] M. K. Raman's 'Star of India' was started in 1926. Other disciples of Keeleri also joined his company. In 1928, while performing in Ceylon, it was harmed irrecoverably in the heavy rains; Thayath Raghavan, 'Kalakeralathinte Romancham', 10.

started running losses that he started his circus *kalari* with the finance he had earned from the Whiteway Circus.[94]

The circus *kalari*, established in 1941 by M. K. Raman,[95] at Chirakkara was, undoubtedly, modelled on the first *kalari* of Keeleri Kunhikannan. In fact, it was built in the memory of Keeleri Kunhikannan.[96] Of the circus *kalaris* mentioned here, this is the only one that still stands. It is approximately 69 feet in length, 23 feet in width, and 30 feet in height. In the beginning, the floor was made of sand, and later mud. The roof of the *kalari*, which is tiled now, was earlier covered with thatched coconut leaves.[97] The walls were earlier made of bamboo poles and thatched coconut leaves, and later stone.[98] One entered the *kalari* through a stone ladder. Framed photographs of Keeleri and Raman along with those of gods and goddesses used to adorn the walls of the *kalari*. Raman built the *kalari* adjacent to his home, the land where he was also laid to rest.[99]

Youngsters were trained in many items such as 'single-wheel cycle', 'cycle', 'wire balance', 'bar', 'rope dance', and 'trapeze' in Raman's *kalari*, while other items such as 'clowning' and performances with animals were to be learned in the circus companies. The male acrobats wore trousers sometimes with a *langoti*[100] inside, while women wore two-piece dresses as in the circus rings. Elementary exercises such as balancing, jumping, *bethak*, *thirichil*, and *dand* were done before practising the items. The bar and the trapeze equipment were fixed at low heights for practicing. Safety nets were not used in the *kalari*, though they were in use in the

[94] The 'Whiteway' Circus was owned by Keeleri's nephew whose name was also Keeleri Kunhikannan. Unlike the Malabar Grand Circus, the Whiteway Circus was a full-fledged company with animals and equipment. It travelled throughout South-East Asia; Thayath Raghavan, 'Kalakeralathinte Romancham', 10.

[95] M. K. Raman is also known as *Moosari* Raman, which refers to the caste of ironsmith.

[96] Sreedharan Paikkatt, 'Sri M K Raman Teacher', *Circus Worker* 1, no. 2 (1980): 17.

[97] Interview, (Late) Bhaskaran, Thalassery, 18 July 2007.

[98] Sreedharan Paikkatt, 'Sri M K Raman Teacher', 17.

[99] Interview, (Late) Prabhakaran, Payyoli, 03 February 2009.

[100] The loincloth (*langoti*) was worn by *kalaripayatt* and *kushti* practitioners during their practice.

circus companies then.[101] Prabhakaran recounts that when he joined the *kalari*, there was approximately 20 students, while Sreehari notes that there were 30 students including 10 girls who kept coming and going in turns.[102] Many pupils went on to become prominent players. Sankaran, owner of Gemini Circus; Balagopalan, owner of the Great Bombay Circus; Sankaran and Narayanan, the brothers who owned the Great Chithra Circus; acknowledged 'bar' players such as Mekkileri Kumaran and his brother Krishnan; Samikutti, V. M. Somu, and Prabhakaran's brother, Krishnan had all received their training in this circus *kalari*.[103]

Just as in his teacher's *kalari*, the acrobatic training was free of charge in M. K. Raman's circus *kalari* too. Former students who had found jobs in circus companies provided financial assistance when they came home on leave. Probably, *gurupuja* (worship of the guru), as was done in *payatt kalaris*, was also observed here but with some differences. At the time of joining, there used to be the practice of giving *dakshina*[104] (offering) of five rupees or so. Having completed their learning in the *kalari* and gotten employment in a circus company, the artistes observed the practice of sending money on the occasion of Navaratri festival. There used to be pujas on every Navaratri; the *kalari* would be decorated with flower garlands and puja would be performed for all the equipment and instruments in the *kalari*. Then, the practitioners would give *dakshina* to their master who would perform the puja. Prabhakaran says that many of the equipment the artistes practised with are still there. On other days, they would light up the holy lamp while beginning the practice and again at sunset.[105] Hardly does a circus acrobat enter the ring without offering prayers to the divine Almighty and touching the floor of the ring. 'Raman, in his later years, would come and spend time in the *kalari* with a watchful eye and go back to his house close by,' remembers Vamakshi, who used to be Raman's neighbour.[106]

---

[101] Interview, Bhaskaran and Prabhakaran.

[102] Sreehari Nair, *Gemini Shankaran & the Legacy of Indian Circus*, 35.

[103] Sreedharan Paikkatt, 'Sri M K Raman Teacher', 15–16.

[104] The practice of giving *dakshina* on auspicious occasions is very common all over Kerala. Santhosh, a *kalaripayatt* practitioner in CVN Kalari, Thiruvangad, told me that it is commonly observed in *payatt kalaris*; interview, Santhosh, Thiruvangad, 14 February 2009.

[105] Interview, Prabhakaran.

[106] Interview, Vamakshi, Chirakkara, 21 January 2009.

Sreedharan Paikkatt says that the changing character of circus items and the new equipment posed a challenge to Raman's son, Viswanathan, who took charge of the *kalari* after his father's death on 31 October 1959. It was at this point that he decided to hand over his father's *kalari* to his friends and disciples. Thus, on 29 November 1959, a meeting was organized in which it was decided to form a 'Circus and Gymnastic Training Hall Building Reorganization Fund' to build a suitable building and buy the required equipment. The target was to collect INR 15,000. The committee was formed with Keezhanthi Gopalan Teacher as the president; K. Gopalan as the secretary; and Viswanathan as the joint secretary. The present building was built with this fund.[107]

Circus *Kalari*: Today

The photographs of M. K. Raman's circus *kalari* will give us an idea about the present condition of this institution. Prabhakaran laments that the circus *kalari* is surrounded by weed and grass since nobody cares for it. No circus artiste or those who desire to join the circus come

Image 1.2 M. K. Raman's Circus *Kalari*
Source: Author.

[107] Sreedharan Paikkatt, 'Sri M K Raman Teacher', 17–20.

there for practice.[108] There was no gate before and the entry was not restricted, unlike now.

The equipment is clearly old-fashioned and shows the lack of advanced technologies. A photograph published in *Chandrika* (10 June 2001) shows that there was a board with the inscription 'Circus Gymnast' kept here earlier, which directly points to the assembling of circus with gymnastics. They use stones and pulleys in contrast to the sophisticated devices used in the Sports Authority of India gymnasium in the town of Thalassery. The rusted tools were assembled in the small room where the photographs of gods were kept. The fungus-infected and torn photographs of exercising persons with healthy, masculine bodies (Image 1.2) that hung inside are reminders of a healthy and energetic period in this circus *kalari*. The absence of women is notable in the photographs. A photo from the 1940s published in *Circus Worker* highlights the presence of young girls and children of 4 to 5 years of age.[109]

Adda

The circus *kalari*s were also a social space for the circus community; a space to gather, chat, and engage in discussions about larger dimensions of their profession and the world around them. The circus *kalari*, which was primarily a training/work space, thus also becomes a community space that could be related to the 'tea-shop gatherings' or what Dipesh Chakrabarty calls an *adda*, an assemblage of young men of the neighbourhood to 'have their noisy *addas*' in contrast to the disciplined *payatt kalari*s.[110] The artistes who came on their annual leave from the circus companies visited the circus *kalari*. These sessions in the *kalari* helped them maintain their fitness with routine exercises during vacations.[111] They would treat the *kalari* students with tea parties

---

[108] Interview, Prabhakaran.

[109] Sreedharan Paikkatt, 'Sri M. K. Raman Teacher', 17.

[110] Dipesh Chakrabarty, *Provincializing Europe: Postcolonial Thought and Historical Difference* (New Delhi: Oxford University Press, 2001), 188; Vasudevagurukkal, *Kalaripayatt: Keralathinte Thanathu Ayodhanakala*, 24–6.

[111] Interview, Rajan, Muzhappilanhad, 17 September 2009.

and exciting stories from their circus life: '[H]e would give them one rupee and with that one rupee, sixteen persons will go together to the restaurant near Manjodi. They will have steamed rice cake with mutton curry and enjoy themselves!'[112]

Physical Cultures

In this section, I will discuss what contributed to the structure of circus acrobatics that exists in India today. I would also be looking at significant contributions and interactions of various physical cultures and the moulding of circus feats. *Kalaripayatt* and *kushti* are traditional Indian physical training systems, while yoga is often regarded as useful for both the physique and the psyche. The Sandow system, the Swedish Drill, and gymnastic practices have contributed to both elementary exercises and have been influential to at least a dozen circus items. I would also look at how various medicinal systems have formed a part of circus medicinal treatments.

Kalaripayatt

> The little girl in the skirt
> biting onto a globe pointer
> may seem to have only one aim,
> to astound me mouth wide open.
> She bends her body like a silk ribbon.[113]

Folding one's body like a silk thread, beyond poetic imagination, demands strong will, painstaking training, and great balance; precisely the traits a circus artiste has to master right from the initial stage. Kandambulli Balan says,

> They [circus acrobats] should begin their training at the age of six or seven. The primary lesson involves the 'boneless folding', a mix of acrobatics and exercising. Strenuous efforts are spent for years for attaining flexibility. Then to each one, different items are taught in accordance with

[112] Sreehari Nair, *Gemini Shankaran & the Legacy of Indian Circus*, 135.

[113] Kondepudi Nirmala, 'Circussukari' [Circus girl], *Kerala Kavitha* (January 1993): 68.

their aptitude and expertise. The training can last from six months to
ten years depending on the complexity of the item. Even after ten years
of practice, there is a possibility of leaving out because of the lack of
perfection.[114]

Valachil, *thirichil*, *marichil*, and *othiram* form some of the elementary exercises of circus acrobatics, apart from jumping and running.[115]
'Boneless' (also known as 'plastic boldness'), one of those first items a
young student learns, is an extended and modified form of these elementary practices. One can easily make out that the terms *othiram* and
nerothiram are used to point out *adavu* (combat strategy) in *kalaripay-*
att.[116] A *payatt* practitioner from Kottayam, K. G. Muraleedharan, deems
that circus in Malabar originated from *kalaripayatt*. He further adds that
in the northern style, there was a *payatt* feat called *njaninmelvela* which
is quite similar to the circus trapeze tricks.[117] T. K. Vijayaraghavan says,

> In the northern system prevalent in Malabar the major three techniques
> are *arappakai*, *pillathaangi* and *vattenthirippu*. ... The leg fight *arappakai*,
> the hand fight *pillathaangi* and dance like fight *vattenthirippu* are assets of
> the northern system. ... In earlier times *vattenthirippu* was a performative
> fight supposed to relax the mind before the combat. Its influence can be
> seen in circus also.[118]

As pointed out earlier, scholars and writers who recognized the links
between circus and *kalarippayatt* did not, however, note the similarities
in the training spaces the *kalaris* shared. The *payatt kalaris* were usually built on the southwestern side of one's house, in accordance with
the *Taccusastra*.[119] The circus *kalari* of Keeleri Kunhikannan had obviously followed this architectural tenet as it was his *payatt kalari* that he

[114] Kandambulli Balan, 'Abhyasikalude Kuude' [With the acrobats],
Mathrubhumi Illustrated Weekly 33, no. 9 (1955): 13.

[115] Interview, E. Ravindran, Neyyattinkara, 12 July 2012.

[116] G. Rishi Natesh, 'Kalamozhiyunna Kalaripayatt' [Kalaripayatt in decline],
Kalakaumudi Weekly 387 (February 1983): 26.

[117] Interview, K. G. Muraleedharan.

[118] T. K. Vijayaraghavan, 'Kalaripayattinte Eettillam' [The birth place of
Kalaripayatt], in *Malabar: Paithrukavum Prathapavum* [Legacy and majesty], ed.
P. B. Salim, N. P. Hafiz Muhammed, and M. C. Vasishtt (Kozhikode:
Mathrubhumi, 2011), 518.

[119] Zarrilli, *When Body Becomes All Eyes*, 62.

transformed into a circus *kalari*.[120] The circus artistes used to wear *langoti* while practicing in the *kalari*, as the practitioners of *kalaripayatt* or *kushti*. In M. K. Raman's circus *kalari*, one can see the images of various gods and goddesses such as Saraswathi, Krishna, and Hanuman. The Navaratri festival was celebrated with much piety in this *kalari*.[121] In the *payatt kalaris*, puja was also done for Saraswati, the goddess of learning, and Hanuman, the lord of physical exercise, wrestling, and yoga, apart from Kaloorika, the goddess of *kalari*.[122] 'On the day of *Vidyarambham* every disciple is supposed to offer the guru a coin or cloth' in the *payatt kalari*.[123] The circus acrobats also offered coins on this day, though it was not at all compulsory.[124]

For *payatt*, it is prescribed to look for persons with a 'small head, narrow waist, torso shorter than legs, strong arms, broad chest and eagle eyes'.[125] K. K. Sreedharan, an acrobat turned trainer, says, 'Circus performance is a balancing act of the body, so people with light hips and body have more fitness and they will be chosen to do somersaulting and jumping in the air while those with a heavy body are trained in *cycling* and *ring dance*. They can take weight and perform on the ground better'.[126]

The resurgence of public interest in *kalaripayatt* began in Thalassery during the 1920s as part of the revival of traditional arts, which characterized the growing agitations against colonial rule.[127] Sreedharan Nair,

---

[120] Interview, Kunhiraman, Melur, 24 January 2009.

[121] Interview, Prabhakaran.

[122] Zarrilli, *When Body Becomes All Eyes*, 60–76; Joseph S. Alter, 'The Body of One Color: Indian Wrestling, the Indian State, and Utopian Somatics', *Cultural Anthropology* 8, no. 1 (1993): 50–4; Vasudevagurukkal, *Kalaripayatt: Keralathinte Thanathu Ayodhanakala*, 20.

[123] R. V. Pothuval, 'Keralathile Kalari' [Kalari in Kerala], *M N Nair Masika* 3, no. 2 (September–October 1937): 104; *Vidyarambham* is a Hindu auspicious day in some parts of South India for one's initiation into languages and arts.

[124] Interview, Prabhakaran.

[125] Chirrakal T. Balakrishnan Nair, 'Keralathile Kaayikabyasakala' [The physical art of Kerala], *Mathrubhumi Illustrated Weekly* 34, no. 33 (1956): 71.

[126] Interview, Sreedharan K K, Meethale Peedika, 10 May 2008.

[127] Zarrilli, *When Body Becomes All Eyes*, 51; different websites on *kalaripayatt* repeatedly talk about how the colonial rule dealt a death blow to this martial system. Lord Bentinck issued an order banning the natives carrying arms and warned them against deportation for life if the rule was disobeyed. The order

a revivalist, writes, 'The one-hundred-and-forty-three years old ban on the possession of weapons and weapons training between 1804 and 1907 succeeded in almost totally destroying the popular appeal and systematic practice of *payatt* all over Kerala. ... The slow journey of its revival started with the Swadeshi (or Freedom) Movement in the early years of the twentieth century'.[128] It was part of a wave of rediscovery of the traditional arts throughout south India.[129] Under the leadership of nationalists such as C. V. Narayanan Nair, the Kerala Kalari Sangham was organized in 1933 and they conducted a number of exhibitions in foreign countries.[130]

Both Vasudevan Gurukkal and Zarrilli have pointed out that pit *kalaris* (*kuzhikalari*) were the most common *kalaris* in 'Kerala', especially in Malabar.[131] Gurukkal further elaborates, 'The pit *kalari* was for the higher castes and the ground level *kalari* was for the lowers. It was to see from afar what the lower castes were learning in their *kalari*, that they were not allowed to dig or wall the *kalaris*.'[132] Vijaya Raghavan points out that even a master *kalaripayatt* practitioner such as Kottakkal

---

was passed on 22 April 1804. Even the display of armed sports was conducted only after securing permission from the commissioners of police in the Presidency town and by the magistrate of the district outside the township. Hence, many a family *kalari* and village *kalari* was transformed into *kalari* temples. Major step was taken by Major Daw, one of the commissioners of Malabar, to destroy the military character of the communities in Malabar. Available at http://choorakkodykalari.com/kalari2.html, http://www.kalaripayattu.org/aboutus. htm, last accessed on 23 March 14.

[128] Chirakkal T. Sreedharan Nair, *Kalaripayatt: Complete Guide to Kerala's Ancient Martial Art* (Chennai: Westland, 2007), xiv.

[129] Zarrilli, *When Body Becomes All Eyes*, 51.

[130] P. Balakrishnan, *Kalaripayatt: The Ancient Martial Art of Kerala* (Trivandrum: CVN Kalari, 1995); Balakrishnan dedicates the book to C. V. Narayanan Gurukkal and writes about his 'untiring efforts for promoting and popularising the art of KALARIPAYATT by bringing it from within the four walls of Kalari on to the stage thus enabling the public to witness it ... not only in Kerala but in other parts of India and even outside India'. We can see how *kalaripayatt* is being 'reformed' as a stage or performing act.

[131] Vasudevagurukkal, *Kalaripayatt: Keralathinte Thanathu Ayodhanakala*, 19; Zarrilli, *When Body Becomes All Eyes*, 28.

[132] Vasudevagurukkal, *Kalaripayatt: Keralathinte Thanathu Ayodhanakala*, 19.

Kanaran Gurukkal (1850–1935) had to go to other regions to train because the lower castes were restricted from entering the pit *kalaris*.[133] Rosmin Mathew and P. K. Sasidharan note that caste was a stumbling block before Kottakkal Kanaran Gurukkal in learning *payatt* as a child and that he could start proper training only at a late age, in his 30s, during the 1880s.[134] He founded *'pothujana kalaris'* (*kalaris* for the general public) in the second decade of the twentieth century, drawing impetus from the nationalist movements and the resultant wave of the revival of *kalaris*.[135] While Sasidharan refers to a 'secular zeal', Mathew notes that entry was 'open to anyone interested'. Probably, the resistance and the wish of a *kalari* for all castes would have been there among many of the 'lower' *kalari* masters of the era.[136] But Keeleri, whose *kalari* came into being during the same time as the revival or even before, found an apt mode of conversion in the modern venture circus. And for him, perhaps, the conversion of his pit *kalari* into a modified ground-level *kalari* justified both his anti-caste position and the suitability for circus acrobatics.

Kushti/Indian Wrestling

A Malayalam synonym for circus is *kasarth*, which can could be traced back to *kasrath* rooted in Urdu. In Malayalam, it denotes all kinds of physical exercises and feats. Watching the training procedures of circus acrobats, Murkoth Kunhappa speaks about their course of exercising 'daanam', 'bethak', 'skippings', 'somersaulting', 'thekkuth', and 'othiram'. According to him, 'these are the primary lessons of any circus acrobat' and 'should be learnt before the bones mature'. These exercises

---

[133] Vijayaraghavan, 'Kalaripayattinte Eettillam', 58.

[134] Mathew, *Kalaripayattu: Ankathattum Rangavediyum*, 58; P. K. Sasidharan, 'Kalarippayatt: Performance Paradigm as Aesthetics and Politics of Invisibility', in *Performers and Their Arts: Folk, Popular and Classical Genre in a Changing India*, eds Simon C. Charlesley and Laxmi Narayan Kadekar (New Delhi: Routledge, 2006), 171–2.

[135] Sasidharan, 'Kalarippayatt', 172.

[136] Later on, during the 1930s, Chirakkal T. Sreedharan Nair propagated that *kalaripayatt* could be trained outside a *kalari*, in a gymnasium or an open ground. Mathew, *Kalaripayattu: Ankathattum Rangavediyum*, 61–2.

are practised for five to six months to gain suppleness and physical strength.[137] The elementary exercises in all the three *kalaris* included *dand* and *bethak*. Kunhappa also recalls elsewhere that *dand* along with dumbbells were practised in the BEMP school.[138] *Mitavadi* (April 1916) reports that Tarabai,[139] known as Lady Sandow, an acrobat and animal trainer and owner of the Tarabai Circus, exercised every day for about one hour and favoured Indian exercises: 'What is good for us are the Indian exercises. The Sandow system is more useful for shaping the physique. For a long time I have been practising that as well. But the better ones are "*dand*" and "*bhattika*" which I practise now. *Kasrath* and *bhasky* are very good exercises.'

John Rosselli gives an account of Bengali wrestlers who joined circuses,

> Priyanath Basu went on from founding *akhra*s to setting up Professor Bose's Great Bengal Circus; a number of other *akhra* leaders, strong men, gymnasts, teachers of physical education in government or private schools (these roles often overlapped) joined his or other circuses or set up their own. Indeed these circuses seem to have been almost as fissile as *akhra*s; they may have worked on a similar *dal* organization even though their Bengali leaders at times joined forces with American, German or British animal-trainers.[140]

Manini Chatterjee notes that many of the early women nationalists in Bengal received training in lathi and swordplay at a gymnasium near Bethune College while they were young:

> [I]n the 1920s girl students in Calcutta, Dhaka, and even smaller towns were keenly aware of the importance of physical exercise not to enhance

[137] Murkoth Kunhappa, 'Circussabhyasam' [Circus acrobatics], *Mathrubhumi Illustrated Weekly* 26, no. 34 (1958), 15.

[138] Murkoth Kunhappa, 'Circussilude Arogya Sambadanam' [Gaining health through circus], *Circus Worker* 1, no. 3 (1980): 23.

[139] According to Prabhakaran, the grapevine has it that Tarabai was a very strong lady who had the strength of an elephant and she could not be defeated by a group of 10 men. Sreedharan says she belonged to the Rajput caste and Ravindran told me that she married a Malayali 'Nair' as her second husband; interview, Prabhakaran, Sreedharan, and E. Ravindran; all these live memories show the significance of the person in their circus life.

[140] Rosselli, 'The Self-Image of Effeteness', 145.

their looks but strengthen their ability to participate in the freedom struggle. Swadeshi-minded girl students formed autonomous groups and physical culture clubs of their own, where nationalist ideology and literature were also imparted in secret. Physical exercise not only improved their ability to face the hardships of revolutionary life; it also gave them enormous self-confidence.[141]

The *BC* (12 March 1914) notes, 'Miss Tara Bai is now on a tour round India with the object of proclaiming to her brothers and sisters what physical culture can do to the feeble Indian womanhood'. The undercurrent of nationalist ideologies in the revival and promotion of indigenous and modern physical cultures is strong.[142] Most of the readings on Bengali circus seem to be along the lines of Roselli, revolving around swadeshi and nationalist movements.[143] It is significant that no records that I have come across relate the circus in Malabar to the discourses of anti-colonial nationalism, while there had been a revival move in the case of *kalaripayatt*. Ian McDonald argues that the resurgence of interest in *kalaripayatt* in the 1920s was part of the reaction against colonial discourses of Hindu effeminacy, and it was celebrated

[141] Manini Chatterjee, '1930: Turning Point in the Participation of Women in the Freedom Struggle', *Social Scientist* 29 (July–August 2001): 46.

[142] Mrinalini Sinha discusses the image formation of the athletic, chivalric, hunting 'manly Englishman' in opposition to the bookish, grave, disorderly 'effeminate Bengali' self. Mrinalini Sinha, *Colonial Masculinity: The Manly Englishman and the Effeminate Bengali in the Late Nineteenth Century* (New York: Manchester University Press, 1995), 1–32; Guha writes that to overcome this colonial stereotype, Bengalis strenuously sought to physical cultures. In accordance with Bankim Chandra Chatterjee's plea for 'bahubol' (physical strength) as the 'key ingredient of Indian nationalism', 'some Bengalis initiated the *akhara* (gymnasium) movement' and in the cricket field, fast bowling. Ramachandra Guha, *The States of Indian Cricket: Anecdotal Histories* (New Delhi: Permanent Black, 2005), 36. Rosselli has also noted the 'effeteness' of the Bengali educated men and the revival of physical cultures as part of nationalism.

[143] Mimasha Pandit, 'Circus, Performance, and Building of National "Self"'; Sarbajit Mitra, 'Bengali Babus on the Flying Trapeze: Circus and Body Culture in Colonial Bengal', paper presented at the international conference on 'Physical Cultures: Bengal and Beyond', Jadavpur University, Kolkata, 21–2 February 2014.

in public discourse as an encapsulation of Kerala's valorous martial spirit and an idealization of Malayali manhood.[144]

Joseph Alter provides a detailed picture of the physical routines of wrestlers and describes the afternoon sessions in which the most common but important exercises called *dand*, a kind of jack-knifing push-ups, and *bethaks*, deep knee bends, were practised. Though separate exercises, referred to as pairs, they constitute a whole-body workout that gives a trance-like mental state and physical strength that develops shoulders, upper arms, chest, and legs. *Dands* especially help to experience enlightenment and a physical experience of muscular development which strengthens the wrists, fingers, palms, neck, chest, and the backbone regions. Alter, while discussing how the notions of masculinity grew as an essential part of the *akhara* culture, points out that the practising of *dand* was believed to cure illnesses relating to semen loss, such as infertility and impotence.[145] *Kasrath* and *bhaski* (squats) are also part of the physical cultures of northern regions in India. *Kasrath* is an exercise composed of sit-ups and pull-ups. A yoga advertising site speaks of *bhaski* and *dhandal* as slow-motion Indian pair exercises with 'maximum muscular contraction'.[146]

It is interesting to note here that the Kollam region in Travancore was famous for *kushti* in the early twentieth century. It had its own wrestlers and also brought in famous wrestlers from other areas for competitions. 'Kollam was to *kushti* as Thalassery was to circus,' says V. Lakshmanan.[147] *MM* (16 October 1909) reports that no day goes without hearing the advertisements of wrestlers on the road. Another report from Thiruvananthapuram mentions a wrestler named Babayi from Attakulangara and his 'ustad' Muneer Khan (*MM*, 24 May 1905). *MM* (13 November 1903) reports the wrestling competition between a circus wrestler and a local wrestler from Alappuzha. It also says that there was a mock wrestling of the children of the circus folk before

[144] Ian McDonald, 'Hindu Nationalism, Cultural Spaces and Bodily Practices in India', *American Behavioral Scientist* 46 (July 2003): 1563–76.

[145] Alter, 'The Body of One Color', 49–69.

[146] Available at http://derekosborn.accountsupport.com/thelibrary/id53.html, accessed on 19 November 2013.

[147] V. Lakshmanan, 'Kusthi Annum Innum' [Kushti today and yesterday], *Janayugam Weekly* 10, no. 35 (1967): 20–3.

it began. The news on the Bengali lady wrestler, Gagubhai, who had come to Thycaud, is especially interesting as it mentions the notice that openly warns her opponent to not touch her clothes and the hair on the top of her head (*MM*, 13 October 1906). *MM* (25 November 1903) reports a wrestler in the Kolappur Kolandas Circus who could carry a girl on his thumb while holding five to six people on his shoulders. Keeleri Kunhikannan, who was also a wrestler, had famous wrestler disciples such as P. Pokkan (*Mitavadi*, January 1914). Australian newspaper reports show that from early twentieth century itself, Indian wrestlers had great presence in their circuses.[148] An interesting picture emerges from all these about the transcultural nature of circus acrobatics in India and how these diverse physical cultures contributed to each other substantially.

At the beginning of the twentieth century, lathi clubs and gymnasia became popular in many parts of India as part of the nationalist movements. Joseph Alter points out that nationalists such as Madan Mohan Malviya, Bal Gangadhar Tilak, and Moti Lal Nehru were staunch advocates of physical education and *akhara* culture for building a free India.[149] In the Maratha region, Bal Gangadhar Tilak started *akhara*s, lathi clubs, and anti-cow-killing societies as part of his Hindu nationalist ideas.[150] Alter strikingly calls this phenomenon 'wrestling nationalism': '[O]n some points there is a high degree of overlap between wrestling values and the ideals of Hindu nationalism. Further historical analysis would undoubtedly show that at various times, and in specific parts of the country, the two have converged and diverged to

[148] *Argus* shows Butta Singh and Gunga Brahmin (not clear), who met at Wirth's Circus, had a tough wrestling competition at the Queen's Theatre in Australia (*Argus*, 30 May 1903). Bud Atkinson's 'Wild West' Circus also included an Indian fighter in their show (*Sydney Morning Herald*, 7 December 1912). *Daily News* (26 July 1904) reports about an adjourned wrestling competition between the Indian wrestler Buttan Singh and foreign wrestlers Mourzouck and Carkeek. *Mitavadi* (December 1914) also writes about the legendary Bengali wrestler 'Gobar Babu' (Guha) showing awe-inspiring tricks in England.

[149] Joseph S. Alter, *The Wrestler's Body: Identity and Ideology in North India* (Chicago: Chicago University Press, 1992), 17.

[150] Mohan Ramanan, *Nineteenth Century Indian English Prose: A Selection* (New Delhi: Sahitya Akademi, 2004), 23.

different degrees.'[151] In an interesting letter to a friend written during his early twenties, M. S. Golwalker, one of the supreme ideologues of Hindu nationalism, provides a list of his own strengths and virtues, and the first item in that list is: 'Malkhambh champion (Malkhambh is an upright post used in gymnastic exercises).'[152] Vinayak Chaturvedi notes, '[C]entral to Hindu nationalism from the 1920s has been the need to set political agendas which rely upon power, masculinity, and strength, both discursively and institutionally.'[153]

Savarkar and Tilak had ties with Maratha circus companies such as the Deval Circus. Babasaheb Deval, who started the company, was a Maratha Brahmin and an active member of the Hindu Mahasabha. Savarkar had made visits to the Deval Circus. In 1948, the Deval Circus tent was burnt down by an angry mob, the backlash of Gandhi's assassination.[154]

It should be noted that circus tents figure in a totally different political scenario too. Two major biographies of the great Dalit leader Mahathma Ayyankali (1863–1941) register that the large peace gathering on 19 December 1915, soon after the legendary Perinadu Rebellion,[155] was held at a circus tent in Kollam Town. When the organizers could not get a suitable meeting place, the owner graciously offered the tent. What is more striking is that both the biographies state that this owner was a Dalit woman of the Cheruma community. While Chentharassery told me that it was Tarabai, Kunnukuzhi Mani and Anirudhan give the name Ratnabai.[156] I interviewed the authors, Chentharassery and Kunnukuzhi Mani, and Chentharassery told me

---

[151] Joseph Alter, *The Wrestler's Body*, 261–3.

[152] Jyotirmaya Sharma, *Terrifying Vision: M S Golwalker, the RSS and India* (New Delhi: Penguin/Viking, 2007), xiii.

[153] Vinayak Chaturvedi, 'Vinayak and Me: Hindutva and the Politics of Naming', in *The Indian Postcolonial: A Critical Reader*, eds Elleke Boehmer and Rosinka Chaudhuri (New York: Routledge, 2011), 141.

[154] Interview, Rajendra Deval, Miraj, 24 January 2013; Kandambulli Balan, *Circus*, 48.

[155] Also known as 'Kallumala Samaram' (stone necklace struggle); Dalits publicly discarded caste marking stone ornaments in the face of violent retaliation from the upper castes.

[156] T. H. P. Chentharassery, *Ayyankali* (Thiruvananthapuram: Prabhath, 2009), 86–7; Kunnukuzhi S. Mani and Anirudhan P. S., *Mahthama Ayyankali* (Kottayam: DC Books, 2013), 110–11.

that there were conjectures regarding her caste that she was a Thiyya. Kunnukuzhi Mani said he has no further details regarding the circus or its owner.[157] By no account have I come across a Dalit woman circus owner, Malayali or otherwise. Tarabai, as we have discussed earlier, was a renowned name. She was born in Bandique in Rajputana (*BC*, 12 March 1914). Neither in the historical records I read nor in the memories of the circus community I could find any information regarding 'Ratnabai', although it could be a misreading of the name Rugmabai, the Lady Sandow from Andhra.[158]

Yoga

Ramamurthy's exercise routine can be divided into five parts: the daily practice of *pranayama*, daily meditation practice that enables deep focus and concentration on any part of the body, vegetarian food, absolute abstention from all kinds of intoxicants, and total celibacy. This is the lifestyle that has produced the modern Bhimasena (*Mitavadi*, January 1917).

Ramamurthy (1882–1942), known as the 'Indian Sandow' and 'modern Bhimsena' (*MM*, 20 February 1909; 5 August 1911), was believed to be amazingly powerful to perform such feats as having an elephant weighing three tons walk on his body, breaking doubly heavy iron chains with bare hands, and lifting a stone weighing three thousand *rathal* (approximately 1400 kgs) on his chest and pushing it off without using his hands (*MM*, 5 August 1911). A celibate, teetotaler, and vegetarian, Ramamurthy was one of the strongest and best wrestlers of his time. He practised *pranayama* (breath control) and *dhyanam* (meditation) in the yoga system and believed that his performances were the result of both physical and mental vigour (*Mitavadi*, January 1917).

---

[157] Interview, T. H. P. Chentharassery, Thiruvananthapuram, 18 July 2014; Kunnukuzhi S. Mani, Thiruvananthapuram, 15 July 2014.

[158] Sreedharan Champad, *An Album of Indian Big Tops*, 28; During the Second World War, when Japan was bombed, Rugmabai Circus and its animals were burnt to ashes. Rugmabai and company returned to India, travelling through forests, starving and suffering. Sreedharan Champad, *Circusinte Lokam*, 155; According to Vanaja, the incident happened in Burma and they travelled on foot to Assam, leaving everything behind; interview, Vanaja, Melur, 23 May 2008.

Yoga has close links with *kalaripayatt* and *kusthi*. Alter, while speaking about 'masculine' body and Indian wrestling, puts forth that for the wrestler, Brahmacharya or celibacy is considered the essence of life and semen loss is a vital anxiety. Meera Nanda points out that Krishnamacharya, one of the major proponents of modern yoga, adopted 'wall ropes and other props' and a 'variety of Western gymnastics and drills' to his yoga routines. She further criticizes the 'Hindu' claim on yoga and says,

> On the contrary, modern yoga was born in the late 19th/early 20th centuries. It is a child of the Hindu Renaissance and Indian nationalism, in which Western ideas about science, evolution, eugenics, health and physical fitness played as crucial a role as the 'mother tradition'. In the massive, multi-level hybridisation that took place during this period, the spiritual aspects of yoga and *tantra* were rationalised, largely along the theosophical ideas of 'spiritual science,' introduced to India by the US-origin, India-based Theosophical Society, and internalised by Swami Vivekananda, who led the yoga renaissance.[159]

Zarrilli notes that the preliminary leg exercises and *vadivu* (a specific posture) in *kalaripayatt* are comparable to the *asana* (meditation pose) in *hatha* yoga (a branch of Yoga) and useful particularly for the vital air to flow equably and harmoniously.[160] Joseph Alter, in his study on yoga, describes *pranayama* and *dhyanam* as two of the most important eight limbs of yoga.[161]

An advertisement of the 'Great Udaya' Circus published in the *Circus Worker* magazine boasts of 'Saleena's *yogasana*s on eleven bottles!'[162] Many veteran circus artistes agree that the items 'frog' and 'thavala [frog] trapeze' have connections with certain exercises done in yoga.[163] An

[159] Available at http://www.openthemagazine.com/article/living/not-as-old-as-you-think, accessed on 22 December 2013.

[160] Zarrilli, *When Body Becomes All Eyes*, 128; Santhosh, one of the *Kalaripayatt* practitioners of CVN Kalari, Thiruvanhad, told me that while practicing *payatt*, it is often preferred to be vegetarians. But it is not strictly followed now. Interview, Santhosh.

[161] Joseph S. Alter, *Yoga in Modern India: The Body between Science and Philosophy* (New Jersey: Princeton University Press, 2004), 57.

[162] *Circus Worker* 1, no. 11–12 (February-March 1981): 19.

[163] Interview, A. V. Karim, Cherakkara, 28 September 2012; Babu, Jumbo Circus, 16 July 2009.

interesting report (*BC*, 13 March 1914) speaks about the 'Human Frogs', De Marlo and Lady De Marlo, who made the audiences in Australia and Africa go 'crazy'. De Marlo's feats included 'turning himself inside out', 'double dislocations on a swinging bar', doubling his limbs in 'weird and wonderful shapes and evolutions that suggest there is not a bone in his body'. Such instances point to the fact that many exercises and feats in various physical cultures were adapted from each other and developed, and none of these can simply be categorized as yoga or gymnastics, 'Indian' or 'Western'. *Mathrubhumi Illustrated Weekly* reports a young yogi, expert in *hatha* yoga, to have travelled all over India and Europe and performed tricks on the rope, eating glass, walking on fire, burying himself in mud, stopping a motor car and such.[164] K. Vasudevan mentions that Subrahmanya Buva, known as 'little Sandow', who had practised and exhibited yoga for more than 30 years, was a disciple of Sandow Ramamurthy. Buva took the mission of promulgating yoga research and established a sanatorium at Olavakkodu in Palakkad.[165] In his autobiography, the renowned playwright Thikkodian (P. Kunhanandan Nair) expresses this confusion better while describing his first meeting with Professor Ramamurthy, an invited guest at the 'Shakthi Mandiram' (Power House): 'Professor Ramamurthy was a physical performer revered by the youth of the time. But I cannot say what he was; whether he was a circus artiste or a wrestler. I can only remember his performance. ... He was famous at the national level.'[166]

V. Parameswaran states that 'the difference between *yoga* and circus can be stated generally; that in circus, items are done swiftly while *yogasana* stays with a position much longer'.[167] Radha Kannan, an old hand in circus acrobatics, said that when she began attending yoga

---

[164] *Mathrubhumi Illustrated Weekly* 19, no. 31 (October 1941): 18; Chitrabhanu, a magician himself, ironically refers to L. S. Rao as a self-proclaimed expert in *hatha* yoga who practised similar magical tricks. Chitrabhanu, *Magikkinte Lokam*, 21–2.

[165] K. Vasudevan, 'Sree Subrahmanya Buva: A *Yoga* Expert', *Mathrubhumi Illustrated Weekly* 31, no. 11 (May 1953): 22–3, 38.

[166] Thikkodian, *Arangu Kanatha Nadan* [Actor who had never been on the stage] (Kottayam: D. C. Books, 2008), 59.

[167] Venkulam Parameswaran, 'Sthreekalum Yogabhyasavum' [Women and yoga exercises], *Mathrubhumi Illustrated Weekly* 35, no. 14 (1957): 35.

classes long after retiring from circus, she recognized many asanas to be quite similar to some exercises she had practised in the circus. Hence, she started a yoga school of her own.[168] But unfortunately, while yoga, *kalaripayatt*, and *kusthi* are recognized as physical cultures, circus is not. This is also because circus does not make a claim on *sidhi*, or secretive powers associated with *kalaripayatt* or yoga. In America, the Ringling Brothers and the Barnum & Bailey group have organized a national fitness programme called 'Circus Fit'.[169] Circus professionals give training to public (including many film stars) at the Cirque School in Hollywood, Los Angeles, which also teaches recreational circus classes.[170]

Sandow System and the Swedish Drill

Noel Daniel says that in American circuses, '19th century jugglers were often strongmen who balanced and even juggled heavy objects like cannonballs, weights and halters, sometimes catching them on their necks or chests'.[171] Weightlifting and pulling trains and aeroplanes with their hair or mouth made them popular in the early twentieth century. While Ramamurthy was well known as 'Indian Sandow', Rugmabai and Tarabai were known as 'Lady Sandows' and Poovadan Kunhambu was known as the 'Malabar Sandow'. These popular name tags show the fame and influence the Sandow system had at the time. *MM* (6 May 1911) reports the Russian Sandow, Mr Kramer's performance in the Victoria Public Hall in Madras, with heavy iron balls and bars and lifting a few people with a single hand. Another report (*MM*, 24 April 1909) says these strongmen cultivated their body with milk and mutton. *MM* (20 February 1909) reports that Ramamurthy had learnt gymnastics in his school in Vijayanagara and the Sandow system having heard of such strongmen as Gulam, but discarded those exercises realizing that indigenous exercises are better. We can see at least a few

---

[168] Interview, Radha Kannan, Bangalore, 17, 18, 19 July 2012.

[169] Available at http://www.circusfit.com, last accessed on 23 December 2013.

[170] Available at http://content.time.com/time/photogallery/0,29307,2108216_2337801,00.html, last accessed on 7 March 2014.

[171] Noel Daniel, *The Circus, 1870s–1950s* (Los Angeles: Taschen, 2008), 314.

reports in *MM* (12 July 1905; 10 June 1905; 24 May 1905) mentioning the visit of Eugene Sandow to Madras. It also says that Ramamurthy had challenged Mr Sandow but the latter disagreed (*MM*, 20 February 1909). Ramamurthy (later known as Kodi Ramamurthy) was a staunch nationalist. The idea of discarding the 'foreign' and taking up the 'native' could have been the adherence to Gandhi and his nationalist call. *Mitavadi* (January 1917) laments, 'How great it would have been if our youth infatuated with white people's physical exercises, began following contemporary Bhimasena Ramamurthy!'

In his autobiography, A. S. R. Chari recounts his youth during the nationalist fervour in the first half of the twentieth century. A friend from Madurai 'taught us to do the Indian *dands* and *baithaks*. At first we did not like it. ... And quite soon the spirit of physical culture had taken firm hold. We wrote to all the famous body-builders in England and America for their courses, Eugene Sandow, Charles Atlas, Erle Leiderman, Lionel Strongfort and above all, Marxick. We studied their systems'.[172] Likewise, Thikkodian, in his autobiography, recounts the establishment of Shakthi Mandiram in his hometown in Malabar as part of the 'Shakthi Movement' started by Acharya T. L. Vaswani in north India to strengthen the youth mentally and physically to uproot the alien domination: 'Training was provided in *Kalari*, *Surya Namaskaram*, bar items and many more.'[173] *Mathrubhumi Illustrated Weekly* reports that in 1952 there was a demand for an organization for weightlifting in Malabar as most of the experts were from there. Another report in the same issue speaks about the 'Bharath Weight Lifting Arena' established at Kozhikode in 1948.[174] All these show the convergence of various strands of bodily practices during that time.

Murkoth Kunhappa mentions that the Swedish drill gained popularity during the First World War period as a system that provided both strength and flexibility to the body, and later the Germans popularized it.[175] The *MM* (7 May 1910) notes that a book named *Elementary School*

[172] A. S. R. Chari, *Memoirs of an Unrepentant Communist* (Bombay: Orient Longman, 1975), 14–15.

[173] Thikkodian, *Arangu Kanatha Nadan*, 58.

[174] *Mathrubhumi Illustrated Weekly* 30, no. 5 (April 1952): 11, 30.

[175] Murkoth Kunhappa, 'Circussabhyasam', 23; *Encyclopedia Britannica* says, 'Gustavus II Adolphus of Sweden accelerated a gradual revival of skill in European

Drill was published from Thiruvananthapuram. Meera Nanda also points out that in the beginning of the twentieth century, the Swedish drill and gymnastics routine developed by a Dane, Niels Bukh, was introduced in India by the British and popularized by the YMCA.[176] In Kerala, all the schools run by the Basel Mission taught Swedish drill exercises. The Swedish drill facilitates the body with flexibility to lean and bend to all sides.[177] Basel Mission schools and the colleges run by Europeans had key roles in disseminating 'modern' education at Thalassery. Madhavan notes the role of Basel Mission in educating the 'lower' castes as part of its evangelical mission and the schools it started in Kasaragod, Taliparamba, Melparamba, Ottappalam, Vaniyamkulam, Vadakara, Koyilandy, Koothuparamba, Kannur, Payyanur, Palakkad, Vadakancheri, Kozhikode, and Thalassery.[178] C. A. Innes, who compiled the gazetteer of Malabar in 1905, notes: 'Elementary schools more than doubled themselves during this period [early twentieth century] and the secondary schools in the district had the largest number of pupils of any district in the presidency, with 58 schools and 18,000 pupils.'[179]

Gymnastics

The influence of gymnastics is also significant. Horizontal and parallel bars and Roman ring exercises practised in the circus *kalari* were derived from gymnastics. Exercises such as vaulting horse, pommel

---

warfare early in the 17th century. His introduction of simplified drill techniques for the use of improved weapons was copied by all Europe'. Available at https://www.britannica.com/topic/drill-military, last accessed on 11 March 2014.

[176] Available at http://www.openthemagazine.com/article/living/not-as-old-as-you-think, last accessed on 22 December 2013.

[177] Murkoth Kunhappa, 'Circussabhyasam', 23.

[178] 'The [Basel] missionaries landed at Calicut on 13th October 1834 and travelling northwards commenced the work with their headquarters at Mangalore in South Canara. Consequently, missionary activities were started in three districts of West Coast comprising Bombay, Karnataka and Malabar with Mangalore as its headquarters.' M. Madhavan, *Social Reform Movements in Malabar*, 54.

[179] C. A. Innes, *Malabar Gazetteer*, Vol. I and II (Thiruvananthapuram: Kerala Gazetteers Department, 1997 [1908]), 295.

horse, balancing on and over the bar, pull-ups, jumping, and floor exercises such as leaps and somersaults are also done in gymnastics.[180] In fact, these exercises form a major part of the Kerala Circus Academy syllabi (syllabus submitted to the managing committee and later on to the government, dated 3 May 2011). We have already seen that many of the early circus practitioners were also drill/gymnastic teachers in the missionary- and government-run schools. They taught the parallel and horizontal bars and the Swedish drill.[181] Sreedhara Menon notes Keeleri's tryst with the 'new', 'modern' physical cultures that came with the colonialists.

He got this opportunity when Overberry, a great sports enthusiast, came to Tellicherry as Deputy Collector. It was a passion for Overberry to invite athletes and gymnasts from the Regimental Centre at Cannanore to display their skill in horsemanship and gymnastics. Keelari [sic] who obtained permission to visit their camp and observe their method of training soon made his own indigenous appliances like Parallel Bars, Horizontal Bars, etc., and made successful attempts at teaching the new techniques to his disciples in the 'circus training school'.[182]

Kandambulli Balan also notes that Overberry was a first-rate sportsman who was enthusiastic in promoting physical sports by all means.

He arranged shows featuring feats on mounted horses and bars by some white soldiers selected from a military camp in Kannur. Mr. Kunhikannan who was a frequent spectator of these shows, was spellbound and decided to self coach those painstaking feats. ... He mastered all of them except for the ones on horseback. He successfully copied the whites and made all the equipments needed for parallel and horizontal bars and roman rings. He practised them himself, and successfully trained some others.[183]

Interestingly, circus artistes use English words to refer to these exercises and items.

[180] Lokesh Thani, *Skills and Tactics: Gymnastics* (Delhi: Sports Publications, 1999), 10; Jean Williams, *Themes for Educational Gymnastics* (London: Lepus, 1974), 74–81.

[181] Murkoth Kunhappa, 'Circussabhyasam', 22–3.

[182] A. Sreedhara Menon, *Kerala District Gazeteers*, 245.

[183] Balan, *Circus*, 49–50.

Throughout India, in the beginning of the twentieth century, various physical cultures and games from around the globe were becoming familiar. For instance, 'Trade Notices' in *TOI* (11 January 1926) show a number of books written mainly by European authors for different classes of people, such as *Primary Gymnastics, Athletics for Girls and Women, Physical Training for Business Men, My Army and Navy System of Free Standing Exercises: A Manual of Physical Instruction for Soldiers, Police Constables, etc.*, and also *Tricks for Self Defence, Weight Lifting Made Easy and Interesting*, and *Text book of Ju Jutsu as Practised in Japan*. The *TOI* (16 January 1926) reports that boys were compulsorily given drill and gymnastics thrice a week in Raja Ram College, Kolhapur. The *MM* reports in 1906 (15 and 19 September) show that in Travancore, St. Joseph's College practised 'bar', and in English Norman School there was a gymnastics instructor. In 1908 (8 April and 3 October), *MM* mentions girls practicing drill in a girls' school in Chegannur, and also a call for the posts of ten gymnastics instructors. Reports show that 'sports practices' were being held every year in the parade ground and prizes were distributed under the Sree Mulam Sports Club where competitions in bicycle and tennis were held with a funding from the government (*MM*, 23 October 1907; 30 October 1907; 21 November 1908). An instructor was brought from George Harriot School, Edinburgh, and INR 5,000 was spent on buying the exercise equipment (*MM*, 19 December 1908; 29 September 1909). In the fourth yearly conference of the Keraliya Nair Samajam, the chairperson lamented the loss of physical training given by the *kalaris* and appealed that the members start them at their houses so that the schools by both the governments would follow the model (*MM*, 11 June 1910). The *MM* notes in as early as 1910 (19 November), a social gathering of a gymnastic club in Kottayam where gymnastic exhibitions and gramophone playing went on, which shows that such 'modern' practices were happening in different parts of the present day Kerala. However, exercising clubs were also established in many parts of north Malabar during the early decades of the twentieth century. The *MM* (27 October 1909) reports about the European gymkhana clubs in Calicut and Cochin and their hockey tournaments. Eleven groups of Europeans and Eurasians travelled by the mail train mail to Kozhikode for a 'ball tournament' (*MM*, 23 October 1909). T. Achuthan's Calicut Athletic Club was established in 1928 with a mission of spreading the merits of physical cultures.[184] *Mathrubhumi* (1 December 1923) speaks about special manual training classes given to about 200 students in the Kannur Training School. While Murkoth Ramunny says that Lord Wellesley was also influential in promoting the circus, S. Muthiah, journalist and historian, notes that the townsfolk 'recently, celebrated the 200th anniversary of cricket in the town, Arthur Wellesley was recalled for everything from being the Sub-Collector to the Hero of the Waterloo, apart from his contributing to the game to the Malabar town. ... The Tellicherry Town Cricket Club was founded ... in 1860'.[185] *Mitavadi* (July 1914) also refers to a cricket club functioning in Thalassery. Physical training was part of the British education, along with other subjects such as Geography, Elementary Science, Drawing, and Indian History.[186] The 'bar' and 'rings' indicate the gymnastic practices that was in the school syllabi for physical education. During the 1940s, the teaching post of a *kalari* instructor was present in many schools in Thalassery, while there used to be a separate post for drill teacher who taught gymnastics and similar physical exercises.[187]

Traditional Medicinal Systems

Kalari Vaidyam has developed as a separate branch of treatment, which includes foot and *marma* (vital point of the body) massage, localized

---

[184] Mushtaq (pseudonym of P. A. Muhammed Koya) says that T. Achuthan learnt circus feats from Kunhikannan Teacher and various other physical exercises from Makkolath Kelu Teacher, Ikkaripparambil Appu and Indian wrestling from Pokkan Gurukkal (from Thalassery), V. Raghavan, Mahe Gopalan Nambiar, and Ajmeer Mirza Jamsheed Fayalman; Mushtaq, 'Calicut Athletic Club', *Mathrubhumi Illustrated Weekly* 33, no. 32 (1955): 34.

'Phayalman' (also 'phayalvan') is commonly used in Malayalam to refer to Hindi 'Pehelwan', meaning 'wrestler'. Pokkan Gurukkal could probably be Keeleri's famous wrestler disciple P. Pokkan.

[185] Interview, (Late) Murkoth Ramunny; S Muthiah, *A Madras Miscellany* (Chennai: East West, 2011).

[186] Proceedings of the Board of Revenue, Malabar District standing order, R-Dis File. 3566, 1919, Regional Archives, Kozhikode.

[187] My paternal grandfather was a *kalaripayatt gurukkal* who worked as a *kalari* instructor at Kathirur High School (a non-missionary school) during the 1940s. Probably this was happening along with the *kalari* revival movements.

application of herbs, and also treatments with *kizhi* (a massage therapy) and herbal steam bath. Therapeutic body massages, such as *thirummal* and *uzhichil* using a specially prepared oil called the *kalari mukkutt* are an essential part of *kalaripayatt* treatments for bone fractures and muscle cramps. In both *kalaripayatt* and Indian wrestling, it is believed that oiling the body increases the volume of blood and muscles, and makes joints and tendons flexible and strong.[188] This practice is not routine with circus acrobats, but they have it for the training of youngsters, mostly girls, for items such as boldness/boneless, which needs great body suppleness. Kausu, who had worked for a long time as a circus artiste in the Great Bombay Circus, told me that *mayilenna* (peacock oil) was used for the purpose. Coconut, gingili, and mustard oils were also used for massaging and bending the bones.[189] Leela, another retired circus performer, who is 99 now, recounts that they had Malayalam (indigenous) medicinal practices. There were two *vaidyan*s (indigenous medical practitioners) employed at the tent for treating the injured. They had an assistant for doing the massaging. Medicinal herbs such as *Muru* and *Chenayakam* were grinded and rolled into balls for long-term keeping. Later, the balls were diluted with water according to necessity and the medicine was applied to injuries.[190] Ravindran says that his first owner, Ambu Master of the Grand Fairy Circus, used to treat them with medicinal herbs and it was prepared in the company itself.[191] Prabhakaran says that in M. K. Raman's circus *kalari*, he treated the injuries with locally available medicinal herbs, but in case of major accidents they depended on hospitals.[192] K. N. Panikkar has pointed out,

---

[188] Alter, 'The Body of One Color', 54; Vasudevagurukkal, *Kalaripayatt: Keralathinte Thanathu Ayodhanakala*, 36–7.

[189] Interview, Kausu, Melur, 28 August 2007; Pushpa, Melur, 14 July 2006.

[190] Interview, Leela, Thiruvangad, 17 January 2012.

[191] Interview, Ravindran E.; Harilal points out, 'In Kerala, however, at least in the medieval period, traditional medical knowledge seems to have extended through many of the major communities located at different levels of the caste hierarchy.' Harilal Madhavan, *Home to Market: Responses of Ayurvedic and Unani Formularies Production from 1830s to 1920s*, Working Paper 408. Trivandrum: Centre for Development Studies, 2008, 11.

[192] Interview, Prabhakaran.

[T]he hospitals, dispensaries and colleges established by the state formed the nucleus from which colonial medicine sought to establish its hegemony and thus to marginalize and delegitimize the indigenous system. In this process, the role of the colonial state went beyond its administrative functions. It not only promoted western medicine, but also sought to assert and establish its superiority over all other systems. ... [I]t [western medicine] was accorded the status of official medicine.[193]

Nowadays, almost all circus companies have allopathic medical stores apart from the stock of indigenous medicines used for minor injuries. The person in charge of the medicine chest would deliver the medicines on demand, and for serious ailments they would seek the help of a local doctor. Currently in big circus companies, two to three drivers would be on alert during the shows in case of an emergency.

Dietary System

For people who perform extraordinary feats with their bodies, the maintenance of a certain constitution is vital. Circus people have their particular methods to keep their physique fit, like in other physical cultures. The daily routine they follow and the rules they observe define circus as a comprehensive discipline, although the code and schedule are not strictly named.

Just as the *kalaripayatt* practitioners are supposed to keep an empty stomach in the morning before the practices, the circus performers have food only after their morning practices, which generally begin at 6 or 6:30 in the morning and last till 11 a.m. The artistes who perform in the matinee would usually take lunch only after their items are over.

Mitavadi (April 1916) provides an interesting account of Tarabai's daily diet:

The representative of the news paper, Bharatha Kesari asked Miss Tarabai, well known as the Lady Sandow, what she eats and when, to which she answered that every morning and evening two cups of milk and almonds and two meals a day. She said she ate only this much and that there is

---

[193] K. N. Panikkar, 'Indigenous Medicine and Cultural Hegemony: A Study of the Revitalization Movement in Keralam', *Studies in History* (August 1992): 286.

no use in overindulging good, nutritious food. What is needed is to eat at regular times minimally and hygienically and exercise properly with conviction. Every morning Miss. Tarabai drinks a cup of clean water.

An earlier piece in *Mitavadi* (December 1913) cites a similar diet followed by the Bengali wrestler Gobarbabu. Studying the 'masculine' body of the wrestler, Alter notes that while the consumption of ghee is supposed to increase semen in the male body, almonds are regarded as the male seed as milk is to female creativity.[194]

Sreedharan says that his father, Mannan Teacher, used to give him *Chyavanaprasam*, *Dasamoolarishtam*, ghee, cod liver oil, and 'English' tonics to make his body fit. Every year, for about three months, he took leave from the company and stayed at home to keep his body in shape. He used to have a mixture of tender coconut juice and sweet toddy for breakfast along with double roti/chapatti. His father advised him to have mutton soup (from the leg piece) later on. His father would treat him till the thrusting bones in his neck (because he is lean) went under the flesh. Sreedharan says 'bar' players seldom oiled their body as they needed to maintain their grip on the bars. And there was also a belief among them that they would lose their muscles if massaged with oil.[195] We may note that 'bar' is a practice adapted from gymnastics, which hardly involves oiling the body.

Ayurvedic practices, north Indian physical-fitness practices, and indigenous medicinal knowledge tend to be combined in the case of

---

[194] Alter, 'The Body of One Color', 54. He also provides the special dietetics of wrestlers:

In addition to the regular fare, wrestlers are enjoined to consume huge amount of milk, 'ghee' and almonds. While actual consumption is restricted to each wrestler's individual means, most wrestlers agree that to drink more than two liters of milk, a half liter of 'ghee', and a kilogram or more of almonds per day is essential for proper physical and moral development. These items are not only regarded as nutritious, but they are also thought of as cooling and 'sattva' by nature. (55–6)

Some of the Indian wrestlers, according to Alter, believed in the therapeutic value of the water drawn from the *akhara* well (Joseph Alter, 'The Wrestler's Body', 31–2).

[195] Interview, Sreedharan.

early Malayali artistes. Even during the 1940s, the immediate treat-ment method they followed was Ayurveda and local medicines. The use of Marathi and north Indian systems in treatments hints at Marathi dominance in circus during a period when most circus companies were owned by them and the regional influences of the places and cultures they roamed around. A mixed use of Allopathic and Ayurvedic systems also throws light on the complex negotiation process in colonies such as India. The constant interaction with divergent cultures and practices, habits and customs, traditions and various modernities has contributed to its open and receptive character; reiterating the transcultural and transnational quality of the enterprise called circus.

In this chapter, I have tried to explore how circus acrobatics came into being as a distinct site and culture of the body during the first half of the last century in Malabar, the northern part of present-day Kerala. Various physical cultures which were historically old and new, dominant and minor, have played a vital role in the configuration of circus acrobatics. But unfortunately, circus acrobatics and acrobats seem to have been confined in rings and tents and could not find a place in the feted annals of the history of physical cultures in South Asia. This could be the reason why a most radical enterprise of its time, the circus kalaris, was also forgotten, while the other kalari, which was an exclusive space, is still celebrated as a glorious element of a shared past of 'Malayali' culture and heritage. Now we shall move from human acrobats to animal performers.

2   Animals, Circus, and the State

Social sciences and humanities have recently begun posing enquiries such as: do animals have histories, memories, and subjectivities? Circus animals hardly figure in the discourses on animals although a wide variety of animals existed in the rings globally as performers and workers.[1] The ban on the training and performance of certain wild animals by the Ministry of Environment and Forests, India, in 1991 was a watershed moment for the circus industry in the subcontinent. This chapter explores the legal battle that followed the ban, various discourses around animals, both wild and captive, the human and non-human association in circuses, and the history of animal training and performance, and critically examines the ideas of rescue, rehabilitation, and conservation. The acquisition, taming, and trade of animals are implicated in the history of hunting and wildlife policies of the colonial and postcolonial states in India. The processes of 'rescue' and 'rehabilitation' of animals from 'private' circus companies to 'public' zoos reveal how the very idea of scientific conservation becomes a violent guile practised by the state and civil society, actively propagating the binary of cruelty and mercy. This chapter will also briefly discuss questions of intimacy and emotions between animals and the

---

[1] Nisha P R, 'Ban and Benevolence: Circus, Animals and Indian State', *Indian Economic and Social History Review* 54, no. 2 (2017): 239–66.

animal trainer beyond the common representations. Can we write histories from a subaltern animal perspective?

Animals have always been an indispensable part of circus around the world until the recent legal proscriptions in many countries and the emergence of new concepts such as 'Noveau Cirque' (New Circus, also known as 'Contemporary Circus'). Despite the fact that Indian circus is almost a century and a half old, its pasts have hardly been explored. Animals in circus bring to the fore a long tradition of animal trade, taming, training, and human accompaniment, raising significant questions regarding their acquisition, captive life, breeding, and changing relation to forests and wilderness over time. They are inextricably linked with a colonial genealogy of the 'exotic' and the 'exhibit'. Social scientists have begun posing the question 'Can animals have histories?' in recent times, recognizing the position of animals as analogous with marginal human groups who are under-represented. Bruno Latour's philosophical perceptions on the agency of non-humans and their rights have been widely influential to the humanities. His observations elucidate that modernity, often defined in terms of humanism, is anthropocentric: 'It overlooks the simultaneous birth of "nonhumanity"—things, or objects, or beasts—and the equally strange beginning of a crossed-out God, relegated to the sidelines.'[2] That circus animals, who are a 'minority' in every sense, hardly figure even in histories on wildlife, environment, and livelihood in India is not at all surprising. On writing animals into social history, Sandra Swart argues that 'drawing on the gendered or women's history paradigm, perhaps historians' first step could be simply to demonstrate that animals have a history at all', and we should explore 'how social history can be enriched by focusing on history from an animal perspective—and equally, how the tools provided by social history reveals the historicity of animals'.[3] This chapter focuses on the historical tale of one of the most marginalized non-human groups, the circus animals. The first section deals with the historical 1991 ban on the

[2] Bruno Latour, *We Have Never Been Modern* (Cambridge: Harvard University Press, 1993), 13.

[3] Sandra Swart, '"The World the Horses Made": A South African Case Study of Writing Animals into Social History', *International Review of Social History* 55, Part 2 (August 2010): 242, 249.

training and performance of certain wild animals and the consequent legal battle between the state and the circus community. Then I will move on to discuss what policies and attitudes had brought animals to the circus historically. In the next section, I will be looking at the colonial and postcolonial state policies of scientific conservation, its emblematic institution, zoo, animal trade, and the ideas of exotic and exhibition.

The Ban

Animals have always been an integral part of circus. Early circuses around the world were in fact itinerant menageries with ticketed exhibitions of caged animals from the wilderness and 'exotic' lands. In the ring, ferocious animals walked on high bamboo rods, leapt through fire rings, played football and cricket, rode bikes, cycles, and trains, and danced to their masters' tunes. Animal lovers and rights activists around the world have always pointed fingers at circus over the cruel methods used to train and tame animals, their life in undersized cages, and transportation from place to place in appalling conditions. Accusations of physical and mental cruelty inflicted on circus animals also include blinding, removal of teeth and claws, deprivation of food and medication, forced breeding, whipping, and electric shock. Over the past few decades, many countries have issued a total or partial ban on animal performances in circus, nationwide and locally. In 2009, Bolivia banned the use of all animals, both wild and domestic, in the circus, an unprecedented action.[4] In November 2018, the Ministry of Environment, Forest and Climate Change in India had also proposed a complete ban on all animals in the circus or mobile entertainment facilities.[5]

On 2 March 1991, the environment ministry of the Government of India issued an order, based on the 1960 Prevention of Cruelty to Animals Act, banning the training and performance of some animals: 'In exercise of the powers conferred upon him under section 22 of the

[4] Available at http://www.theguardian.com/world/2009/jul/31/bolivia-bans-circus-animals, last accessed on 23 March 2012.

[5] Notification, GSR 1142(E), Ministry of Environment, Forest and Climate Change, New Delhi, 28 November 2018.

Prevention of Cruelty to Animals Act, 1960, the President is pleased to order that no person shall train or exhibit the animals specified below:—1. Bears 2. Monkeys 3. Tigers 4. Panthers 5. Dogs.'[6] (In the corrigendum dated 7 August 1991, the ban on dogs was withdrawn.)

The Legal Battle

In less than three weeks, on 20 March, the Delhi High Court granted a stay on this order on a petition filed by the Indian Circus Federation, and the animals continued in the ring. Six years later, after hearing the case at length, on 21 August 1997, the court ordered the government to consider their ban order afresh. Thus, an expert committee[7] was constituted and in accordance with their report, recommendations of the Animal Welfare Board of India, and other relevant material pertaining to the case, a new notification was issued on 14 October 1998: '[T]he Central Government hereby specifies that the following animals shall not be exhibited or trained as a [sic] performing animals, with effect from the date of publication of this notification, namely:—1. Bears 2. Monkeys 3. Tigers 4. Panthers 5. Lions.'[8] Both the Indian Circus Federation and the Indian Circus Employees Union moved court, challenging the order. On 16 December 1998, the Delhi High Court dismissed the petition of the Indian Circus Federation, and consequently the Indian Circus Employees Union withdrew its petition in February 1999.

Many cases were filed by circus companies in courts around the country against the seizure of the animals and seeking compensation from the government. The most significant ruling came from the High Court of Kerala in a petition filed by the employees of Jumbo Circus. Dismissing the petitioners' plea, the division bench, comprising Justice

[6] Notification file no. F 26-7/91 WL-I, Ministry of Environment and Forest, 2 March 1991.

[7] The committee members were addl. Inspector General of Forests (IGF) (Wild Life) as the chairman, director of animal welfare as member secretary, and director of Wild Life Institute of India (Dehradun), member secretary of Central Zoo Authority and S. C. Dey, addl. IGF (Rtd.).

[8] Notification file no. 9-9/97-A. W., Ministry of Social Justice and Empowerment, 14 October 1998.

K. Narayana Kurup and Justice K. V. Sankaranarayanan, asked in their telling judgment: 'If humans are entitled to fundamental rights, why not animals?'[9] We will come back to this significant ruling in the concluding section. The petitioners appealed to the Supreme Court of India, but to no avail. The apex court dismissed their appeal on 1 May 2001.

The ban, fateful in the lives of thousands of circus artistes and workers roaming around the country, has become a significant moment in the collective memory of the community. Even those who had retired from the trade long before the ban would usually start telling their life stories with some statement about the event's aftermath. V. M. Prabhakaran, secretary of the Indian Circus Employees Union at the time, said that about 400 animals had been taken away from Indian circuses altogether: 'An animal has at least three keepers including the animal trainer. Thus at least 1200 trainers and keepers have become jobless with that order. The animal keepers and trainers who have been looking after the animals haven't got any compensation either from the circus owners or from the government.'[10]

The central argument of the petition is that 'the Notification dated 14th October, 1998 issued by the Government arbitrarily threatens the livelihood of around 40,000 animal trainers/caretakers/handlers/performers',[11] and that 'the petitioners herein are carrying on their trade/occupation/art/profession for nearly 109 years'.[12] Another petition states, '[T]here are more than 3500 animals who are involved and are participating in the exhibition of circus shown in various parts of the country.'[13]

---

[9] Judgment dated 6 June 2000, *N. R. Nair and Others* v. *Union of India*, Original Petition No. 155 of 1999 (hereafter, 'Judgment 2000'). I am grateful to the late K. V. Raghavan, former president of the Indian Circus Employees Union, for providing me with a copy of the complete case file.

[10] Interview, V. M. Prabhakaran.

[11] Special leave petition (civil) of 2000 in the matter of Original petition (O.P.) no. 155 of 1999 R (hereafter, 'Special leave petition').

[12] Argument notes, O.P. no. 2636 of 1999, *M. A. Sasidharan and Others* v. *Union of India and Another* (hereafter, 'Sasidharan, 2636').

[13] Amended writ petition, O.P. no. 155 of 1999.

Circus owners and workers also argue that the circus animals which are born and brought up in the circus are accustomed to only the circus way of life and, therefore, cannot survive in the wild or with any other animal or in any other surroundings, whether the zoo, sanctuary, or jungle. They cited instances of the deaths of two circus animals from the Golden Circus within just two months of their rehabilitation at the Borivali National Park, Mumbai, and also the deaths at the Alipore Zoo where animals from mobile petting zoos were rehabilitated. They pointed out that the animals were kept in the same cages in which they had been brought for more than six months. They also raised before the court the plight of race horses and elephants used in temple festivals, bullocks used for pulling carriages, donkeys used for carrying weights in hostile climates, and the animals being transported to slaughter houses, cramped in vehicles for many hours.[14]

The petitioners assert that the breeding rate in circus tents is far higher than that in zoos and sanctuaries, and this is evident from the substantial increase in the number of animals in spite of the ban on the acquisition of animals since 1972.[15] They further state that not only is breeding more productive in circuses but death rates are much lower too compared to the zoos.[16] They complain that the 'existing animals with the various zoos are not provided for proper food, shelter and surroundings'.[17]

---

[14] O.P. no. 155 of 1999, N. R. *Nair and others* v. *Union of India and Another*.

[15] The Wild Life (Protection) Act, 1972, instructs that 'No licensee under this Chapter [v] shall … (b) (i) capture any wild animal'.

M. Krishnan critically notes, 'The act does not seek to prohibit the hunting of all animals, but only their unlicensed poaching' and 'the definitions of "animals" and "wild life" are needlessly inept'. M. Krishnan, 'The Wild Life (Protection) Act, 1972: A Critical Appraisal', *Economic and Political Weekly* 8, no. 11 (1973): 565.

[16] S. Abu states that 'the breeding in the circus is so effective that we are looking at it with open eyes. It must be mainly because of the relationship between the animal trainer and the animals. We are always facing difficulty to breed animals in captivity while in circus, there might also be other reasons, but they breed and produce lots of cubs'. Interview, S. Abu, Thiruvananthapuram Zoo, 19 May 2010.

[17] Sasidharan, 2636.

Interestingly, the judgment of the High Court of Kerala quotes the report of the committee[18] constituted to review the ban on the exhibition and training of performing animals and criticizes the attempt to draw a parallel between the zoo and circus: 'Contrasting differences in the case of zoos and circuses are that the latter have capture, transportation, training, rehearsal and performance whereas the former have capture/seizure and translocation.' It further argues that the circus groups have 'failed to appreciate the total changes in the zoo ethics of late' and shows their concern regarding 'an adverse impact on the animals on display mostly in unnatural environment' in circuses.[19]

Along similar lines, the Review Committee Report argues that 'the circuses may never be able to achieve the standards of housing and upkeep of animals that the modern zoo provides'. The Review Committee that looked into the ban further reports, '[B]reeding in circuses is only accidental, or incidental, and in no way helps a national conservation program. It needs to be pointed out that inbred stocks lose their heterogeneity and vigor.'[20] On the other hand, circus employees of various circuses argue, 'Circus Units are from 1971 prohibited to purchase sale or transfer their wild animals without the written permission of Wild Life Authorities. However, the circus animals retained [sic] enjoy good health and longevity and an increase in numbers,' and allege, 'the Government does not have the means, the capacity or ability to look after the healthy animals which are being fully cared for and owned by the circuses.'[21]

The Review Committee Report further states,

> [W]hile banning the use of tigers, panthers, bears and monkeys in circuses, always had in mind that the circuses have been the source of many livelihoods and that it would cause hardships if the use of all the animals is banned abruptly. Therefore, the animals like elephants and lions which are held by circuses in large numbers, were not covered in the list of banned animals in the first instance.[22]

---

[18] Report of the committee constituted by the Ministry of Environment and Forests, Government of India, to review the ban on exhibition and training of performing animals, CWP 890/91 (hereafter, 'Review Committee Report').

[19] Judgment 2000.

[20] Review Committee Report.

[21] Special leave petition.

[22] Review Committee Report.

It is worthwhile noting here that the government was confused about its compassion and conservation policy. It has not been made clear how dogs got into that list or why they were excluded later. This predicament is conspicuous in the circular issued for the rehabilitation of circus animals that explains the purpose of the ban thus: '[I]t was time society realized and [sic] importance of animals and their crucial role in ecology.'[23]

In August 2013, the Animal Welfare Board of India (AWBI) issued a ban on elephant performances in circus.

> The Board decided to stop registration of elephants for performance under Performing Animals Rules in view of huge cruelties and abuse suffered by them. The Board also decided that a proposal for inclusion of Elephants in the list of banned animals under The Performing Animals (Registration) Rules 2001 be sent to the Ministry for consideration and there should be no performing animals in circuses.[24]

The Board also 'directed to issue legal notices to all circuses for using sick, injured and unregistered animals in their circuses as Performing Animals' and 'seize them after making arrangement for rehabilitation with some of the AWOs [Animal Welfare Organizations] and Zoos'. The AWBI has stopped the registration of circus elephants under the Performing Animals Rules cited above. *Captive Elephants in Circuses: A Scientific Investigation of the Population Status, Management and Welfare Significance*, a report that focuses on the conditions of elephants maintained in circuses, notes the need 'to change and improve living conditions of these magnificent animals' and recommends that since the 'basic welfare needs of elephants cannot be met within circuses', banning elephants from circuses is the 'progressive and humane step'. This report, which contributed largely to the ban of elephants in circuses, though it acknowledges the long history of performing animals in circuses, has hardly paid any attention to the human–animal relationship there. In line with the early bans, it negates circus as a space where 'animals are trained or conditioned to exhibit specific behaviors

[23] Circular no. 9-9/97-AWD, Animal Welfare Division, Ministry of Social Justice and Empowerment, Government of India, dated 23 June 2000 (hereafter, 'Circular no. 9-9/97-AWD').

[24] Minutes, 39th general meeting of the Animal Welfare Board of India, Chennai, 23 August 2013.

with no option to do otherwise', and 'the sole purpose of the elephants' existence in circuses is their ability to generate revenue'. The report, on many occasions, fails to understand circus elephants as working animals and circus as the zoos or temples where humans benefit from animal works.[25] However, as per the Central Zoo Authority's legal restrictions, elephants do not perform in circuses now. Many of them were kept on the private estates of circus owners as there were regulations around keeping elephants in tents and the management anticipated a complete ban. The elephants were also sold to Hindu temples and private parties. Dogs, horses, ponies, camels, and parrots still work in Indian circuses. Since a great number of circuses are being closed down in recent years, many of the owners sell off their camels and horses when offered a lump sum.

It is worthwhile noting in this context that elephants figure dominantly in the animal policy of the nation. Project Elephant was launched in 1992 and the Elephant Task Force was constituted in 2010 by the Ministry of Environment and Forests. As Mahesh Rangarajan, who headed the task force, notes elsewhere, 'The fact that a species is unique as well as rare has eventually played a role in nationalist projects to protect, review and propagate it.'[26] Eric Scigliano notes that the species included in the Association of Zoos and Aquariums' 'Species Survival Plan Mission' are often flagship species, well-known animals which arouse strong feelings in the public.[27]

Generating measures for the conservation of elephants, the report of the Elephant Task Force notes, 'Conservation policies that may diminish the status of the captive elephant should effectively integrate them into India's wildlife protection laws. This is especially important given that the vast majority of captive elephants today were born in the wild and subsequently taken into captivity.' The report recommends replacing 'ownership' with 'guardianship' and suggests that 'service conditions of mahouts' should also be addressed, and training and

[25] Surendra Varma, S. R. Sujata, Suparna Ganguly, and Shiela Rao, *Captive Elephants in Circuses: A Scientific Investigation of the Population Status, Management and Welfare Significance* (Bangalore: Compassion Unlimited Plus Action, 2008).

[26] Mahesh Rangarajan, 'Region's Honour, Nation's Pride: Gir's Lions on the Cusp of History', in *The Lions of India*, ed. Divyabhanusinh (Delhi: Black Kite, 2008), 258.

[27] Eric Scigliano, *Love, War and Circuses: The Age-Old Relationship between Elephants and Humans* (Boston and New York: Houghton and Mifflin, 2002), 293.

certificates should be granted to them. It also recommends that the usage of elephants in circuses and for collection of alms should be discouraged/banned, and should follow the precedent of phasing out as per the 1991 ban.[28]

From Circus to Zoo: The Aftermath

Soon after the court rulings upheld the government order, zoo authorities around the country were instructed to raid circuses and take away the animals. Various animal rights NGOs gave a helping hand in the raids and strengthened campaigns against circuses, posting reports and requests widely on the internet.[29]

A 2001 *Telegraph* report about a starving couple of royal Bengal tigers, a monkey, a bear, and 20 lions, including four babies and an old lion, which were abandoned in Patna by Ajanta Circus after a surprise raid by the central wildlife officers and an order of cancellation of ownership, gives a picture of the aftermath. Another news report from the *TOI*, 2001, notes that the seizure of these animals by zoo authorities could not take place in the first phase. The circus owners claimed that the action by the authorities was not legal as the case by the circus regarding the compensation for the upkeep of animals was still pending before the High Court of Patna. On the other hand, the authorities claimed their actions were within the law legality. The circus moved to Bokaro, the authorities left 'empty handed', and the poor animals were left starving.[30]

---

[28] Mahesh Rangarajan et al., *Gajah: Securing the Future of Elephants in India: The Report of the Elephant Task Force* (New Delhi: Ministry of Environment and Forests, 2010), 108, 117.

[29] Spencer's thesis discusses the role of visuality as a distinct mode of activism with regard to the animal activist movements where visual representations are created and distributed to give certain meanings. Moore Spencer, *From Magazines to Twitter Memes: The Visual Methods of Animal Activist Social Movements 1860–2018* (Canada: Queens University, 2018).

[30] Available at http://www.telegraphindia.com/1010725/front_pa.htm, last accessed on 29 July 2014; also see http://timesofindia.indiatimes.com/city/patna/Circus-animals-Ordeal-ends-for-a-better-deal/articleshow/1320569066.cms, last accessed on 29 July 2014; it is noteworthy that according to the latter, the animals were left with some circus animal keepers.

The circular issued to all chief wildlife wardens for the rehabilitation of circus animals specified five shelters spread over various states:

1. Sri Venkateswara Zoological Park, Tirupati
2. Indira Gandhi Zoological Park, Vizagapatam
3. Bannerghatta National Park, Bangalore
4. Nahargarli Biological Park, Jaipur
5. Arignar Anna Zoological Park, Vandalur, Chennai

It further added that the construction of the sixth shelter located at Nandankanan Biological Park, Bhubaneswar, would be completed shortly.[31] (See Table 2.1, compiled based on information from the official website of the Central Zoo Authority [CZA] for the number of animals 'rescued', the circuses they were taken from, and the zoos to which they were transferred.)

Circus animals at the Tirupati Sri Venkateswara Zoological Park are kept in two rescue centres. These enclosures are not part of the zoo itinerary and hence not accessible to the public.[32] Funded by the Central Zoo Authority, Animal Rescue Centre–I was constructed during 1999–2000 and the second centre in 2004–5. The CZA also bears the upkeep of the animals and the funding is reduced in accordance with the decrease in the number of animals. The curator added that these enclosures (that seemed like old-age homes with aged lions) would become part of the regular zoo space after all the circus animals cease to exist. Deliberate measures such as castration and separating the males and females are undertaken to prevent breeding. She further said that most of the animals were hybrids, so breeding has to be regulated. However, accidental breeding has happened and those cubs have been moved to the safari park for display.[33]

Current details regarding the circus animals that came to the Tirupati Zoological Park, provided by the zoo curator's office, show that 45 animals have already perished and that all the tigers and tigresses are dead too. The report says:

The first batch of 12 Nos. of rescued Lions (5 male + 7 female) was received from Rambo Circus on 26-09-2001. In the next batch, 12 Lions

[31] Circular no. 9-9/97-AWD.
[32] I am grateful to the zoo curator, Yesoda Bai IFS, for granting access.
[33] Interview, Yesoda Bai, Tirupati Zoological Park, 28 August 2014.

Table 2.1 List of Seized Circus Animals at the Central Zoo Authority

Circuses/Other Sources from Where the Animals Were Received	Capacity		Current Position		Name of the Circus Surrendered
	Lions	Tigers	Lions	Tigers	
Arignar Zoological Park, Vandular	40	20	53	8	Johnson Indian Variety Entertainment; Royal Mobile Circus, KallaKurchi; Private Circus, Kanyakumari; Great Rayman Circus, King Bharath Circus, Satur; Great Royal Circus, Chennai; Great Bombay Circus, Polur Taluk; and Gemini Circus, Kancheepuram
Bannerghatta National Park, Bangalore	70	30	97	3	Mobile Circus, K.G.F, Kolar; Mobile Circus, Kundapur, Mangalore; Geeta Circus, Gulbarga; Komal Circus, Faridabad, Haryana; Golden Circus, U.P.; Sangli Zoo, Maharashtra; Asiad Circus, Bijnor, Uttaranchal; Bharath Circus, Madhya Pradesh (Nimuch); Nandankanan Zoo, Orissa; Shalimar and New Golden Circus; Grand Prabhath Circus; and New Grand Circus
Sri Venkateswara Zoological Park, Tirupati	15	15	25	1	Rambo Circus and Grand National Circus
Indira Gandhi Zoo, Vizagapatam	30	30	26	12	Ajanta Circus, Patna; Saibaba Circus; Famous Circus; and Suresh Circus
Nahargarh Biological Park, Jaipur	30	20	23	12	Great Geeta Circus; Jamuna Circus; Empire Circus; Indian Circus; and Mobile Zoo

Source: Central Zoo Authority website (http://www.cza.nic.in/rescue.html, last accessed on 30 November 2019).

(4 males + 8 females) and 2 Tigresses were received from the National Circus on 31.03.2002. In addition to the above 26 animals, 18 animals i.e., 9 Males and 9 Females were received from the Western circus, Appollo circus and Royal Circus during the year 2004–05. On 15.8.2005, 2 Lions and 3 Lionesses (total 5 Animals) were received from Sangli- Miraj- Kupwad, Mahanagarapalika Zoo, Sangli, Maharashtra. On 31.8.2005, 3 Lions, 16 Lionesses and 1 Tiger (Total 20 Animals) were received from Jumbo Circus, Jaipur (Mishra farm house) and 7 Lions (5 males and 2 females) from Amar Circus, Jaipur (Mishra farm house) on 30.9.2006. At present there are 36 animals being maintained in the Animal Rescue Centre at Tirupati.[34]

Circus owners complain that they found large numbers of animals taken from them missing when they reached the zoos. Sujit Dilip, who runs Rambo Circus, says, 'I'm afraid of dogs, but I've never been afraid of lions. They were let loose in my house and they were not *wild*, they were bred in our own circus, and I was brought up along with them, in their company.' He added that Rama Master, a tiger trainer, committed suicide after his animals were taken away. Another ringmaster, Rajan, left the job.[35] Babu, a ringmaster from Gemini, told me that many of his senior ringmasters quit the job and some did not even have a home to go to.[36] Sujit says that he had requested those officials who came to take away the animals to keep a single trainer with them, which was not allowed, and now he knows that all his animals taken to Tirupati Zoo are dead and gone. He laments that even the very old lions were made to travel long distances, which led to their deaths.[37] Animal trainers and helpers in other circuses have similar tales to tell. Another significant allegation about the state policy was that the zoos in Junagadh, Mysore, and Tirupati were revamped with the animals taken from various circuses.[38]

There are many news reports that throw light on these animals' afterlife at the zoos. A *Telegraph* (7 June 2008) report about circus animals

---

[34] Note given by the zoo curator's office, Tirupati Zoological Park, 28 August 2014.

[35] Interview, Sujit Dilip, Pune, 13 December 2011.

[36] Interview, S. Babu, Gemini Circus, 19 June 2012.

[37] Interview, Sujit Dilip.

[38] Interview, E. Ravindran.

at the rescue centre in Tirupati's Sri Venkateswara Zoo states that lions numbering 70 were kept in packed same-sex cages, and the zoo warden admitted that the animals were kept tranquilized most of the time so that they did not get violent. We must bear in mind that the law clearly states, '[S]edatives or tranquilizers or steroids or any other artificial enhancers are not administered to or inserted in any animal except the anesthesia by a veterinary doctor for the purpose of treatment of an injured or sick animal.'[39]

The *Telegraph* report describes the management of circus animals at the rescue centre and zoo animals at Tirupati's Sri Venkateswara Zoo as 'a caste system': 'Some are pampered, allowed as much sex as they want, and are hailed as the finest of the Asian breed. The other set survives in jam-packed same-sex cages, fed but not cared for, denied copulation rights, objects of pity that is mixed with contempt.' The report further adds that circus animals, which are mostly hybrid, are not considered 'wildlife', and wildlife laws do not allow sex between hybrid and 'pure' breeds. But the wildlife warden makes clear that these animals 'eat more', which shows that they were not underfed in circuses. The story criticizes the attitude of zoo authorities which feel that 'these animals must be allowed to live as long as they can. That's all'. 'Lions and lionesses were kept separately to prevent breeding. The lions were neither pure Asiatic nor African,' says a report on the transfer of circus animals to Bannerghatta National Park.[40] It must be noted here that most of the animals in circuses are procured through exchange deals with the zoos, private parties, and markets. So, 'an unknown percentage of animals classified as captive-bred in circuses were actually bred in other private facilities'.[41]

In 2015, Mexico introduced a federal ban initiated by the Green Party on animal performances in circuses, including tigers, lions,

[39] Available at http://envfor.nic.in/legis/awbi/awbi19.html, last accessed on 30 July 2013.

[40] Available at http://www.indiadivine.org/content/topic/1928663-animals-rescued-circuses-banned/, last accessed on 30 July 2012.

[41] G. Iossa, C. D. Soulsbury, and S. Harris, 'Are Wild Animals Suited to a Travelling Circus Life?' Available at http://www.savezooelephants.com/pdf/WILD%20ANIMALS%20IN%20CIRCUS.pdf, last accessed on 22 December 2012, 131.

elephants, and zebras. Echoing the condition in India, there have been many reports about the Mexican state failing to facilitate the upkeep and provide living spaces for the approximately 3500 'saved' animals. Reports say that the public zoos in the country are already full with animals, while some of the private zoos have shown interest—all of which indicates the country's limited capacity to provide sanctuaries. Associated Press reports that six tigers, seven baboons, four camels, and three dromedaries were found abandoned without food and water.[42] *The Guardian* report hints at the long history of black market trade in exotic species, increasing doubts regarding the actual 'protection' of animals. It adds that the circus owners are desperate to sell their animals (with a thriving black market outside), while many of them are putting them to sleep as there is hardly any other way.[43]

In 2014, hundreds of workers in the circus industry, apprehensive of the consequences of such a ban, had staged public protests and protest performances in the Mexico City Square.[44] Just as in the case of 'traditional' practices such as Jellikettu in India, Mexico does not prohibit the use of animals in a rodeo known as Charreadas.[45] Bull fighting, cock fighting, and dolphin shows are also legal in the country. The international NGO Animal Defenders International brags that Mexico is the 29th country to ban animals in circuses through their incessant campaigns.[46] It probes questions such as what does it actually mean to be an animal in postcolonial lands such as India or Mexico and what do legal proscriptions and animal rights activism really come to mean for the non-human beings at the end.

[42] Available at https://www.pri.org/stories/2015-07-02/mexico-bans-wild-animals-circuses-theres-no-place-them-go, last accessed on 28 November 2018.

[43] Available at https://www.theguardian.com/world/2015/mar/27/mexico-deadline-ban-circus-animals-looms, last accessed on 28 November 2018.

[44] Available at https://www.ibtimes.co.uk/mexico-circus-ban-will-leave-thousands-tigers-elephants-camels-homeless-1492365, https://www.bbc.com/news/world-latin-america-27788291, last accessed on 28 November 2018.

[45] Available at https://www.theguardian.com/world/2015/mar/27/mexico-deadline-ban-circus-animals-looms, last accessed on 28 November 2018.

[46] Available at https://www.stopcircussuffering.com/news/latin-america/mexico-bans-wild-animals-circuses/. Last accessed on 28 November 2018.

Animal Defenders International records that the government rescue centres did not have the capacity for the 'exceeding number of animals' collected from Indian circuses. This throws light on the fact that the state did not have accurate data about the number of animals they were going to deal with. It notes, 'In addition, some states don't support the ban, whilst others do not have the finances to enforce it.' The website, critical about circuses, clearly mentions that a lion died before it could be rescued from the Olympic Circus, and adds, 'After a lengthy campaign it was agreed that the animals would be moved to rescue centres that would be expanded to house them, but the Government lacked any funds for transport and holding cages.'[47] The *Hindu* also reports how the Vandalur Zoo authority was reluctant to take circus animals at first, since they were apprehensive about the letter of credit from the state government.[48] So, we may ask whether a change in ownership from the 'private' circus to the 'public' zoo makes any difference in the real suffering of animals.

It is noteworthy that the Wild Life (Protection) Act of 1972 defines zoo as 'an establishment, whether stationary or mobile, where captive animals are kept for exhibition to the public [and includes a circus and rescue centre]'.[49] Though substituted later on, it shows that there was only a thin line of demarcation between the zoo and the circus as a space for exhibiting animals. Just like zoos, early circuses had ticketed exhibitions of their menageries during the breaks between performances. A notice of O. C. Appa's Grand Kerala Circus from early twentieth century announces that 'From morning 8 to evening five wild animals will be exhibited for a ticket price of 3 paisa each'.

These ticketed exhibitions of caged wild animals were prevalent in Indian circuses well into the latter half of the twentieth century.[50]

[47] Available at http://www.adinternational.org/animals_in_entertainment/ go.php?id=212&ssi=10, last accessed on 30 July 2014.

[48] Available at http://www.hindu.com/2002/03/15/stories/2002031507140300. htm, last accessed on 30 July 2014.

[49] The Wild Life (Protection) Act, 1972 (53 of 1972). Subs. by Act 16 of 2003, Section 3, as 'but does not include a circus and an establishment' (w.e.f. 1 April 2003).

[50] Interview, Radha Kannan; Pushpa; Sukumaran, Kolassery, 12 November 2012.

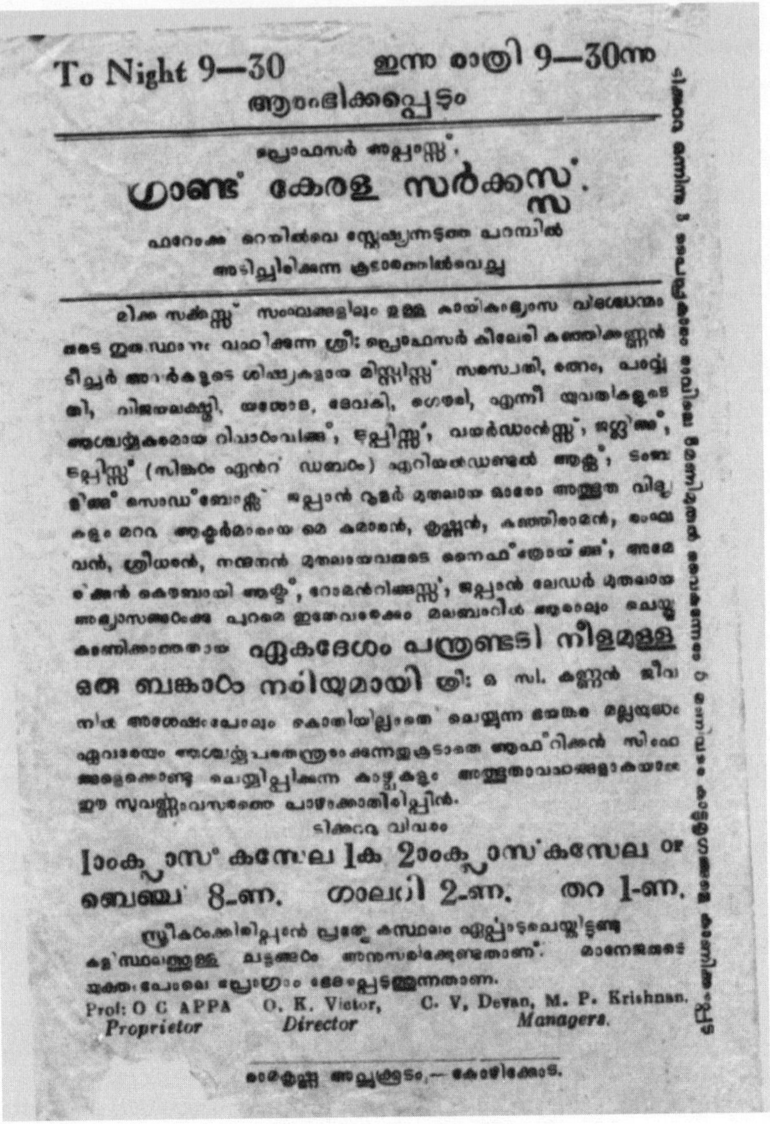

To Night 9—30 ഇന്നു രാത്രി 9—30ന്നു
ആരംഭിക്കപ്പെടും

ഗ്രാണ്ട് കേരള സർക്കസ്സ്.

ഏകദേശം പന്ത്രണ്ടടി നീളമുള്ള

ഒരു ബങ്കാറം നരിയുമായി

ടിക്കററ വിവരം

1ാംക്ലാസ് കസേല 1ക 2ാംക്ലാസ് കസേല or

ബെഞ്ച് 8-ണ. ഗാലറി 2-ണ. തറ 1-ണ.

Prof: O C APPA O. K. Victor, C. V, Devan, M. P. Krishnan.
Proprietor *Director* *Managers.*

Image 2.1 Publicity Flyer, Grand Kerala Circus

Source: Private collection of Edward Williams.

Performances in zoos have a different history, which we will discuss soon. But we may observe here how a sudden shift from familiar surroundings to cramped zoos or zoological parks with large areas would have affected the circus animals and resulted in the deaths of the more vulnerable cases.

H. Hediger, who served as the director of Zoological Gardens, Zurich, observes in his seminal work *The Psychology and Behaviour of Animals in Zoos and Circuses* that the surroundings in which zoo animals and circus animals are brought up are quite different with respect to spatial territories and association with humans.

> In circuses nearly every animal is almost continually in close contact with people. ... The circus animal is, as it were, never alone. In the zoo on the contrary, each keeper is responsible for a large area containing many animals and he has little or no time to devote to separate individuals, consequently the intimacy of the circus between man and animal is seldom possible.[51]

Circus animals are accustomed to movement and music, lights, and mechanical and human noises. He further adds, '[W]hen in the past I included a circus ring in reconstruction plans for Basle Zoo, the overriding considerations were biological ones. Many animals turn stupid when shut up in cages and left to themselves'.[52] Hediger's observation resonates with Thiruvananthapuram Zoo's former curator's remark quoted earlier regarding more productive breeding among circus animals: 'It is mainly because of the more intimate relationship between the animal trainer and the animals unlike as in the zoo'.[53]

This is significant when both the state and animal rights NGOs construct and delegitimize circus as an 'other' of zoos, sanctuaries, national parks, and reserved forests. The relationship between the animal trainers and the animals in circus that comes across in the above-mentioned observations is significant. In the legal battle that ensued from the ban, this intimacy has not been talked about even by the petitioners who raised the problem of the livelihood of animal trainers and keepers. Dr M. S. Gopal, a senior veterinarian who claims to have treated circus

---

[51] H. Hediger, *The Psychology and Behaviour of Animals in Zoos and Circuses* (New York: Dover, 1962), 117.

[52] Hediger, *The Psychology and Behaviour of Animals in Zoos and Circuses*, 118.

[53] Interview, S. Abu.

animals in various circus companies for more than 20 years, mentions in his letter dated 4 October 1997 addressed to the review committee, 'There is almost a one to one relationship, personal attachment and affinity between the animal and the trainer in the Circus.'[54]

The animal keepers in zoos are selected through employment exchanges and people are appointed with no previous experience or training, although the rules stipulate a minimum two years of experience. Sadasivapillai, curator at the Trivandrum Zoo, sarcastically notes, 'Most of the people who come here for the job may not have looked after even a cow in their lives.'[55] Both Pillai and the curator of the Tirupati Zoo, Yesoda Bai, stated that no animal trainer from any circus company has ever joined their zoos to the date. There was no effort on the part of the ministry that banned circus animals to rehabilitate trainers/keepers along with the animals. Nor did they find it necessary to give any compensation to the animal trainers or their assistants.

Maneka Gandhi, the environment minister during the 1991 ban, is startlingly condemnatory about those in the circus trade: 'If their "fundamental right to carry on their trade and business" has been infringed … then smugglers, pickpockets and poachers can also argue on the same lines because their arrest by the police infringes their ability to carry on their nefarious trades as well!'[56] Meena Radhakrishna points out, what she calls 'Civil Society's Uncivil Acts', how the Kalandar community's livelihood was shattered following the ban on their traditional occupation of bear dancing.[57] These instances point out how those who argue

---

[54] Case file, Indian Circus Employees Union, Thalassery.

[55] Interview, Sadasivapillai, Thiruvananthapuram Zoo, 18 May 2010.

[56] Maneka Gandhi, *Heads and Tails* (Mapusa, Goa: The Other India Press, 1994), 96–7.

[57] '[E]ven after the Wildlife Protection Act, 1972, came into force, possession of a bear for entertainment or as a pet was legally permitted till as recently as 1993'. Radhakrishna further observes that by 2001 the community became not only prone to deprivation and poverty and large-scale starvation but also vulnerable to undertaking antisocial jobs. Meena Radhakrishna, 'Civil Society's Uncivil Acts: Dancing Bear and Starving Kalandar', *Economic and Political Weekly* 42, no. 42 (2007): 2; Amrita Talwar reports that INR 50,000 was given to each Kalandar family as compensation to find an alternate livelihood. Amrita Talwar, 'Go Home Teddy', *Outlook* (30 October 2006): 50.

for proscriptions seldom pay any attention to the rehabilitation of the lives of humans and animals caught in the game. Maan Barua reminds us with regard to elephants that the key issues facing those who cohabit with elephants, some of whom are among the poorest people in the world, are often ignored.[58]

Marthe Kiley Worthington sharply notes, '[I]t is often argued that zoos are *not necessarily* cruel and wrong, ... whereas circuses are *by their nature cruel*' (italics in the original for emphasis).[59] Now, organizations such as People for the Ethical Treatment of Animals (PETA) and the International Organization for Animal Protection in India (OIPA) are demanding the closing down of zoos as well.[60] All of these point towards the fact that when screaming for bans, the very ideas such as conservation need to be looked at critically so as to understand the tactful way with which we construct and relish our 'modern', 'humanitarian' image and ideal. As Eric Scigliano scathingly points out, '[D]on't despair over dying rain forests and coral reefs; your neighborhood zoo will save the last tigers from the gathering darkness. This mission justifies the pleasure we get from viewing captive animals and the enrichment zoos derive from exhibiting them. Exploitation becomes salvation.'[61] Worthington argues, 'Ethically, ecologically and ethologically acceptable ways of inter-species associations are possible and desirable, and they could develop even in zoos and circuses. For this to happen, though, such institutions must change, not be banned.' If this change occurs, she thinks, just as we keep a watch on human rights, we will also develop our own understanding of animal rights.[62]

[58] Maan Barua, 'Between Gods and Demons', *Seminar* (651) (2013): 75–9.

[59] Marthe Kiley-Worthington, *Animals in Circuses and Zoos: Chiron's World?* (Essex: Little Eco-Farms, 1990), 12.

[60] For instance, see the petition available at https://www.change.org/en-IN/petitions/shut-down-all-zoo-and-circuses-in-india-sukanya-kadyan, last accessed on 29 July 2014.

[61] Eric Scigliano, *Love, War and Circuses*, 293.

[62] Marthe Kiley-Worthington, *Animals in Circuses and Zoos*, 223; Though the publisher claims that this book 'was commissioned by the RSPCA to carry out an independent, scientific study of circus animals, in comparison with animals in zoos and other husbandry systems and in the wild', the Review Committee Report dismisses it, saying, 'RSPCA has categorically stated that they have not

The Janus-Faced Law

It should be noted that both our laws and the colonial laws which we had followed have been specious in the case of forests and animals. Besides promoting hunting as a 'manly' sport, the colonial government had cash awards for those who killed wild animals, issued guns to interested parties, and levied taxes on grazing for domestic animals.[63]

Ironically enough, this was part of their forest policy—clearing forests and slaughtering wild species. This very structure established the Society for the Prevention of Cruelty to Animals. Mahesh Rangarajan notes the Raj's project to eliminate ferocious beasts, 'They were a scourge to be wiped out. Such practices were new to India: no previous ruler had ever attempted to exterminate any species.'[64] The major goal behind these forest policies was to promote valuable timber, such as teak and sandalwood, collect specimens for scientific purposes, and export skins, teeth, and nails of animals for commercial purposes.[65]

---

endorsed the conclusions made by the author and the views expressed in the book can at best be considered as the views of an individual and not as the views of RSPCA'. This book was submitted by the Indian Circus Federation as an additional document as part of their Transfer Petition (Civil) no. 361 of 2000 in the Supreme Court of India. The author's son, Jake Rendle-Worthington, told me that the book had been commissioned by the RSPCA, but they backed out in the final phase because the findings were not in congruence with their official line. Interview, Jake Rendle-Worthington, London, 22 June 2016.

[63] M. S. S. Pandian, 'Gendered Negotiations: Hunting and Colonialism in Late 19th Century Nilgiris', Contributions to Indian Sociology 29 (1–2) (January–December 1995): 239–63; Mahesh Rangarajan, India's Wildlife History: An Introduction (Delhi: Permanent Black, 2001), 22–3; M. P. Sivadasa Menon, a hunting enthusiast from Malabar, narrates known hunters, methods of hunting, and varieties of animals found in Malabar forests and opines that the hunters in Malabar were of lower castes and lacked education, which contributed to the perception that hunting is inferior. This glaring casteist observation shows that caste dimensions of hunting discourse needs to be looked at just as race or masculinity. M. P. Sivadasamenon, Malabarile Shikar [Hunting in Malabar] (Palghat: Udaya Publications, 1959), 14.

[64] Mahesh Rangarajan, India's Wildlife History, 23.

[65] There are ample archival records that show the colonial British attitude towards animals and their forest policies in Malabar, Mysore, Coorg, and

Sujit Sivasundaram points out that the British colonial state used elephants in the military and traded, exhibited, and exchanged them as gifts in the colonies as well as their homeland. They adopted the natives' knowledge to mark, trap, train, and medically treat elephants in India. But the native acts were considered less benevolent:

> The British therefore prized benevolence in their entrapment of elephants rather than coercion, just as Britons hoped to use gestures of generosity as an aide to subjugating the Indian. Indians' relations to the environment, in the meantime, were presented as violent and savage. Yet beneath this rhetoric of difference the reality was that Britons learnt to capture elephants from local potentates.[66]

The Prevention of Cruelty to Animals Act came into force in 1890 and the Society for the Prevention of Cruelty to Animals (SPCA) was established by the colonial state under the Societies Registration Act, 1860.[67] The *TSR* Records, 1911, show the government sanctioning fines levied under Section 5 of the Towns Nuisance Act to the local branches of the SPCA where they executed prosecutions for cruelty to animals. One superintendent, two chief inspectors, two chief agents, one 1st-grade, two 2nd-grade, four 3rd-grade, and eight 4th-grade agents were the servants of the society. An official memorandum dated 13 August 1910

Canara districts. For instance, a revenue department order, dated 13 December 1886, about granting rewards for the destruction of wild animals instructs that a register be kept for recording the details of the rewards and the body parts of the animal killed. It further suggests that an extract from this register be sent along with the skin of the animal to the Huzur office. Revenue Board standing order, 13 May 1886, Tellicherry sub-collectors' office records (hereafter, '*TSR*'), List-1, File no. 4631, Regional Archives, Kozhikode.

[66] Sujit Sivasundaram, 'Trading Knowledge: The East India Company's Elephants in India and Britain', *The Historical Journal* 48, no. 1 (2005): 42.

[67] The Act notes, 'The Committee for the Prevention of Cruelty to Animals appointed by the Government of India drew attention to a number of drawbacks in the Prevention of Cruelty to Animals Act, 1890', which was a consolidated form of various local Acts and was confined to roads or streets in towns as well as certain types of cruelty only, and suggested its replacement by a more comprehensive Act. The new Act of 1960 contained provisions for the establishment of an Animal Welfare Board.

suggests that to make the operations of the Act more beneficial, it should be made clear before the public that 'the agents of the Society are not merely men of local position drawing adequate pay, but are also possessed of sufficient veterinary knowledge and appliances to be able to advise the owners of sick animals and afford some help in their treatment'. To endorse the view of the government that 'the people must learn to look upon the Society's agents as friends and assisters, instead of merely prosecutors', the SPCA has kept the 'educational part of its work in the forefront'. The society established a veterinary hospital and a lethal chamber, and organized annual animal shows, essay competitions, and bands of mercy. It also brought out a magazine called *The Tit-Bits of Animal Life* in Tamil and Telugu.[68] *Mathrubhumi* (5 April 1923) reports that the British Parliament passed a law that only certain animals could be exhibited and trained in circuses and that only certain types of equipment could be used while training them. Janet M. Davis points out that orientalism represented Asian and Middle Eastern regions as irrational and ahistorical in the European and American imperialist thinking. For the American animal advocates, colonial 'India primarily served as a field for humane education—as a model of nonviolence and vegetarian animal kindness on the one hand, and as a subject for moral uplift on the other'. She further adds,

> American and British empire builders believed in animal protectionism as a linchpin of higher civilization, which suggests that humane advocates around the world shared a common teleological language of animal protectionism. However, the colonial India example underscores the ways in which cultural and political differences bear on transnational histories of animal advocacy. The experiences of caste, religious pluralism and British colonialism shaped South Asian ideologies of animal kindness and nationalism in culturally specific ways, helping to sow the seeds of Hindu cultural nationalism and Muslim demonization in the twentieth century.[69]

[68] Government of Madras order, Judicial Department, communicated to all sub-divisional magistrates, 24 March 1911, *TSR*, List-II, File no. 2264, Regional Archives, Kozhikode.

[69] Janet M. Davis, *The Gospel of Kindness: Animal Welfare and the Making of Modern America* (New York: Oxford University Press, 2016), 152–3.

Faithfully following the duplicitous colonial laws, the Prevention of Cruelty to Animals Act, 1960, in India puts certain restrictions on the exhibition and performance of animals. In this Act, the word 'exhibit' has been defined as the exhibition of animals at any entertainment through the sale of tickets and training them for the purpose. The interesting thing to be noted here is the exemptions to this Act:

a. the training of animals to bona fide military or police purposes or the exhibition of animals so trained; or
b. any animals kept in any zoological garden or by any society or association which has for its principal object the exhibition of animals for educational or scientific purposes.

Keith Thomas examines how historically the English world entertained itself with sportive killings and animal fights, while the mischief of children extended to killing and inflicting pain on animals since 'it was a world in which much of what would later be regarded as "cruelty" had not yet been defined as such'. He notes pithily,

> Yet contemporaries were surely wrong to think of people as being more or less humane at one period in history than at another. What had changed was not the sentiment of humanity as such, but the definition of the area within which it was allowed to operate. The historian's task is to explain why the boundary encircling the area of moral concern should have been enlarged so as to embrace other species along with mankind.[70]

He points out how 'benevolence' and 'charity' were 'the most favoured words in literary vocabulary' in the eighteenth century, while with the emergence of towns and the industrial order, animals became highly marginalized and the early modern period realized the 'concern for animal rights'.[71]

---

[70] Keith Thomas, *Man and the Natural World: Changing Attittudes in England 1500–1800* (Harmondsworth: Penguin Books, 1983), 148–50.

[71] Thomas, *Man and the Natural World*, 175–81.

The 'Exotic'

The European love of the 'exotic' has its root in the territorial, political, racial, and environmental imperialism that colonialism exercised in its colonies. The new-found lands and things, people and animals, which were in great demand in the native lands of the colonizer, became part and parcel of this 'craze'. Paul Chambers throws light on how the very idea of the African elephant Jumbo as the 'greatest elephant in the world' invokes the obsession that was prevalent throughout Europe to see 'the longest, biggest, and the most abnormal and extraordinary' from its colonies.[72] The autobiography of the circus animal agent, Charles Mayer, describes how he was sent to Bombay by P. T. Barnum, the circus baron, to find an Asiatic elephant with 14.5 feet height.[73] *Gippsland Times* (27 July 1922) reports the adventures of Charles Mayer who caught animals from Malay forests, adopting the native ways. Three natives were killed and twelve injured when he trapped sixty elephants in a single undertaking. Mayer describes his first meeting with Mahommed Ariff 'who held a monopoly on the animal trade' in Singapore along with Gaylors, Barnum's other agent. They bought 'a tiger, several monkeys and a pair of leopards' from him.[74]

Christopher Plumb points to a rapid increase in animal trade and shipping between Britain and Asia during the mid-eighteenth century, many of them 'originating from newly acquired lands'. 'Animal dealers were selling a broader range of species' such as monkeys, tigers, and camels, and 'in the 1760s, a distinct geography of animal exhibitions and commerce emerged in London'.[75]

Animal trade from the colonies was one of the most prosperous enterprises for the colonial empire. They were exported for scientific experiments, to be showcased at zoological gardens and parks, and to

---

[72] Paul Chambers, *Jumbo: The Greatest Elephant in the World* (London: Andre Deutsch, 2007).

[73] Charles Mayer, *Trapping Wild Animals in Malay Jungles* (New York: Duffield, 1921), 22.

[74] Mayer, *Trapping Wild Animals in Malay Jungles*, 12.

[75] Christopher Plumb, *Exotic Animals in Eighteenth-Century Britain*, Doctoral Dissertation, University of Manchester, UK, 2010, 53–5.

be stuffed in the museums of London and Paris.[76] In Germany, there were companies which specialized in capturing animals from colonies such as Africa to be sold around the world. In Africa, animals such as monkeys, elephants, wild horses, dogs, and porcupines were collected in the form of taxes by the colonial administration (*Mathrubhumi*, 9 August 1923). In Asia, 'wild animal and plant products have been major trade items between South and Southeast Asia and China for more than two millennia'.[77] Chambers describes how Jumbo was purchased by the superintendent of Regents Park Zoological Gardens by offering an Indian rhino, two dingoes, a jackal, a pair of eagles, a possum, and a kangaroo.[78] W. W. Hunter remarks, 'In 1882-3, 475 elephants were captured in Assam yielding revenue to government of 8573 pounds.'[79] Blyth exhibited 16 full-grown fighting tigers, purchased from the government sale in Lucknow at Calcutta's Tiretta Bazar. Other animals include trained cheetahs, hunting leopards, and wild dogs from the hill jungles of Assam.[80] From the animal market at Calcutta, one could easily get monkeys, bears, leopards, and fish for the coloring the fish'.[81] Indian circus companies bought elephants, horses, and camels from *mela*s (fairs) at Assam, Calcutta, and Bihar. Elephants, chimps, monkeys, bears, camels, birds, and different types of horses,

---

[76] Plumb, *Exotic Animals in Eighteenth-Century Britain*, 233, 254.

[77] Available at http://www.ecologyandsociety.org/vol9/iss3/art3 [PDF], last accessed on 18 October 2014.

[78] Chambers, *Jumbo: The Greatest Elephant in the World*, 155.

[79] W. W. Hunter, *The Indian Empire: Its People, History and Products*, 1886 (New Delhi and Chennai: AES, 2009), 655–6.

[80] Christine Brandon-Jones, 'Edward Blyth, Charles Darwin and the Animal Trade in the Nineteenth Century India and Britain', *Journal of the History of Biology* 30, no. 3 (1997): 168–72.

[81] 'Coloring the fish' is a circus item in which the performer swallows small fish of different colours such as silver or gold. The performer would then drink coloured water and disgorge the fish and water before the public. Sreedharan from Melur, who used to perform this item in various circus companies, told me that in preparation he would have to skip his lunch and empty his stomach for a long time before the performance since he is supposed to bring back nothing but the fish. The performer would suffer from stomach ache and vomiting later on; Interview, Sreedharan K. K.

such as the Persian horse, were regularly bought from the Sonpur *mela* in Bihar.[82]

The practice of exchanging animals as gifts and tokens of appreciation was also common amongst rulers. Margaret Stuart Lane writes:

> [T]he King of Ashanti was anxious to please the English Governor, and knowing that the white man had a great fondness for animals of all kinds, he sent him the panther cubs to tame and keep. ... The Governor took him out of the cage, put him on a chain and made him free of the house. The panther cub grew up ... and became, next to the Governor, the most talked-of being in the town.[83]

When Lord Wayles came to India, many such species were sent to him from Nepal (*MM*, 19 August 1905). Jose Saramago's poignant novel *The Elephant's Journey* narrates the elephant Solomon's travel on foot from Lisbon to Vienna as a wedding gift from the King of Lisbon to the Hapsburg Archduke in 1551.[84] This type of exchange has continued well into the twentieth century. For instance, in 1982, 34 elephants were sent from Thrissur to Delhi in a jumbo train for the Asian Games. The Kerala chief minister inaugurated the journey that began on 1 November. The elephants were made to stand for the entire journey that lasted almost a week. The veterinarian, Dr Radhakrishna Kaimal, who accompanied the elephants recounts that one of the elephants got sunburnt and another had an early onset of *musth* [rutting] in the Delhi winter.[85] Nehru gifted a baby elephant named after his daughter, Indira, to Japanese children in 1948.[86] From the Ethiopian kingdom, India received two lion cubs in 1957.[87]

Examining the correspondence between Edward Blyth, curator of the Asiatic Society Museum at Calcutta, and Charles Darwin, the

---

[82] Interview, Moreswar, Melur, 5 June 2006. On request the name has been changed; Kumaran, Kannur, 12 March 2009.

[83] Margaret Stuart Lane, *The Big Book of Animal Stories* (London: Oxford University Press, 1928), 5–6.

[84] Jose Saramago, *The Elephant's Journey* (London: Harvill Secker, 2010).

[85] Dr Rajan Chungath, *Aana Manushyante Aathmakatha: Dr K Radhakrishna Kamailude Jeevitham* (*The Autobiography of the Elephant Man: The Life of Dr K Radhakrishna Kaimal*) (Kozhikode: Mathrubhumi Books, 2015), 23–8.

[86] 'Indira', *Mathrubhumi Illustrated Weekly* 35, no. 35 (1957): 20.

[87] 'Photograph', *Mathrubhumi Illustrated Weekly* 35, no. 16 (1957): 13.

scientist, Christine Brandon-Jones has brilliantly described the animal trade between colonial India and the British Empire in the nineteenth century. The mushrooming of menageries in London was the result of this animal trade which lasted over a century. Like silk and spices, wild animals from colonized lands also crossed the seas; from hunts-men to intermediaries to buyers employed by the European zoological gardens and menageries. She notes further that 'the establishment of natural history museums and the popularity of zoological gardens gave a veneer of scientific legitimacy to a trade in live and preserved exotic animals that originated in the much older sport of wild-fowling and big-game hunting'.[88] Thus, the zoological gardens and parks, which we consider a 'safe' haven for animals today, were established for pastime hunting and the white man's quest for the preservation of exotic flora and fauna found in their colonies.

The Asiatic Society had a significant role in shipping animals to colonial centres such as London. Wild animals from many places were brought to Calcutta, which was a major port and disembarkation point. Moreover, European soldiers liked to take back home exotic animals as pets. Scottish soldiers who had come to Lucknow to quell the 1857 rebel-lion took back parrots, guinea pigs, mongooses, dogs, and cats, which often landed up in the zoos of their native lands. The wealthy upper castes in Calcutta also kept exotic animals in their homes.[89] The official website of Central Zoo Authority states, 'The first zoo was probably the one started by Raja Rajendra Mallick in 1854. It is popularly known as the Marble palace Zoo and is still in existence in Calcutta.'[90] Newspaper reports from early-twentieth-century Kerala also show that affluent individuals kept wild animals in their homes (*MM*, 20 March 1901 and 20 March 1912). A 1905 news report about a circus company purchas-ing a tiger cub from an assistant superintendent of the Public Works Department at Trivandrum throws light on the open private ownership and trade of wild animals that existed at the time (*MM*, 13 December). The zoo in Thiruvananthapuram, considered as the first public zoo in

[88] Christine Brandon-Jones, 'Edward Blyth, Charles Darwin and the Animal Trade in the Nineteenth Century India and Britain', 145–78.

[89] Christine Brandon-Jones, 'Edward Blyth, Charles Darwin and the Animal Trade in the Nineteenth Century India and Britain', 152–8.

[90] See http://www.cza.nic.in/history.html, last accessed on 22 September 2014.

the country, was also established in 1857 by the king of Travancore. By the end of the nineteenth century, zoos had been established in many major centres and transactions between these zoos were usual.[91]

Donna Haraway observes, 'Once domination is complete, conservation is urgent. But preservation comes too late.' She notes how gorillas were shot with guns and cameras by Carl Akeley when 'science had already penetrated' and taxidermy emerged as a scientific expertise.

> What followed was the return to the United States and active work for an absolute gorilla sanctuary providing facilities for scientific research. Akeley feared the gorilla would be driven to extinction before it was adequately known to science. ... Between 1921 and 1926, he mounted his precious gorilla specimens, producing that extraordinary silver back whose gaze dominates African Hall.[92]

It is worthwhile noting here that the Natural History Museum in Thiruvananthapuram established in the nineteenth century, adjacent to the zoo, possessed a large number of animals and birds stuffed by the known Asian taxidermists, Van Ingen and Van Ingen.[93] This must definitely have been part of the idea of becoming a 'modern' state.

Performing Animals

Helen Cowie notes that London had a long tradition of trade and exhibition of animals: 'In the eighteenth century this was mainly the preserve of small-scale dealers, showing rare creatures on their premises, in the streets or in traditional social spaces like coffeehouses. In

---

[91] 'Mr. Sankaranarayana Pillai, sent to zoos at Madras, Bombay, Baroda, etc., from Trivandrum on government expense has disembarked from the British Indian steam navigation ship, "S S Saradhana" at Alapuzha last Saturday and has left for Trivandrum with new breed monkeys, birds, deer, etc. brought from Bombay' (*MM*, 26 April 1905). Records from the Kerala State Archives show that these regular exchanges were done through bargaining with dealers to get animals at the lowest price; EDUCATION (1940–5), F-1584, B-234, dated 7 December 1940.

[92] Donna Haraway, 'Teddy Bear Patriarchy: Taxidermy in the Garden of Eden, New York City, 1908–36', *Social Text* (11) (1984–5): 28.

[93] K. Rajendrababu, *Nammude Museum* [Our museum] (Trivandrum: Directorate of Public Relations, 1978), 42.

the second quarter of the nineteenth century, the zoological garden emerged as the fashionable venue for viewing exotic beasts.' She further adds, 'They have also been seen as playing an important role in showcasing Britain's commercial prowess and imperial power, displaying simultaneously man's domination over the animals and Britain's growing influence around the globe.'[94]

The first state-owned zoo in colonial India, the Thiruvananthapuram Zoo, was modelled on the London Zoo. It is interesting that a 'temple city' (as the zoo brochure of 2008 calls it), which remained a royal state until the mid-twentieth century, had established such quintessential 'modern' institutions such as the zoo, a museum, botanical gardens, a hospital for women and children, and a mental asylum. A newspaper report from 1904 puts it succinctly: 'the city by all means is a perfect blend of "tradition" and "modernity"... the most "modern" among the cities and thus fit to be selected as the premier city in the State' (*MM*, 1 February 1904). 'The zoo was started in 1859 with the gracious gift by His Highness Maharaja' from the palace menagerie.[95] Madhava Rao, devan of Travancore, promises John Allan Brown, the curator at Trivandrum Observatory, in 1859, 'I shall ascertain and let you know shortly what selections from His Highness the Rajah's menagerie can be made for the zoological garden.'[96] In architecture as well, the zoo was modelled on its colonial predecessor.[97]

Philip T. Robinson observes that animal performances such as tightrope walking, tortoise riding, elephant riding, dining chimpanzees, and motorcycle riding by the bears were regular show items in zoos in the United States of America in the nineteenth and early twentieth centuries:

> The big male gorilla [at the Lincoln Park Zoo in Chicago] occupied a bare cage whose only internal fixtures were a resting bench and a platform scale ... [which] permitted the public to verify how much he weighed,

[94] Helen Cowie, *Exhibiting Animals in Nineteenth Century Britain: Empathy, Education, Entertainment* (London: Palgrave, 2014), 30.

[95] T. K. Velu Pillai, *The Travancore State Manual*, Vol. IV (Trivandrum: Government of Travancore, 1940), 275.

[96] Cover files (Napier Museum), 2 July 1859, File no. 239/1859, Bundle no. 30, 1859–60, Kerala State Archives, Trivandrum.

[97] Pattom G. Ramchandran Nair, *Thiruvananthapuratthinte Ithihasam* [The legend of Thiruvananthapuram] (Thiruvananthapuram: Sahityavedi, 1996), 513.

a play upon our pop-culture fascination with mega apes such as King Kong and Godzilla. At about the same time, the Cincinnati Zoo still had trained chimpanzees that entertained visitors by riding little motorcycles, while the chimpanzees dressed up as members of a swing band, wielding trombones and drumsticks. ... Even earlier, numerous zoo featured young apes and monkeys in people clothes in tea parties, while they demonstrated their abilities to drink milk from a glass, eat with a spoon from a bowl, and perform other examples of human etiquette.[98]

The most famous among these items was 'the chimpanzees' tea party' in the London Zoo, which started around 1928.[99] *Mathrubhumi* (9 August 1923) reports how large gatherings assembled every day to watch the ape in the London Zoo wash its clothes and take a bath. Chuny, an elephant imported from Bengal in 1809, was one of the London Royal Menagerie's main attractions.[100] Kay Anderson has noted the introduction of a circus in the Adelaide Zoo in 1939, 'A trainer was employed, chimpanzees were trained to hold tea parties, and when the circus commenced "shows", members of the society observed that "animals enjoy the performance as do the many adult spectators who usually outnumber the children"'. The circus stopped in 1942 after criticism from some visitors but was replaced with a bicycle-riding act by an 'Orang-outang'.[101] A publicity notice from September 1838 in the collection of the British Library on the performance by the American animal trainer Issac Van Amburg of Astley's Circus features a Bengal tiger, lions, and leopards.[102] Another notice of December 1839 titled 'Ryan's amphitheatre' shows an Asian elephant in performance.[103]

[98]   Philip T. Robinson, *Life at the Zoo: Behind the Scenes with Animal Doctors* (New York: Columbia University Press, 2004), 92.

[99]   Koothattukulam M. S. Pillai, *Mrigasalayil* [In the zoo], Vol. I (Kottayam: NBS, 1962), 44.

[100]   Available at http://www.vam.ac.uk/content/articles/d/development-of-circus-acts/, last accessed on 3 August 2014.

[101]   Kay Anderson, 'Animals, Science and Spectacle in the City', in *Animal Geographies: Place, Politics, and Identity in the Nature–Culture Borderlands*, ed. Jennifer Wolch and Jody Emel (London and New York: Verso, 1998), 44.

[102]   Available at https://www.bl.uk/collection-items/circus-poster-full-grown-living-tiger, last accessed on 22 September 2014.

[103]   Available at https://www.bl.uk/collection-items/circus-poster-full-grown-living-tiger, last accessed on 22 August 2014.

Photos published in *Mathrubhumi Illustrated Weekly* show that joy-riding for children, circus-like feats where the elephant carries the performer in the trunk, and group dancing and performance on stools were staged by elephants in the Colombo Zoo during the 1950s.[104] I could watch similar performances by elephants and a sea lion in 2016.[105] In Thailand too, elephants perform similar tricks at the Nong Nooch Botanical Garden and as part of private tourism packages. In many parts of the world, feeding baby elephants with a milk bottle and bathing them in the river in sanctuaries and national parks is part of tourism. Some of the private zoos, such as the Dar es Salaam Zoo in Tanzania, have donkey carts, tortoise and camel riding, and performances by wild animals. During the first few decades of the twentieth century, there was an orangutan ape at the Thiruvananthapuram Zoo who entertained the spectators with his avid smoking. Apart from that, '[h]e used to give most of the gifts he received from the thrilled onlookers to his keeper and he also performed some special items to obtain incentives for the keeper'.[106] Pillai also notes enthusiastically about the donkey cart meant as a joyride for children at the Thiruvananthapuram Zoo: 'the colourful cart driven by the brisk foal adorned with genie and saddle along the park road was an exciting amusement for the young ones!' Without a tinge of emotion, the author concludes that since this poor foal died prematurely, some other healthy donkey might hopefully come forward to take the place.[107] S. Abu recounts that his colleague's father, an early-generation tiger keeper, welcomed the royal members to the zoo by carrying the tiger on his shoulders.[108] It is interesting to note that a report by The *Hindu* (30 December) in as late as 1963 shows photos of the 'masterly dumb show at Kerala Forest Sports Festival' by Sankaran and Rangan, the captive baby elephant in the Nilambur Forest Division. The babies, hardly 2.5 years of age, were trained for 5 months. They played a mouth organ apart from acting like a Ganapathy-pujari and performing drunkard roles. 'Holding

[104] 'Aanakal Colomb Mrugasalayil' [Elephants in the Colombo zoo], *Mathrubhumi Illustrated Weekly* 31, no. 51 (1954): 24.

[105] Fieldwork, Colombo Zoo, August 2016.

[106] M. S. Pillai, *Mrigasalayil*, Vol. I, 58–9.

[107] M. S. Pillai, *Mrigasalayil* [In the zoo], Vol. II (Kottayam: NBS, 1963), 134.

[108] Interview, S. Abu.

it [mouth organ] in their mouth they blow hard into it and produce well-modulated sounds, moving their right and left legs in rhythm with the sounds.' The news further states, 'These pachyderms also execute acrobatics of the type that one sees in a circus, like pushing a roller around, with their forelegs.' The report also mentions Ramavarman and Bhaskaran, two other elephants trained similarly. Thomas Trautman, who observes that circuses have a 'more discontinuous history' unlike that of zoological gardens, points out, 'For modern zoos and circuses, the flow of captive elephants to places far away from their habitat was made possible by the transportation revolution, occasioning a huge rise in numbers from the second half of the nineteenth century. Before then the number of elephants in Europe or America was very small indeed.'[109] Susan Nance observes,

> While seemingly ephemeral, combs and the exhibition of a baby elephant were politically rich moments in the early republic, highlighting how early Americans understood patriotism and free trade to be two sides of the same coin. Certainly, Britain and France used tariffs and embargoes to wage war and jockey for political power. Well into the antebellum years, various Anglo-American political thinkers would contend that citizens' access to global products and the requisite sea trade were issues of national security and, from a consumer's point of view, proud economic liberty.[110]

Animal Transactions

Exchanges of animals between zoos and circus companies were common in India. There were also exchanges and sales between zoos in various countries and between zoos and private parties. Kandambulli Balan complains that surplus animals born in Indian zoos were sold entirely to the rich foreign circus companies. He says a lion or tiger cub was priced at INR 3,500–4,000, which was not affordable to Indian

---

[109] Thomas R. Trautman, 'Towards a Deep History of Mahouts', in *Conflict, Negotiation and Coexistence: Rethinking Human–Elephant Relations in South Asia*, ed. Piers Locke and Jane Buckingham (New Delhi: Oxford University Press, 2016), 68.

[110] Susan Nance, *Entertaining Elephants: Animal Agency and the Business of the American Circus* (Baltimore: Johns Hopkins University Press, 2013), 21.

companies. He emphatically demandeds that the export of wild animals should be legally banned and they should be made available to Indian circus companies.[111]

On 28 October 1987, the Environment, Forest, and Wildlife Department of the Indian government instructed forest secretaries and wildlife wardens of all states and union territories thus:

> Instances have come when the State Governments and Directors of all Zoos have requested to allow them to sell their excess animals to circus parties on the plea that they are having excess animals like lions, leopards and tigers, etc and due to limited accommodation, there excess animals are maintained in small cells. Moreover, feeding expenditure on these animals is also stated to be a problem. ... After careful consideration, it has been decided not to allow the sale of excess animals of Indian Zoos to Circuses. However, such zoos may exchange their excess animals with other Indian zoos authorised by Government of India or State Government/ Municipal Corporation. It would also be appropriate to curtail or stop breeding of those animals which are getting surplus.[112]

It is interesting to note that the order acknowledges 'the excess animals', 'small cells', 'limited accommodation', and the state policy to curtail/stop 'breeding of those ... getting surplus'. A 1990 order to the chief wildlife wardens of all states categorically prohibits 'any

---

[111] Kandambulli Balan, *Circus*, 128.

[112] It further mentions that 'the surplus animals should invariably be disposed of through exchange programmes between different zoos'; such bartering of animals among zoos around the world is common even now; Central Government Orders Prohibiting Sale of Animals by Zoos, G.O. no. 3-52/87/ WL-1, Department of Environment, Forest and Wildlife, Government of India, dated 28 October 1987, *The Wildlife Protection Act 1972*, 2008, 144–5. Recently, an anaconda from Sri Lanka was exchanged with a pair of Indian bison in the Trivandrum Zoo; available at http://www.thehindu.com/sci-tech/ energy-and-environment/sri-lanka-gifts-anacondas-to-thiruvananthapuram-zoo/article5893355.ece, last accessed on 22 September 2014. The archival files unravel the story of the bushbuck from Nairobi—how some of its companion animals died, the suffering during the travel, at the port, and in the hands of human administrative officers; letter from the honorary director, Government Gardens, Trivandrum, to the chief secretary to government, 29 May 1941, Confidential Files, National Museum, Education Department (1940–5), File no.1584, Bundle no. 234.

commercial dealings of scheduled animals' and, in respect of other animals, 'any dealings of wild animals can be done only under license under section 44 of the [Wild Life (Protection)] Act. Therefore, zoos are not entitled to carry out any trade in respect of any wildlife species'.[113]

Doctor Charles Chandra, retired veterinary chief of Thiruvananthapuram Zoo, recounts that transactions of animals between the zoo and certain circus companies were regular before the aforementioned orders. The stock records of Thiruvananthapuram zoo during the decade prior to the ban orders attest to this fact. Gemini Circus provided the zoo with a pair of male and female Himalayan black bears on 30 September 1974 and another male bear on 25 September 1984. Though there is an entry in the stock records regarding the transaction of another female bear and two pelicans by Gemini Circus, the date has not been entered. A female camel came from Jumbo Circus on 20 October 1985 and a male camel on 9 March 1987.[114]

Dr Chandra says that circus companies from outside Kerala also used to come to buy animals. There were also agents. But he says that it was mainly Gemini Circus which had regular transactions with the Thiruvananthapuram Zoo:

> We used to get about twenty lion cubs and about ten tiger cubs every year. Gemini especially used to ask us if we were in need of any animals when they toured in such areas like Rajasthan and Delhi. In Delhi they used to get lots of bears. In fact, all of the stock of bears in the Zoo is from them only. Earlier we had deals with other circus companies as well. Just for one lion cub they used to give lots of animals and birds as exchange. They collected migratory birds of all kinds from Jaipur. They used to bring water birds of beautiful feathers, and I used to pinion them so that they do not fly away.[115] We used to exchange our surplus animals with their lot. The barter was always a gain to both parties, we were happy, they were also happy.[116]

An old photograph (circa 1960) from the collection of Dr Chandra shows him with Leo, a 1-year-old lion, on the day it was exchanged to

---

[113] G.O. no. 3352/87-W L-I, dated 14 November 1990.

[114] Stock register, Thiruvananthapuram Zoo.

[115] Pinioning is not allowed now. The doctor said that he had performed it for both zoos and circus companies.

[116] Interview, Charles Chandra, Thiruvananthapuram Zoo, 16 May 2010.

Gemini Sankaran, the proprietor. While giving the lion, Dr Chandra
had insisted that since the lion was brought up in his own house as a
pet, Sankaran should not train or let him out in the ring, but use him
only for breeding. Dr Chandra said that sometimes the animal trainers
of circuses used to stay in the zoo for about a week before taking the
animals to get acquainted with them.

There was an additional advantage for zoo authorities with circus
animals; they were more tame than any other animal they possessed.
Like the Thiruvananthapuram Zoo, many major zoos in India had
active animal bartering with various circus companies. The *International
Tiger Studbook* has data about the exchanges of Bengal tigers between
various zoos in India and the circuses. Male and female tiger cubs born
on 10 April 1971 in Nandankandan Zoo, Orissa, were transferred on
13 November 1971 to a 'CIRCUS'.[117] A 1-year-old male tiger, captured
from the 'wild' in Assam in 1976, was transferred to a circus on 23
May 1978. Two female tiger cubs born on 20 October 1979 in the
Mysore Zoo were moved to a circus on 25 June 1980. The transaction,
of course, was not one way. Krishna, a male tiger, was born in a circus
in 1965 and was transferred to the zoo in 1968. It died there on
3 September 1984.[118]

There were also occasional exchanges between private individuals
and zoos. S. Abu and Charles Chandra stated that such exchanges have
also happened in the Trivandrum Zoo. The *Tiger Studbook* notes an
exchange in the late 1980s where a male tiger, born on 18 June 1986 at
Nandankandan Zoo, was haggled to a private party on 20 August 1986.
However, the animal was given back to the zoo on 27 March 1987. The
tiger lived there till its death on 9 December 1988.[119]

---

[117] The book only mentions 'CIRCUS' and does not mention the
name of any of the circus companies. *International Tiger Studbook* (Leipzig:
Zoologischer Garten Leipzig, 2002), 89, 121, 122; the data provided shows
that such exchanges are common in many countries around the world
even now.

[118] *Tiger Studbook*; details of the death of the animals that the zoos have
exchanged to circuses are not given, which obviously means that little information was known to the zoo authorities about the animal once the exchange
happened.

[119] *Tiger Studbook*, 86.

Animal Acrobats in the Ring

In early circus companies established by the Marathis, human performers had a lesser role compared to their animal counterparts.[120] Champad
notes elsewhere that this could have been because many of the circus
owners of early Maratha companies were animal trainers. He adds that
as acrobats from Keeleri Kunhikannan's circus *kalari* in Malabar began
to join circuses in Maharashtra, Bengal, Andhra, and Karnataka, animal
performances were surpassed by humans.[121] Although acrobats started
dominating the ring, animals remained to be a major attraction to the
circus spectators. Kandambulli Balan observes thus about the failure of
Malabar Circus, the first circus company of the region established by
Parayali: 'In spite of the fact that Malabar circus kept a high standard
in performance, there were no animals or other required technical
instruments.'[122] Champad notes, 'Maharashtrian Circuses imported
many more animals and eminent artists from abroad. Parayali could
not stand up to the competition.'[123] Balan describes Whiteway Circus
as a 'perfect' circus formed later on with animals.[124] Ravindran and
Bhaskaran, who were workers and partners of the Akhil Bharath Circus,
a cooperative circus company formed by circus workers in the 1960s,
point out the absence of animals as a significant reason for its failure.[125]

The importance of animals is very much evident in circus publicity
fliers, posters, and advertisements. A notice of O. C. Appa's Grand Kerala
Circus of the early twentieth century proclaims, 'Never performed in
Malabar until now—O C Kannan's spectacular duel with the twelve feet
long Bengal tiger with the least botheration about his own life. And
also amazing shows by African lions.' The Grand Fairy Circus notice,
dated 15 March 1956, describes '[t]wo special trains carrying circus
Equipments and Animals'. The Rayman Circus notice, announcing its
performance for 1 January 1958, is embellished with illustrations of
elephants in procession, doctor–patient performance of a chimpanzee

---

[120] Champad, *Circusinte Lokam*, 131.

[121] Champad, 'Circussinte Eettillam', 149–50.

[122] Balan, *Circus*, 52.

[123] Champad, *An Album of Indian Big Tops*, 14.

[124] Balan, *Circus*, 52.

[125] Interview, Ravindran; Bhaskaran.

couple, and a host of zebras and lions. The Kamala Circus programme book has Koran, the trainer, and his dog who adds up mathematical figures on a board.[126] Another programme book of the Kamala Circus describes 'Champa, the tiger' as one who 'was found in the jungles of Madhya Pradesh. The little cub was named Champa by the girl artistes of the circus. The artistes used to keep her in their laps while feeding her with the bottle'.[127] A Gemini Circus advertisement on the back cover of the *Big Top* (1965) showcases their hippopotamus with the following copy: 'Though I have reigned as the Lord of the Great Tropical Rivers of Africa, at present I am happily installed in GEMINI in my watery abode—a tank containing 2,000 gallons of water and fed on 3 mounds of potatoes daily.'[128]

Photographs of circus owners with lion and tiger cubs in their hands are ubiquitous in their offices and official and personal albums. Companies often printed their letterheads with images of animals and their items.

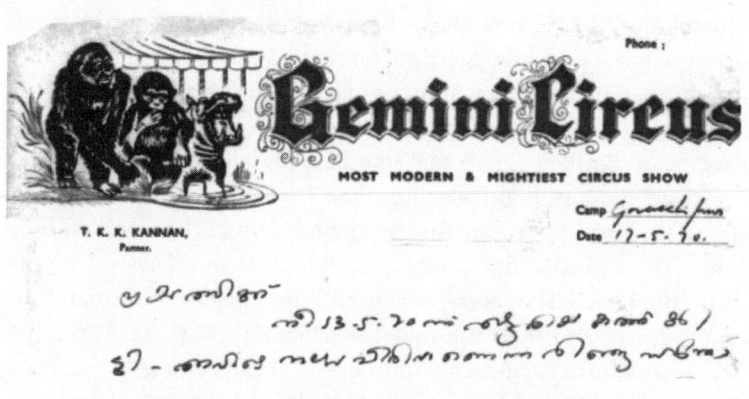

Image 2.2   Letterhead, Gemini Circus, circa 1970

Source: Private collection of E. Ravindran.

[126] Kamala Circus programme book, circa 1955, private collection, M. Sreedharam, Muzhikkara.

[127] Kamala Circus programme book, circa 1955, private collection, Gloria Vanderwielen, Kolassery.

[128] *Big Top* 1, no. 1 (1965).

Circus animals appear very often in Malayali newspaper reports from the early twentieth century, which suggest their significant role both in the ring and for the enjoyment of the public. *MM* (1 April 1905) reports that an acrobat in a circus was bitten and clawed by their tiger in Kannur. A judicial verdict was passed with a fine of INR 500 to the circus manager and three-months imprisonment to the animal trainer; while in Kochi, a tiger at Deval Circus killed a child (*MM*, 25 July 1908). Another report reviews that the performances of elephants, dogs, horses, and tigers in a circus group from Bombay were in good quality (*MM*, 25 November 1905). A report announces the opening of a circus in Puthan Kacheri ground, Trivandrum, which possesses two monkeys, a goat, a dog, and two horses (*MM*, 3 November 1906). One report (*MM*, 11 March 1903) mentions a circus with excellent horse items done by children. Another circus group was denied permission for the ground and they performed at the Jubilee Town Hall in Kozhikode without the horse items (*MM*, 6 June 1903). It is interesting to note that the Malayalam newspapers most often do not mention the names of circuses in their reports.

The report (*MM*, 7 May 1910) that two horses of Deval Circus fell into a river and died while travelling on catamarans throws light on the various human means of transport used for the transportation of circus animals and the dangerous situations they were exposed to. An elaborate report on Karliker Circus that travelled via rail mentions that they had a bigger wild animal collection than Deval or Chatre. The report goes on, 'The lion entered the ring on elephant back. The elephant rode bicycle … lions, bears, tigers, leopards, dogs and monkeys sat on the stool in affinity. … They were driven back by horses. … A small bird filled the pistol and fired the matches to shoot' (*MM*, 11 December 1909). A report on a Parsi circus group speaks about bears and elephants that rode cycles (*MM*, 1 December 1909). The tricks of elephants and parrots are specially mentioned by another enthusiastic report (*MM*, 24 November 1909). There are various reports over the years about Great Indian, Parasuram, Excelsior, and a branch of Chatre Circuses performing at Kozhikode and Kollam (*MM*, 20 March and 13 October 1909; 27 January 1912; 5 February 1913). A report about the 'Kolappur Kolandas' Circus Company states that they had received certificates and medals of appreciation from the kings of Mysore and Hyderabad, and their animal collection included horses, monkeys, dogs, tiger, leopard, and a python. It adds with more astonishment, 'The entertaining and astonishing acts these animals perform succumbing to the mastering of the circus manager, might make one think that there is nothing impossible to humans' (*MM*, 25 November 1903).

A report from Thrissinappally about the performance of the European Hippodrome Circus notes that they had 'a type of horse with lines (zebra) which no other company that visited here had'. It describes the performance of a young man with his lions: 'he uses them as bed to sleep, as eating companions, as a parallel bar on which he can play, as a vehicle that could carry him, as a weight he could carry and as a fellow wrestler to fight with' (*MM*, 19 February 1908). From these reports one can assume that there were regular tours of circus companies, both Indian and foreign, during that time. It should be noted here that the somewhat-elaborate news reports about circuses in *Mitavadi* and *Mathrubhumi*, both published from Malabar, hardly mention circus animals in native circuses in the first few decades of the twentieth century. This throws light on the absence or the insignificant number of animals in the early Malabar circus companies pointed out earlier.

Animal Training in the Early Maratha Circus

Parasuram Mali has preserved all the medals, certificates, photos, newspaper cuttings, and other documents he inherited from his grandfather, father, and uncles who were known animal trainers and proprietors of Parasuram Lion Circus. Parasuram Elappa Mali, his grandfather, had established the circus in 1897 and it was in the business until 1957.

I met Mali, who was also an animal trainer, in his ancestral home at Tasgaon in Sangli district, Maharashtra. The present Sangli district, comprising Tasgaon and Miraj, had been the region where many of the early circuses in Maharashtra were established, including Chatre Circus—supposedly the first circus company in the subcontinent. He kindly took me to meet his three brothers, who were also animal trainers, and the place which was the animal training centre during the heyday of their company. It was called the *shikarkhana* (animal training zone).

The structure has been revamped and it is the home of one of his brothers now. This training place was established along with the company. The trainers at the time were Nirmal and Yeshwant Rao. When they grew up, Mali and his younger brothers also got trained here. They had a white tiger, 59 horses, 11 elephants, and 40 other animals including lions and tigers. According to Mali, these animals used to roam in

Image 2.3   Animals Training at the *Shikarkhana*, circa 1930

Source: Private collection of Parasuram Mali.

the large field around the house and some mischievous ones crawled into the bedding of the kids and slept there.

The *shikarkhana* had three enclosures. One each to train, keep, and wash the animals. New animals that arrived in were kept separately. Those who had finished their training were also kept apart until they were taken to the circus. Horses used to be tied outside the house, while elephants were maintained in another place nearby. Sometimes they got animals from the royal menageries as gifts.[129]

Bhagwantrao D. More, a retired director general of police, told me that his ancestral house in Sangamner also had a similar *shikarkhana* as part of the Grand Indian More Circus established by his great-grandfather, Yeshwant Rao Gangaram More, in 1881.[130] Built on a large area

[129] I gathered all the above information from my interviews with Parasuram Mali, Tasgaon, 25 December 2012 and 6 May 2013.

[130] Interestingly, Bhagwantrao D. More claims that this was the first circus enterprise in India. He says that the company was sold to some Malayali proprietor in Bangalore in 1960–1. Ravindran states that the buyers were the owners of Sagar Circus which was later turned into Venus Circus in the hands of Kunhikannan. Interview, Bhagwantrao D. More; E. Ravindran.

of his land, the big house dome building, called *wada*, was divided into two halves; one for keeping the animals, called the *shikarkhana*, and the other for giving them rehearsals, the *khelwada*. The place for elephant-keeping and training was called the *hathikhana*. There was also a training place for acrobats in the house, called *talim*. During the recess of the circus, the trained circus animals were also kept here. There were about a hundred wooden bullock carts for transportation. The whole village became a circus locale with animal trainers and helpers living around. The More family still keeps the cages of lions and tigers as a fond memory of the circus. A letter dated 17 May 1905 from Hajee Esmail Aboobaker Jhaveri addressed to 'Prof Morey of Grand Indian Circus in appreciation of splendid performances' states:

> I had the pleasure of witnessing the performances of the Grand Indian Circus more than once during its stay at this place and am very happy to say that the acrobatic feats, and the horse, especially the tiger and the elephant performances were simply marvelous. ... I heartily wish him success in his endeavours and hope he will receive full encouragement at the hands of well-to-do people.[131]

A significant fact is that none of these animal trainers are from any traditional castes associated with animals. Proximity of dense forest areas is definitely a considerable point. That Vishnupanth Chatre was a royal horse trainer throws some light on the early occupations of these masters. Parasuram Elappa Mali was an animal trainer in Chatre's Circus.[132] An interesting fact is the absence of women from the families in this trade. However, that Avdabai, Chatre's wife, was a well-known acrobat and animal trainer is noteworthy.[133]

Divyabhanusinh notes about the cheetah trainers of colonial times:

> In Jaipur, Bhavnagar and Kishangarh they were Muslims. Information from Baroda and Hyderabad are unavailable, though photographs of the

---

[131] Private collection, Bhagwantrao D. More, Mumbai.

[132] Champad, *Circusinte Lokam*, 130.

[133] Balan, *Circus*, 40; renowned circus artistes and company owners of early twentieth century, such as Tharabai and Rugmabai, were also wild-animal trainers. They trained lions, tigers, elephants, and jaguars and performed with them. It should be mentioned here that animal trainer has been a common metaphor for patriarchy, flaunting a brutal masculinity—a point we shall discuss soon.

keepers at Kolhapur show them wearing the Maratha state's court dress including the turban. Hence it is more likely that they were Marathas, though as per the practice of the time, Muslim retainers, if any, would have worn the same dress.[134]

He also points out that in ancient India, 'dappled cats took part in royal processions, and Indians brought them as gifts to their kings' and an amazing variety of animals and birds such as 'the mighty elephants to the African grey parrots [were] trained to fire ceremonial golden and silver cannons at Baroda'.[135]

Venkita Rao Deval, who established Deval Circus in 1856, was born in a village called Mysag near Miraj. The owner brothers donned many roles in the early phase: managers, ringmasters, jokers, and acrobats. Rajendra Deval (Venkita Rao Deval was his grandfather's uncle) said the company was handed over to Kamala Circus in 1956 and his uncle and father entered the film exhibition business. 'With the entry of Malabaris, glamour, show business and acrobatics came in, but our circus was rooted in animal performances. That was why Deval Circus was decided to wind up.'[136] Deval's grandfather, Bandopant Deval, has written a memoir in Marathi called *Circus Barobal Chaleez* (Along with circus for forty years), which was published in 1982.

Marathi animal trainers went to work in circus companies in the West too. Of these, the most illustrious is definitely Damoo Dhotre (1902–1972) who worked in the popular American circus company, the Ringling Brothers. Likewise, there were European animal trainers in Indian circus companies. They brought animals such as chimpanzees, sea lions, and horses, and exotic birds, such as the multicoloured parrots, with them to the companies they worked for.[137] There used to be dance performances in Indian circuses until the 1950s, and one item

---

[134] Divyabhanusinh. *The End of a Trail: The Cheetah in India*. (New Delhi: Oxford University Press, 1999), 118.

[135] Divyabhanusinh, *The End of a Trail: The Cheetah in India*, 114, 113.

[136] Interview, Rajendra Deval.

[137] For instance, rainbow-coloured parrots mostly came from Australia and Singapore. One Australian parrot costs about a lakh in Indian currency. Later, when parrot-capturing and trade flourished in Singapore, the circuses could easily buy them; interview, Moreswar.

had been with serpents that the American performers—done by men and women jointly—trained and brought with them.[138]

Another noteworthy aspect is the bizarre cross-breeding of animals. The Great Royal Circus had ligers, a cross-breed of a female tiger and a male lion. The owner of the circus, Narayan Rao Walavalker, himself did the breeding of these animals in his company during the 1960s.[139] Photographs of a liger riding a three-wheeled cycle and six ligers lined up figure prominently in a programme book of the company with the description that 'Prof. Walavalkar rightly boasts of being the only one in the world to have such crossed animals'. However, except for a couple of instances, this kind of cross-breeding was not a common practice in Indian circus.[140] Interestingly, such breeding—donkey with horse, horse with zebra, lion with leopard—was routinely practised in the royal menageries and zoos in India and all over the world. Alipore Zoo had the 'world's last tigon', Rangini, crossed between a royal Bengal tiger and an African lioness in 1974. Her predecessor tigon, Rudrani, produced seven litigons (crossed between a lion and a tigon) in as late as 1985.[141]

On the other hand, the Breeding of and the Experiments on Animals (Control and Supervision) Rules, 1998, clearly state that experiments on animals shall be conducted for the purpose of 'advancement by new discovery of physiological knowledge which will be useful for saving or prolonging life or alleviating suffering or for combating any disease whether on human beings or on animals'.[142] The Central Zoo Authority decided to put a ban on the experimental breeding of big cats after a

---

[138] Posters of the Ringling Bros in the early twentieth century show that performances with snakes were common. A 1938 American circus poster shows the performances of a 'Hindu fakir' hypnotizing reptiles. Noel Daniel, *The Circus, 1870s–1950s*, 228.

[139] Interview, Prabhakaran.

[140] Great Royal Circus programme book, circa 1970, private collection, late Shyamala Shirolkar, Pune.

[141] Available at http://indiatoday.intoday.in/story/worlds-last-tigon-waits-for-death-at-calcutta-zoo/1/265829.html, last accessed on 17 September 2014.

[142] Available at http://envfor.nic.in/legis/awbi/awbi10.html, last accessed on 17 September 2014.

huge hue and cry from animal lovers and vigorous campaigns by World Wildlife Fund.[143]

Trainers from Malabar

Animal trainers of the early circus companies in Malabar were also Marathis. Kairu Thorath, who had worked in Grand Fairy and Rayman Circuses, was one of the best in tiger fighting, while Kashinath was counted as par excellent in horse training. Narayan Chouhan and Balvand Chouhan were other well-known Marathi trainers in wild animals. Premsigh Rathore, who married a Thalassery circus artiste, was another known animal trainer. Many of them later moved on and went on to become ringmasters in other circus companies.[144] The programme book of the Great Royal Circus also mentions the animal trainers Manohar and Nishikant Walavalkar.[145]

Only later did the circus people from Malabar venture into animal training. Each animal group had about three to four caretakers who would feed and bathe them. A ringmaster was in charge of both the assistants and the animals. Though it must have been a matter of livelihood for the majority, for some the profession had been born of sheer passion. The best instance would be the acrobat-turned-wild-animal-trainer, Parammel Kesavan. Gopi, nephew of the Grand Circus owner, Ambu master, was another. A notable trainer of horses and elephants, Gopi lost one of his legs during a training session, but he continued with the job until his death. Sekharan from Kannur, an elephant specialist, had his training from Parasuram Circus.

Krishnan, the owner of Jubilee Circus, was another ringmaster who trained wild animals. His wife, Kalyani, renowned as a ringmaster in training lions and tigers, surpassed her teacher–husband as her fame spread beyond the country. Krishnan had also taught his sister-in-law, Lakshmi, who by the time had become a famous wild-animal trainer. However, during a performance a lion attacked her. Luckily she survived

---

[143] Available at http://expressindia.indianexpress.com/ie/daily/19980708/18950374.html, last accessed on 17 September 2014.

[144] Interview, E. Ravindran.

[145] Great Royal Circus programme book, circa 1970, private collection, Shyamala Shirolkar, Pune.

and underwent treatment for a long time in Calcutta.[146] After Krishnan's death, Kalyani remarried and renamed the circus 'Indra', and she began to be known as 'Indrani'. She was also popular as 'Kalyani Bai' in Uttar Pradesh and Bihar.

The Kamala Circus programme book states, 'Madhavi, the unassuming, quiet-natured animal trainer of Kamala circus is the only one of her kind in Asia. She ranks high among the small fraternity of women animal trainers in the world.'[147] Madhavi, referred by the programme book as 'fearless Madhavi', was an excellent trapeze artiste and stunt cycle-rider before she became a wild-animal trainer. Photographs in a very popular Malayalam magazine show her taking a full-grown tiger on her shoulder, riding another tiger, and her company of three tigers performing 'namaste' in obedience and sitting on stools on their hind legs, with the caption. 'Madhavi who all by herself make ten lions and seven tigers perform—is also a Malayali'.[148]

There were other women trainers and performers who worked with animals. One of *Mathrubhumi Illustrated Weekly*'s cover photograph is of Revuutty, an animal trainer of the Great Eastern Circus, with her two tigers. The inner pages introduce Revuutty who trained and performed with tigers and also Devaki who performed with elephants in the Great Eastern Circus, established in 1931.[149] Sharada was such a great performer on horses that she had earned the nickname 'Kuthira' Sharada (Malayalam for 'horse'). A photograph of her dancing on horseback was is published in the *Mathrubhumi Illustrated Weekly*.[150] Photos of Keezhanthi Krishnan's (Grand Fairy) and Kumari Rekha's (Great Bombay) popular item of an elephant passing over their chest have also appeared in the magazine.[151] The accompanying text of a photo of

---

[146] Interview, Prema, Chirakkuni, 23 October 2006.

[147] Kamala Circus programme book, circa 1955, private collection, Gloria Vanderwielen, Kolassery.

[148] 'Madhavi: Lokaprasasthayaaya Mrugasikshika' [Madhavi: the world famous animal trainer], *Mathrubhumi Illustrated Weekly* 33, no. 43 (195): 16.

[149] *Mathrubhumi Illustrated Weekly* 33, no. 3 (1955): 1, 22, 23–6, 70.

[150] The photograph is published as part of Kandambulli Balan's article, 'Circus Indiayil' [Circus in India], *Mathrubhumi Illustrated Weekly*, 32, no. 45 (1956): 70.

[151] *Mathrubhumi Illustrated Weekly* 34, no. 11 (1956): 20; 'Aana Nenchil' [Elephant on the chest], *Mathrubhumi Illustrated Weekly* 33, no. 47 (1956): 31.

Gemini Circus's gorilla informs the reader that the animal was not there in any Indian zoos during the time and had been bought in exchange of 60,000 rupees. There are eight photographs of a fight performance between the gorilla and its trainer, Krishnan.[152] Though Krishnan's name is not given, Radha Kannan, a Gemini veteran who still fondly keeps Krishnan's and his gorilla's photos, says playfully about their act: 'You wouldn't know who is gorilla and who is Krishnan; their performances merged so intimately'.[153]

Kittan was one of the topmost trainers of bears in circus. Bears and Kittan were so well associated that he had earned the nickname 'Karadi' Kittan (Bear Kittan). Kittan had a special recipe for feeding bears that involved jaggery, ghee, and roti. The bears hung about him mesmerized by this dish. He was in such demand that he would keep moving from one circus to another. Circus people from far off came in search of him to get their bears trained by him.[154]

The bears performed items such as 'dental', 'motorcycling', 'rolling', 'beating the drum', and 'imitating a woman with an umbrella'. Renowned animal trainers such as Gunter Gebel-Williams and Damoo Dhotre have noted that accidents with animals often occur when the master is not attending to his animals. 'Kittan became a little inattentive to his bear during one of the performances. And the bear, unlike the lion that attacks from straight in front or the tiger who strikes on back neck, hits on legs. Kittan was attacked and lost the thumb of his foot.'[155]

Circus people believe that every species has some general traits and that certain physical attributes of animals can help us understand their nature; the tusk of an elephant, ears of horses, or the nose of a bear.[156] Gunther Gebel-Williams notes, 'I never trusted them [leopards] the way I trusted the tigers,' though he acknowledges that there were compliant and nicer leopards in a herd. On another occasion, he observes, 'When tigers become too old and weak, or

---

[152] 'Gorrilla Circussil' [Gorrilla in circus], *Mathrubhumi Illustrated Weekly* 45, no. 50 (1968): 29–32.

[153] Interview, Radha Kannan.

[154] Interview, Nazeer, Royal Circus, 13 June 2008.

[155] Interview, E. Ravindran.

[156] Interview, Sreedharan.

too sick to defend themselves, the others go for them. That is their nature.'[157]

Kandambulli Balan has devoted two chapters in *Circus* to discuss animals and their trainers—'Animal Trainers' and 'An Autobiography of a Tiger'. Although he discusses Damoo Dhotre in the former chapter, he does not mention any other well-known Indian animal trainers of the time.[158] In the second chapter, written in the form of a soliloquy by the tiger, true to his circus self, he narrates the thoughts of an animal craving for a performance in the ring.[159]

Sreedharan Champad (2008, 2012, 2013) mentions some prominent animal trainers only in passing and certain incidents concerning animal training, such as accidents. A section in the last chapter of *An Album of Indian Big Tops: History of Indian Circus* briefly discusses the battle of animal lovers against circuses and its aftermath. In his memoir, Gemini Sankaran (2012) briefly refers to the wild animals being moved to one of his estates after the ban. Sreehari Nair's (2013) biography of Gemini Sankaran also mentions the same effort by him to keep the animals at the Varayal estate in Wayanad, Kerala. There are two photos of Sankaran's children with the chimpanzee, Raja. The book also describes some loving moments the animal and its owner shared.

The Marathi artiste, Moreswar, who lives in Thalassery now with his Malayali wife and family, told me that he used to eat, sleep, and

[157] Gunther Gebel-Williams and Toni Reinhold, *Untamed: The Autobiography of the Circus's Greatest Animal Trainer* (New York: Williams Murrow and Company, 1991), 51, 311.

[158] Balan, *Circus*; although Dhotre's autobiography was published in the same year, Balan's source is the book *Circus Doctor* by J. Y. Henderson. Henderson writes about his first meeting with Damoo Dhotre: 'He combined the qualities of the physical daredevil and the Hindu philosopher and mystic. He studied his animals thoroughly and he knew them theoretically as well as personally.' J. Y. Henderson, *Circus Doctor* (Boston: Little, Brown and Company, 1951), 22.

[159] A similar but 'normal' narrative from around the same time could be seen in a soliloquy to children who come to see the circus. Here, the caged lion is worried about the animal trainer who torments with the whip. C. Achuthanunni, *Bharam Vahikkunna Kuunanmarum Circusssukaran Rajavum* [The little people who bear the load and the circus king] (Kottayam: Vidyarthimithram Book Depot, 1963), 2–3, 26–48.

wake up in the company of his animals. He has literally put his head in the mouths of lions, hippos, leopards, and tigers as part of his performance in various circus companies. He used to perform tiger-fighting in the ring during the late 1940s. The tiger would be let loose in the ring and the performer would engage in a mock wrestling with it. 'The tiger will drag you and will lie on you, and in the end you will ride on the tiger.'[160]

Animal trainers would wake the animals up early in the morning at about 4 a.m. and train them in the ring for about two hours. At times, there would be practice at night too for about an hour. The duration of the practice session would vary according to the items an animal performed. In the first phase of the training, they were taught to sit, walk, stand up, 'go', and 'come'.[161] Two helpers would stand on either sides with a rope tied to the animal and make it repeat these actions. A piece of meat or some other favourite food was provided so that the animal would cooperate. In the second phase, it would be trained to climb on top of tables or bamboo rods or on other animals. The younger ones would practise on tables in accordance with their height.

While moving from one place to the other, separate trucks would be arranged for horses, elephants, and wild animals. Their masters and caretakers would travel along with them. In case of trains, animals would have separate cars. Food was prepared according to the needs and orders were placed in advance for fruit, meat, and milk at particular stations. The programme book of Kamala Three Ring Circus, the largest circus in Asia in its heyday, from the mid-1950s mentions that it had 125 animals, including 20 elephants, while the book also admits that an equal number of them perished during the 1950s.[162] Similarly, Shyamala Shirolkar notes that during the American tour of Kashinathpanth Chatre's Grand Indian Circus, a number of horses, deer, monkeys, and elephants succumbed to the severe cold.[163]

[160] Interview, Moreswar.

[161] Vladimir Durov, the Russian animal trainer, observes, 'The cubs learn very quickly and are usually easy to train, although things do not always run smoothly.' Emmanuel Dvinsky, *Durov and His Performing Animals* (Moscow: Foreign Languages Publishing House, 1960), 56.

[162] Kamala Circus programme book, circa 1955, private collection of Edward Williams, Chirakkara.

[163] Shirolker, *Circus! Circus!*

The first lesson Moreswar said he learnt was that one should never be afraid while dealing with wild animals; that animals are nothing before humans. He says that he grew up with these animals, which used to sleep beside him as any other pet animal would. But mishaps have happened. Once, he got a deep bite on his thigh from a tiger with which he used to perform. He narrated a poignant incident about a colleague and his chimpanzee in Jumbo Circus. Gigantic and a little naughty, the animal attacked the trainer, Babu, whose right arm was almost severed. Then, the animal silently lay beside him. Babu still trains elephants, camels, and horses in the circus. Jason Hribal pointedly observes,

> Every captive animal knows, through learned response and direct experience, which behaviors are rewarded and which ones are punished. … Captive animals know all of this and yet they still carry out such actions? often with a profound sense of determination. This is why these behaviors can be understood as a true form of resistance. … They have a conception of freedom and a desire for it. They have agency.[164]

Everyone who has lived in tents will have similar heartening tales to tell, whether they were associated with the animals or not. The chimpanzee named Raja in Gemini Circus was a lovable prankster. He was the star of his item, but he would never appear on stage on time. And the moment his item was over in the evening show, he would escape the ringmaster's notice somehow and go straight to the proprietor Kunhikannan's tent where he and the managers would have a drink. Raja would jump and sit on the owner's lap and demand his drink. Once a manager gave him plain water and Raja threw away the glass in anger. Before he threw more tantrums, somebody fixed him a nice drink.[165] 'A tamed animal is like a human child,' said Leela, a retired circus artiste.[166] Peta Tait argues that 'political campaigns for social change and ethical behaviour that appeal to reason and intellectual principle' should take into account the 'visceral and sensory experiences'. She observes, 'Animal–human connections, however, are potentially as short-lived and tenuous as any human social relationships derived

[164] Available at http://www.counterpunch.org/2011/01/18/a-message-from-tatiana/, last accessed on 16 September 2014.

[165] Interview, Babu.

[166] Interview, Leela, Thiruvangad, 17 January 2012.

from emotions. In developed societies there is the emotional freedom to leave a lover—and an animal.'[167]

Food and Medical Care

In the mornings, the carnivores got beef; it had been mutton in better times. Each animal got 10 kgs of mutton at about eight in the morning and 6 litres (later three) of milk in the evening. During rainy season, liquor—usually local arrack—was mixed with milk and given to both elephants and horses, but not to wild animals.[168] For six elephants, about 2 kilos of ghee was added to 12 kilos of jaggery, which was then mixed with bread crumbs and *aval* (rice flakes). This was served only at night. Early in the morning, eggs mixed with milk was served to both horses and elephants to strengthen the body's inner unit. Fresh grass and carrots made the best meal for horses. Otherwise, they were provided with soaked *chana* (chickpeas) and *muthira* (horse gram). Dogs were given fresh eggs and bread in the morning and a light lunch. After the evening show, they got a heavy meal of rice and meat. Dog food was cooked with turmeric and without salt.

Experienced mahouts and indigenous medical practitioners qualified in elephant treatment from Kerala, Bihar, and Assam were employed in circuses to look after the elephants. An allopathic doctor's help would be sought only as a last resort or when a surgery was needed. Elephants were selected according to certain features that supposedly mark character and quality.

For a camel, summer season was not a period to worry about. But once the rains and dirt appeared, infections started. 'Unlike horses, camels easily get affected with infections since its milk is very sweet,' Ravindran says. Mustard oil was given to them to resist the cold and to clear the stomach. There was a special cup made out of bamboo to pour the oil into their mouth. Just before the rains, *pachakarppooram* (edible camphor), coconut oil, and *neelam* (indigo dye) were stirred together and applied all over their body, fully shaven. This medicine was applied to all other animals as well for the treatment of minor infections. For

---

[167] Peta Tait, *Wild and Dangerous Performances: Animals, Emotions, Circus* (London: Palgrave Macmillan, 2011), 199, 197.

[168] Interview, Wilson, Jumbo Circus, 22 April 2007.

the treatment of wild animals, zoo doctors or other veterinary specialists in the city where they camp were consulted. In case of minor wounds, they were washed and cleaned, and some antiseptic liquid or powder was applied.[169] All these point to a blend of both indigenous and European practices adopted by them.

The Interstices of a Metaphor

The animal trainer has always been a typical metaphor of supremacy and cruelty. In literature, especially in certain strands of feminist literature, the animal trainer personifies a brutal and violent masculinity that tames, controls, and inflicts pain on the feminine/nature/wild. Nationalist literatures often deploy this metaphor to represent the colonizer, while the wild animal signifies the colonized. It is in the grey expanse between the metaphor and the lived experience of an animal trainer that one finds the pain and peril in taming and training an animal, and the fear, intimacy, and love the two beings share. In this context, let us look at a rare autobiographical piece from an animal trainer from India who made his mark in the West, Damoo Dhotre.

Wild Animal Man, as told to Richard Taplinger, was published in the United States of America and Canada in 1961. This pioneering memoir offers a view into the culture of animal training from early twentieth century in India, Maharashtra to be precise. It is also definitely a contribution to the field of wildlife history in India, where circus animals hardly appear. Significantly, the book was translated into Dhotre's mother tongue, Marathi, only two decades later, in 1982, as *Wagh Sinha Maze Sakhe Sobati* (My Tiger, Lion Companions).

However, the transnational character of this work explores the author's life in Indian as well as foreign circuses, especially his decade-long stint with the Ringling Brothers' Barnum and Bailey Circus in the United States of America, hyped as the 'greatest show on earth'. The book, of course, revolves around animal training, taming, and intimacy with his subjects. It shatters many of our preconceived notions of trainer–animal relationships and those concerning circus itself.[170]

---

[169] Interview, Ravindran; Wilson.

[170] Damoo Dhotre, *The Wild Animal Man* (Boston and Toronto: Little, Brown and Company, 1961); all citations are from this edition.

Image 2.4   Damoo Dhotre and Sonia

Source: Private collection of Kamala Damodaran.

Interestingly, accounts about his personal life are more or less absent. But from my fieldwork I know that almost every circus veteran in Malabar who holds him in great esteem remembers his marriages, his bungalow in Pune—'Circusvilla', his retirement from the American circus, and the last days he spent in Maratha circuses. A three-page interview with Dhotre when he was camped in Paris, published in *Mathrubhumi Illustrated Weekly*, describes many of his personal moments and the fame he attained outside India. The accompanying photographs include Dhotre's spouse at the time, Bess Jaxon.[171]

A fascinating aspect, true to the spirit of the book, is that it has been dedicated to 'Sonia, the most beautiful of them all', his darling leopard with whom he shared the applause of circus audiences of various continents. To him, Sonia represented 'the complete fulfilment of a trainer's dream'. The last chapter, 'Dance of Death', movingly describes the passionate love of Sonia and Damoo: '[I]n all my life I've never met another animal like her.' And in all her life, as it turned out, she never performed for another trainer.

The book, divided into 11 small chapters, has a non-linear structure. The first chapter opens with the devastating fire accident in Cleveland.[172] Dhotre recounts the moment thus: 'my first reaction was one of relief when I found that only the menagerie tent, the tent housing the untrained animals was on fire. But this was followed by two violent reactions: first my concern for the animals that had been caught in the fire and second my concern for the effect this might have on my own animals' (4–5). He movingly narrates that, following the show business dictum, he performed with his frightened and panicked wild animals in the next show that very evening.

The next section turns to Dhotre's childhood where we see him as the 9-year-old boy who desperately wanted to join his uncle's circus. One of the largest circuses in India, it toured across Asia by rail, the only company to do so at the time. The professional writer-collaborator of the book, disappointingly, has not cared to name this Indian circus or the full name of Dhotre's uncle. Tukaram Ganapat Shellar was a known acrobat in Karleker Circus and later became a partner in the company.

---

[171] Balan Vyloppilli, 'Dhomthar Damoo Dhotre' [Strong Damoo Dhotre], *Mathrubhumi Illustrated Weekly* 31, no. 16 (1953): 18–24.

[172] Though the book does not mention the date, this fire, considered to be one of the worst disasters in circus history, happened on 4 August 1942 when the menagerie tent of Ringling Brothers Barnum and Bailey went up in flames, killing hapless animals including lions, tigers, leopards, elephants, giraffes, and camels. Approximately a hundred animals perished, some of them shot by the police.

After Karleker's death, the company was divided and he formed his own company, Shellar's International Great Indian Circus.

The second chapter narrates the growing fascination of young Damoo for wild animals, especially an enormous lioness named 'Mumma', his grandmother's pet. Damoo learnt his first lessons about wild animals from his grandmother, which paved the way for him to becoming a master animal trainer:

> The greatest triumph, it seemed to me, was to make each wild animal my friend. This has been the pattern of my life, not the *mastering* of a wild animal, not the taming of a ferocious jungle beast, but the development of a friendship, of mutual trust and confidence between the animal and me. That enabled me to perform tricks most people considered impossible. (17)

The third chapter is aptly titled 'Getting to Know Them'. Dhondiram Chavan was the wild-animal trainer in Shellar Circus. Chavan sensed the young boy's potential and took charge of him. Damoo started training with two lion cubs, holding a stick with dangling pieces of meat. A dialogue between the master and his pupil opens up a new sensitivity and understanding that the wild beings possess individuality:

> 'If two lions can be different', I asked, 'how can they be the same?'
>
> 'Their basic characteristics are alike,' he told me, 'for instance if a lion wants to attack you he will come at you in short rushes. He will not, like a leopard or a tiger spring at you all at once. He will not, like a bear, pretend to be friendly and then suddenly attack you. These traits are common to all members of the species. But *within* the species each animal is an individual. One is mean; one is generous; one is loving; one is a killer. You must become intimately acquainted with each animal personally to know what kind of a *person* he really is'. (34–5, emphasis in original)

Obviously, Damoo Dhotre never forgot this great lesson.

Later on, Damoo got an offer from Isako's Russian Circus and joined them. He travelled to Hong Kong, Tokyo, Afghanistan, Indonesia, Bali, Siam, Malaya, Burma, and Indonesia. Many of the circus artistes consider touring their greatest bliss. 'Leopards in the Garden' speaks of his excitement while joining the Ringling Brothers' Barnum and Bailey Circus.

Chavan, Damoo's trainer, found out from his experiences as a trainer of animals that a trainer does not beat his animals unless he is not smart and patient enough to train them properly. Dhotre trained his animals according to their habits. He believed that a trainer should observe deeply and learn an animal's personality, then train what comes to them naturally. Many circus people still recollect with awe Dhotre's daring act in the open ring with a tiger, a leopard, and a lion together—three animals that have completely different characters. Following Dhotre's method, his friend, Dick Clemens, trained his lion with 'the biggest yawn' for the famous *head-in-the-mouth-of-lion* act.[173]

This perception is interesting especially in a context where social history is yet to note that 'each animal has an individual history, a history often written on their bodies'.[174] These distinct approaches and methods also show that it is not simple to frame them all within 'cruelty'. For example, Mathew Scott, the keeper of Jumbo, believed that 'any person who wanted to gain the total trust of an animal had in return to forfeit some aspect of their own life',[175] while Arstingstall, the trainer of Barnum, regarded his animals as 'working wild animals' and not pets.[176] In the legal battle discussed earlier, only Alfred Court's biography, *Wild Circus Animals*, was cited as instance to conclude that there are only three weapons—fear, hunger, and pain—enforced, with which an animal is made to perform.[177] Just as our systems do not regard each animal as an individual, each animal trainer is also dismissed as cruel without considering his or her distinctive methods and approaches.

Animal as Citizen

In a short piece titled 'The Moral Status of Animals', philosopher Martha Nussbaum, citing the legal battle concerning circus animals in India, argues,

> It has been obvious for a long time that the pursuit of global justice requires the inclusion of many people and groups not previously

[173] Interview with Parasuram Mali, Tasgaon, 25 December 2012.

[174] Swart, 'The World the Horses Made', 249.

[175] Chambers, *Jumbo: The Greatest Elephant in the World*, 55.

[176] Nisha P R, 'Jumbo Minorities', *Conservation and Society* 8, no. 2 (2010): 151–2.

[177] Review Committee Report.

included as fully equal subjects of justice: the poor; members of religious, ethnic, and racial minorities; and more recently women, the disabled, and inhabitants of poor nations distant from one's own. But a truly global justice requires not simply looking across the world for fellow species members who are entitled to a decent life.[178]

On the other hand, political theorist and ethicist Alasdair Cochrane says that sentient animals have a right not to be made to suffer and not to be killed, but not a right to liberty. He argues that humans have no moral obligation to 'liberate' them, since animals are unlike humans who 'are autonomous agents who should be able to frame, revise and pursue their own life goals and ambitions, ... thus questioning whether a commitment to animal rights necessarily entails an acceptance that all animals have a right not to be owned'. He points out that complete liberation of animals, which 'entails a duty to abolish their use, ownership and exploitation of animals', is not necessary to recognize their rights. While the human right not to be owned by another is uncontroversial, in the case of animals, it is sceptical.[179] Historian Jason Hribal argues that 'animals are part of the working class' as 'animal rights movements are part of the working class movement, for their formations have always been linked', although he hardly mentions performing animals.[180]

The ruling of the Kerala High Court in the circus animal ban case has some telling ethico-legal observations that compellingly challenge positions such as Cochrane's. Incidentally, it is from this judgment that Nussbaum's take quoted above begins. The bench comprising of Justice K. Narayana Kurup and K. V. Sankaranarayanan stated,

If humans are entitled to fundamental rights, why not animals? In our considered opinion legal rights shall not be the exclusive preserve of the humans which has to be extended beyond the people thereby dismantling

---

[178] Martha Nussbaum, 'The Moral Status of Animals', *Chronicle of Higher Education*, 3 February 2006, available at http://3quarksdaily.blogs.com/3quarksdaily/2006/02/martha_c_nussba.html, last accessed on 21 March 2012.

[179] Available at http://www.casj.org.uk/blogs-archive/animal-welfare-vs-animal-rights-false-dichotomy/; http://www.cupblog.org/?p=8131#more-8131, last accessed on 5 August 2014.

[180] Jason Hribal, '"Animals are Part of the Working Class": A Challenge to Labor History', *Labor History* 44, no. 4 (2003): 453.

the thick wall with humans all on one side and all non-human animals on the other side. While the law currently protects wildlife and endangered species from extinction animals are denied rights, an anachronism which must necessarily change.[181]

But speaking of 'anachronism', it is this very judgment that categorically endorses the merit of zoos for their 'conservation and education purpose', and hails them as 'excellent places for captive breeding'. Eric Scigliano points to an interesting statistic from the Association of Zoos and Aquariums (AZA) that 'the zoos could maintain just 16 of earth's 2700 or so snake species and 141 of 9672 birds', and scathingly remarks, 'zoos breed the animals that draw people to zoos'.[182] Peter Singer has sharply argued that the anti-cruelty movement of the nineteenth century is based on the assumption that non-human animals need to be protected only when human interests are not at stake. He puts forth the apt ethical dimension of the idea of conservation thus:

> So African human beings could be captured, shipped to America and sold. In Australia white settlers regarded Aborigines as pest and hunted them down, much as kangaroos are hunted down today. Just as we have progressed beyond the blatantly racist ethic of the era of slavery and colonialism, so we must now progress beyond the speciesist ethic of the era of factory farming, of the use of animals as mere research tools, of whaling, seal hunting, kangaroo slaughter and the destruction of wilderness.[183]

The idea and language of animal rights and conservation become menacingly calculating in the contexts of racism and casteism. A glaring instance would be the recent beef bans in India by the Hindu majoritarian government in the name of conservation of cattle and protection of 'holy' cows. Beef, in India, is a staple diet of the Dalits and Muslims, as opposed to the 'vegetarian' castes who feast upon chicken and mutton. The vegetarian compassion in India is often caught up, obliviously or otherwise, with the regressive politics of Hindu Brahminism. In many awful incidents, people belonging to Dalit and minority communities

---

[181] Judgment 2000.

[182] Scigliano, *Love, War and Circuses*, 293.

[183] Peter Singer (ed.), *In Defense of Animals* (New York: Harper and Row, 1986), 10.

are publicly lynched for the mere suspicion of eating beef, working on leather, or slaughtering a cow.

The 1991 ban directly affected a marginalized group of people but, at the same time, hardly affected certain other dominant exhibition spaces, such as the elephants in religious places or the 'traditional' animal-fighting for sport. It has to be noted here that a ban on elephants would not have been easier, since elephants are associated with powerful institutions with 'traditional' and religious aura, such as the temple management body called the Devaswom Board. The most ironical fact is that these exhibitions are not even considered as animals in 'performance'. What makes certain performances and spaces illegitimate is a triggering question. We may remember in this context how, in the southern state of Tamil Nadu recently, following a mass agitation, the central and state governments sought to lift the Supreme Court ban on the agrarian sport of bull-fighting, Jallikkettu, by amending provisions in the law related to the prevention of cruelty to animals. The major argument was that Jallikkettu upholds Tamil traditional and cultural values and has historical significance. Similarly, Animal Welfare Board of India (AWBI) has filed a report in the Supreme Court alleging that Thrissur Pooram, a globally well-known Hindu temple festival in which about 80 elephants are paraded annually, violates various rules and court orders. The AWBI inspection team had found elephants with heavy chains around all four legs and the belly during the events of the entire two-day festival. Many of these pachyderms had impaired vision, cracked nails, and wounds which were deliberately covered with some black paste. The team also found the use of banned control devices such as *ankush* (elephant goad) at the Pooram. Fitness certificates were issued to elephants in the aforementioned conditions, while the AWBI team was denied permission by state authorities to enter the fitness inspection camp.[184] The Kerala High Court did not even consider AWBI's plea that the firework ceremony is often harmful to the elephants who are made to stand for long hours, often drugged, amidst the terribly loud noises.

---

[184] Animal Welfare Board of India, Ministry of Environment, Forests and Climate Change, Reprot [*sic*] on Inspection of Captive Elephants Used in Thrissur Pooram 2016, dated 23 April 2016, 1–33.

The state government of Kerala had also issued a government notification on 26 February 2016 and distributed the ownership certificates
of elephants against the provisos of the Wildlife Protection Act, 1972.
The Supreme Court's intervention has barred the state government
from further action for the time being (The *Hindu*, 5 May 2016). Thus,
it turns out that certain spaces and practices are 'sanctioned' and certain
work/performances become 'accepted', while 'others', such as the circus
or the poor snake charmer in the street, are branded 'cruel' and banned.
It is this historical duplicity in the name of love and law that has to be
challenged and redefined for a fair and sincere ethico-legal policy for
our fellow beings.

3 Tenting the Circus

The towering tents are striped in white and black, no golds and crimsons to be seen. … Black-and-white stripes on grey sky; countless tents of varying shapes and sizes, with an elaborate wrought-iron fence encasing them in a colorless world.

—*The Night Circus*[1]

Circus lives in tents, literally and figuratively. One cannot imagine circus without those big tops spreading over on tall poles. No wonder the architecture of most permanent circus venues around the world is modelled on tents. Literary and filmic representations about circus in Malayalam are often titled with various terms meant for the tent; for instance, G. Aravindan's classic film, *Thambu* (1978), and Sreedharan Champad's novel, *Koodaram* (2007). The opening of a contemporary American novel, *The Night Circus* (2011), quoted at the beginning of the chapter shows that postmodern phantasmagorical fiction also prefers to enter the circus through those magnificent tents. In this chapter, I will discuss the major components and technologies of the circus tent and the spatial structure of a circus camp. I shall also look at tents of the earlier era used for administrative purposes and as itinerant entertainment sites.

Many historical explorations in recent times have looked at how modernity has been shaped/experienced/transformed with 'things' from South Asian societies. For instance, there are socio-economic-cultural

---

[1] Erin Morgenstern, *The Night Circus* (London: Harvill Secker, 2011), 3.

histories of tea, coffee, and rice that brought to light remarkable accounts of the relationship of these 'things' with colonial empires, nationalist movements, global capitalism, religion, caste, the politics of consumption, and so on.[2] On the lines of Orhan Pamuk's wonderful novel *Museum of Innocence*, which preserves the sweet little artefacts of a broken love, one may also ask what stories of affect and intimacy do these 'things' have, and their association with humans and animals. Analysing the past and present of the Malabar biryani, to cite an example, could unravel the trajectories of the 'global food' it has become, its intimate affiliation with the Mappila community, culinary cultures, and local/global demands. A China cup or a mobile phone or an ATM machine will have different tales to offer: the users, manufacturers, transnational movements, and also their demand in the global market. Hence, by thinking through things, this chapter could weave together various objects, themes, and disciplines through a history of the circus tent.

These historical enquiries have close links with philosophical thoughts that examine the agency and state of being of objects. The philosophical branch of knowledge popularized as Object Oriented Ontology acknowledges and values non-human existence in contrast to 'anthropocentrism' that prefers humans over all other beings; as philosopher Levi Byant puts it effectively, Being *as such* is relegated to Being for humans.[3] In his 1999 lecture, Graham Harman called it Object Oriented Philosophy which later gets termed as Object Oriented Ontology (OOO).[4] Harman explains, 'Numerous intellectual methods already exist that involve subtracting the object from its holistic interweaving with other things and thereby liberating its solitary power.' He further adds that if his work could contribute anything in this process, it is by not treating object in terms of dynamic wholes but by 'look[ing]

[2] A. R. Venkatachalapathy, *In Those Days There Was No Coffee: Writings in Cultural History* (New Delhi: Yoda Press, 2006); K. T. Rammohan, *Tales of Rice: Kuttanad, Southwest India* (Thiruvananthapuram: Centre for Development Studies, 2006).

[3] Levi Bryant, *The Democracy of Objects* (Ann Arbor: Open Humanities Press, 2011), 35.

[4] Graham Harman, 'Object Oriented Philosophy (1999)', in *Towards Speculative Realism* (Washington: Zero Books, 2010), 93–104.

instead at how individual entities disrupt or resist or withdraw from those wholes'.[5]

In his philosophical debate on 'Interobjectivity', Bruno Latour observes, 'Objects do *do* something, they are not merely the screens or the retroprojectors of our social life. Their sole function is not merely to "launder" the social origin of the forces that we project onto them.'[6] Latour, who believes we need to give rights to non-humans, quasi-objects, and hybrids, argues that 'because it believes in the total separation of humans and nonhumans, and because it simultaneously cancels out this separation, the Constitution has made the moderns invincible'. Perhaps it was necessary at one point 'to increase mobilization and lengthen some networks'; this divide has now become 'superfluous, immoral' and 'anti-Constitutional'. To have (what he calls) 'the Parliament of Things' defined, we need to understand that 'there are no more naked truths, but there are no more naked citizens, either. The mediators have the whole space to themselves', and let us 'take up the two representations and double doubt about the faithfulness of the representatives', thus 'in its confines, the continuity of the collective is reconfigured'.[7] An implication of Latour's stance 'is that the power asymmetries addressed in studies of political economy should be possible to trace to specific kinds of human-object relations'.[8] In his working paper, Rammert, who looks at the distributed agency between humans, machines, and programmes, critically approaches Latour to argue that we need 'levels and degrees of agency'.[9]

[5] Lucy Kimbell, 'Object Strikes Back: An Interview with Graham Harman', *Design and Culture* 5, no. 1 (2013): 11.

[6] Bruno Latour, 'On Interobjectivity', *Mind, Culture and Activity* 3, no. 4 (1996): 236.

[7] Bruno Latour, *We Have Never Been Modern* (Cambridge: Harvard University Press, 1993), 37, 144.

[8] Alf Hornberg, 'Artefacts, Agency and Global Magic: How Amazonian "Ontologies" Can Illuminate Human–Object Relations in Industrialized Modernity', available at hornborg_artefacts-agency-and-global-magic.pdf, last accessed on 28 November 2018.

[9] Werner Rammert, 'Where the Action Is: Distributed Agency between Humans, Machines, and Programs', The Technical University Technology Studies Working Papers, 2008, 10.

Isabel Hofmeyr, leading scholar of African literature and the Indian Ocean world, observes that in this 'post-humanist object-oriented age', the question of how objects are governed is very much important. She notes in the South African context, 'Given that Customs and its governance of objects long pre-dated systems of bureaucratically classifying people, this question becomes pertinent, more especially so, when one considers that the roots of colonial customs rests with Company rule at the Cape where slave bodies were treated as dutiable commodities', which opens up debates such as who is objectified and whose objective it is, what constitutes an object, and if an object is really what it looks like.[10] She, unlike the OOO exponents, is looking at objects in their relation to other objects, their mobility, and the networks in which they are embedded—quite the transnational historian's way. For me, it is these networks, exchanges, intimacy, and skilled knowledge that the circus tent demands from its humans and animals, enabling a whole world particular to that of the circus that is most remarkable. The affinity, terror, and myth associated with this object—for example, in the pujas performed or in a belief, such as if a king pole falls down and harms someone in the tent it is unfortunate for the whole circus—marks how fateful the circus tent could be.

The very structure of circus is embedded with the idea of temporariness, of constant movement; the most obvious symbol being the tents.[11] A tent could simply be defined as a shelter consisting of sack or cotton material attached to a frame of poles or supporting ropes. Circus tents must be some of the largest tents used for habitation and exhibition. Tents are as inevitable to circus as humans and animals, the ring in which the circus feats take place, the galleries for the audience, the

[10] Isabel Hofmeyr, 'Object-oriented Reading: The View from the Custom House', available at https://wiser.wits.ac.za/system/files/seminar/Hofmeyr2018.pdf, last accessed on 28 November 2018.

[11] 'Any permanent structure is to be considered a house, which, on land, serves, or would serve, for the accommodation of human beings, or of animals, or goods of any descriptions provided always that it cannot be struck, and removed bodily like a tent, or a mat house.' Census of the Bombay Presidency, 1872, General Report and Tables of the Population, Houses, & C., enumerated in the Bombay Presidency on 21 February 1872, Part-II (Bombay: Government Central Press, 1875), 25.

*ravuttee*s (small residential tents) where the members live—all of these are tentage. The configuration of tents defines the space in which circus is lived and performed, distinctly marking the hierarchy and power within. These tents will obviously have amazing tales of lives and technologies to tell. But when circus in India has hardly been documented and historicized, there is no need to specifically mention that the tales of tents are yet to be told.

Kandambully Balan wryly notes that to experience the real wonders of circus, one should see the numerous activities which do not figure in the programme book—tenting, dismantling, and transporting—and hence without 'audience' and 'applause'. He provides an account to put across the magnitude of this operation, comparing it with a major military manoeuvre:

> In just 42 hours an iron fence with a 2000 foot diameter and the canvass city within it shall be dismantled, transported to a destination 100 miles away and reset. And add to this, 150 animals including 20 elephants, 500 people and 1000 ton equipment! … As soon as the last show ends the tent master deploys the 200 expert staff under him and 100 temporary local laborers. While one group would fold the 4000 chairs another would disassemble the makeshift gallery for 2000 spectators. Gates, electrical equipments, fences, decorations, gallery, poles and small tents are attended to by some others. 50 trucks would be ready by then to load these. The last one to fold is the big tent which is 50 feet high and 2000 meter canvass spread over six large iron poles. Only the tent master and some trustworthy assistants would handle it. The steel ropes would be carefully loosened and the tent will come undone like a gigantic parachute. … Next morning the school kids would stand looking at that empty ground with mouths agape.[12]

From another part of the world, the authors of the book *The Love of the Circus* point out this lack in historical writing about circus in general, and especially aspects such as the tent:

> There are numerous aspects of the history of the circus which are not well documented—and the question of who first used a tent for his circus shows is one of them. According to George Speaight, Astley himself experimented in 1788 with the 'Royal Tent' for his shows in Liverpool, but the idea does not seem to have been successful as the tent was auctioned at

---

[12] Kandambulli Balan, *Circus* (Kottayam: NBS, 1961), 61–2.

the end of the season. Probably the first circus to tour with a tent was one in America. In an article in *Bandwagon*, journal of the Circus Historical Society, Stuart Thayor records that J. Purdy Brown was touring his circus with a tent there in 1825. By the time of the Golden Age of circuses, in the late nineteenth century, the touring big top was commonplace on both sides of the Atlantic.[13]

Brenda Assael notes the gradual progression of British circuses to tents from the semi- permanent wooden amphitheatres and permanent amphitheatres, pointing out that tenting became popular in British circuses after the 1850s. The different spaces the circus occupied during the nineteenth century depended on the company's size, status, and wealth. She further adds, 'Since the change away from tenting and towards residency was gradual, it became common for companies between 1840s and 1880s to alternate between tenting and residing in amphitheatres during the summer season.'[14]

Entertainment Tents in the Subcontinent

Touring entertainment had become popular in cities and towns around the subcontinent by the beginning of the twentieth century, and tents figured prominently on the scene. An *MM* correspondent reports from Calcutta in 1909 that the city has been welcoming the autumn season with a lot of fanfare and the 'ground is packed with the tents of bioscopes, circus players and drama artists' (3 April). Another news of the same year briefly mentions the tenting of a Tamil drama troupe in Kayamkulam (*MM*, 2 June 1909). While discussing the formation of film audiences in Madras during the first decades of the twentieth century, Stephen P. Hughes notes that itinerant entertainment companies, depending on the season and weather, pitched tents on open grounds in the city. He points out instances of independent cinema exhibitors performing 'two shows every night at 6.30 p.m. and 9.30 p.m. mostly at outdoor locations in Madras with their own large and well ventilated tents', and also notes that 'the circus visited the town at

---

[13] David Jamieson and Sandy Davidson, *The Love of the Circus* (London: Octopus, 1980), 88.

[14] Brenda Assael, *The Circus and Respectable Society in Victorian Britain*, Doctoral dissertation, University of Toronto, Canada, 1998, 65.

least once a year'.[15] The Madras Presidency Cinematograph Act specifies that 'the word "building" shall be deemed to include any booth,
tent or similar structure'.[16] *Mitavadi* (May 1918) and *MM* (13 October,
17 February 1909) report the use of 'expansive tents' by the bioscope
and cinematograph exhibitors. One of the prominent Malayalam film
producers of the early era, Shobhana Parameswaran Nair, remembers
his first cinema going experience during the first half of the 1930s in a
'round shaped big tent erected in a paddy field by people from Tamil
Nadu'.[17] Padwardhan Circus, which had come to perform in Puthen
Kacheri ground, Thiruvananthapuram, for two weeks, did not start on
the day fixed for opening because of some unfinished tent work (*MM*,
20 and 23 October 1909). Tents were used for *kushti* competitions
as well (*MM*, 28 November 1903). The *kushti* competition between
a Bengali woman wrestler, Gangubhai, and her male counterpart,
Muhammed Ismail, took place in the tent pitched in Puthan Kacheri
(*MM*, 3 November 1906). From this period, one can find a number
of news items in *MM* on the tenting of circus companies in various
grounds in present-day Kerala.[18] While there were play houses (*nadaka
shaala*) for drama shows in Travancore, the Puthan Kacheri ground was
active with circus performances at regular intervals.

In 1910, *MM* (30 July) advertises: 'A tent for sale, without any damage,
with all equipments, a verandah around and can comfortably accommodate three hundred persons.' The *TOI* (11 January 1926) advertises:
'Waterproof Canvas Materials—Including the well-known "Dux" qualities are available at reduced prices in 36", 60" and 72" widths. Sample
on application to ELGIN MILLS, CO., LTD., Cawnpore.' This shows
the demand for water-proofed tents in the market during the time.
Elsewhere, the same company has published: 'A DELIGHTFUL CAMP is

[15] Stephen P. Hughes, 'The Pre-Phalke Era in South India: Reflections on the
Formation of Film Audiences in Madras', *South Indian Studies* 2 (July–December
1996): 165, 169.

[16] Notification, Cinematograph Act, 1918, 25 June 1920, *TSR*, List-1, File
no. 2579, Regional Archives, Kozhikode.

[17] K. J. Johny and Venugopal C., *Cinemayude Kalpadukal* [Footsteps of cin-
ema] (Thrissur: Current Books, 2009), 138.

[18] For example, reports published in *MM* on 24 October, 25 November, and
26 December 1903; 14 June, 9 August, 20 December, and 4 and 25 November 1905.

the universal verdict when "Elgin" Tents are used to accommodate your guests' (*TOI*, 6 January 1926). It is interesting to note that the government provided tents to those visiting Delhi (*MM*, 8 November 1911).

Many retired circus artistes in Malabar recount that tents as living quarters for artistes and workers were popularized by K. Damodaran of the Kamala Three Ring Circus during the 1950s. He must have got the idea from the foreign trips he made to South East Asia at that time. Damodaran had introduced many changes in the make-up, attire, and presentation of animals after this tour. Till then, artistes and others found accommodation in rented houses near the camp site.

Tents and Colonial Administration

Tentage had been a usual practice with the British officials in India during the nineteenth century. The revenue and military officials and officers of salt, abkari, railway, geological survey, and forest departments, who had to travel constantly for tax collections and inspections, made the most of tents. A letter to the collector of Vizagapatam from the Board of Revenue proves that almost everyone, regardless of hierarchy, depended on tents.[19] Different kinds of tents were in use for different places, departments, officers, and purposes. The inspectors and conservators of forest by and large deployed the 'hill tents' (usually 12' × 12'), 'sleeping pal', 'servants' tents' (usually 10' × 10'), and the 'necessary tents' (usually 4' × 4').[20] The travelling colonial officials drew tentage and *batta* (maintenance/travelling expense) accordingly.[21] At the same

[19] Letter from D. F. Carmichael, collector of Vizagapatam, 2 July 1864, R-Dis files, Vol. 24, File no. 10, Regional Archives, Kozhikode.

[20] Letter from A. W. Peet, conservator of forests, north circle, to the secretary to the commissioners of land revenue, 15 May 1897, *TSR*, List-1, File no. 1670, Regional Archives, Kozhikode.

Letter from A. G. Cardew, Imperial Civil Service (ICS), inspector general of prisons, Madras, to the secretary to the commissioners of land revenue, 1 April 1898, *TSR*, List-1, File no. 1701, Regional Archives, Kozhikode.

[21] Letter from the collector of Malabar recorded in the board's proceedings, 23 April 1863, R-Dis files, Vol. 20, File no. 95, Regional Archives, Kozhikode.

Letter from G. W. Dane, acting collector of Malabar, to the secretary to the commissioners of land revenue, 26 May 1897, *TSR*, List-1, File no. 1666, Regional Archives, Kozhikode.

time, the superintendent and assistants of the geological survey were 'also obliged to keep their tents in repair and good working order during the whole of five years, no matter what exposure or injury they may have had, out of the same [travelling] allowances'.[22]

Men were employed to accompany these officials with the tents. F. C. Harrison, Officiating Accountant General to the Government of Madras, writes to the secretary to the commissioners of land revenue to reprint the 'Bill-iii of Contingencies (Forest Department Code)' in a revised form, which includes such headings as 'Carriage of tents' and 'Cooly to tent lascars'.[23] G. Balachandran notes that the word 'lascar' in its Persian origin meant 'an army' or 'a camp', while the Dutch and the Portuguese used it to refer to Indian seafarers. He further adds that until the twentieth century, it described 'porters, and other unskilled manual workers employed in the army, the railways and the public works department'. He also cites examples where the word stood for 'a common coolie'.[24]

The Home Department proceedings, 24 September 1870, mention the reduction of expenditure upon tent *khalasi*s at one rupee a month as remuneration for the extra duty. One of the most interesting aspects of this file is the use of the term words 'tent lascar' with relation to Hyderabad and Madras and 'tent khalasie' in relation to regions such as Punjab, Coorg, and British Burmah. Another file describes tent *khalasi*s as 'men entertained for purely tent work'.[25] The archival sources throw light

---

[22] Letter from Oldham, esq. LLD, Supdt. Geological Survey of India, to the under secretary to the Government of India, Home Department, Home Department proceedings (expenditure on account of Tent Khalassie establishments in India), Public branch, 20 August 1870, Home Department files, File nos 17–36, National Archives, New Delhi.

[23] Letter from F. C. Harrison, officiating Accountant General to the Government of Madras, to the secretary to the commissioners of land revenue, 16 February 1897, *TSR*, List-1, File no. 1654, Regional Archives, Kozhikode.

[24] G. Balachandran, *Globalising Labour?: Indian Seafarers and the World Shipping; C. 1870–1945* (New Delhi: Oxford University Press, 2012), 28–9.

[25] Home Department proceedings (expenditure on account of Tent Khalassie establishments in India), Public branch, 20 August 1870, Home Department files, File nos 17–36, National Archives, New Delhi; it is interesting to note that in Malabar the traditional community called 'mapillah khalasi' is still very active

on the fact that in all districts 'fixed tentage' was allowed to meet the expense of keeping up tents and 'extra tentage' to cover the additional charges incidental to travelling.[26] In special cases, extra tentage was allowed without the prior possession of tents.[27] The Census of India, 1901, mentions the presence of 'tent makers' and 'tent sellers' as four and two males respectively.[28]

Tents were popular among the Indian royalty for their hunting excursions. A scenic description in *TOI* (4 January 1926) about the Christmas camp of 'His Highness Maharaja Saheb of Alwar' at Vijay Mandir Palace goes thus: '[T]he tents forming three sides of a large quadrangle in the centre of which there were many beautiful flower beds. At night the whole camp was lit up with electricity; and looked like a fairy scene.'

---

in executing highly skilled jobs involving great weights and depths. Musthafa Haji, a Mapillah Khalasi, notes in his autobiography that 'khalasies were a special contribution of the mappilas'. They work with 'high end machinery that weighed a ton and a length of forty feet with simple steel ropes and pulley tied to a bamboo (called *silanki*)'; C. M. Musthafa Haji Chelambra, *Mappilah Khalasi Kadha Parayunnu* [Mappilah Khalasi telling the tale] (Kozhikode: Pratheeksha Books, 2011), 37.

All these descriptions point out the 'skilled' nature of their work, the regional variety of the expertise, and a technology developed by them with simple technical instruments but needing high expertise and team work. The fact that these technologies have meaning more or less only in their special context, as in the circus tents, probably contributed to their marginalization and ignorance to the outside world.

[26] This allowance was allotted only when an officer possessed or kept a suitable set of tents. The latter was made possible except in some special cases when the officer moved about in his district on duty, carrying his tents with him and providing accommodation for his cutchery in the absence of a government building; proceedings of the Board of Revenue to J. D. Bourdillon, secretary to government, Revenue Department, copies to the collectors of Canara and Malabar, 1 September 1859, R-Dis files, File no. 35, Regional Archives, Kozhikode.

[27] Letter from G. A. Ballard, collector of Malabar, to W. Huddleston, secretary to the Board of Revenue, Madras, 7 August 1862, R-Dis files, File no. 66, 1862, Regional Archives, Kozhikode.

[28] *The Census of India*, 1901, Volume XIA, Bombay (Towns and Island), Part VI, Tables by S. M. Edwades, ICS (Bombay: Times of India Press, 1901), 134.

The collectors and sub-collectors on the coast took advantage of the sea and kept a boat and crew to carry the tents from place to place.

In the monsoon, which is peculiarly heavy on the western coast, tents cannot, of course, be carried about, and would be useless if they could. The revenue officers, however, rarely have occasions to move about that season, and when they do, it is generally to make a rapid journey to some one place, the expense of which is not fully covered by the extra tentage allowed by the rules.[29]

A circus veteran from Thalassery, K. K. Sreedharan, recounts that in the early part of the twentieth century the side poles of small single-pole circuses that roamed around south India used to be made of bamboo while the main king poles were of strong woods such as teak.[30] In a complaint letter to the commissioner of land revenue, E. P. Poppert, the conservator of forests, says that the servants' tents supplied to him were torn and stained with oil. It also mentions the unseasoned condition of the bamboos supplied with the tents—a significant information that bamboos were used as poles in the early construction of tents. The secretary of the board, in his reply, convinces Poppert that the tents were probably torn during transit and that the superintendent, Central Jail, Vellore, has been instructed to take more care about the 'seasoning' of the bamboos:

All bamboos are now being thoroughly soaked before use, which is the method followed by the Ordnance Dept. … From information received, however, it appears doubtful whether any amount of soaking will prevent the attacks of the borer, if the eggs have already been deposited in the bamboo. I shall be much obliged as if the Forest Officers under the Board's control can tell me of any way of seasoning bamboo as to render them safe against the borer. At the instance of Govt., I'm in

---

[29] Proceedings of the Board of Revenue to J. D. Bourdillon, secretary to government, Revenue Department, copies to the collectors of Canara and Malabar, 1 September 1859, R-Dis files, File no. 35, Regional Archives, Kozhikode. The circus companies avoid the monsoon season as they schedule their performance in accordance with the seasons. This points to their knowledge of the seasons and climatic conditions about the places where they roam around. Moreover, the major festivals and *melas* in the subcontinent are mostly in summer and winter.

[30] Interview, K. K. Sreedharan.

correspondence with the Chemical Examiner regarding the best means of preventing the occurrence of mildew in tent cloth.[31]

The fact that the state was charging tax for the bamboos highlights the wide use of it for various purposes at the time.

> Salem has always been a district noted for the excellence and quantity of its bamboos, and large quantities are hourly and daily cut for the purpose of supplying the Madras and the Banglore markets. Our tax on them was not oppressive (12 Annas per bandy-load), and was only imposed on those who cut them for sale. Ryots and villagers were allowed to cut as many as they chose for the erection of their houses and not one complaint having come to my notice on this head.[32]

Sandal trees grew in bamboo jungles and they had to be protected with the shade and moisture of the bamboos until they grew to a certain height, after which the bamboos were felled. Tax was imposed not only to make money out of the felling of bamboo but also to protect 'the more valuable sandal trees' from 'unnecessary damage' in the hands of the local people. It gave the British not only the patronage of a local knowledge, which they could direct to their own use to make tents and sheds, but also a tight hold over the local market where these bamboos were being sold. That the villagers used bamboo for the construction of their houses highlights the local technique of building houses that was prevalent in the southern part of the subcontinent.[33] This invariably shows the demand for bamboo in the local market and also hints at its use and the users. It is clear from the fact that only the trees that had market value were being taxed by the British administration. It was also perhaps because they did not want to deprive the local people of their right to build houses using bamboo, which could have resulted in

[31] Letter from A. G. Cardew, ICS, inspector general of prisons, Madras, to the secretary to the commissioners of land revenue, 1 April 1898, *TSR*, List-1, File no. 1701, Regional Archives, Kozhikode.

[32] Letter from Lieutenant C. J. Walker, deputy conservator of Salem and S. Arcot Forests, to Captain R. H. Beddome, officiating conservator of forests, 3 September 1865, R-Dis Files, Vol. 31, File no. 42, Regional Archives, Kozhikode.

[33] Letter from Lieutenant C. J. Walker, deputy conservator of Salem and S. Arcot Forests, to Captain R. H. Beddome, officiating conservator of forests, 3 September 1865, R-Dis files, Vol. 31, File no. 42, Regional Archives, Kozhikode.

resistance against the alien state. The expansion of railways and other modern modes of transportation made it easy for the market and its users to access it.[34]

The Tellicherry sub-collector's office records contain the government order on the board's proposals regarding the size of tents supplied to the various classes of officers of the forest department, and its request to the government to reconsider orders in the matter of the supply of 'Shooting Pal' instead of 'Swiss Cottage' tents. The file has been submitted with four tent catalogues.[35] These files throw light on the different types of tents used by different classes of officials for their movement during the colonial period. Swiss cottage tents seem to be a common practice at the time among forest and range officers who had the risks of working in the interiors. Another file in the same office proposes that Swiss cottage tents may be made with rectangular verandahs and bathrooms. Mr Peet, the conservator of forest, northern circle, Madras, urges that tents in this style would be much 'more commodious and that could be more easily pitched by untrained lascars'.[36] Probably, it was this practice of cottage tents and transportable bathrooms and toilets that the circus people utilized to make their *ravuttee*s. It also makes one think whether there were different technologies involved in the making of cottage tents and the tents used for the ring.

Sheds, bungalows, and government buildings were the other temporary arrangements of accommodation. The proposals for building bungalows in various districts show that they were limited in number. However, later records about constructing fixed sheds, bungalows, and rest houses throw light on the fact that these buildings were being constructed permanently for government business. Records on 'fixed tentage' show a somewhat new attitude of the British government towards movement and settlement, pointing to the emergence

[34] Letter from the officiating conservator of forests, to the acting secretary to government, Revenue Department, 11 October 1865, R-Dis files, Vol. 31, File no. 55, Regional Archives, Kozhikode.

[35] Order (furnishing certain catalogues of tents), proceedings of the Board of Revenue, Forest, 8 December 1896, Tellicherry Sub-collectors' Office Records, List-1, File no. 1647, Regional Archives, Kozhikode.

[36] Board proceedings, Forest, 1 April 1897, Tellicherry Sub-Collectors' Office Records, List-1, File no. 1666, Regional Archives, Kozhikode.

of a new political economy with the colonial power spreading its tentacles. It also shows the rapid processes of urbanization and town building.

Small and Big Circuses

Small circus companies usually set up business during religious festivals in towns and villages and built their small tents on the shrine grounds. Big circus companies also performed during such festivals, depending on the size of the ground, but generally could not build their large tents on the festival grounds. Big circuses stayed at a place for one to two-and-a-half months, while small ones moved as soon as the festival season was over. David Jamieson and Sandy Davidson point out that the Americans traditionally looked for three ring circuses, the size, the spectacle, and the multitude of performers and animals. European circuses, on the other hand, featured a single ring that provided a closer proximity to their spectators.[37] It seems the early circuses in India were modelled after the British circuses.

The classification based on 'size' is determined by not only the humans and animals involved but the structure of the tents too. Generally, the size of a circus is calculated based on the number of its major poles, known as the king poles. There are one-, two-, four-, six-, and eight-pole circuses. According to Champad, six king-pole tents with 100–150 artistes, other workers of around the same number, and 80–100 animals/birds would come under the premier category. The ban on many wild animals has resulted in a substantial reduction in their numbers. Four king-pole tents with approximately 50 artistes, 50 workers, and 30 animals would be the second category, while two king pole tents with around 50–60 staff would fall under the third category. The last one in the order are the single-pole tents with about 20 personnel and no animals.[38] The increase in the number of king poles naturally would mean more side poles, quarter poles, canvas tent, and in total a larger tent area. Let us look at some of the key specificities of the tent, the poles, and the rings.

---

[37] David Jamieson and Sandy Davidson, *The Love of the Circus*, 10.
[38] Champad, *Circusinte Lokam*, 188.

THE BOMBAY CHRONICLE, MONDAY MARCH 24, 1913.

DOUBLE-POLED TENT.

The Oldest Goverment Tent Manufacturers.

Best Material and workmanship guaranteed.

Dining tent, double pole, double fly, with four folds of cloth throughout. The tent is provided with 4 ft. verandah all round, and is complete with durrie, purdahs, chicks, ropes, double gunny Sulleeths, bags, poles, mallets, pins &c.

For further particulars apply to

ADAMJEE PEERBHOY'S

SPINNING

AND

WEAVING MANUFACTURING MILLS, TARDEO.

The Adamjee Peerbhoy Tent Factory.

Tardeo, BOMBAY.

Image 3.1   Advertisement of a Double-poled Tent Given by the Adamjee Peerbhoy Tent Factory in Bombay

Source: BC (24 March 1913).

Many single- and double-pole circuses were converted into four- and six-pole circuses by the first half of the twentieth century. One of the most glaring instances being 'Kamala' Circus, the second largest circus in the world and the biggest in India at one time, which started as a double-pole circus and later upgraded to four, six, and finally eight poles with three rings.[39] The programme book of Kamala Circus states proudly under a photo of its tent featured on the opening page that '[t]he six pole tent of Kamala Circus, which can accommodate a maximum crowd of 10,000, is the only one of its kind in Asia. It takes nearly 15,000 feet of canvas and costs 40,000'.[40] In the beginning of the twentieth century, these circuses mainly depended on bullocks and carts for travel and transportation. These single-pole circuses of Kerala usually travelled to neighbouring regions in Tamil Nadu or Karnataka.[41] But, of course, there were Malayali-owned double-poled circuses which did business mostly in certain parts of north India. For instance, the 'Indrani' circus roamed around Bihar, U.P., and the neighbouring places.[42] Largely, 10 to 20 bullock carts carried the tent and two to three carts carried the people. These circuses had limited number of artistes and hardly any animals. They stopped at places where they found water to take bath or for other primary necessities.[43] The side poles of these circuses used to be of bamboo while the main king poles were made of strong wood materials, such as the teak.[44]

Pole

The normal distance from one king pole to another is about 70 feet. The major reason for this is to fix the flying trapeze net.[45] A 2.5 foot pit is dug about 10 feet away from the ring. A metal bar similar to fishplates is fixed under the pole. Iron spikes are hammered down to the earth.

[39] Interview, Govindan, Thalassery, 25 January 2011; E. Ravindran.

[40] Interview, Sulu, Thiruvangad, 17 January 2012; Kamala Circus programme book, circa 1955, private collection, Gloria Vanderwielen, Kolassery.

[41] Interview, Sulu.

[42] Interview, Babu.

[43] Interview, Leela.

[44] Interview, Sreedharan.

[45] Interview, E. Ravindran.

Four heavy wood pieces of six to eight inches thickness and two feet length are laid on it. The poles are erected on these. Once the pole is raised, these are loosened and taken out. The heavy pole that usually has a 60 foot height is laid slanting on an iron box so that this can be pushed to standing straight with the help of an excavator or a tractor. In fact, the poles are not strongly fixed in the mud as we see in permanent buildings where the pillars might be fixed deep inside the soil. The strength of the poles actually depends on the wire ropes (iron and plastic) which tie them. A pole is made of iron in four pieces of 19 feet length and 12 inches width. The top portion of the pole is called the cap. Four feet goes inside while joining. The same methods were applied to wooden poles of earlier times. A shock absorber is separately fixed to the iron poles. There is a wire rope and a pulley tied on each pole. The length of the tightening wire rope is one *gaerope*, about 120 feet. These two wire ropes come from 60 feet above, about the top of the pole. They are called *kada gaerope*, which is of 300 feet. Through these wire ropes the pole is pulled slowly and directly using a heavy pulley with the help of manpower and once it is perfectly straight to the satisfaction of the tent master and others, the pulley is tightened and tied. Ring boys and other labourers take part actively in these actions. Two wire ropes on opposite sides hold the pole in balance. There is an extra wire rope on the first pole on which a pulley is used for the second pole. The second pole is pulled straight in the same way but in the opposite direction so that it in no way affects the standing and balance of the first pole. However, the second pole is made to stand on the strength of the first pole. The same process is followed with other poles in the case of a circus with more than two poles.[46]

With the third and fourth poles, the wire rope, which is fixed at 60 feet above, is drawn from below. The interesting thing about a single-pole circus is that the ring is not in the middle but either to the left or right of the circus tent. To give strength and support above and in the middle, along with the wire ropes at 60 feet, two other ropes are fixed at 45 feet on the pole, and two at the back side. This is to withstand strong winds that can topple down the poles and the canvas. In total, there are six wire ropes tied on each pole from all sides to keep the balance.

[46] Interview, E. Ravindran.

There are two thick iron *kada gaerope*, two thick plastic *aada gaerope*, and two comparatively thin plastic wire ropes called 'clamps' that are tied at the sides of the pole. Thus, in total, 24 wire ropes are attached to the four poles. The terms *kada gaerope* and *aada gaerope* seem to be local alterations of their English equivalent, guy line and eave line. The stability and security of the tent depends mainly on these wire ropes. Physical and chemical deterioration can affect their stability. A book on tents published by the US military department observes that 'physical damage is caused by surface wear or from internal friction between the fibers. Chemical damage is caused by exposure to weather conditions and acids'.[47] An extra wire rope is also added to each pole to provide additional support. The clamp is also a wire rope fixed at 45 feet high on the pole so as to fasten the 'flying trapeze' net and equipment for items such as the 'ring of death' or 'sky bath' with the help of two pulleys. The poles become straight only when the weight of these devices balance out, otherwise there can be a slant of about 10 degrees, said Narayanan, the tent master in Royal Circus.[48] A tent master, as the title denotes, is the body and soul of a circus tent. Big companies usually have two tent masters. Tasks such as waterproofing of tents, determining the appropriate ground, setting up and shifting of tents, and daily supervision of tent safety come under the tent master. The safety of thousands of spectators who walk into the circus tent, hundreds of circus artistes, personnel, and animals is all dependent upon the tent master. There are about 10 to 20 assistants closely working with him, apart from others and the local contract labourers. Big companies have two to three tailors exclusively to stitch the tents. Tailors are also hired from outside to stitch according to the instructions of the tent master.

Although the writers on circus in India have hardly acknowledged the significance of the technologies involved in a circus tent so as to write about them, they seem to be aware of the fact that even minor negligence can lead to fatal mishaps. For instance, Sreedharan Champad says that although treachery within the circus ring is unheard of, there has been one dreadful incident in his experience. A tent master who had some squabble with the others intentionally or unintentionally left

---

[47] *Tent Pitching* (Washington: Military Department, 1956), 101.
[48] Interview, Narayanan, Kannur, 9 June 2008.

a screw undone in one of the poles. While an acrobatic performance was going on, the pole came down and instantly killed two innocent spectators.[49]

Sreedharan, who owned Great Gemini Circus, told me that they used to acquire the poles and gates from the iron factories at Meerut and Gorakhpur. The circus company would provide the measurements to the factories. However, the factories cannot always make all the hardware needed by a circus company, because they may not possess the equipment to meet the special requirements. Hence, big circus companies appoint their own blacksmiths, carpenters, and welders. The company ironsmith works in accordance with the idea and requirement given by the company or the artistes for a special item. Apart from him, there is a painter and a carpenter who move along with the company. They have two or three assistants. Many of these skilled labourers come from the caste occupations of their native places. It is significant to note that even in a 'modern' form such as circus the caste structure is live in some way or the other. This shows not only a multilateral exchange of knowledge as modern skills are combined with 'traditional'—read caste—occupations but also the terrifying plasticity of caste. When I visited a major circus company, I was told that the carpenter had gone to the owner's house to make chairs and showcase materials. The artistes told me that it was because the labour in circus is cheaper. The owner could pay some extra 50 or 100 rupees and employ them in his service at half the price compared to the payment drawn by the carpenters outside.

The company carpenter makes tables and equipment for the show, beds, benches, gallery, and so forth. Sunandan K. N., whose study includes the carpenter castes of north Malabar, has pointed out that these caste groups, whose knowing practices were different from the colonial system of knowledge production, cannot be defined under the binary of 'tradition' and 'modernity'.[50] The painter paints all the poles, tables, show equipment, and gates.

---

[49] Sreedharan Champad and Suresh V. K., *Thamb Paranja Jeevitham* [Life told by a tent] (Kottayam: DC Books, 2012), 52.

[50] Sunandan Kizhakke Nedumpally, *Ways of Knowing: Asaris, Nampoothiris and Colonialists in Twentieth Century Malabar, India*, Doctoral dissertation, Emory University, Atlanta, 2012, 3–4.

G(K)ally, Top, and the Central Top

A colourful canvas is one of the most attractive elements of a circus. Earlier, though, the tent cloth used to be made of drab military cotton. The canvas of military troupes used to be of '9 ounce olive-drab sateen cotton cloth'.[51] Impoverished single-pole circuses used sacks as tent material.

The canvas of the tent for a four-poled circus usually contains 20 pieces. This consists of 12 pieces of *g(k)ally* (triangular pieces of tent canvas) and eight pieces of 'top'. Top would usually be at the two sides and at the back and front gates of the tent, and the rest are *g(k)allies*. Below them hang pieces of unbleached cloth (usually different in colour compared to the top and the *g(k)ally)* called *korathuni*. The circle around it that acts as a fence is called *kenaath*. Besides the canvas cloth, attractive colourful cloth pieces are hung at the front and back gateways, usually made of curtain clothes, called *purdah*. Cloth filled with sand in the shape of a ball, called *bori*, acts as weight balance to keep them steady.

Plastic ropes are stitched underneath the canvas cloth to give it support and strength. This part, however, is done by the tent master himself. The wire ropes of the *g(k)allies* and the top, three and two respectively, are tied on the welding of the ring bell. The rectangular top at the topmost part of the circus tent is called the 'central top'. It covers the four king poles. The two extra wire ropes of 300 feet, left free at the time of the erection of poles, are used now to tie and tower the circus tent. A pulley is used to pull the wire ropes to lift the tent up. Long wire ropes are necessary during the un-pitching of the tent, and hence the length of these wire ropes is around 300 metres. A 7-foot bar is set and Ds are fixed at the bar. The pulleys on the poles help pull the tent sideways to form a triangle. The rest of the tent comes to be at a height of 45 feet on the pole, while the central top goes up to 55 feet. Once the tent and the central top have been erected, 110 side poles are erected. Side poles are usually 16 feet in length, and there are six or eight side poles for each king pole. After that, 36 quarter poles are built inside the tent. These are in a ratio of two quarter poles to a king pole. Poles with a height of 36 feet are fixed in a slanted way so that strong winds do not lift up the tents.[52]

---

[51] *Tent Pitching*, 32.

[52] Interview, E. Ravindran.

Ring Bell

The use of the ring bell seems to be a common technique used in all types of tents.[53] The ring bell is an iron circle of about 18 inches width, and within it there are two circles and rods of 1 inch thickness. The borders of the tent cloth are inserted and fastened with a rope in the ring bells. It is put on the pole from the lower side, while the first two pieces are joined and it is attempted to straighten them out. Two Ds are fixed on each side of the ring bell. While the pole is made to stand, wire ropes of approximately 120 feet length are fixed and lowered on which two pulleys are fixed. These wire ropes are some of the longest ropes in the tent as they have to reach the lower end and be tied securely. On this, the four pieces of the tent are spread on the top. It should be noted here that all this work is usually done at night time.[54]

The process of disassembling a tent usually begins a week before the circus company is to shift from a camp. Animal tents, coverings around the ring, extra tents, and decorative clothes are the first to go and would reach the next camp before the major disassembling. During the evening of the last day, while the last show would be still on, this work would be in progress. The audience sitting inside has little clue about the tents and side poles being removed and loaded into trucks. When the show is over, the 'big top' is removed and the king poles are loaded along with the *ravuttees*. People, animals, and equipment move to the next destination in a train or trucks.[55]

Ring

As we have already discussed in Chapter 1, the word 'circus' has a Latin origin and comes from the Greek word *kirkos*, meaning circle, oval, or ring.[56] The etymology itself points to the fact of how important and

[53] See images in *Tent Pitching*, 8–15.

[54] Interview, E. Ravindran; Sreedharan.

[55] Interview, George, Royal Circus, 29 May 2008.

[56] Praveen Walimbe has also observed, 'The word circus has the same root as circle and circumference and therefore also recalls the distinctive environment in which such entertainment is presented.' Walimbe, *The World of Circus* (Pune: Tanaya–Esha, 2003), 3.

central the ring is to a circus; circus is but the circus ring. Hovey Burgess claims that 'the one thing that has remained constant and universal is the diameter of the circus ring, which Astley set at about forty-two feet', and further adds that this was something which gave the maximum balance of centrifugal and centripetal forces to a person riding the horse.[57] However, the Indian circus ring does not seem to agree with this 'universal' measurement and belief. The diameter of the ring in an Indian circus is 45 feet. It is a standard measurement the tent master makes. The radius of the ring is 22.5 feet on each end.[58]

The Rambo Circus programme book claims to have a revolving ring.[59] The circumference of a ring measured like this is marked by painted iron boxes. These equal-sized iron boxes are called *kokkappetti* in Malayalam. This is to separate the performing area from the parading circle for animals and artistes, and also the viewers. (A rope or a line would have done the job, but it seems this is an attractive way to do it.) An interesting thing about the boxes is that they contain colourful images of various circus feats, animal and clown acts. The parading area will be five feet away from the ring and 10 feet from the poles. The parading circle is 5 feet in width so that the performers and animals, such as horses and elephants, can pass by comfortably. Another 5 feet in between is left without digging to give strength to the poles. (When the poles are fixed inside and taken out, the mud in this area is supposed to give it strength). The height of the ring from the ground varies with the nature of the ground, whether it is rocky, sandy, or muddy.[60]

Digging is done according to the nature of the ground; if it is a rocky area, only 4 feet is dug, otherwise 5 feet. The place where the pole is to be positioned is dug for 2.5 feet. Digging the ring also has its peculiarity; it is not a levelled digging, but more often at a 30 feet slope from the gallery side. The mud that is dug out is sloped from 30 feet to 65 feet so that the spectators in the extreme back can have a clear view of the performance in the ring. The soil that is dug from the side of the

[57] Hovey Burgess, 'The Classification of Circus Techniques', *The Drama Review* 18, no. 1 (1974): 66.

[58] Interview, Narayanan.

[59] Rambo Circus programme book, circa 2010, private collection, Sujit Dilip, Pune.

[60] Interview, Narayanan; E. Ravindran.

ring would go to the back, the gallery side.[61] For example, if we are digging 3 feet, we will also distribute the mud to the back side. After that, with the mud the slope is shaped and polished using newspapers. The military system of tent-building made sure that trenches are made nearby their tents: 'When the tent is pitched on heavy soil, clay or a flat rocky surface, a trench should always be dug. When the tent is set up in very sandy soil, which absorbs water as fast as it falls, or when it is located on a mound which slopes off in all directions, a trench may not be necessary.'[62] One can see a trench with an outlet, often made near the *ravuttee*s and the main tent of the circus ring.

The Madras Cinematograph Act (1918) specifies that the chairs and galleries should be arranged in the last phase. The seating in the building is so arranged as not to interfere with free access to the exits.[63] The Madras Cinematograph Act describes rules for building galleries for travelling shows,

Any galleries must be:

a. Strongly built,
b. Provided with access by not less than two stairs or approaches at least 4 feet wide, and
c. Divided into separate blocks by clear gangways at least 4 feet wide running from front to rear at intervals of not more than 30 feet apart.[64]

Ground

A ground could be of different shapes. The elementary aspect is whether it is suitable for the construction of a circus tent with separate tents for artistes and labourers and open tents for the animals. A tent master should have the expertise to foresee whether he would be able to include all the required tents within the available space, where the elephants or horses could be tied, where the women's quarters could be set up, or where the toilets for the staff and spectators could be

---

[61] Interview, George.

[62] *Tent Pitching*, 94.

[63] Notification, Cinematograph Act, 1918, 25 June 1920, *TSR*, List-1, File no. 2579, Regional Archives, Kozhikode.

[64] Notification, Cinematograph Act, 1918, 11 May 1922, *TSR*, List-1, File no. 2596, Regional Archives, Kozhikode (hereafter, 'Cinematograph, 2596').

constructed.[65] If the manager who books the ground for the company has any doubts regarding the size of the ground, he would request the owner to send the tent master to have a look.[66] It is up to the tent master to finalize if the ground could be of use. In usual cases, the tent master is sent only 15 days in advance along with the necessary articles. The next set would be the publicity group, extra tents, wooden planks, iron cables, and so on.

But, of course, the primary decision is where the 'big top' could be built. The next priority is whether the tents for animals and humans could be built adjacent to it. Then, his helpers (tent boys/canvas men, also referred to as ring boys) mark the identified positions of the king poles with iron rods. The book on pitching the military tent repeatedly instructs that the ground plan should be examined perfectly before pitching the tent. It directs that the ground for military tents should be made level and free from projecting tree roots and rocks.[67] Though circus tents are not built on mountains or the riverside, as would military tents often be, they keep an eye on the character of the ground site nonetheless. However, circus companies do occasionally play in high-range towns, such as Shillong in the Khasi hills or Kattappana in the Western Ghats.[68] Gopal Yadav and his team members of Gemini Circus told me that local people would always gather to see them work and turn the empty ground into a canvas town. Janet M. Davis notes the curiosity of audience groups to see the tents in progress and the technological changes in labour being replaced by machines in United States of America:

Audience members travelled ... just to observe how circus workers (aided by horses and elephants) created a magical movable city on an empty lot. At the turn of the century ... human–animal labor still performed virtually all the on-site jobs, before gasoline-engine stake drivers and other motorized machines began replacing some of the human labor in 1910–20. The creation of the tented city was a thrilling physical feat in which human labor functioned as a seemingly seamless corporate body.[69]

[65] Interview, E. Ravindran.

[66] Interview, Madhu, Jumbo Circus, 12 April 2009.

[67] *Tent Pitching*, 49, 57, 93.

[68] Interview, Sukumaran.

[69] Janet M. Davis, *The Circus Age: Culture & Society Under the American Big Top* (Chapel Hill: University of North Carolina Press, 2002), 67.

In his work on the American circuses of late nineteenth century, Noel Daniel observes that construction is done with extraordinary precision and speed, and in front of hundreds of townspeople:

> While the number of tents depended upon the size of the circus, the basic construction of the tents was similar. The huge center poles travelled with the circus on specially built extra-long wagons. … Ropes were attached to various sections of the canvas tent and poles, and then attached to stakes. Finally the canvas roof was raised by a bale ring around the centre poles and then attached to stakes. Finally, the canvas roof was raised by a bale ring around the centre poles. Bleachers were erected, chairs unfolded, animals unloaded, from the wagons or trains and exercised and fed.

It is also interesting to note that, unlike in Indian circuses where circus elephants were seldom used in this process, in the United States of America the circus elephants 'unroll[ed] the massive heaps of canvas and move[d] the tent poles'.[70] S. Narayanan observes, 'To erect the tent, fixing the galleries, leveling the ground and to pitch their own living tents within a day on arrival is a herculean task. Accidents are bound to happen.'[71]

Many circus labourers told me that manual labour in circus is cheaper. A job that would need 10 to 12 men in any other workspace would be done with 5 to 6 people in the tent, that too for lower wages. To pitch a single-pole military tent, the approximate time required is 90 minutes and manpower is 9 men.[72] It takes only 2 to 3 hours to build a circus tent, which may be triple the size of a medium-sized military tent of habitation. The programme book of Kamala Circus notes about the spectacle:

> The greater feat is the 'pull down' and 'pitch up' of the Big Top. It is the trailers and the caravan and the cages and all the paraphernalia of the circus items. The 'pull down' and the 'pitch up' require as much split second timing as the feats. For when the circus decides to take to the road and open in the next town it has to pack up in record time at the place of showing and unpack in as record a time to keep the date with the new town.[73]

[70] Noel Daniel, *The Circus, 1870s–1950s* (Los Angeles: Taschen, 2008), 428.

[71] S. Narayanan, 'Survey of Circus in India', *Circus Worker* 1, no. 5 (August 1980e): 13.

[72] *Tent Pitching*, 11.

[73] Kamala Circus programme book, circa 1955, private collection, Shyamala Shirolker, Pune.

Belief and Technology

A very interesting aspect of tent construction is the blend of 'belief' with 'technology'. The day on which the first plank is laid on the ground is very important. It should be a 'good' day, an auspicious day in the astrological calendar. Wednesday, Thursday, and Friday are considered as most auspicious to start the work on tents in a new ground. But it varies with each circus company and its owner, says E. Ravindran of Gemini circus.

> There are circuses which even let the pole rise on Tuesdays, supposed to be 'worst', but in Gemini circus and all other circuses owned by Sankarettan[74] it is mostly on Wednesdays, if not on Monday, Sunday and other days, but never on Tuesdays and Saturdays.

Usually on Wednesdays, the *rahukalam* (inauspicious time by Malayalam calendar) is from 12 to 1 o' clock. In Gemini Circus, after 1.30 p.m., the pole is erected and the tent spread, while the opening of the circus takes place on Fridays. There is a puja before each opening in each camp. Any mosque, church, or temple nearby is presented with offerings. The circus people would always make a detailed enquiry about the religious places of the town in which they will be performing. For example, 'if the camp is in Thalassery town, Mattaambram mosque, Thiruvanhad temple, Andalur Kavu are places the necessary offerings are made', confirms Ravindran.[75] It should be noted here that Thiruvanhad temple is one of the well-known upper-caste temples, while Andalur Kavu is famed as a Thiyya Kavu, and the Mattambram mosque is one of the oldest mosques in the town.

Pujas or gifts, such as a *nilavilakku* (ceremonial oil lamp), in the name of the company are the common offerings made. Five coconuts are broken as an offering, one each to the four poles and the ring. *Kumkum* is applied on the poles, and laddu, bananas, and *kumkum* are distributed among the labourers. *Karppuram* (camphor) is burnt as another offering to God. On the opening day, another five coconuts are broken after the puja. The interesting fact is that the circuses owned by Muslims also

---

[74] One of the most senior circus owners in India who used to own three circus companies—Gemini, Jumbo, and Royal.

[75] Interview, E. Ravindran.

follow these 'Hindu' practices. This assorted nature and cross-cultural paradigm could be seen in almost all the activities of the circus people. In the context of the jute mill factory workers in Calcutta, Dipesh Chakrabarty describes the sacrifices and pujas offered to machines:

> In fact, the worker's relationship to the machine, instead of being mediated through a technical knowledge, was mediated through the North Indian peasant's conception of his tools, whereby the tools often took on magical and godly qualities. A religious outlook rather than 'science' determined this relationship, with the difference that in a jute mill, the laborer's tools were far more powerful and malign than the peasant's implements and were capable of taking lives at the shortest notice.

He argues that the 'man-machine relationship in a factory always involves culture and a techno-economic argument overlooks this'.[76] Another interesting element would be the relations of the circus tent with other objects, such as the pole or the ring; it is, in fact, all these that constitute the tent and also the obvious object–human relationships, deciding the beliefs and lives of the human actants.

The Circus Is Tenting

As pointed out earlier, it is the circus manager who would first visit the proposed camping sites. Once he finds a suitable ground, he would seek permission in writing from the district collector or the municipal chairperson for camping and obtain a 'no objection' certificate from the sanitary and electrical engineers of the local administration.[77] One of the two main objectives of the Cinematograph Act in India had been the licensing of cinema houses (the other, of course, the censoring and certification of films).[78] The Cinematograph Acts show that such licences were necessary for all touring entertainments. But Acts particularly referring to circus shows and tents do not seem to exist. It is such passing references as 'itinerant', 'travelling shows', or 'touring industries' that include circus shows.

---

[76] Dipesh Chakrabarty, *Rethinking Working Class History: Bengal, 1890–1940* (New Jersey: Princeton University Press, 2000), 89, 90.

[77] Interview, Madhu and Sahadevan, Jumbo Circus, 12 April 2009.

[78] Hrishikesh Mukherjee, *Censorship of Films* (Pune: Board of Extra-mural Studies, University of Pune, 1982), 4.

Mitavadi (September 1917) notes that a law would be enacted in the next Indian Legislature Assembly to be held at Shimla, stating that bioscope companies could only operate with licences and nothing without government permission should be shown. *Mathrubhumi* (11 January 1924) and *MM* (15 April 1911) show the regulatory licences and warning orders given to theatre groups. 'The Ernakulam Municipality has decided that the license of any drama, cinema or circus group who perform anything that is detrimental to the morality of the audience will be canceled' (*Mathrubhumi*, 10 May 1924). A letter from J. F. Hall, additional district magistrate, Malabar, to the secretary to the government, judicial department, states that under the Madras Presidency Cinematograph Act, the manager of every such cinema company must give to the district magistrate 'not less than seven clear days' notice in writing' every time he proposes to change the place in which his performances are to be given; 'these companies move from place to place throughout the district and do not stay for so long in any one town or village'. The letter from E. J. W. Greenwood, electric inspector to the joint secretary, Public Works Department (PWD), points out that this notice is necessary for 'efficient police control'. The electric inspector here mentions that the continuous movement of the cinema companies is creating problems for him. The letter also mentions that 'the intention of the Act and the Govt. order seems to be that each plant should be examined by the Electric Inspector and that in case he reports unfavourably the District Magistrate may ... request the local Govt. to issue an order under section 34 (2) of the Act'.[79] The licence is granted, subject to the provisions of the same Act of 1918 and the rules made thereunder.[80] It is evident from these communications that the state has always found it difficult to 'control' these constantly moving tents. James Scott points out that for communities which were out of the state's bounds, the latter formulated its own clever strategies to discriminate and marginalize.[81] He says that 'everything about these

[79] Notification, Cinematograph Act, 1917, 18 January 1917, *TSR*, List-1, File no. 2559, Regional Archives, Kozhikode.

[80] Cinematograph, 2596.

[81] James Scott, 'The State and People Who Move or Why Civilizations Can't Climb Hills', lecture delivered at Indian Habitat Centre, New Delhi, 19 December 2008.

people's livelihood, social organization and ideologies and (more controversially) even their largely oral cultures, can be read as strategic positioning designed to keep the state at arm's length'.[82] I feel this is particularly relevant in the case of the circus community. Their constant movement has enabled them to often slip away from the fists of legality. But this has, in turn, contributed to some extent to its depiction as a realm of all kinds of exploitation.

Many laws concerning touring tents have become outdated now, especially in a context where circus might be the only industry which widely makes use of tents. Some files in the Kozhikode Regional Archives dealing with cinematic shows also throw light upon the emergence of permanent auditoriums and the instructions given to theatre owners in the matter of building theatres.[83] The traveling cinema companies had to get a 'clearance notice' which the circus people have to do even now to set up show at a place.

If the ground is owned by a private party, the job is easier, managers say. If it is under the municipality, they have to wait till the municipality members meet to take a decision. Seeking support from the political party in power for fast and favourable decisions is the usual method. Sometimes, not only the leaders in power but also those from the opposition would come in handy.[84] It should be noted here how circus thrives on conferring the legal formalities of the state and the competitive relationship of the political parties. More than a century ago, *MM* (6 June 1909) reported that since the collector did not give permission to pitch their tent, a circus company was running its show at the Jubilee Town Hall without the horse items. Another report states that when the *peshkar* (chief revenue officer) refused to give permission to play at Kanjirappalli, Bombay Grand Circus telegrammed the *divan* (minister to the ruler in the erstwhile princely states) and sought permission (*MM*, 28 December 1901). Things have not changed much for circus even after a century.

No objection certificates from the police and electrical inspectors are compulsory. The managers say that the opening day of a camp is an

---

[82] James Scott, *The Art of Not Being Governed: An Anarchic History of Upland Southeast Asia* (New Haven: Yale University Press, 2009), x.

[83] Notification, Cinematograph Act, 1918, proceedings of the Board of Revenue, R-Dis file no. 7178/21, 10 September 1921, Regional Archives, Kozhikode.

[84] Interview, Sahadevan and Mohandas, Jumbo Circus, 14 April 2009.

edgy day for them as certificates of the electrical inspector and the PWD can be attained only then. The electrical inspector and the PWD officers are driven in the car in the morning itself. While the latter would check the gallery and the 'building', the former would examine the electrical connections in the camp.[85]

Sanitation

Most circus people whom I interviewed complained that circuses lacked the necessary sanitary facilities. In towns and cities, water tanks are bought from the municipal water authority. The circus camp could have their lines connected to the municipal or corporation drainage system only if the camping site is nearby those lines. When the plan of the ground is given, the sanitary officials provide information on the position of drainage pipelines. These connections and the types of toilets and bathrooms are checked by the sanitary inspectors. If it is a ground without drainage lines nearby, a deep pit is dug and concrete slab pieces are used to cover it. When the tent is dismantled after the show season, the excreta is covered with mud to compost. 'But the real adversary is the rain. All these are in the ground and when the water level comes up ... and we are living here only,' says Shobha.[86] (When I went to Gemini Circus in Kottayam in 2010 for fieldwork, it was raining heavily and I noticed the terrible conditions with dirt, urine, and muddy water flowing together all over the ground.) In metro cities, circus companies follow the flush-out toilet system. Earlier, 'scavengers' used to be hired by the companies from the localities they visited, and big companies would mostly have a 'scavenger' accompanying them. Although manual scavenging, one of the most dehumanizing occupations imposed and sanctioned by the caste system, has been banned by the law it still exists in many parts of the country.

Office Administration

Office administration of a circus company is by and large a male domain. This department consists of accountants, cashiers, ticket-in-charges,

---

[85] Interview, Manoharan, Jumbo Circus, 14 April 2009.
[86] Interview, Shobha, Gemini Circus, 19 June 2012.

store officers, and clerks. The programme book of Jumbo Circus includes managers, assistant managers, wardens of company girls, and booking assistants under office administration.[87] Around 30 people come under this division, among whom only one of the wardens of the girls' hostel is a female. Reservations and advanced bookings are done in the office via phone and in person. The ticket-in-charge and his two to three assistants take care of ticket-selling during the peak hours of the show. The ticket-in-charge makes sure that no malpractices happen while selling and that the cash boxes are safe until the counters are closed. When the entertainment tax for circus was in force, it was his duty to stamp and tally the tickets in accordance with the rules: 'Tax was generally paid by the sale of tickets of admission. So, they used to be stamped to show that the tax had been paid.'[88] It was a known secret at that time that tickets with the same numbers used to be repeated to cheat the authorities. Entertainment tax was levied in India from 1922 'on performances in which the performers were actually present and their words or actions constituted the entertainment (for example, a play, concert, lecture or circus)'.[89] On constant request by circus owners of the Indian Circus Federation, circus was exempted from entertainment tax when Indira Gandhi was the prime minister.[90] *Kerala Kaumudi* (6 February 1978) reports that the chief executive councillor, Kedarnath Sahni, declared that circuses are spared from paying the entertainment tax in Delhi. Entertainment taxation is decided by each state government, and over the years circus has been exempted from this in all states in India.

Publicity-in-charge

For a new camp, the publicity group of a big circus company reaches the town about two weeks in advance, making an estimate of the

[87] Jumbo Circus programme book, circa 2007, private collection, E. Ravindran, Eranjoli.

[88] Interview, Shivaprasad, Royal Circus, 18 May 2008.

[89] Subhash P. Khamkar, *Entertainment Tax in Maharashtra State: Its Economic Impact and Analysis*, Doctoral dissertation, University of Mumbai, Maharashtra, 2000, 22.

[90] Interview, Sujit Dilip.

population and the span of the town. If it is a town area and the camping is to be for 30 to 40 days, posters are put up and announcements are made in a radius of approximately 6 kilometres.

Usually, announcers are hired locally. In fact, circuses have their own announcers in every locality who are hired whenever they reach there. Kareem from Thalassery and Lohithakshan from Kunnamkulam are old-time circus announcers. 'Thankathin varnna shobhayaarnna thaliru polatha tharuni manikal, minnal pinarinte vegathayil thakitam mariyunna kazhcha kaanuvan [To see the golden-coloured tender beauties somersaulting with lightning speed]', thus goes the usual announcement hinting at sexuality and the female body. Kareem says that it was even more 'vulgar' earlier and students used to walk away with embarrassed faces while he announced near the colleges, but they would definitely come for the evening show. The major difficulty a new announcer has to face is to know each and every circus item and the descriptions to be given in ornamental rhetoric. Kareem received 12 rupees a day in 1972, which is now 250 rupees. He is almost 80 now, but his voice remains youthful. He has also been recording cassettes for circuses.[91] The publicity-in-charge pays the local bus and auto owners to put up boards and vehicle stickers on them. Legally, they have to attain permission from the Regional Transport Office, but the managers tactfully deal with such formalities. Advertisements are published in the local editions of major newspapers.

Lighting

As mentioned earlier, the managers would obtain a 'no objection' certificate from the electrical engineers before the show opened. The line superintendent would check the electrical connections and issue a certificate. All companies have a team of electricians. Harish, the main electrician of Royal Circus, told me that they need to be alert all the time as a short circuit can destroy the whole tent area in no time. All connections are secured under the ground with the use of pipes as soon as the tent master finishes his job.[92]

[91] Interview, Kareem, Galaxy Circus, 23 March 2007.
[92] Interview, Harish, Royal Circus, 12 June 2008.

Electricians operate the lighting arrangements for each item. The lighting outside the tent is also done by them. Specific lights are switched on for particular items, and lights with coloured papers as filters are used for the desired effect. For example, for an item such as the fire dance, all lights should be switched off. It is important that they put the surroundings in complete darkness.[93] The number of lights varies according to the size of the camp. In earlier times, petromax lights were used in the circus rings. Three or four lights used to be put at the centre and also at the sides where the performance happens. During that time, a single person was allotted the charge of lighting.[94]

Harish has not received any formal training in electrical work. He learnt the trade watching his supervisor, an electrician, in Rambo Circus where he began as a ring boy and later assisted him. He has been working in Royal Circus for the past 12 years. He ran away from home and joined the circus. The major difference he finds nowadays is that earlier, the electricians could do things on their own, but now they are supposed to do everything in accordance with the law, as they are held responsible for any mishap that might occur. However, it is not that laws were not in place during earlier times.

Rules for travelling cinematograph shows mention the lighting arrangements inside the tent. The rules also say that smoking and carrying inflammable articles are prohibited within the tent, and that the operator should make sure that all cables, leads, connections, and resistances are in proper working order before the commencement of each performance. We can see in circuses, as per the rules, general lighting is capable of being controlled from inside and outside, and away from the enclosure. As per the Cinematograph Act, every cinematograph installation should be inspected by the government electrical inspector, who would then issue a licence. This too is obliged by the circus companies. In Madras, before the issue of licences, the commissioner of police, Madras city, and the district magistrate were officially informed.[95]

---

[93] Interview, Rajan, Gemini Circus, 19 July 2012.
[94] Interview, Harish.
[95] Cinematograph, 2596.

Tent Fire

The major hazards the circus people have to confront are storms, fires, and rain. During a storm, the first protective measure they take is to tighten immediately the lines on the tent and close all possible corners. If the wind is too strong, they spread the canvas on the ground. Sometimes during rainfall the tent absorbs so much water that it becomes too heavy for the canvas men to carry it, remembers Kalicharan.[96] Although they are fire-proof, they do burn: 'they usually do not burst into flame, but smolder and char'.[97] The Madras Cinematograph Act clearly defines the measures to be taken to prevent fire in a tent. A bucket of dry sand and a portable fire extinguisher should be kept in the enclosure. Six buckets of water and four portable fire extinguishers are kept in an auditorium. One can see the red buckets of sand and water kept orderly in any circus ring. It is also mentioned in the notification that these appliances should be so disposed as to be readily available for use, and that the buckets should have round bottoms with handles and shall be capable of holding at least two gallons of water. They should be painted red with the word 'Fire' on them in large black letters in English and the vernacular. It is also mentioned in the rule that before the commencement of each performance the cinematograph operator shall satisfy himself that the fire appliances in the enclosure are in working order. One or more persons, as may be necessary, shall be specifically nominated to have charge of the fire appliances in the auditorium during a performance.[98] In both circus and cinematograph exhibitions, the opening is fitted with a screen of fire-resisting material.

Waterproofing

Rain is a constant threat to circus tents. Waterproofing is the only long-term solution. Waterproofed canvases of earlier times were so heavy that it needed many people to lift up and carry them. Although tents are made water repellent, rain causes the canvas and lines to shrink,

[96] Interview, Kalicharan, Galaxy Circus, 18 March 2007.
[97] *Tent Pitching*, 99.
[98] Cinematograph, 2596.

and the shrinkage leads to tearing.[99] The only solution to this problem for both military and circus troupes was to loosen the tent lines sufficiently so that they hardly became tight. In order to compensate for this shrinkage, they always left an extra free swing of tent cloth at the eaves and edges. But nowadays, cotton tarpaulins with a thin plastic coating are used.[100] Canvas, though lighter and cheaper, wears out after four to six seasons. So, plastic tents, according to David Jamieson and Sandy Davidson, which have a prolonged life are being used by the Cannobio organization of Milan, which has produced dozens of big tops.[101] The tent masters of Royal and Jumbo Circuses spoke to me at length about the method of using wax and kerosene oil in a ratio of 1:2 to waterproof their tents. The use of kerosene or fuel usually depended on the economy and size of the circus. Petrol or diesel contained the element of iron, which made the tent cloth rust. So, aviation fuel was used by big circuses who could afford it.

A Tent Tragedy

The tragic end of Kelappettan,[102] a renowned tent master in Kamala Three Ring Circus who was an expert in making waterproof canvas, needs to be mentioned here. Kelappettan had spent the prime part of his life stitching tents and lifting poles in the circus. Kelappettan had built a tent with a whopping capacity of around 12,000 for Kamala Circus. His skills impressed the legendary Professor Damodaran, the owner of Kamala Circus, so much that Kelappettan was sent to China to learn the Chinese style of cutting tents. In 1955, K. S. Menon, the owner of Bharat[103]

[99] Interview, Gopal Yadav, Gemini Circus, 23 June 2009.

[100] Interview, Ashok Kumar C. C., Thalassery, 17 February 2011.

[101] Jamieson and Davidson, *The Love of the Circus*, 90.

[102] The intimacy and reverence of 'ettan' (elder brother), like 'dada', shows the communitarian feelings within the tent. We can see artistes referring to many of their known predecessors in the field adding 'ettan' to their names, at the same time, referring to circus gurus such as Keeleri Kunhikannan and Ambu by adding 'teacher' and 'master' to their names.

[103] In Gemini Sankaran's memory, the incident takes place in Gemini Circus in Kurnool, Karnataka. According to him, the fire must have started from a discarded cigar; Sankaran and Madai, *Malakkam Mariyunna Jeevitham* [Somersaulting life] (Kottayam: DC Books, 2012), 69–70.

Circus, had come to Delhi for the Indian Circus Federation's meeting of circus owners. He desperately needed Kelappettan's services and requested Professor Damodaran for him. Bharath Circus had four new canvases perfectly stitched, but needed waterproofing. It was a tough task that required the master because the waterproofing work had to be done before sunrise. Kelappetten took up the challenging assignment. In the wee hours he began work, melting hot wax to perfection. While pouring the hot wax into the fuel with utmost care, he must have had no idea what destiny had in store for him. Kelappettan was busy working on the canvas. Accidents and mishaps were not unfamiliar to him; he had lost a leg under the train engine of Kamala Circus. But that day, at Bharath Circus, was irreparably tragic. A fire broke out and spread all of a sudden, burning Kelappettan to death along with his most beloved items, the tents.[104]

The Venus Fire

The fire that engulfed Venus Circus in 1981 at Bangalore while the show was going on was the most horrible circus tragedy in India to date.[105] On 7 February, Venus Circus had arranged a matinee show with special discount rates for the school children in the city. The circus camp was scheduled to move to Krishnagiri two days later. Approximately 2,000 school children from various schools accompanied by their teachers attended this matinee. By 6.30 p.m., the show ended and while the spectators were leaving the tent, the tragedy struck: 'The cause of the fire was speculated to be a discarded cigarette or an electric short circuit.'[106] Sixty-six people lost their lives. *New York Times* (9 February 1981) reports that at least 500 people were critically injured. Except for a hippopotamus, all the animals—including 17 lions, 10 elephants, 9 horses,

[104] Interview, Sreedharan M.

[105] 'The worst fire in the circus history [which] totally consumed the big top, eventually killing 169 people and injuring 682' had been 'on July 6, 1944, while 8,000 people gathered in Hartford, Connecticut under the big top of the Ringling Brothers, Barnum and Bailey.' Available at http://www.tcr.org/tcr/essays/Web_Hartford.pdf, last accessed on 23 November 2012.

[106] Available at http://en.wikipedia.org/wiki/1981_Bangalore_circus_fire, last accessed on 23 November 2012.

7 dogs, and a bear—were saved from the flames. Another report notes that '[s]urvivors said the fire quickly spread through the canvas top and wooden bleachers' (*Lakeland Ledger*, 10 February 1981). *Kalakaumudi* reports from the accident site: 'The ground between Platform Road and Mirage Line was in [*sic*] not at all suitable for tenting the circus. There are heaps of metal for the construction of a railway quarters. Had the circus been in a much more spacious and open site there would have been more exits for the people to flee'.[107]

Some big companies have shifted to advanced material and technologies which are supposedly safer. But for small companies, these are not yet viable and accidents still happen. For instance, the circus tent of New Golden Circus during the last show at Chunabhatti went up in flames (*TOI*, 30 October 2011) and the tent of Crown Circus, made of cotton, was destroyed in a fire in Mullipalayam on Bangalore Road (The *Hindu*, 8 November 2012). The circus labour union leaders point to possibilities of fraud in many such minor mishaps, which they allege is the handiwork of the proprietors to cheat the insurance companies.

Fireproof Tents

Sujit Dilip, owner of Rambo Circus, claims that they introduced fireproof tents in India in 2009, just as they introduced air-conditioning in 1992.[108] The material cost was INR 45 lakhs and the tent was erected at about INR 1 crore (*Indian Express*, 26 February 2012). The programme book of Rambo Circus claims it has 'the first self custom built tent in India'.

> The tent was made in 2009 with the help of Mr. Bruno Loyale, Magic circus of Samoa and it was magnificent experience for all our tent masters as they have always stitched the cotton tent. It is the largest tent having 210 Ft. diameter with four king poles, 16 queen poles, and 32 poles and 136 side poles. It helps our air conditioning system as it is black out and it is India's 1st fire proof tent. The tent has a capacity of 4500 audiences.[109]

[107] Surendran, 'Thambil Maranam Vithacha Theenaambukal' [The fire flames which sow death in the tent], *Kalakaumudi* (287) (February 1981): 4.

[108] Interview, Sujit Dilip.

[109] Rambo Circus programme book, circa 2010, private collection, Sujit Dilip, Pune.

The tent master of Royal Circus, Narayanan, said that their circus tent costs about INR 2.5 lakhs with an approximate rate of INR 85 per metre, thus INR 4,500 per tent piece.[110] Since there had been heavy rains in previous camps in various places in Kerala, they were unable to do the waterproofing and instead opted for tarpaulins worth INR 106,000. With this they could manage for about six months in the rain. But waterproofed tents have a longer life.

Trucks are used to load and unload the circus tent; a truck each for tents, poles, pipes, and two gallery sides. For the camp at Kannur, where I visited them, Narayanan master and his crew had come 18 days before the opening. They cleaned and marked the assigned ground with lime before the levelling work began. Usually, local contract labourers are hired to do such work. Narayanan (who is addressed as 'Narayanan Master' by everyone in the circus, including the owner) has six assistants who always accompany him. Narayanan master started his career at Hercules Circus in 1954, doing various jobs. He has 18 years of experience as a tent master in Gemini Circus and has also served for the same management at Vahini and Jumbo Circuses. He has also worked for Amar, Rayman, and Rambo Circuses. He was invited to Rayman Circus to make tents while he was working for Royal Circus. It is a usual practice amongst circus companies to use the expertise of experienced tent masters of other companies.

Spatial Structure of a Circus Tent

The gate has at least three security guards who work in shifts. Usually, at both ends of the gate, there are boards with the timings of the three shows, and ticket counters with ticket rates. About two hours before the show begins, recorded music is played on high volume to attract the attention of the town's people. The disc jockey collects and plays both popular Hindi and regional film music. For ticket reservations and related enquiries, one or two ticket staff is often in or nearby the counters almost all the time. No outsiders are allowed inside the circus tent without permission before or after the show timings.

---

[110] Interview, Narayanan.

Posters

One cannot enter the premises of a big circus company without noticing the big colourful posters, which used to be on paper and are nowadays in flex print. Earlier, there used to be metal boards with painted pictures. The images displayed would be of the circus numbers—animals in performance, colourfully made-up clowns, and women. Flex posters of the present-day big circuses are double the life-size and are pasted onto wooden boards and fixed on the grilled iron gates.

Posters and notices pasted around a town announce the upcoming camp. These are printed in Shivakashi, Tamil Nadu. Irulappan's and Taskin's families have been traditionally printing for circus companies, especially Gemini, Jumbo, and Royal. Nowadays, circus companies fax or email the details of the camp to them and they deliver the materials on time. There are also posters that can be used anywhere. The date, camp, and timings are pasted on them accordingly. These are called 'location posters'. For grand camps, they print the posters along with the location of the camp. Besides these are the telephone stickers and vehicle stickers. All of these are printed in both English and the language of the region where the camp is set up.

Once we cross the gate, we enter the 'red carpet area'. It is a spacious lounge area where long coir mats (often) of red colour are spread. One would find the managers reading newspapers, counting cash, or relaxing in the lounge. The moment we step inside the circus tent, the air changes, literally and figuratively, and we find ourselves in a multilingual, cross-cultural human space with horse, camel, and elephant stables on both sides. The strong smell of animals, palm leaves, hay, and excreta surrounds us. Animal tents, which are open and built in the spacious yard, are our first sight; it serves a definite purpose—the animals of the circus mark its glory. Before the wild animal ban in 1991, this animal space would be more populated with various species, a mini-zoo with tigers, lions, chimpanzees, panthers, and leopards lined up all the way around to the back of the tent. In earlier times, tickets were sold to visit this 'zoo' during non-show timings. Beyond the animal world are the living tents or *ravuttees*.

Ravuttees

The cottage tents for habitation are referred to by circus people as *ravuttees*. They are A-shaped tents. They are built when the work for the major tent for performance is done with. This also comes under the work of the company tent master. The difference in the living tents more or less reflects the status of the inhabitant: the biggest and finest *ravuttees* would be those of the owner or the proprietor. Some owners choose to live in their tents while others rent rooms in hotels. The owner of Great Bombay Circus recollected his father's days when they used to stay at the Oberoi Grand Hotel in Calcutta when the circus camped there.[111] Next in line would be those of managers, if at all they chose to live in tents. The managers and the pricey male artistes would usually rent hotel rooms, for which the company paid.

The quarters for single women are usually the largest living tents in the circus. These quarters are guarded and separated with iron-plate walls, all of these arranged in a circular manner, and a guard is usually appointed at night. A company girl is not allowed to go out of the circus premises and interact with male artistes and labourers. Usually, an elderly woman is appointed as the caretaker.

Women live in a single tent with single beds. Children also share the quarters, trained and guarded by the grown-ups. Many old women artistes I interviewed fondly remembered those good old days where 60 to 75 girls and children lived in the single women quarters, spending the leisure time playing cards and carrom. They did the washing for the little ones, and looked after the sick ones and accident victims. Another favourite pastime in the single women quarters was doing embroidery works on their costumes.

This could be one reason why many retired circus women choose embroidering and tailoring as a profession back home. However, the stitching of these clothes is done by professional tailors appointed by the company. A company might also make use of the expertise of popular tailors in other circuses, invited as guests for a period of two to three months.[112]

[111] Interview, Dilipnath.
[112] Interview, Velayudhan, Rajkamal Circus, 12 May 2010.

Image 3.2   Women's Quarters, Great Bombay Circus, circa 1970
Source: Private collection of Pushpa.

Married couples are provided separate tents of their own. These are called 'family tents', or simply 'family'. There are small televisions, stoves and utensils for cooking, and a bed for two to four people. The equipment for various performances are usually kept inside the family tents of artistes. Children playing around is a familiar sight near the family tents. In early circuses, family troupes with parents and children as performers were common.

Attached to the quarters for single women is the 'company girls' mess' (also known as the 'artistes' mess') where all company girls, male artistes, and family members have food. Managers and proprietors also take food from here when they prefer. Their food is substantially different from the food provided to the labourers. Earlier, chicken or mutton used to be part of their diet every two days or at the weekends, while eggs and milk formed a compulsory part of their everyday meal. The labourers are provided with only simple *daal* and rice. In small circuses of earlier times, artistes used to make food for themselves, while big companies had cooks for the company artistes and labourers separately. In these single- and double-pole circuses, charges were seldom given to somebody in the company to cook rice, while the rest of the artistes and labourers were supposed to cook on their own.[113] The circus party gives contracts to meat, vegetable, and grocery sellers in the local markets. The ownership of the company usually determines the region of the menu. The tents used as kitchens are also A-shaped like the *ravuttee*s. They are often made of cheap military cotton. It is worth mentioning that 'Bhayyaji's [elder brother's] mess' in Gemini Circus was once famed among the circus people. Bhayyaji, who is 94 now, began his circus mess career at the age of 10, and has been running the artistes' mess for more than 60 years.[114] The mess was so popular with the food and the way he served it that he became Bhayyaji for everyone, and his kitchen became 'Bhayyaji's mess'. He still moves with Gemini Circus long after his retirement and is warmly looked after by his colleagues.

Then there are tents of tent masters, animal trainers, their assistants, electricians, band staff, tailors, generator operators, a staff mess, and the mess staff, which are on either side of the main circus tent. The masters usually have their own living space, while the assistants share tents. On the right side would be the tents of carpenters, ironsmiths, and ring boys. The most insignificant tents are those of the labourers. It should also be noted that labourers hardly bring their family along, as the artistes do. S. Narayanan observes the deplorable circus tents of labourers: '[A]dult persons of both sexes married and unmarried huddled together in a small tent maximum (20' × 15') size' and 'workers are overcrowded in tents without any hygiene and sanitation, it becomes the breeding place of all those epidemics'.[115]

In between or near the family and the company girls' quarters are attached toilets and bathrooms for women. Near the family and labourers' quarters are the men's toilets. Outside the ring, there will be only a few urinals for the spectators. It seems that living tents of a similar type were used by the British military troupes: 'The tent is an A- shaped, square-ended, rectangular tent. ... Both sections [back and field] have a similar contour, sloping gently to each side of a central ridge.'[116]

---

[113] Interview, Leela.

[114] Interview, Bhayyaji, Gemini Circus, 23 June 2012.

[115] S. Narayanan, 'Survey of Circus in India', 13.

[116] *Tent Pitching*, 54.

Circus Flavours

Let us continue with our walk through the circus tent. Circus arenas around the world have their peculiar gastronomic aromas, differing according to the place. One cannot get away from the delightful fragrance of popcorn, green chilly *bajji*s (fritters), ice-creams, *kurkure*s (masala munchies), and fried peanuts. An array of cold and hot beverages would also be there to wash down these delicacies.[117] The canteen vendors would roam around the tent doing brisk business. Circus canteens, also made in tents, are usually stationed outside the main gate or at the corners to the convenience of the circus-goers and the staff. Running the canteen in major cities, such as Madras, Calcutta, Bangalore, and Delhi, is a flourishing business for which canteen contract parties from different regions look forward to. The proprietor would collect good money by bargaining with and sealing contracts to those who offer the most. Sometimes though, they run the business as a tradition, as in Royal Circus. However, all the arrangements and positions mentioned above are made in accordance with the size and availability of the ground. Local street hawkers would find business around the outer walls of the camp.

Seating Arrangement

Crossing the brightly coloured silk purdahs on either side, we enter the ring through a smoothened passage that leads to the performing arena. The name of the circus is embroidered on the purdahs in golden or silver lettering. The smooth passage, often referred to as the 'front gate', has descending steps leading to the seats, first- and second-class chairs, and the gallery.[118] Earlier, there were no second-class chairs, only

---

[117] Bailey, one of the protagonists of the novel *The Night Circus*, bonds with the mysterious 'Circus of Dreams' through the mesmerizing smells and tastes the tents emanate, of 'apples dipped in caramel so dark they appeared almost darkened but remained light and crisp and sweet, Chocolate bats with impossibly delicate wings [and] the most delicious cider Bailey had ever tasted'; Erin Morgenstern, *The Night Circus*, 50.

[118] *Mathrubhumi* (10 April 1923) reports an accident during a drama performance due to the collapsing of a gallery where more than 400 people were seated.

'peanut-crunching groundlings' who sat on the ground, reminding one of the Shakespearean theatre. Performers enter the arena through the back gate at the other end of the ring, also covered with purdahs. On the passage to the ring, we can see the mud slope made for motor-jumping feats.

An exclusive section with a few chairs is cordoned off with a cloth for the VIP spectators. Earlier, cloth coverings were used to demarcate the space for lady spectators, especially in certain parts of north India.[119] A notice of Grand Kerala Circus, an early twentieth-century company, mentions: 'Special seating arrangements have been made for ladies'. It is customary among circus owners to invite the dignitaries of the place for the opening ceremony. Legislators, collectors, police officers, municipal chairpersons, judicial officials, journalists, electrical and sanitary engineers are all invited. It is part of their negotiations with the officialdom and media. They expect the officials to help them get through official formalities easily and provide excellent media promotion. Free family passes are generously handed out to them. Passes are also given to retired circus artistes and their families, especially when a circus performs in places such as Thalassery or Pune, where circus has its roots. Kandambulli Balan notes that the Czechoslovakian Circus that visited India made a seating arrangement for 10,000 people, consumed electricity of 1 lakh watts for illuminating both the interior and exterior of the tent, and spent INR 2 lakhs on publicity. All technical arrangements for the programme were done with the help of their Bengali partner, A. L. Chopra, especially for the Indian tour.[120]

Bandmaster

Music plays a key role in circus performances, both spectacular and jocular ones. In earlier times, many big circus companies had their own live music bands, which, nowadays, have either shrunk or been replaced by

[119] Interview, Ravindran;

None of the artistes whom I interviewed remember any kind of caste-based seating arrangements in early circus arenas and I have not yet come across any source regarding this. But there is ample evidence about such tensions from the first half of the twentieth century at the exhibition sites of drama and cinema.

[120] Kandambulli Balan, 'Czechoslovakian Circus', *Mathrubhumi Illustrated Weekly* 38, no. 8 (1960): 6.

disc jockeys. Just as circus is a hybrid form, so is its music. Indian circus music includes mainly Western music, but is often mixed with anything that's interesting. This choice is mainly because of the energy of Western music, says Digpal Singh, a Punjabi musician with 22 years of experience in a circus band. During the golden era of live bands, Goan musicians had the lead. Europeans of early times, he says, insisted that only Western music should be played while they were performing.[121] For the African dance, the performers play their own music CDs. Hindi, Punjabi, Tamil, or any other music is mixed and played in accordance with the location of the camp. Digpal, a diploma holder from Allahabad University, plays the flute, drums, saxophone, keyboard, and trumpet. His uncle was a police bandmaster who had played for a couple of Hindi films. Music is selected according to the pace of the item. For those with dialogues, especially the comic scenes, no music is played. 'Baby Elephant Walk', the music from the film *Hatari* (1962), is played during the elephant numbers. The music of *Wonder Boys* (2001) is another popular mix in the circus. Kim Baston observes that circus music functions 'not only to accompany acts in the ring, but also to produce that action'.[122]

Sometimes, Indian music is mixed with Russian or other Western music in accordance with the rhythm. The composing is done by the bandmasters themselves, but individual tastes mark the music of each company. There are six to seven people in a circus band. Keyboard, drums, pad, violin, saxophone, and guitar are the major instruments used. It is mostly electrical instruments, such as the keyboard, that are played now. The accordion, Hawaiian guitar, Spanish guitar, saxophone, trumpet, and blow horn were the instruments in use in early circus bands, says Dileep, whose father is a drummer and two brothers are keyboard players in Rajkamal Circus.[123]

Circus Vernacular

People from different continents, geographies, and cultures living and performing under the same tent, travelling extensively to faraway lands,

---

[121] Interview, Digpal Singh, Royal Circus, 17 May 2008.

[122] Kim Baston, 'Circus Music: The Eye of the Ear', in *The Routledge Circus Studies Reader*, ed. Peta Tait and Katie Lavers (London and New York: Routledge, 2016), 129.

[123] Interview, Dileep, bandmaster, Royal Circus, 23 May 2008.

coexisted with each other in the dilemma of various unfamiliar languages—how is this possible without a 'common' tongue?

Amitav Ghosh talks about the Laskari language, language of the lascars on the ship, drawn from such different languages as Malay, Malayalam, Hindustani, English, Chinese, and many others spoken on board.[124] Interestingly, just as the Laskari language that resembles Hindustani/Urdu, the language used by circus people is commonly a mix of many tongues. I have seen many retired circus couples from Kerala interacting with each other in Hindi in their daily life, not to speak of those who have had inter-regional marriages. They randomly mix Malayalam, English, Hindi, Urdu, and many other unfamiliar languages when they speak of certain things and relationships closer to their performance and training. Just as Laskari was the language of command on the ship, its usage by the circus people is more visible when they hint at technical words concerning the construction of the tent and naming certain items. Amitav Ghosh notes:

> [W]hat really sets a sailship apart from other machines is that its functioning is critically dependent on language: underlying the intricate web of its rigging, is an unseen net of words without which the articulation of the whole would not be possible. To work a sailship efficiently, dozens of men must respond simultaneously, the failure to do so could make the difference tacking a vessel neatly or tipping her over on her beam ends.[125]

This would have been the same with a circus where so many people are needed to respond efficiently and simultaneously to work out the construction of the tent. In circus performances, a timely response from the group involved is a requisite and one has to trust the other in life-threatening situations, which also would have contributed to the development of a mixed language. The circus techniques also involve this kind of teamwork and collaboration.

[124] Amitav Ghosh, 'Of Fanas and Forecastles: The Indian Ocean and Some Lost Languages of the Age of Sail', *Economic and Political Weekly* 43 (25) (2008): 58.

[125] Amitav Ghosh, 'Of Fanas and Forecastles: The Indian Ocean and Some Lost Languages of the Age of Sail'. *Economic and Political Weekly* 43, no. 25 (2008): 58.

It should be noted here that whether it was Laskari or the mixed language of the circus people, Malayalam formed a significant part of their language. It not only throws light on the history of Malayali migration but on the supremacy and power they held on the consecutive areas too. In the United States of America, circus lingo has been identified and accumulated. Websites such as goodmagic.com[126] on British/ European and American circus lingo show the wide acknowledgement of these usages and the peculiarity of the circus vernacular. It should be noted here that earlier, when Marathis dominated the circus world, Marathi was spoken by many of them. I was surprised when Omana, a Kannadiga by birth, spoke to me in Malayalam, that too in the slang particular to Thalassery, with the least tinge of Kannada when I met her at Royal Circus in 2008. Omana told me that it was not at all surprising as she joined the circus as a child during a time when almost all the artistes and company owners were Malayalis from north Malabar. Same is the case with the Belgium nationals, Gloria Vanderwielen and her brother, Minni. Sreedharan Paikkatt also notes that Gloria could speak English, Hindi, Urdu, and Malayalam.[127] While they talked to me in English, they interacted with each other and their family in Hindi. East-African acrobats from Tanzania, Kenya, and Ethiopia spoke Hindi. While many of the Ethiopian artistes spoke Hindi in bits, the Swahili-speaking acrobats from Tanzania and Kenya were very fluent in Hindi. Swahili is highly influenced linguistically by Arabic and Persian, both powerful in the case of Hindustani as well.[128] However, the circus people seem to have always been masters of almost all 'Indian' languages. Almost all the circus people whom I have been interacting with claimed that they could fluently speak Punjabi, Assamese, Bengali, Tamil, Telugu, Nepali, and Kannada, apart from Hindi, Malayalam, and Marathi. Many of them who had spent some years abroad knew English, Arabic, and

---

[126] See http://www.goodmagic.com/carny/c_a.htm, last accessed on 10 June 2014.

[127] Sreedharan Paikkatt, 'Miss Gloria', *Circus Worker* 1, no. 3 (June 1980): 6.

[128] Please see https://www.britannica.com/topic/Hindustani-language, last accessed on 1 December 2018; James De Vere Allen, *Swahili Origins: Swahili Culture and the Shungwaya Phenomenon* (Nairobi: East African Educational Publishers, 1993), 3–6; also see https://www.britannica.com/topic/Swahili-language, last accessed on 1 December 2018.

Russian. Susan Seizer, who identifies the 'Drama Tongue' to 'a community centered on mobility' in her study on 'Special Drama' artists, notes, 'The Drama Tongue is a way of getting by, getting through, and getting away with some things, but it is a way out of outsiderness.'[129]

Touring

Indian circuses, in early times, made use of ships, flights, and trains, other than circus wagons, for their trips. The souvenir programme book of Kamala Circus was published 'to mark the triumphant return to India after ten years' tour abroad'.[130] The circus covered many parts of Asia. Another programme book of Kamala Circus has published a photo at the Burmese harbour where they arrived from Rangoon in the S.S. Sangola. The message well-wishing by the Indian ambassador in Burma wishing them well mentions that it had been performing in Rangoon and lower Burma.[131] Great Royal Circus toured in Asia and East Africa. Gemini Circus has also been to African lands, Russia, and the Gulf. During the first half of the twentieth century, even a small circus such as Rugma Bai Circus was travelling in South Asian lands, such as Burma. N. N. Pillai, renowned playwright and actor, recounts in his autobiography meeting a 'very poor circus company' from Malabar in the Penang province in Southeast Asia during 1938.

> A house full of people; 4–5 men, more women than men and more children than women. But there were no children more than about seven years of age. In the front yard there were cloth lines with several outlandish garments hanging on them. There were also quite a few instruments here and there. A strange community!
>
> They performed at crossroads and villages; not only acrobatics but also songs, dance and skits.

Pillai notes with his characteristic sarcasm that 'there was a uniqueness to that circus troupe. There were no animals other than humans

[129] Susan Seizer, *Stigmas of the Tamil Stage: An Ethnography of Special Drama Artists in South India* (Durham: Duke University Press, 2005), 300.

[130] Kamala Circus programme book, circa 1955, private collection, Shyamala Shirolker, Pune.

[131] Kamala Circus programme book, circa 1955, private collection, Sreedharan M., Muzhikkara.

in it', and that 'humans were mostly from Malabar and a couple of Tamilians'.[132]

However, the touring of a company is decided exclusively by its owner with the help of a map. But it is executed by the managers who look out for the availability of camps in accordance with his/her decisions. Three to four managers of the same company are sent in different directions months before to do the booking. The circus moves in accordance with the availability of grounds, calculating the collections, the nearest distance, and suitable climate. The programme book of Kamala Circus notes, 'The tour programme itself of the circus has to be drawn up with great foresight, for bad weather in any town can be an upsetting factor and put the circus to great loss.'[133] Circuses have their travelling preferences; for instance, certain circuses travel only in north India. Nowadays, the competition of circus owners over the ground has largely contributed to the monopolizing of certain regions.[134] For instance, in Kerala, only some Malayali-owned circuses have been touring for the past 10 years. In recent times, in many major cities—for instance, in the capital, Thiruvananthapuram—the circus has to move to the outliers in Neyyattinkara or the Government Homeopathic Medical College ground, while earlier it used to be the Putharikkandam ground in the heart of the city. We will now move on to examine the route of a circus with the help of a map.

Asoka Circus, a double-pole company, travelled from Jadcherla to Mettur from February to November in 1969.[135] P. K. Balakrishnan joined the camp at Jadcherla, present-day Telangana. This map shows the route of a small company sticking to small towns and places. The travel route is given below:

---

[132] N. N. Pillai, *Njan* [Me] (Kottayam: Current Books, 2012), 115–16.

[133] Kamala Circus programme book, circa 1955, private collection, Shyamala Shirolker, Pune.

[134] Interview, Sujit Dilip.

[135] P. K. Balakrishnan's diary, private collection of Kausu, Melur; late Balakrishnan had been the tent master's assistant in various circuses such as Asoka and Great Bombay from where he retired. I got the diary from Kausu, his wife, who worked with him.

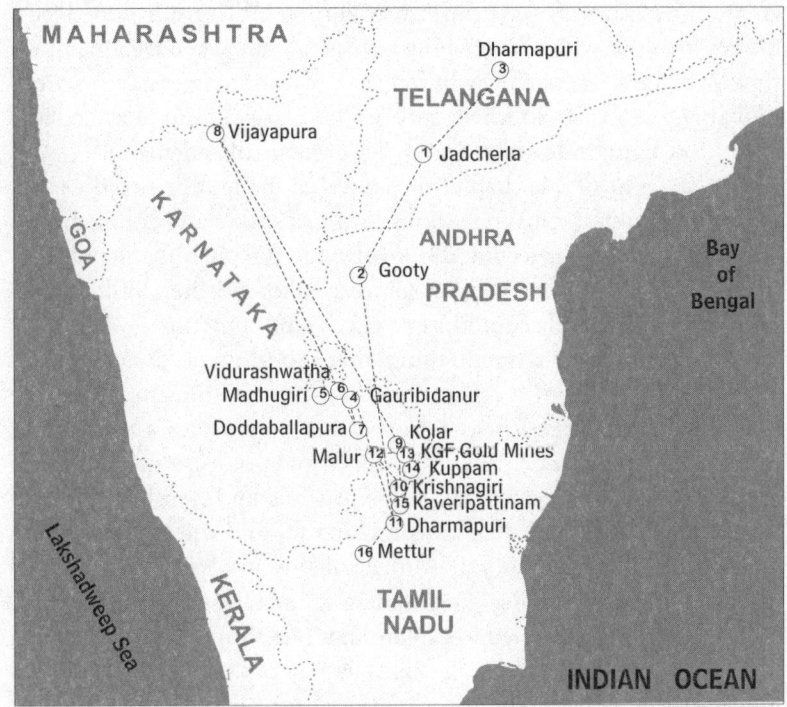

Image 3.3   Travel Route of a Small Circus Company

Source: Author.

Disclaimer: The map is for representative purposes only and is not drawn to scale.

(1) Jadcherla, Telangana; (2) Gooty, Andhra Pradesh; (3) Dharmapuri, Telangana; (4) Gauribidanur, Karnataka; (5) Madhugiri, Karnataka; (6) Vidurashwastha, Karnataka; (7) Doddaballapur, Karnataka; (8) Vijayapura, Karnataka; (9) Kolar, Karnataka; (10) Krishnagiri, Tamil Nadu; (11) Dharmapuri, Tamil Nadu; (12) Malur, Karnataka; (13) KGF Gold Mines, Karnataka; (14) Kuppam, Andhra Pradesh; (15) Kaveripattanam, Tamil Nadu; (16) Mettur, Tamil Nadu.

David Arnold has pointed out that '[t]echnological transfers are more likely to take the form of a "dialogue" rather than a simple process of diffusion or imposition, and this was especially the case in India, which had a wide range of existing technologies and a physical and social environment far removed from that of Europe'.[136] These dispersed techniques involved with tent pitching in India might also have undergone timely changes, interacting with indigenous technologies and practices. Probably, the words attached, such as 'tent lascars' and 'tent khalasi', also throw light on regional and community involvements.

The first part of this chapter speaks about the tenting practices during colonial times, tents for various itinerant shows and competitions, and also the complex techniques involved in the pitching of a big top. In the second half of this chapter, I have tried to walk literally and metaphorically through the contours of a circus tent, sometimes missing out something and finding certain things that appeal to me. Different types of tents have different social and cultural connotations in circus. The spatial structure has been so arranged that it generates a meaning in accordance with hierarchies based on occupation or gender and much more. I have also tried to look at the humans and non-humans who live in these tents and their lives moving around the big top. Those who have perceived agency and intentionality in objects have already discussed their roles in deciding human–animal lives. Through the stories of the tent, I have tried to explain the roles things have in deciding the human and non-human destinies by way of their connections and hierarchies that enable the circus itself to function as a whole. Now we will move on to look at some daring acts off the ring; attempts, both futile and successful, to form labour unions for circus workers.

[136] David Arnold, *The New Cambridge History of India: Science, Technology and Medicine III: Science, Technology and Medicine in Colonial India* (Cambridge: Cambridge University Press, 2004), 92.

4 Circus Workers and Trade Unions

Although circus figures in the common sense as a realm of extreme exploitation with dangerous working conditions, wretched living conditions, miserable wages, irregular working hours, physical and mental harassment, and insecure employment and life, if one looks at the history of trade unions in India, one would hardly find circus workers' unions. We may bear in mind here that circus flourished in north Malabar along with the communist movement and trade unions in the first half of the twentieth century. E. M. S. Namboodiripad, the legendary leader of the communist movement from Kerala, notes that 'starting as Congress Socialists and then becoming Communists we naturally worked hard to develop trade union and kissan [farmer] unions'. He further states, 'The progress in both was rapid. In less than half a decade we were able to form a number of trade unions in the entire Malabar District of the then Madras Presidency. In Cochin and Travancore too we were able to forge links with the existing trade unions and organize several unions.'[1]

---

[1] E. M. S. Namboodiripad, *History, Society and Land Relations* (New Delhi: Left Word, 2010), 109. It is worthwhile mentioning here that the first organized trade union in India was established in Madras Presidency, of which Malabar was a part. The Madras Labour Union was founded in April 1918; D. Veeraraghavan, *The Making of the Madras Working Class* (New Delhi: Left Word, 2013). The first organized labour union in Kerala is the Thiruvidancore Labour

Labour unions of circus workers are rare in other countries also. But they are part of larger unions encompassing performance arts. For instance, the American Guild of Variety Artists (AGVA) meant for all touring shows and theatrical revues includes circus performers. The American Federation of Labor and Congress of Industrial Organizations (AFL-CIO) was formed by merging several performance groups. The British Actors' Equity Association, popularly known by its short name—'Equity', is a trade union for 'professional performers' and 'creative practitioners' that includes circus artistes as well.[2]

Another significant aspect in the context of unionization is the delineation between performing artistes and other workers, an unsettling division of 'high' and 'low'. Of the latter, there is a further demarcation based on skilled and unskilled labour. We shall come back to this later.

Theodore Bhaskaran pointedly notes while writing about trade unionism in the Indian film industry: 'It is observed that of all the industries of our times, it is in the entertainment industry that trade unionism was late to appear and had to struggle through to strike roots.' He further adds, 'Entertainment industry traditionally has been stigmatized and looked down upon, in Asia; such an attitude was much more accentuated in India because of the rigid stratification of the society on caste basis.'[3]

Association (later, Thiruvidancore Coir Factory Workers' Union) established in 1922; Molly Varghese, *Dynamics of Trade Unionism in Kerala with View to Find Gandhian Alternative to the Industrial Problems in Kerala*. Doctoral dissertation, Mahatma Gandhi University, Kerala, 2000, 101–2.

[2] Please see http://www.britannica.com/EBchecked/topic/19681/American-Federation-of-Labor-Congress-of-Industrial-Organizations-AFL-CIO01/12/13 and http://www.nationaltheatreofvariety.org/variety.pdf, last accessed on 1 December 13.

The *Labor Tribune* reports, 'Teamsters Local 688 has represented as many as 235 workers at Ringling Bros. and Barnum & Bailey circus for over 50 years representing virtually every facet of work required to bring "The Greatest Show on Earth" to life in your town, including the elephant handlers'. Available at https://labortribune.com/the-greatest-show-on-earth-going-going-gone/, last accessed on 9 December 2018.

[3] Theodore S. Bhaskaran, *Trade Unionism in South Indian Film Industry*. Working Paper 36, Noida: V. V. Giri National Labour Institute, 2002, 1–2.

In this chapter, I will discuss two circus labour unions, the Akhil Bharath Circus Karmachari Sangh and the Indian Circus Employees Union, organized under the tutelage of two major political parties, the Communist Party of India and the Indian National Congress respectively. A remarkable outcome of the Akhil Bharath Circus Karmachari Sangh was the establishment of a circus company called the Akhil Bharath Circus—a circus owned, managed, and worked by circus workers. I will also briefly examine the few early attempts, mostly futile, to form labour unions in Indian circus and the organization formed by circus company owners, the Indian Circus Federation. The class battle between the worker and the owner in the circus industry will be explored through various narratives gleaned from interviews and publications, including notices, booklets, and the mouthpiece periodicals—the *Circus Worker* and the *Big Top*.

Those who have written on Indian circus do not mention the circus workers' unions as a significant aspect, if at all they are mentioned. Sreedharan Champad briefly notes the formation of Akhil Bharath Circus in his autobiography, *Thamp Paranja Jeevitham* (Life told by tent) (2012), *Circussinte Lokam* (The world of circus) (2008), and *An Album of Indian Big Tops* (2013). Although he mentions some of the leaders and incidents, he does not see Akhil Bharath Circus as a major labour movement and a significant attempt in the history of world circus where the workers formed a company of their own. Same is the case with the Indian Circus Employees Union, some of its leaders and the magazine *Circus Worker* published by them, which gets a brief mention.[4]

Kandambulli Balan states in the article 'Prasnanhal-Circus Mothalaliyudeyum Thozhilaliyudeyum' (Problems of the circus owner and worker) that 'there is no other industry in India which is as disorganized like the circus' and foresees that 'as in every other sphere the circus workers will unite, today or tomorrow'.[5] Balan mentions about the futile attempt to form a union called 'Akhilendia Circus Thozhilali Sangham' (All-India Circus Labourer's Organization) without providing any data.

---

[4] Sreedharan Champad, *An Album of Indian Big Tops* (Houston: Strategic Books, 2013), 134–5.

[5] Balan, *Circus*, 125, 132.

Unsurprisingly, the trade unions are not mentioned in the two life-histories of the circus entrepreneur Gemini Sankaran. Joyiamma Varghese, in her master's degree dissertation, 'Problems of Retired Circus Artists in Thalassery', does not mention any of the trade unions for circus workers or the pension received by the retired circus artistes in Kerala, which was made possible by the constant battles of the unions. It is interesting to note that in this work that tries to register the labour problems faced by the circus artistes, no differentiation is made between artistes and labourers. One cannot but strongly disapprove of whimsical statements such as 'there are inter caste marriages also among the circus artists and most of the time they are failures' or 'there is a gymnastic instructor, an ordinary labourer, generally what is called a bad lot, a scape-grace, unsteady drunkard'. Grand theories such as 'nowhere in the world minors are employed except the circus in India' are thrown around.[6] This, I would say, represents a stereotypical outlook that dominates the common perception about the world of circus, which ironically is one of the things the unions want to do away with.

The Owners Unite

It is interesting to note in this context that long before a circus workers' union came into being, circus company owners had formed an organization, the All India Circus Association, way back in 1953.[7] This organization was later renamed as 'Indian Circus Federation' in 1964.[8] The federation was registered under the Societies Registration Act XXI of 1860, with its head office in New Delhi. Though the owners say that the federation is inactive now, Ashok Shankar, a lawyer and son of Gemini Sankaran, and Dilip Nath, owner of Great Bombay Circus, are included in the administrative and syllabus committee of Kerala Circus Academy as representatives of the federation.[9]

[6] Joyiamma Varghese, *Problems of Retired Circus Artists in Thalassery*. M.A. dissertation, Calicut University, Kerala, 1992, 8, 9, 41.

[7] Interview, C. M. Ramachandran, New Delhi, 12 February 2010; Sankaran, Kannur, 29 October 2012.

[8] Interview, Ashok Shankar, New Delhi, 18 January 2013.

[9] Ashok Shankar and Dilip Nath have been the president and the secretary of the federation respectively for the past decade.

The major reason, Ravindran recounts, for organizing this federation was the problem with the availability of a circus ground, a perennial one, in Calcutta. A wealthy circus contractor in Calcutta called Vijay Babu did not allow any other circuses except those of Bengali owners to set up tent in the Howrah ground. To compete with him, Damodaran of Kamala Circus found a ground in the interiors of the city for his company's shows. Damodaran sent an invitation to Vijay Babu for the show's opening, but the latter died of heart failure that very evening. Owners of various circus companies had come to join hands with Damodaran that evening, which laid the foundation for the owners' federation.[10]

Mathrubhumi Illustrated Weekly reports under the title 'Circussukarkku Orakhilendia Sanghatana' (An all-India association for circus people), '[A] meeting of owners and representatives was held in Calcutta under the Chairmanship of Murkoth Kunhappa to organize an association for the circus people in India, most of whom are Malayalis.' There are two photographs along with the report. One is a group photo taken during the inauguration of the Circus Owners' Association with Damodaran of 'Kamala', K. M. Kunhikannan of 'Great Bombay', Subodh Banerjee of 'International', K. K. Achuthan of 'Oriental', Kandambulli Balan, 'Gemini' Sankaran, K. S. Menon of 'Bharath', and Murkoth Kunhappa who inaugurated the function. Another photograph is of Kandambulli Balan, the secretary of the association, delivering the welcome speech.[11] Balan mentions that as the secretary of the association, he was officially invited to visit the Soviet Circus College by Aleksandar Voloshin, the principal.[12] However, Balan caustically notes elsewhere that 'after one year's inertia the owners arrived at a unanimous choice—to disagree on all matters!'[13] The annual meeting of the federation was held in Madras on 18 and 19 July 1965, presided over by K. Damodaran, chairman of the federation, and was attended by those owners who were present in the first meeting. It was in this meeting that the owners decided to

---

[10] Interview, E. Ravindran.

[11] 'Circussukarkku Orakhilendia Sanghatana' [An all-India association for circus people], *Mathrubhumi Illustrated Weekly* 31, no. 48 (1954): 16.

[12] Kandambulli Balan, 'Circus Soviet Naattil' [Circus in Soviet land], *Mathrubhumi Illustrated Weekly* 34, no. 49 (1957): 27.

[13] Balan, *Circus*, 128.

publish a quarterly journal, *Big Top*, to air the 'problems of Circus' and 'to educate the public and the Government on the role Circus plays in the cultural life of the country'.[14]

Big Top, professed by the publishers as the 'the mouth piece of those engaged in the circus art', was by all means an exclusive crusader for the company owners. The editorial in the inaugural issue of the *Big Top* has many glaring contradictions that illustrate the predicament of the proprietors. The editorial, 'Plea for better deal', nostalgically laments that 'during the pre-independence days circus had enjoyed better facilities and assistance from the then Government' and 'if anything, it was only the Princely States, now no more in existence, which had evinced some interest in the development of circus art and helped it before the country attained independence'.[15]

The editorial then goes straight for the jugular: 'It may seem paradoxical, but the conclusion is irresistible, that circus art rarely prospers in democratic countries.' After pointing out the bankruptcy of some major American and European circus companies, the writer(s) urge us 'to compare this with the growth of circus in Russia'. 'Under the Czarist regime circus had only an anemic growth, but after the Revolution when the state started taking direct interest this art was revitalized and as the time advanced the Russian circus improved so much that today it is claiming first place in world circus.' So, is the federation craving for a Soviet model nationalization wiping out private property? The editorial hastily dismisses any such untoward thought and clarifies: 'We may not be misunderstood as advocating State control over circus in this country. We have referred to the growth of this art in Democratic and Socialist countries only to bring home the point that without

[14] 'Editorial', *Big Top* 1, no. 1 (1965): 33.

[15] Interestingly, this longing for the golden days of colonial rule and princely states is preceded by a blatantly nationalist rallying call from the chairman K. Damodaran to donate to the defence fund in the wake of the war with Pakistan. The chauvinistic rhetoric that lambasts the nation's enemy concludes by citing a telegram sent to the president, prime minister, and defence minister: 'Unanimously resolved by the Indian Circus Federation to render full support and solemnly assure co-operation and help to defend the Mother land. Proprietors and employees of all circuses numbering over 20,000 condemn jointly naked aggression by Pakistan'; 'Editorial', *Big Top*, 3–4.

State patronage and assistance circus in democratic countries has little chance of survival.'[16]

The editorial then strategically moves toward another thorny issue which had been raised consistently by circus workers at the time, that all the labour laws and rules in the country should be applicable to them. The owners' mouthpiece shrewdly states that 'the Government

Image 4.1   Indian Circus Federation Members with Morarji Desai,
the then Prime Minister

Source: Private collection of C. M. Ramachandran.

[16] 'Editorial', *Big Top*, 3–4. In a speech delivered on the occasion of the reception given to Bharath Circus by the Patna Kerala Cultural Association, K. S. Menon—its owner and secretary of Circus Owners Association—said, 'Unless the government takes special note the future of Indian circus will be worrisome. ... This "little travelling world" might disappear from India and that fatal negligence could push about twenty thousand families into destitution'; U. Chandrasekharan, 'Bharath Circus', *Mathrubhumi Illustrated Weekly* 44, no. 28 (1966): 22.

should think of a separate legislation for circus' as 'by its very nature a circus, its workers and artistes cannot be brought under the ambit of any one of the various legislations now in force'.[17] This is undoubtedly a direct response to the establishment of Akhil Bharath Circus Karmachari Sangh and a bill titled 'Protection of Circus Employees Bill' brought before the lower house of the Indian parliament by K. Anandan Nambiar, veteran communist trade union leader, on 10 March 1964, three days after the union's registration.

A *TOI* (27 February 1979) report shows that even in as late as 1979, the federation members was actively holding meetings with Morarji Desai, the then prime minister, and P. C. Chunder, the education minister, to review the problems and difficulties of Indian circuses. There is a snapshot of this meeting in the private collection of C. M. Ramachandran, who has worked as the secretary and cashier of the federation. First, let us briefly look at some futile early attempts to form a circus workers' union.

Failed Moves

M. Sreedharan, a veteran circus artiste, told me that he had gone along with some other workers of Kamala Circus to meet the eminent communist leader A. K. Gopalan in New Delhi with the idea of a workers' union in 1955. He states that their plan was to organize a workers' union to take on the circus owners' Indian Circus Federation that was recently formed. Unfortunately, this effort did not work out further. According to Sreedharan, Kamala Circus was tented in Delhi at the time and he went along with other workers to meet AKG at his Delhi residence. He says, although AKG welcomed them warmly, promised all help to form the union, and had lunch together, some days later, they saw him visiting Kamala Circus along with the owner, Damodaran.[18] Sreedharan alleges

---

[17] 'Editorial', *Big Top*, 3–4.

[18] Noted theatre actor and playwright Ibrahim Vengara recounts in the autobiography, *Green Room*, his life as a menial labourer and occasional clown in the Gemini Circus while he was a wandering youth in Madras city. Ibrahim goes to the ground where the Gemini Circus was tenting, looking for a job, and sees and recognizes the legendary left leader A. K. Gopalan there speaking to the circus manager, Balakrishnan. With the recommendation of AKG, Ibrahim is hired by

that they had a feast together in the owner's tent and when the leader went back, his car boot was filled with gifts.[19] Sreedharan Champad notes in his blog that 'some opposition leaders promised on requests of artists to form their union in several occasions' and 'they also had collected funds for the expenditure for forming committees and registration of union'.[20]

Champad mentions that a union for circus workers was established at Thalassery in 1956 but closed shop within two weeks. He states that it was organized by some circus workers themselves without support from any political party.[21] The only other historian of circus in Kerala, Kandambulli Balan, also notes that a meeting of circus workers was held at Thalassery and that they had organized the 'Akhilendia Circus Thozhilali Sangham' (All India Circus Employees' Union). He warns ominously that some company owners are operating to nip the union in the bud.[22] E. Ravindran says that this short-lived union had been the brain child of M. K. Balan, son of the legendary circus master

---

the company. (It is worthwhile mentioning here that all three protagonists in this story and the circus company are from the north Malabar district of Kannur.) Remarkably, AKG tries his best to dissuade the young men from working in the circus: 'when we see their acrobatics and all we will think their existence is just like the shining attire they wear, absolutely wrong. Have you any idea about the hardships they have to endure? The lives of humans and animals in a circus tent are almost similar.' Ibrahim Vengara, *Green Room* (Kottayam: NBS, 2014), 96. But Ibrahim sticks to his decision and AKG gives in: 'well … there is no use in my deterrence if your fate is to go through hellish suffering' (*Green Room*, 97). But contrary to the great Marxist's dire prediction, young Ibrahim seems to have enjoyed his brief stint at the circus and was heartbroken when he had to quit when the company left for an overseas tour next (*Green Room*, 102–6).

The crucial question that arises here is why a daring and sincere leader such as A. K. Gopalan, who was well aware of a sector where both humans and non-human beings undergo 'hellish suffering', did not make any effective move to organize and bring about significant changes.

[19] Interview, M. Sreedharan.

[20] Available at http://sreedharanchampad.blogspot.in/search?zx=fd163843656e3145, last accessed on 12 September 2012.

[21] Sreedharan Champad, *Circussinte Lokam* (Kozhikode: Mathrubhumi, 2008), 161.

[22] Balan, *Circus*, 132.

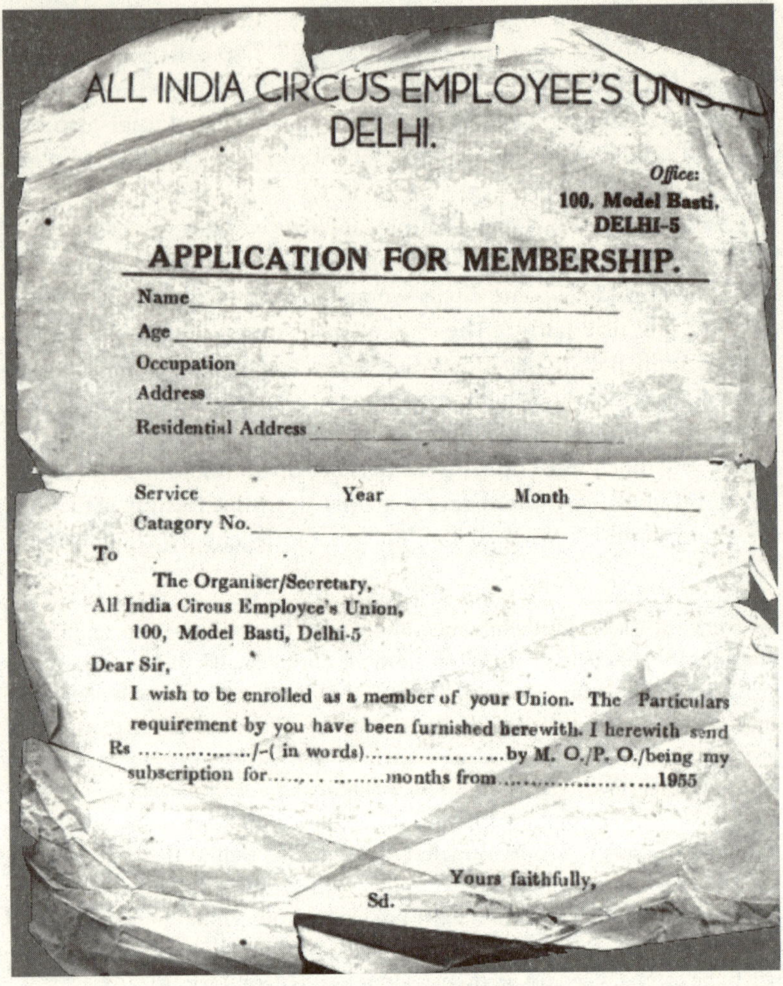

ALL INDIA CIRCUS EMPLOYEE'S UN

DELHI.

Office:
100, Model Basti.
DELHI-5

APPLICATION FOR MEMBERSHIP.

Name________________________
Age________________________
Occupation________________________
Address________________________
Residential Address________________________

Service__________ Year__________ Month__________
Catagory No.________________________

To
The Organiser/Secretary,
All India Circus Employee's Union,
100, Model Basti, Delhi-5

Dear Sir,

I wish to be enrolled as a member of your Union. The Particulars requirement by you have been furnished herewith. I herewith send Rs ..../-(in words)......................by M. O./P. O./being my subscription for.............months from.....................1955

Yours faithfully,
Sd.__________

Image 4.2 Membership Form for the All India Circus Employees Union, circa 1955

Source: Private collection of M. Sreedharan.

M. K. Raman.[23] Luckily, Sreedharan has preserved a blank membership application form (Figure 4.2) of this stillborn union, 'All India Circus Employee's Union, Delhi'. The address in the form is 'The Organiser/ Secretary, All India Circus Employee's Union, 100, Model Basti, Delhi-5'.

23 Interview, E. Ravindran.

Interestingly, the only existing circus union now, formed in the late 1970s, has a similar name.

By all accounts then, 'Akhil Bharath Circus Karmachari Sangh', established in 1964, was the first proper union with backing and goodwill from a major political party, the Communist Party of India. But we must remember that for the CPI 1964 had been a watershed year. At the end of that year, the party would split right—almost—in the middle.

Akhil Bharath Circus Karmachari Sangh

On 16 March 1964, E. Ravindran, a circus artiste and activist camping with Rayman Circus at Bilaspur in Madhya Pradesh, received a telegram from his home town, Thalassery in north Kerala. The message from his fellow comrade, P. Krishnan, was as terse as possible: 'UNION REGISTRATION OVER'. Eighty-year-old Ravindran still keeps that ragged paper bit from half a century ago.[24] Like Ravindran, this news was momentous for many who had been toiling in the tents erected in various towns and villages around the country.

'Akhil Bharath Circus Karmachari Sangh' was registered in the nation's capital on 7 March 1964 with a local address (xvi/10211, Western Extension Area, New Delhi–5), and the area of its operation has been given as 'the whole of Bharat'. The membership was open to 'all employees of all Indian Circus Companies irrespective of the size and shape of the Circuses' and the membership fee varied in accordance with the gender, status, and salary of the workers: 'Every male member shall pay Re. 1/-, girl member 0-50 np. as monthly subscription, but Ring Boys, animal attendants and such low paid workers shall pay only 25 np. per month.'[25] The bylaws of the union state that it shall be governed by a managing committee, which included a chairman, a deputy chairman, a general secretary, a treasurer, and four joint

---

[24] Personal collection, E. Ravindran, Thalassery; P. Krishnan, a local Communist party leader, was the office secretary of the union in Thalassery.

[25] 'Rules of Akhil Bharath Circus Karmachari Sangh', *In Memory of Keeleri Kunjikkanan Teacher* (hereafter, *IMK*) (Thalassery: Akhil Bharath Circus Karmachari Sangh, 1964), 1–4.

secretaries, and the managing committee shall be elected at the annual general meeting.[26]

In the very beginning of the union's bilingual publication, *In Memory of Keeleri Kunjikkanan Teacher*, Akhil Bharath Circus Karmachari Sangh states that one of their principal objectives is 'to get the Indian Govt's recognition of these workers classified under workmen's category'.[27] In the Malayalam introduction, T. V. Balakrishnan Nair makes the point forcefully:

> Circus owners seem to have misreckoned that circus does not belong to the category of industry like other industries and hence circus does not come under the labor laws or worker compensation laws. They have bullied the workers into believing that no labor law would come for their protection. The workers were forced to suppose that their lives are to be solely determined by the contract or agreement given by them or their parents to the owners. Even if a worker loses his or her life the owner would take it merely as the loss of a piece of furniture.[28]

The spirit with which the laws of the country are invoked is definitely not just rhetorical. Just three days after the union registration, a bill titled 'Protection of Circus Employees' was brought before the lower house of the Indian parliament, the Lok Sabha, by K. Anandan Nambiar. He was a veteran communist trade union leader elected from Tiruchirappalli, Madras, who had been instrumental in the formation of the circus union. The role of Akhil Bharath Circus Karmachari Sangh in this endeavour is duly acknowledged in the introduction of the union publication.[29]

---

[26] M. C. Raman from Thalassery, who earlier worked in Singapore, was very active in this union's office work. He was the chairperson of the union for some time. He had an affiliation with the Communist party. Interview, K. K. Sukumaran; A .V. Karim says that Madhavan Nair, who was a circus manager, had also been its chairperson, and Rayman Gopalan, owner of the Rayman Circus, having noted this, caught him once and warned him against helping the labourers. Interview, A. V. Karim.

[27] *IMK*, 1.

[28] 'Introduction', *IMK*, 20.

[29] Balakrishnan Nair's Introduction concludes thus: 'For presenting the tales of circus workers soaked in tears before the nation's parliament let us thank the union leaders and the Member of Parliament Sri K. Anandan Nambiar.'

The Bill and the Debate

The bill presented on 10 March 1964 on 'Protection of Circus Employees' generated a heated debate in the Lok Sabha with several members chipping in, including those with open leanings towards the circus company owners. The deliberation went on to the session next day at the end of which Anandan Nambiar's motion was negated. The arguments in Nambiar's bill and the points which came up in the debate for and against them are in many ways significant. Unfortunately, or should one say bizarrely, these are precisely the arguments which are still played out regarding the circus industry, even after 50 years.

Anandan Nambiar opens formally with a brief description of the bill and the requests, 'the Bill to protect the Circus employees by bringing them under the operation, of the Industrial Disputes Act, 1947 and the Workmen's Compensation Act, 1923, etc. be taken into consideration'. He then makes a crucial strategic move differentiating the workers from the owners and their respective demands: 'this is not a bill about the circus industry. This bill only seeks protection to be given to the tens of thousands of employees working in the circus industry.' Thus, the proposed bill is marked off from the Circus Owners' Federation's claims being made on behalf of the *entire* circus industry, squarely placing them in the opposition.

Nambiar also addresses the crucial problem of 'region' embedded in the class structure of the circus industry: 'Ninety percent of the circus proprietors come from Malabar in Kerala and ninety-five percent of the artistes and employees are also Malayalees.' He deploys this 'regional' affiliation, even stating his own identity as a 'Malayalee', in defence of the objectivity and fairness of the bill: 'I have no animosity towards these proprietors. As I have said most of these people come from Malabar and I will naturally have a soft corner for them because I am also a Malayalee'.

Anandan Nambiar, born in Malabar in 1918, represented Tiruchirappalli constituency in the erstwhile Madras state in the first (1952–7), the third (1962–7), and the fourth (1967–70) Lok Sabha. *IMK* carries the parliamentary debate on this motion in extenso, both in English and Malayalam. All citations of the debate are from this source.

The Bill proposes that circus workers should be included in the category of 'workman'[30] and demands a better clarification of the category 'industry' in the Industrial Disputes Act,[31] 'An artiste of the circus company may be working on the trapeze or doing any other work in the company or he may be riding a tiger or tiger in the cage on the motor cycle, etc. the employee may be taming or breeding some dangerous animals. These people do not come under the term "workman"'.[32] There is no mention in the Payment of Wages Act that the circus workers will benefit and there is only a remote mention of them in the Workmen's Compensation Act. The Member of Parliament suggests that the management should maintain a muster roll where the employees in their company should be listed.[33] Although, no circus worker need to work

[30] The circus workers have complained that though general laws and orders exist, the circus somehow seems to escape these laws. This is mainly because of the bribing of owners, the roaming nature of the circus industry, and the fear and disunity among workers. Interview, Salman, Jumbo Circus, 29 April 2007; Rajan; Babu.

[31] Anandan Nambiar points out that circus owners are capable of escaping the hands of the law by spending lots of money so that their employees do not get the benefit of the legislation, 20; on the back inside cover of the *IMK*, there is a call to join the union: 'To get the Industrial Disputes Act, the Labor Disputes Act, and other labor laws to the benefit of the circus workers, join Akhil Bharath Circus Karmachari Sangh formed by the circus workers of India.' The front inside has a subscription call for a 'Circus and Cinema monthly magazine', *Chithrarajyam*, 'the official publication of Akhil Bharath Circus Karmachari Sangh', priced at 25 paisa excluding postage fee. Although Ravindran states that there was a magazine, he does not remember its name. Sreedharan Champad says it was 'Circus'; available at http://sreedharanchampad.blogspot.in/search?q=akhila, last accessed on 12 September 2012.

[32] 'There is no fixed salary for the circus artistes or workers and no security of work. The salary is paid in accordance with the number of items they do. If the owner does not like you, he can dismiss you for no reason'; interview, C. C. Ashok Kumar.

[33] Radha Kannan showed me a monthly payroll of circus artistes at Gemini circus during the 1960s, a simple sheet of paper with nothing official about it. Radha, a child artiste of about ten at that time, does not figure in that list. Rajan told me that though they keep the ledger nowadays, neither all the company girls nor all the items they perform are entered. Usually, the salary shown will be less so that they need not pay much to the provident fund. Interview, Radha Kannan; Rajan.

more than eight hours a day and 48 hours a week, 'right from 10 in the morning up to 12 or 1 in the night the employee, he or she, is engaged in some or the other'. They have no holidays in a week and for that they do not get any double pay either.[34]

Anandan Nambiar refers to a memorandum submitted by Damodaran, the owner of Kamala circus, in which he argues that children below 12 years must be brought in as bending of the body can only be trained at that age. Nambiar contends this citing the example of Russian circus where only children over 14 years perform. When another member sensitive to Nambiar's cause points out that the Russian children perform along with their family, he responds that in Indian circus 'orphans are brought so that nobody sheds any tears over the children's sufferings'. He mentions that the circus industry should flourish with the exemption of entertainment tax and providing railway facilities but at the same time the employees' problems should also be taken into consideration.[35]

Nambiar again mentions the Russian circus for their safety measures for artistes contrasting it with the circus in India citing examples of trapeze artistes who lost their lives in the Gemini and Kamala circuses. He quotes the leader of a Russian circus team that visited India recently,

[34] Anandan Nambiar notes the excuse given by Damodaran, owner of the Kamala Circus, that there is two to three days' leave while shifting camps and argues that this, in fact, is more work and, therefore, they should be allotted a month's leave with full payment annually. Suniti told me that more than the artistes, the ring boys are the ones who suffer 24 hours' work, especially while the tent is being pitched in a new camp or the camp is being shifted. Interview, Suniti, Elayidathu Mukku, 9 February 2012.

[35] As in the case of troupes of theatre, magicians, music and dance, and artists of bonafide entertaining companies or parties, the Northern Central Railway of India specifically provides allowances of travel to circus parties. 'Bonafide professional circus artistes/parties ... travelling to participate in specific performance sponsored or approved by Dept. of Youth Affairs & Sports (Ministry of Human Resource Development)' having a 'Certificate from Department Of Youth Affairs & Sports, Ministry of Human Resource Development through Indian Circus Federation' are given fifty percentage for first class and seventy-five percentage for second or sleeper class reduction; available at http://www.ncr.indianrailways.gov.in/view_section.jsp?lang=0&id=0,1,283,363,682, last accessed on 10 September 2012.

Mr. Valoshin, who suggested nationalization of the circus industry and adds strategically: 'I do not say now to nationalize it … let the industry thrive. My intention is to see that the industry thrives with all the help that government must give to it'. His idea regarding the course of action the law should take is unambiguous: 'A circus tent is a place where the circus proprietor alone rules. The rule of law does not reach there. … if anything happens to anybody, if he is beaten he could be buried in the tent'.[36]

Nambiar did get some responses which were sensitive towards his arguments. While some members engaged in the debate for the sheer pleasure of playfulness, one member had the explicit objective of speaking on behalf of the other party, the circus company owners. Joachim Alva proclaims his 'humble support of the bill' and then cheekily states: 'I come from a place not far off from Malabar. I pay a tribute to the Malabar artistes – they are also communists, but for us they are good artistes – these Malabar boys and girls'. S. M. Banarjee speaks passionately favouring the bill and demands that stringent steps should be taken by the government to protect the circus workers. A couple of members criticize the anthropocentricism of Nambiar's class analysis by pointing out that circus consists not only of the employees and employers, but also animals and he has not made any mention about them.

Manoharan of the Dravida Munnetra Kazhagam (DMK), elected from Madras South, opens his speech making it perfectly clear as to where his sentiments lie: 'it is my duty to bring to the kind attention of the house certain difficulties the circus management is undergoing'. He speaks at length and challenges the very purpose of the bill:

> If Mr. Nambiar wants through this bill the complete abolition of the circus I can understand it. But on one hand he wants the circus to grow because it is one of the cultural institutions of the country and on the other he wants to introduce restrictions on the employees of the circus which will virtually paralyze the circus company.

[36] Radha Kannan told me that while she was chosen to perform in the cultural exchange programme in Russia during 1963, they made them sign the agreement that they were performing at their own risk since they were performing such risky items on the top without any safety measures; interview, Radha Kannan.

He plunges the knife in deep: 'I would like to point out that our circus companies are not looked after by the government'. Owner's raj or perish seems to be the unambiguous message.

R. K. Malvia, deputy minister for Labour and Employment, responds to the bill from the government amid sarcastic comments such as 'Is he the minister for circus?', which in fact bare the crux of the critique in Nambiar's bill that laws of the land do not reach the tents. The minister, naturally, dismisses the arguments in the bill categorically stating that circus workers are 'covered by the existing labor legislations and absolute protection is available to them'. And taking off from the member Manoharan who spoke for the circus owners, the minister puts the onus back on Anandan Nambiar: 'The Employment of Children's act definitely provides that children below 12 years should not be employed in any industry. My hon. friend can take advantage of that provision and also move for banning children below 12 years being employed in the circus industry'. The predicament of Nambiar is apparent all over in his feeble response:

> I ought not to be accused that I am provoking some sort of an action whereby the circus industry will be at disadvantage because it will be deprived of the service of the children; I should not be attacked in that way. ... My purpose was never to do any harm to the industry and I made it clear. It is an industry which is built by private sector and poor people had to suffer untold hardship to build an industry of the type and our circus industry is second to none in any part of the world. That is a great achievement and this industry should flourish. Therefore whatever lacuna is there it may be removed so that these employees are protected.

The motion about the unseen plight of a space that ironically thrives on 'show', which was brought for the first time before the highest law-making house in the country was summarily dismissed.

The dilemmas of class antagonism and tactical alliances have obviously continued over the decades in the circus industry, especially with regard to children and animals; two key moments being the banning of the performance of wild animals in 1991 and children below 14 in 2011. The Indian Circus Federation filed a petition in the Delhi High Court challenging the animal ban and the Indian Circus Employees Union supported the move by filing another petition simultaneously. But significantly, years later, on 18 April 2011 when the Supreme Court of India banned the employment and performance of children and adolescents from the Indian circus on a petition filed by the NGO Bachpan Bachao Andolan, the position of the Indian Circus Employees Union had been wavering. In a letter addressed to the Central cabinet minister A. K. Antony, the union concedes, 'As a responsible national trade union with conscientious ideals and actions, the Indian Circus Employees Union understands and appreciates the legal and ethical spirit of the honourable court's ruling. The fundamental rights of children should be held high in any democratic society, indisputably'.[37]

'Circus Workers, Don't Get Cheated'

The union had no plans to restrict its actions to parliament parliamentary motions and pin all their hopes on the guarantees the labour minister offered in the Lok Sabha. But they did make use of the assurances from the state two months later when they came out strongly against a labour contract drawn in Kamala Circus that was signed by the concerned parties on 15 June 1964. The union published the entire contract consisting of 14 clauses along with a stringent critique as a Malayalam notice aptly titled 'Circus Jeevanakkar Vanchitharaakaruthu' (Circus workers, don't get cheated).[38] It opens with 'The contract drawn by Professor K Damodaran, the owner of Kamala circus which is going on with its show now at Ahmadabad in Gujarat State and has a head office at the Prakash building at Mahatma Gandhi Road at Ernakulum in Kerala State', 'on 15 June 1964', followed by the 14 items listed one by one.

The critique by the secretary of the Akhil Bharath Circus Karmachari Sangh addresses 'the young men and women' and cautions that 'today this contract has its beginning in Kamala circus. Tomorrow it will be implemented in all the circus companies.' Then it goes on stating boldly that 'this place is not ruled by the circus owners, but the government elected by the people of India' and reminds of the debate in the parliament two months ago and the protection the state laws guaranteed to the circus workers: 'Not many days have gone since the Government assured in the Parliament that Industrial dispute Act and other state

---

[37] Letter draft, Indian Circus Employees Union, Thalassery, n.d.

[38] The address given is 'Secretary, Akhila Bharat Circus Karmachari Sangham' and printed at 'Krishna Printing Works, Thalassery', n.d.

rules cover the circus' and 'this contract is made to snatch away the rightful benefits provided by the law for the circus workers in India'. The notice then severely criticizes the policy of the Kamala Circus management that tries to wash of its hand from responsibilities such as accidents and declares that the contract is 'beastly, hitherto unheard in this civilized country'. The notice criticizes the policy of the Kamala Circus management that takes its hand off from responsibilities of fire or other accidents that might harm the lives of the workers, from providing the place for practice inside the circus, and making the performers wear the dress of the owner's taste. The Union warns the labourers that even if they perform with all their sincerity only if it satisfies the owners, they will be paid as per the contract and at the end, the labourers will have to put their show equipment to auction for the money to return home. The workers are denied of their deserving gratuity, casual and weekly leaves, and even if a parent died, they cannot go home: 'Without any concern to your health, you will have to perform end number of times to the satisfaction of the owner. Or else, your salary will be cut and for the loss of the owner you will be trapped in cases legally'. The notice reminds that 'millions of organized working class is with you in this struggle for justice' and appeals to

> declare at the top of your voice that no male or female artiste will sign the contract. You will recognize the dark hands behind this contract sooner or later. Raise your voice against this contract which will pull the circus workers of India deep in misery and tears. In this struggle of justice and injustice, justice will have the ultimate victory.[39]

Again, this was not mere political rhetoric richly developed in Malayalam by that time and could be found in umpteen notices of its kind. This tough position against a top circus company and its mighty owner and the way in which Anandan Nambiar kept a distance from the standard 'socialist' slogan of the time, 'nationalization', in the parliament points to a glorious plan the union had in mind. In the back cover of their publication *In Memory of Keeleri Kunjikkanan Teacher* (1964), this dream venture had been announced: a circus company of the workers.

---

[39] 'Circus Jeevanakkar Vanchitharaakaruthu' [Circus workers, don't get cheated], Secretary, Akhila Bharatha Circus Karmachari Sangham, printed at Krishna Printing Works, Thalassery, n.d.

The Akhil Bharath Circus Company

The announcement was thus:

> Akhil Bharath Circus Company (Private Limited), Main Road, Thalassery. On the 17th anniversary of Indian Independence day August 15th, the circus company formed by the circus workers in India with a capital of one lakh rupees from forty members with Rs. 2500/ shares each has begun. For the few shares that remain eligible persons are invited.[40]

This endeavour was by no means idealistic. The Akhil Bharath Circus Karmachari Sangh had before them at least two exemplary successful models: The Milk Producers' Co-Operative established in Anand, Gujarat, in 1946, and the Indian Coffee Workers' Co-Operative Societies, established in 1957, who owned and managed Indian Coffee Houses all over the country. One of the founder members of the coffee co-operative, N. Parameswaran Pillai narrates the famous tale in his book *Coffee Housinte Katha* (The story of coffee house). In May 1957, the Coffee Board decided to shut down all the 43 coffee houses in various cities. This would have affected more than a thousand workers and the workers went on strike under the leadership of A. K. Gopalan. The Coffee Board came up with the alternative to transfer the coffee houses to private owners which lead to the historic decision of forming workers co-operatives and taking over the establishments.[41] But significantly, the circus workers were going for a private limited company: a circus company owned and managed by circus workers. The first shareholders were Narayanan, Mekkileri Kumaran, Undakuppi Ananthan, and Vijayan.[42]

---

[40] Akhil Bharath Circus Karmachari Sangh, *In Memory of Keeleri Kunjikkanan Teacher*, Thalassery, 1964, back cover.

[41] N. Parameswara Pillai, *Coffee Housinte Katha* [The story of coffee house] (Thrissur: Current Books, 2005), 21–46. Another great movement closer home with the same political backing is the Beedi Workers' Co-operative. After some failed attempts, the Kerala Dinesh Beedi Co-operative Society established in 1969 became an extraordinary enterprise of its kind; Thomas Isaac, Richard W. Franke, and Pyaralal Raghavan, *Democracy at Work in an Indian Industrial Cooperative: The Story of Kerala Dinesh Beedi* (London and Ithaca: Cornell University Press, 1998).

[42] Interview, Sreedharan.

It should be noted here that the workers' circus came in existence at a time when while its contemporaries in theatre or the film industry were also toiling with labour issues. But none of these organized a company of their own. The Kerala People's Arts Club (KPAC), a drama group established in 1950 that was formed following the model of IPTA (Indian People's Theatre Association), a drama group of Communist artists formed in 1943 in Mumbai, is the only distant resemblance. It was organized and run by the Communist party for propagating the party ideals mainly. While an organization for film producers was formed in 1968,[43] a labour union was fruitfully organized in the Malayalam film industry only as late as the 1970s.

Bhaskaran, who was an active member in the Akhil Bharath Circus Karmachari Sangh, told me that the major pull behind organizing such a union exclusively for workers was the non-payment for the matinee shows. He added,

> Circus owners made the workers perform for three shows and paid for only two. Once the owners found out the strength and unity behind all those workers who were associated with the Union, they were dismissed from various circus companies. They would send telegrams to each and every circus company, which was about three hundred then, that such and such persons performing such and such items should not be given jobs in any of the circus companies.[44]

At Madras, some of the circus people were arrested from Kamala Circus on the accusation that they stole fish from a nearby pond. But the actual reason for the arrest was union membership. Bhiman Kittan who was a Sandow wrestler in Kamala, was assaulted and attacked at Thalassery for being a union leader. An ambassador car was sent to follow him wherever he went and hit if possible. He was very cautious and he managed to escape each time. Bhaskaran was also dismissed from the Kamala circus with regard to his union work.[45]

---

[43] 'Nirmathakkal Sanghadikkunnu' [Producers organize], *Mathrubhumi Illustrated Weekly* 46, no. 32 (1968): 43.

[44] Interview, Bhaskaran.

[45] Bhaskaran remembers that it had an office at Thalassery, in north Malabar, Kerala, at the old bus stand area. That was the only concrete building in that

It was thus the idea of a circus company owned, managed, and worked by labourers came to their mind. Hence, the Akhil Bharath Circus was started by those artistes who were dismissed from various circuses. He says that all of them did not take shares of 2500 rupees, but some 100, some 500 and so on. The peculiarity of this circus company was the marked absence of animals.

The company was inaugurated on 30 December 1964 by V. R. Krishna Iyer, who was the minister of law and social welfare in the first ministry in Kerala headed by E. M. S. Namboodiripad in 1957. He was also one of the leading lawyers in Thalassery. It is interesting to note that while many of the circus union members dearly keep the memory of his inauguration and speech, Iyer does not remember either the union or his inauguration of the circus.[46] By all means, the union and the circus were communist.[47] Although the party had split a month ago, it had not affected the trade union affiliations directly at the time. Bhiman Krishnan (also known as Bhiman Kittan) who was in the 'right' wing was chosen as the leader by the workers.[48]

Having opened the performance at its hometown, Thalassery, the company performed mainly in Kerala and Tamil Nadu for the next two-and-a-half years. Major artistes from various circus companies joined the company. The company played at Mananthawadi, Kozhikode, Kanjirappally, Pathanamthitta, Thengashi, Palayamkotta, Thirunelveli, Sathur, Shivakashi, and Thuthukkudi. There were about 60 workers including children, men, and women who worked as part of it. But there were no animals. Sreedharan Champad recounts in his autobiography the performance he saw at Thalassery: 'The four poled tent with a forty five feet long canvas was not at all bad, along with equipments such as the cross flying trapeze and others. Although without animals

---

area then, which also throws light on how well the union must have functioned. It functioned for about five years; interview, Bhaskaran.

[46] Interview, V. R. Krishna Iyer, 22 July 2013.

[47] It is interesting to note that during the parliamentary debate where Anandan Nambiar speaks about the recent formation of the union, one of the members asks whether it was affiliated to the Communist party, to which Nambiar does not give any direct answer.

[48] The break up in AITUC came years later in 1970, and Centre for Indian Trade Unions (CITU) was formed.

Image 4.3   Inauguration, Akhil Bharath Circus, 30 December 1964
Source: Private Collection of E. Ravindran.

there was the acrobatics by well-known artistes, both men and women. Several unparallel items; 'seven bar' by Mekkileri Kumaran and Antoli Divakaran; Comic juggling by the famous Antony.'[49]

But problems began to mount. E. Ravindran, who owned 2 of the 40 shares and also served as the company's director in 1966, narrates the incidents that lead to the downfall:

> For two three camps the collection was good. The salary and *batta* [special allowance] could also be given properly. But in between the agents of the circus owners somehow managed to get inside the circus. The owners had assembled at Thalassery behind closed doors to discuss how this circus could be ruined. P. T. Nanu popularly known among the circus folk as Engineer Nanu who had been a major force behind the forming of this circus, got angry. Then a rumor began systematically circulating that Nanu was a cheat. Nanu beat up a person who spread this gossip. There

---

[49] Champad Sreedharan and V. K. Suresh, *Thamb Paranja Jeevitham* [Life told by tent] (Kottayam: DC Books, 2012), 119.

were other minor issues also such as food in the artistes' mess was not good and healthy, and that salary was not being given properly. It turned into quarrels and created a serious crisis.

Another crisis had occurred in between. The circus was playing at Thirunelveli in Tamil Nadu and the tents were torn in the strong wind coming from Thengasi. And there were heavy rains. From there the circus went to Pathanamthitta in Kerala. Nanu contacted Anandan Nambiar, the MP and with his help some money was arranged and *korathuni* [hard cotton sheet] was bought for the tents. There was only average collection and nobody had money for two square meals. I had to pawn my golden ring to meet the expenses. The company travelled to Tamil Nadu for some time and came back to Kerala. By the end of 1966 almost all have left the company and it was shut down.[50]

Ravindran says there were several reasons for the failure of their circus company. A major problem must have been the embitterment of the workers. When he left after six months, he got only 50 rupees as the total remuneration. During those times as an acrobat he was getting a salary of 600 rupees. An article published in the *Circus Worker* magazine years later notes the case of a circus worker Raman and his family, deceived by the union: 'Raman who had worked day and night for the Akhil Bharath Circus Union says that the union betrayed the workers. Once they realized this hard truth, forty workers including Raman left the union at Kozhikode. It did not take much time for the union to become "vacant"'.[51]

Ravindran believes the absence of animals had also been a major reason for its failure. Champad sees an accident being the beginning of misfortune for the workers' company. 'The circus went from Thalassery to Mananthavady. There, while pitching the tent, the king pole fell down and a worker died. There began the misfortune of the circus company.' The strike which began with an injury on Nanu's forehead continued for 17 days and with declarations that the circus would not be allowed to move to another camp. The situation went out of their hands that organizers did not have money for their own daily expenses. He adds that a kind acquaintance offered his vehicle and a driver to move the canvas and equipment.[52]

---

[50] Interview, E. Ravindran.
[51] Nikhil, 'V. M. Raman', *Circus Worker* 1, no. 4 (July 1980): 28.
[52] Champad and Suresh, *Thamb Paranja Jeevitham*, 120–1.

It is indeed a historical irony that a circus company formed by the workers themselves had to shut down because of a workers' strike. Even after the extinction of both the union and the company, those who were part of them remained in the 'black' list of many of the owners and haunted in every way possible. A letter in the Gemini Circus letter pad dated 13 March 1968, Ahmadabad, addressed to E. Ravindran by a friend informs, 'A warrant is issued in your name. It seems to be from K. S. Menon. Beware, it is non-bailable. It was sent back saying you are no longer here.[53] When they come to know where you are, they will send it there, so be careful.' Ravindran could not join the Bharath circus as per the agreement was the reason for provocation. At the same time, another owner, late T. K. Kunhikannan was sympathetic towards the workers, says Ravindran. Kunhikannan cautions Ravindran in the same case, 'Only after finalizing the agreements with K. S. Menon, think about joining. Else it might lead to troubles'.[54]

Now we shall move onto the Indian Circus Employees Union, the only existing trade union of circus workers. I will also briefly look at a splinter union called the Circus Labour Union.

Indian Circus Employees Union

The central committee office of the Indian Circus Employees Union is situated in the new bus stand, a public square at Thalassery town, near the open market and the Fashion Street. Although the Union office was a separate room next to the Congress Party office, the three men in white *khadar mundu* (a traditional dhoti of Kerala made from khadi) and shirts, the room with big coloured photographs of Indira Gandhi and Rajiv Gandhi and new posters of Malayali Congress leaders with Sonia Gandhi, made me feel I had come to another Congress Party office. After taking a seat, I glanced again and noticed a small, black-and-white framed photograph of a young girl performing upside down on horseback in one of the corners. In another corner, there was a small old notice board with a torn notice with illegible print.

The three men in *khadar* were Raghavan, the first president of the Union, his office assistant Ramdas, and a party member. They were

---

[53] Private collection, E. Ravindran, Thalassery, Kerala.
[54] Private collection, E. Ravindran.

quite unlike the circus people I had met. People in the circus community were always warm, welcoming, intimate, and eager to tell their stories. Initially, they seemed a bit disturbed about my Delhi University credential and did not allow me to record the interview although later Raghavan generously handed over copies of all the case files, the *Circus Worker*, and the letters in his collection, and introduced me to other key leaders. Raghavan passed away on 2 March 2011.[55]

I met the other founding leaders J. F. Stephen[56] at Pallur in his house where he is staying with his wife Daisy, and A. V. Karim[57] and his family at his house in Chirakkara. But the most memorable and intimate relationship that grew into a family friendship was with V. M. Prabhakaran and his wife, Ramani, both retired circus performers. A trapeze artiste for decades, Prabakaran lived a healthy and cheerful life and fought for the circus workers' rights until he passed away on the May Day in 2012.[58]

[55] K. V. Raghavan joined the Congress party at the age of 14 through the Bala Sangh. In 1942, he became the state secretary of INTUC and the district administrator in 1946. With no other personal connection with circus, he was also the president of a number of trade unions in various sectors, such as cashew, timber, plywood industries, and head-load workers. After Raghavan passed away, C. C. Ashok Kumar was directly appointed as the president, though the bylaws of the union clearly mention that the selection of executive members should be through election.

[56] J. F. Stephen has worked in various circus companies of India as circus manager and retired from the job before 10 years. He was also the secretary of the union but left (though not officially) the union after his quarrel with Raghavan. He was a member of the Kerala Student Union (KSU) and has participated in its meetings and discussions at various places in Kerala.

[57] A. V. Karim joined the circus at an early age and worked in various companies as an artiste performing comic juggling, trapeze, and frog. He was active in union activities from its early phase. He left circus after the labour strikes and consequent dismissal, and migrated to the Persian Gulf where he spent almost a decade. Now he spends his retired life being disenchanted with union politics.

[58] V. M. Prabhakaran was the joint secretary of the Indian Circus Employees Union. He was from Gopalpetta, Thalassery, and joined circus as a young boy of 9 years along with his brother, Krishnan. He had about 50 years of experience as a trapeze artiste in various circus companies and also as an *ustad* (master) who taught his juniors.

On the other side of the town near the old bus stand, overlooking the Arabian Sea, is the office of another circus trade union by the name, 'Circus Labour Union'. The leaders of the Indian Circus Employees Union insist that it is a mere splinter group. But Dayanandan, who introduced himself as the president, told me that it was registered in 1998. The certificate framed and hung on the wall just behind Dayanandan's seat in the union office says that it is 'registered under Indian Trade Unions Act 1926' on '5th December 1998'.

The office, facing the pier port, is in one of the many old warehouse rooms built earlier by the British East India Company for the storage and export of goods. The ladder leading to the office was in a very bad shape that one had to literally cling on the rope tied to it. The moment one enters the room, one catches the big garlanded photo of Keeleri Kunhikannan Teacher. Dayanandan also clad in white *khadar* told me that he was moved by the deplorable situation of the circus workers and has no other connection with circus.[59] He also showed me the tailoring unit started for circus women in an adjacent room which is no longer functioning.

Raghavan told me that Dayanandan was the follower of the late A. C. Shanmughadas, former state minister and Nationalist Congress Party (NCP) leader. He alleged that Dayanandan collected the details of circus artistes from their office records, sent letters to the artistes, organized meetings independently, and formed a separate union splitting from the Indian Circus Employees Union. While C. C. Ashok Kumar, the present president of the Indian Circus Employees Union snubs 'Circus Labour Union' as 'a co-operative society', Dayanandan categorically states that it was registered as a trade union and functions as such.[60] We may note here that although the Indian Circus Employees

---

[59] Dayanandan's second wife, Komalam, was a circus artiste and, in fact, led the tailoring unit with a few retired circus artistes from Thalassery and Melur areas. Interview, K. V. Raghavan, Thalassery, 11 March 2010.

The unit was started when it was part of the Indian Circus Employees Union but later on after the split, the group of women moved with Komalam and Dayanandan to the new union. Interview, Dayanandan, Thalassery, 15 March 2010.

[60] Interview, K. V. Raghavan, Thalassery, 14 March 2010; C. C. Ashok Kumar; Dayanandan.

Union is supposed to be a national trade union and circus workers are spread across the country, trade union activities are limited to in and around Thalassery.

Since there have been only a few attempts to unionize circus artistes and labourers, one would generally expect a certain collective memory at work, but surprisingly not. The Akhil Bharath Circus Karmachari Sangh, interestingly, has been well documented by the circus community itself. In contrast, the remembrances regarding the circumstances that led to the formation of the Indian Circus Employees Union—the only existing 'national' union for circus artistes and labourers—about two decades later is astoundingly fragmentary. Let us look at how conflicting memories create varying stories with different key leaders and incidents.

A Tale of about a Strike

Only five days were left for the New Grand circus camp to shift from Belgaum. Small loads were already being sent in trucks to the next camping site. Though a workers' union had already been born by the time, not much happened publicly. It was a secret known only to a few people. But the owner of the New Grand circus, Anif, had his doubts regarding the existence of the union. The coolies from Andhra and Tamil Nadu were always complaining that they were being punished and tormented only because of the union membership. They were becoming the wrong doers in the eyes of the owner and the management.

And then one day the fateful happened. The ringmaster of the circus, Shivakumar was dismissed by the owner, Anif. No particular reason given and obviously the coolies and the ringmaster believed that it was because of the union membership. The 'union leaders' J. F. Stephen, V. M. Prabhakaran, A. V. Karim (incidentally, all Malayalis), and J. B. Swami (Sri Lankan Tamilian) went to meet the owner Anif. Their only request was to take the dismissed ringmaster back. But Anif was stubborn.

The leaders were in a tight spot. What should be the next move? It was then that the desperate leaders noticed the labourers who were removing the front tent of the circus animals. With not much hope they approached those workers and explained the situation. The workers agreed to stop their work and stand by the cause. It was a bold assurance and action for a circus tent of the times.

The circus was camped opposite the Belgaum Central Railway Station. The striking labourers who numbered about 20 went to the railway station to seek help from the CITU leaders there. Unfortunately, they were in some meeting. The next step was to contact the district collector or the superintendent of police (SP). The railway enquiry should know the whereabouts of the collector's bungalow. The railway staff understood that the circus workers were in trouble. Not only did they help with the details of the collector and the SP, they also informed the police control room that the circus workers were on strike.

None of the strikers had any prior experience of being in a protest or rally. With the escort of the police they walked towards the collector's bungalow. The only marking sound of the rally was the siren from the police jeep. The townsfolk gathered here and there and watched the proceedings. By then the news had reached the collector and he had ordered to redirect the protestors to the SP office.

As per the complaint of the strikers, the owner of the New Grand circus was called to the police station. He sent a manager and his nephew instead. This angered the police inspector and he decided to arrest the owner. But the strikers cooled him down and told him that they were willing to meet the owner at his place. They went back to the circus tent with the police. No sooner had the owner seen the police vehicle than he disappeared to the backyard of the tent. The inspector met him there and repeated the demand of the circus workers. But to no avail. Thus, it was decided that they would sit at the entrance. The inspector explained the legalities concerning the strike to them: a copy of the strike notice should be provided to the circus owner, the collector, the SP, and the local police station. But none of the strikers knew how to write a strike notice. The young inspector drafted a notice for them on his own letter pad.

As the circus was nearing to an end in the town, it had been running houseful for the last two weeks. The striking workers sat in front of the circus. No 'zindabad' or slogans. None of them had eaten anything. They had no money either. It was show-time and the record started playing at full volume. There was a military cantonment nearby and lots of soldiers were coming to see the circus with their families. The strikers requested them to show solidarity by boycotting. The first show of the day began before an almost vacant house. The only artistes who performed were the company girls. The next two shows were cancelled. By the time the whole city knew that there was a strike in the circus. The local media carried the news. There was an aluminium factory at Soppa nearby and the CITU workers from the company arrived at the tent and arranged food for the striking comrades; simple daal and rice. The railway CITU workers also came in solidarity. They threatened the circus owner that if he did not agree the demands of the labourers, his circus would die in Belgaum. The Belgaum district collector and the SP also visited the tent.

The CITU lawyer suggested that they list the demands of the strike. But there was no demand apart from that the dismissed had to be taken back. The CITU labourers and the advocate argued that 'there was no strike without demands' and a list of demands was prepared:[61]

a. The dismissed must be taken back.
b. The daily food allowance should be raised from Rs. 2 to Rs. 5 (the CITU people were of the opinion that it should be raised to Rs. 10 but the circus strikers felt that it would be injustice).
c. The labourers should not be bullied and beaten up.
d. Leaves and bonus had to be given properly.

The demands were presented to the owner and a settlement was prepared. The owner Anif who was from Andhra sobbed in Tamil, 'ennada ithukk thaannai ...' (Is it for this that you guys ...).

I have attempted to tell the tale above in a proper linear style, with a beginning, middle, and an end and without annoying blockages. But the memories of circus artistes and union members from which I have gleaned this narrative are full of conflicts and complexities. This is interesting because this is not something from a distant past. Still memories are in disarray and other sources scarce. For instance, the precise date of the decisive strike narrated above seems to have faded away from the memory of even the key players. For many it happened 'some months before the union registration'. Notably the year of the formation is also uncertain in 'official' memories. While the certificate of registration that hangs on the wall of the union office has 28 April 1979, Stephen

---

[61] Interview, Prabhakaran.

says the union was formed in 1977 and Raghavan 1966.[62] In another interview, Raghavan told me that the formation was in 1964 while he writes in his article, 'Sufferings of Circus Workers: Past and Present' that it was formed, registered, and is functioning from 1977.[63] Prabhakaran once said it was around the 1980s that it was organized, but in a later interview he told me that it was during 1977 that the Union got registered and was formed two–three months before that.

To cite another instance of significant discrepancy, as in the case of the year of the union formation, narratives of the founding members and office bearers mention different reasons for that crucial strike at the New Grand circus camp. According to Stephen, a motorcycle jumping artiste, Shivakumar's dismissal was the immediate reason for the strike and that he was dismissed for holding a union membership. Prabhakaran says that immediate call for the strike had been the dismissal of Shivan, an animal trainer, and some coolies. Though the names and incidents they refer to have some similarity, the occupation they attribute to the person are entirely different.[64] Quite in contrast to what these retired circus artistes remember, Raghavan states that it was the accident of the animal trainer Krishnan, which gave the impetus to the strike.[65] A. V. Karim, who was a comic juggler in the New Grand remembers that although Shivakumar, the animal trainer was dismissed from New Grand circus, the immediate reason for the strike was the poor quality of food served in the mess of the circus artistes.[66]

[62] Interview, J. F. Stephen, Pallur, 12 December 2010; K. V. Raghavan.

[63] K. V. Raghavan, 'Circus Jeevanakkarude Durithanhal Annum Innum' [Problems of circus workers: yesterday and today], Circus Worker 1, no. 11–12, (February–March 1981): 18–19.

[64] While Prabhakaran says he is a ringmaster, Stephen says he is a motorcycle-jumping artiste. Stephen does not refer to the coolies at all in his story.

[65] Raghavan's account goes on like this: a ringmaster named Krishnan was attacked by a leopard in his charge while he was sleeping near its cage. As a result, he lost his leg and was dismissed by the company owner; interview, Raghavan. It should be noted that all the narratives agree on one thing. The theatre was the New Grand Circus camp in Belgaum.

[66] Interview, A. V. Karim; Karim was the vice-president and J. B. Swami the president of the organization urgently formed at Belgaum in the New Grand Circus. Before INTUC took up the charge of the union, it was an association run only by circus labourers. Swami could not continue in the position when

J. F. Stephen's article in the *Circus Worker* annual edition carries with it a photograph of 13 persons with a caption that says, 'The first comrades who went on strike in India for circus workers'.[67] It is interesting that while many of the circus workers have preserved the photograph of the Akhil Bharath Circus inauguration, none of the key leaders of the Indian Circus Employees Union have this photo in their albums. Stephen remembers in his article his meetings with the comrades in a lodge room in Coimbatore and recognizes some of those in the photograph: 'A V Karim, V M Prabhakaran, J V Swami[68], catcher Vasu, K Ramadas known as clown Dasan, R Damodaran and Durgadas'.[69] When I enquired about the others in the photograph none of the leaders could recall any of the names and could refer to them only as 'the coolies'.

In the introduction of her remarkable book, *The Other Side of Silence: Voices from the Partition of India*, Urvashi Butalia succinctly notes the predicament of the historian working with memories:

> I am deeply aware of the problems that attach to the method I have chosen. There has been considerable research to show that memory is not ever 'pure' or 'unmediated'. So much depends on who remembers, when with whom, indeed to whom, and how. But to me the way people choose to remember an event, a history, is at least as important as what one might call the 'facts' of that history, for after all, these latter are not self-evident givens; instead, they too are interpretations, as remembered or recorded by one individual or another.[70]

As I have pointed out in the introduction, memories and memorabilia of the circus community and their oral narrations form the

---

he was terminated from the company and also when the organization became affiliated to INTUC at Thalassery. According to Prabhakaran, it was Stephen's association with the Congress party which affiliated the 'unorganized' organization to INTUC; interview, Prabhakaran.

[67] J. F. Stephen, 'Indian Circus Employees Union: Uthbhavavum Pravarthana Panthavum' [Indian circus employees union: origin and functions], *Circus Worker* (annual issue): 137.

[68] 'J. B.' Swami in Prabhakaran's narrative, and 'J. V.' Swami in Stephen's narrative.

[69] Stephen, 'Indian Circus Employees Union', 136.

[70] Urvashi Butalia, *The Other Side of Silence: Voices from the Partition of India* (New Delhi: Viking, 1998), 8.

crux of my primary sources. Though I cannot place my project on oral history alone, it is definitely a useful method to tell the tale of circus. Indira Chowdhury points out, 'oral history, which was regarded as being based on unreliable memory, actually demonstrated a complex connection between memory and identity and between individual and collective memory. The relationship between subjectivity and history could no longer be ignored'.[71] Pierre Nora says, 'With the appearance of the trace, of mediation, of distance, we are not in the realm of true memory but of history'.[72] For Brereton, memory is important since it 'allows for the retrieval of life stories of women (and men) as they themselves conceptualize and tell them: real people, real lives'.[73] Paul Thompson opines how oral history has transformed both the content and the process of history writing: 'History becomes more democratic. The chronicle of kings has taken into its concern the life experience of ordinary people.'[74]

Oral histories mainly speak of experiences of historical trauma and pain; the Holocaust or the Partition or the race and caste experiences. In the case of the circus people, the memories are mostly about everyday lives which are always on the move, shifting in places and periods; even if they build it around a location, along with a point in time, they move exploring other sites of memory. This constant move is evident in their recording and recollection. For example, an entry in Balakrishnan's diary from 1968: 'In Ranchi there was heavy rain and storm. In Jharsuguda, there was a terrible fight. While returning from Sampalpur saw the largest mountainous river in India. A must see spectacular scene.'[75]

[71] Indira Chowdhury, 'Speaking of the Past: Perspectives on Oral History', *Economic and Political Weekly* 49, no. 30 (2014): 40.

[72] Pierre Nora, 'Between Memory and History: *Les Lieux de Memoire*', trans. Marc Roudebush, *Representations* 26, no. 7 (2014 [1989]): 8.

[73] Bridget Brereton, 'Gendered Testimony: Autobiographies, Diaries and Letters by Women as Sources for Caribbean History', in *Slavery, Freedom and Gender: The Dynamics of Carribean Society*, eds Brian L. Moore, Carl Campbell, and Bryan Patrick (Jamaica: University of West Indies Press, 2001), 233.

[74] Paul Thompson, 'The Voice of the Past: Oral History', in *The Oral History Reader*, eds Robert Perks and Alistair Thompson (London and New York: Routledge, 1998), 26.

[75] Diary, P. K. Balakrishnan, circa 1965, private collection, Kausu, Melur.

Memories vary, obviously. What women remember is often strikingly different from that of their male counterparts. For instance, body is a significant presence in the memories and recounting of many women. Accidents in the tent and the banning of children and animals form an inevitable part of their narrations. Same is the case with memorabilia. The urge to historicize the union and their lives and be part of the historical narrative, could be seen as a salient feature with the circus trade union stories. But it is significant in itself that the remembrances of forming a trade union during late 1970s, just after the infamous Emergency, are packed with fragmentary narratives. D. Veeraraghavan notes,

> The growth and development of labour movement cannot be considered in isolation as an autonomous process. Its interaction with political movements under non-working class leadership, the impact of the changes in the economic situation and technologies on the objective formation of the working class, the attempts of the state to suppress, control or co-opt the labour movement, the influence of the various formations that relate their activities to control and leadership the labour movement—all these aspects are to be taken into account.[76]

Women's Strike

Another strike followed at the New Grand Circus. But unlike the earlier strike where women remained on the margins, this strike was carried out by them. Prabhakaran states that women were deliberately excluded from the first strike because of the apprehension about the consequences.[77] And besides, getting access to the company girls was a really difficult task. In this battle situation the only male worker who could interact with them in private was the company tailor. And the tailor at the New Grand Circus was none other than J. B. Swami, one of the key players in the first strike. Swami was the link between the union activists and the company girls.[78] About 15 Malayali girls became union members, but obviously it remained a closely guarded secret.

---

[76] D. Veeraraghavan, *The Making of the Madras Working Class* (New Delhi: Left World, 2013), 23.

[77] Interview, V. M. Prabhakaran.

[78] Interview, A. V. Karim.

The strike happened when the company was camped at Trichinapally, Tamil Nadu. The news that the women artistes had joined the union somehow got leaked. Karim points out that the food served for the company girls was of very bad quality. The girls, as planned, went on a hunger strike. The owner, Anif was out of station and when he was back his 'elder wife'[79] informed him that the girls have joined the Union. And the dismissals started.[80] J. F. Stephen notes, 'We continued with this underground operation for one year. In November 1977 while New Grand Circus was camping at Kannur, one of our letters sent to another circus company landed up in the hands of the management. They sent it to the owner of the New Grand.' In a sharp sarcastic tone, Stephen notes that 'in the court of the New Grand owner Mr. M D Anif' the ruling was that 'J V Swamy has committed the gravest crime in the Indian circus criminal code by enlisting the company girls as union members and hence he should be sentenced to life imprisonment'.[81]

At that time, unjust dismissals were common practice in circus companies. Police and other state officials would be bribed so that they would overlook such matters. Prabhakaran says, 'Nobody will stand up for you even when you were close with each other. Once you are on the other side, you will be all alone'. He points out that the circus owners and their Indian Circus Federation came out with support for the New Grand Circus management. They even sent a manager to destroy the Union.[82]

The New Grand Circus then moved to Kerala, Kozhikode, and Kannur. The next camp was in Mangalore. On the day of the Mangalore

---

[79] Prabhakaran says that Anif had five wives. Prabhakaran sometimes mentions that the owner was from Andhra, while some other times that he was a Tamilian. Whenever he quoted him, it was in Tamil; interview, Prabhakaran.

[80] Interview, Prabhakaran.

[81] Stephen, 'Indian Circus Employees Union', 137–8.

[82] Interview, V. M. Prabhakaran; Stephen and his wife recount that the owner of the New Grand Circus came to his home at Gopalpetta, Thalassery, along with some of his men and promised Stephen that he would get him whatever he wanted, money or job. But the condition was that he should break up with the union. But Stephen decided to stay with the union and the workers just as his wife had advised him. His wife told me that his decision left her and their children with no means to live, but she did not want him to cheat his fellow workers. Interview, Stephen; Daisy, Pallur, 12 December 2010.

opening the police arrived in large numbers. The owner had filed a complaint at the local police station against the union troublemakers. The union members had been in constant touch with the local INTUC offices in every town they had camped. The Congress leader in Mangalore whom they contacted was reluctant to help them and so, the union members approached the Janata Party leader who was a young man and willing to help.[83] He advised them not to go to the police station since he was sure that they would be beaten up. He contacted the Prime Minister's office—the Janata Party was in power in the central government at the time—and made necessary arrangements. At the police station, the camp manager was waiting for the arrest of the union people, blissfully unaware that they had managed the support from the highest office in the country. Naturally, the poor guy was admonished by the police inspector. While at the tent, the *flying trapeze* net[84] was being untied as the others also thought that the union activists would be arrested and jailed.

It is interesting to note that though INTUC had formed the circus workers' union, the circus workers actually had to negotiate with political leaders of almost all the parties directly. K. V. Raghavan, the INTUC leader and the former president of the Union, believes that only INTUC could have formed a circus union because it was a 'national' organization. Karim is of the opinion that though Stephen belonged to the Congress party, he and Prabhakaran believed in Communist ideals, as is apparent from their reference to fellow members as 'comrade'.[85]

Before long Stephen was dismissed from the New Grand Circus for organizing the union though it was not openly stated.[86] He was given about INR 5,000, the balance amount of his salary. He was without a job for the next 10 years.[87] But definitely the situation changed with the two

---

[83] Prabhakaran says that the Congress leader was leaving for Shivakasi and he introduced the Janata Party leader to them.

[84] 'Flying trapeze' is the first item in all Indian circuses.

[85] Interview, A. V. Karim; Prabhakaran told me that he does not believe in any political ideologies. Interview, Prabhakaran.

[86] Stephen did not tell me what reasoning the owner gave for the dismissal. Prabhakaran says it was 'drinking and smoking', interview, Prabhakaran.

[87] Later he joined 'Rambo', the circus company of his friend, Dileep; interview, Stephen.

successive strikes. Things would never be the same. Stephen remembers that from then if the coolies did not work properly the owner would approach the union and complain. Whenever they shifted base the union leaders' first duty would be to find a labour office because it was sure that there will be problems.

Other Strikes

Stephen organized a strike in the Bharath Circus owned by K. S. Menon when he was dismissed from the New Grand with the help. The reason again was the senseless dismissal of one of the labourers. Stephen ran the strike along with about 15 supporters of the Congress Party at Palayam Kotta in Tamil Nadu where the company was camping. Stephen was arrested and spent about seven days in the Palayam Kotta jail. According to his narration, none of the political leaders came to help him. He arranged bail with the help of some strangers (who were the local people) whom he paid a large sum of money for standing his surety. He continued with the same strike at Ottappalam in front of the house of K. S. Menon and the Bharath Circus went out of business. A similar strike happened in the Great Bombay Circus against the dismissal of some labourers. In the National Circus camped at Gundur in Karnataka a publicity worker died in an accident, but the management refused to pay compensation. Stephen filed a case in the Court and INR 70,000 was granted as compensation.[88]

The *Circus Worker*: Class Conflict in Print

The union launched a periodical, the *Circus Worker*, in April 1980. The union had been publishing pamphlets before this transformation into a magazine format with monthly periodicity. The anger and desire of the workers found expression on the pages of the magazine.

In the very first issue, J. F. Stephen compellingly notes, 'All the 295 circus companies operating in India and the 48,000 laborers working in them come under the acts and rules in the country regarding labour disputes, compensation, gratuity, bonus and provident fund.

---

[88] Interview, Stephen.

But since circus is an industry that keeps moving from one place to another the circus owners violate all these laws'.[89] In his letter addressed to the Employees' Provident Fund Commissioner, New Delhi, dated 8 February 2011, Prabhakaran complaints that the 'Rajkamal' and 'Amar' circuses were sold without the knowledge of the workers and that many of them have not been included in the provident fund scheme: 'Some of them are still working there for a salary of Rs. 300/-. The owners deceive the laborers by showing lesser salary so that they do not have to pay a large sum for their P F'.[90] The memorandum filed by C. C. Ashok Kumar, present president of Indian Circus Employees Union, puts forth that to avoid this complexity, 'it is necessary that before issuing license for performance of each camp, there should be certain verification of registers and records regarding provident fund, list of employees and salary registers etc., pertaining to relevant labour laws'.[91] He further demands, 'there should be fixed minimum wages and circus workers have to be included in the schedule of minimum wages act 1948' and requests the government to bring out a special legislation for circus employees.

The article pointedly titled 'Sarkassukar—Ayitha Jathikkar' (Circus workers—untouchable castes) notes that while the deaths and accidents in cinema are highlighted in media, none of the accidents in circuses are reported. The government has established certificates and academies to promote and honour artistes from various fields, but it has completely neglected the circus people.[92] Almost all the issues of the *Circus Worker* magazine refer to instances of unexplained dismissal of labourers in various companies. Kandambulli Balan's book *Circus*, written half a century back, has an entire chapter on the problems of circus workers and owners. He points to the 'merciless training given to children by the uneducated trainers'. He opines that not only the artistes but other labourers such as 'managers, clerks, ticket sellers, animal trainers, ring boys and others' work for more than 15 hours a

---

[89] J. F. Stephen, 'Maattuvin Chattnhale' [Change the laws], *Circus Worker* 1, no. 1 (April 1980).

[90] Private collection, V. M. Prabhakaran.

[91] Private collection, C. C. Ashok Kumar.

[92] Thalayi Padmanabhan, 'Sarkassukar Ayitha Jathikkar' [Circus workers untouchable castes], *Circus Worker* 1, no. 4 (July 1980): 16.

day. 'Insecure employment, rough living conditions, irregular working hours, harassment and physical torture' are some of the major problems faced by the circus workers.[93] The artistes have a different menu and mess. The ring boys, animal trainers, and contract labourers have to do with a substandard mess and its food.[94] Prabhakaran's letter notes that the only people who benefitted from Indira Gandhi's decision to exempt circuses from entertainment tax are the circus owners.[95] Many of the owners prefer to stay in expensive hotels while they use their tents only while they visit their companies.[96] Likewise, the management staff and sometimes the male stars of the ring will stay in hotel rooms. The *Circus Worker* reproduces a news report about 150 workers held captive in Bihar by the local people because the company owner who owed them INR 30,000 fled.[97]

Laws and Circus Workers

Raghavan points out that because of some minor loopholes in the law, on many instances, the circus workers do not get the deserved gratuity, workmen's compensation, and maternity benefits like other industrial workers. He further adds that there should be some kind of legal amendments particularly for circus workers as in the case of mine, estate, or railway workers to solve this problem.[98]

But loopholes in the law do not seem to be the guilty party in all instances. 'The Maternity Benefit (Mines and Circus) Rules, 1963'

---

[93] Balan, *Circus*, 130–1.

[94] Interview, Pushpa; Kausu; Leela.

[95] Translated from the Malayalam letter addressed to K. G. Balakrishnan, chief justice of India (n.d.). A copy was also addressed to Solicitor General Gopal Subrahmaniam (private collection, late V. M. Prabhakaran).

[96] Interview, Babu; Dilip Nath, owner of the Great Bombay Circus, told me that he has stayed at the Oberoi hotel in Calcutta and Nirulas in Delhi as a child while his father and uncle managed the circus. Interview, Dilip Nath, New Delhi, 19 December 2012.

[97] *Circus Worker*, August 1980, 28.

[98] K. V. Raghavan, 'Indiayile Thozhil Niyamanhalum Circus Thozhilalikalum' [Labour laws in India and the circus workers], *Circus Worker* 1, no. 2 (May 1980): 23.

clearly states that each company should keep a muster roll and enter all the particulars of women workers employed in mines and circuses: 'the employer shall make payment of the maternity benefit and any other amount due under the Act' and 'medical bonus shall be paid along with the second instalment of the maternity benefit'. But even after such laws came into force, none of these benefits are given to a circus woman and she goes for delivery without any benefits. Kausu told me that she had performed in the ring for seven months while she was carrying.[99]

Benefits

For those employed in the circus companies the foremost advantage of the union formation has been that they have certain rights and bargaining power with managements and state bodies.[100] Pension, provident fund, gratuity, retrenchment compensation, and all other benefits to be provided under the Statutory Act are given to the artistes of a circus company now. Raghavan writes that before the collaboration with the union, the circus workers hardly knew bonus, gratuity, and compensation for accidents and dismissals. He claims that the Indian Circus Employees Union made the government recognize the circus as a mobile industry and bring it under the Shops and Commercial Establishment Act.[101] Raghavan told me that Kerala is the only state in India that provides pension to retired circus artistes and that is because of the union and INTUC.[102] The state government allotted the monthly pension scheme for the circus workers of Kerala in 1980. It was INR 150 at the time and has been increased recently to INR 1200.[103] The *Circus Worker* notes in its editorial, 'At last the Kerala Government has decided to give pension to the poor and ailing circus artistes who have sacrificed their golden

[99] Interview, Kausu.
[100] Interview, Stephen.
[101] Raghavan, 'Circus Jeevanakkarude Durithanhal Annum Innum', 20, 19.
[102] Interview, Raghavan.
[103] GO (MS) no. 134/2009 under the Department of Education, Youth, and Sports, Thiruvananthapuram, dated 18 June 2009, shows that the pension has been revised to INR 500 and an order has been passed permitting 99 'disabled circus artists' eligible for pension. This order has been passed with reference to the GO dated 15 May 1980 (MS) no. 201/80/G.A.D.

adolescence and youth for the glory of circus art, which will be a relief in the twilight of their lives.'[104] But this scheme only includes circus performers and leaves out circus managers, animal trainers, and caretakers, ring boys, entrepreneurs, contract labourers, tent masters, and also the circus clowns. It is interesting to note that while the membership is 'restricted to the workers employed in the Circus establishments all over India' as per the bylaw of the union, it now gives membership and certifies eligibility for the State Government pension to only Malayali circus performers. Artistes from other regions who married Malayalis and settled in Kerala are excluded from the pension scheme. But Karim insists that the union takes action from the complaint of any circus worker.[105] Salary structure and daily allowances have been modified considerably. For instance, the average salary a female artiste receives nowadays is INR 4000–5000 while it had been a paltry INR 100, couple of decades ago. This is how Raghavan explains the modus operandi of the union: 'There is a Unit of the Union in all the circus companies, big and small. This unit is the Division Committee; if there is any problem in any Division Committee, we will be informed and the Union will look into it.'[106]

'Art' and 'Labour'

The American circus historian Janet M. Davis sharply notes, 'the social structure of the railroad circus was built upon an occupational hierarchy akin to a caste system, in which musicians ate and slept with musicians, and candy "butchers" with candy butchers.'[107] Division of labour and hierarchical status plays a very important role in circus life. This is more than evident in the spatial arrangement of the tents in a camp. Ramani notes sharply that ring boys are just like 'untouchable low castes' in the hierarchy. They are unorganized, bound by unjust contracts, and lead a life of poverty and suffering without proper sleep,

---

[104] 'Editorial', *Circus Worker* 1, no. 3 (1980): 3.

[105] Interview, A. V. Karim.

[106] Interview, Raghavan.

[107] Janet M. Davis, *The Circus Age: Culture and Society under the American Big Top* (Chapel Hill: University of North Carolina Press, 2002), 62.

food, and clothing. Owners easily wash their hands of responsibility if any serious accidents happen to them.[108] Balan points out that in Soviet circuses, major artistes would change into the uniform of labourers and assist the ring boys soon after their performance, in hope that this would be an eye opener for their Indian counterparts.[109] One can see here how 'art' and 'labour' are differentiated and 'art' is held as something more significant. Here, it is notable that skilled jobs, such as circus performances, animal training, or even a tent master's job that requires expertise, are valued more while the unskilled job of the ring boys (that could be anything from picking the hat from the ring to erecting the pole) is not defined. Ring boys and helper boys who reach circus are those who have tried their hands at various unskilled jobs and many of them are from 'lower' castes.[110]

Ring Boys

As the name indicates, the major duties of the ring boys are concerning the ring. They arrange the equipment used for performances in the ring, such as pulling the ropes for *Dental*, untying the flying trapeze net, and checking the tickets, apart from the loading and unloading, carrying the heavy poles and galleries, and other construction works around the tent, such as 'watering the rings, dusting the galleries, attending the animals for bathing and feeding'.[111] The ring boys I met in Gemini, Jumbo, and Royal Circuses were mostly from the North-Eastern states, West Bengal, Uttar Pradesh, Bihar, Odisha, Bangladesh, and Nepal. Ramani

---

[108] Ramani Thalassery, 'Circussile "Ring Boyi" kal' [Ring boys in the circus], *Circus Worker* 1, no. 5 (August 1980): 14, 16–17.

[109] Kandambulli Balan, 'Soviet Circus Indiayil' [Soviet circus in India], *Mathrubhumi Illustrated Weekly* 34, no. 51 (1957): 21.

[110] It is worthwhile to note that in USA, a circus labourer is often referred to as a 'roustabout', an unskilled or casual labourer, most probably because of the popular Disney animation film *Dumbo* (1941) and its television spin-off *Dumbo's Circus*. The song sequence in the film, 'Song of the Roustabouts' featuring faceless black circus workers is considered to be one of the most explicit racist portrayals in American popular culture.

[111] S. Narayanan, 'Survey of Circus in India', *Circus Worker* 1, no. 4 (1980): 13.

notes that they are a powerless community that cannot bargain with the owners for even their basic needs.[112] When the tent is being built, during the loading and unloading sessions, the ring boys hardly sleep; many of them work 24 hours a day.[113]

Unlike the circus performers, musicians, or animal trainers, the ring boys hardly have a family lineage in the circus, obviously related to the 'unskilled' nature of their job. For example, Ali Aktar from Siliguri reached the circus after doing petty jobs in various cities such as Guwahati, Nagaland, and Ernakulam.[114] Umesh of the Royal Circus was doing labour work in the metro railway, Delhi, before.[115] Both their parents are peasants in their native places.

Anne Phillips and Barbara Taylors who notes that skill is an 'ideological category on certain types of work by virtue of the sex and power of the workers who perform it', points out that women workers with 'their family responsibilities' and 'partial dependence on a man's wage' were regarded as 'secondary workers who can be pushed back into their primary sphere-the home' and this contributed to their vulnerability as workers,

> When knowledge and training are required to make a product, the worker who has that knowledge ... also has power over the speed and quality of the work. If however, that craft knowledge can be transferred from the worker to the technical experts or managers, and the worker reduced to the performance of routine operations within a process s/he no longer fully comprehends, capitalist control over production is greatly increased. The worker becomes 'de-skilled', as the knowledge which was once part of the job becomes part of the power of capital itself.[116]

Women and Children

In a letter published in the *Circus Worker*, Ramani, daughter of a circus artiste, says, 'It is a fact that our society is scornful of women circus

[112] Thalassery, 'Circussile "Ring Boyi" kal', 17.

[113] Interview, E. Ravindran; Ajitha, Melur, 12 March 2006.

[114] Interview, Ali Aktar, Royal Circus, 12 May 2008.

[115] Interview, Umesh, Royal Circus, 12 May 2008.

[116] Anne Phillips and Barbara Taylor, 'Sex and Skill: Notes towards a Feminist Economics', *Feminist Review* 6 (1) (1980): 79–88.

artistes,' and asks, 'Isn't it a fact that the majority of public are not ready to marry a circus woman?'[117] Ramachandran argues that it is not just films that have 'sex appeal', but that circus has it too: 'A recent survey says that seventy percent of the spectators come to see voluptuous female bodies up close.'[118] Vasantha, a retired artiste, says that the contractors made agreements with their parents for meagre amounts, while they collected hefty sums from the circus owners in exchange for them, and the artistes were forced to stay on for years after the completion of the agreement period.[119] Ramani says that many parents send their children to circus, thinking they would get good food and salary.[120] Yamuna, a retired artiste, living in a charity old-age home, says that she was left without a single paisa upon retirement as her owner looted her of all her money and gold.[121] A report in the *Circus Worker*, aptly titled 'Avar Swathanthryathilekk!' (Towards freedom!), is about three circus couples united by the Chief Magistrate Court, Thrissur. When the Venus Circus management came to know about their love affair, it kept the girls in their custody and dismissed the young men, who moved court.[122]

In the same issue of the magazine, J. F. Stephen notes, 'The dependents [of the circus women] in their native places may not be getting the money mentioned in the agreement. The letters sent by friends and relatives might be resting in the iron treasury of the circus owner.' He goes on, 'It seems the circus owners have forgotten that bonus is an amount kept separate from the salary which is rightful to the workers.'[123] The 'Union News' says, 'As per the complaint of the six children in Aroma Lion Circus, the Union members went and saved them and entrusted them into the hands of their parents.'[124] A. V. Karim mentions many

[117] Ramani Thalassery, 'Circus Kalakarikalekkurich Oralpam' [A little about circus women artistes], *Circus Worker* 1, no. 3 (August 1980): 27.

[118] Nedunhanda Ramachandran, 'Circus Koodarathil' [In the circus tent], *Janayugam Weekly* 44, no. 12 (June 1969): 23.

[119] Interview, Vasantha, Melur, 29 May 2008.

[120] Thalassery, 'Circus Kalakarikalekkurich Oralpam', 27.

[121] Interview, Yamuna.

[122] 'Avar Swathanthryathilekk!' [Towards freedom!], *Circus Worker* 1, no. 1 (1980).

[123] Stephen, 'Maattuvin Chattnhale'.

[124] 'Union News', *Circus Worker* 1, no. 1 (July 1980): 2.

such complaints.[125] Kandambulli Balan notes that small children are not seen in Russian circuses and to employ them, the companies need to seek permissions from the labour unions and industrial departments.[126] Joseph Peter speaks about the crude and cruel training given to children by the trainers.[127] The bylaw of the union states that '[m]embership is limited to such worker who has attained the age of 16', while child performers were always an integral part of the circus industry.

The Indian Circus Employees Union pointed out in recent times, after the ban on children under 14 came into force,

> Children of circus workers, by and large, travel with their parents to wherever the circus company moves. The constant shifts from place to place pose great challenges before the parents in imparting formal education to their children. Since every child below fourteen years has the constitutional right to compulsory education, alternative educational provisions may be arranged for the children of circus workers and children above fourteen should be allowed to get professional training under the supervision of experts.[128]

Owners' Rule

Since circus is a wholly private enterprise, the owners exercise tyranny in the tents—as reiterated by workers and unions alike. If anybody defies or shows disobedience, s/he is dismissed undoubtedly, but there are also incidents of physical assault.[129] Prabhakaran's letter addressed to the chief justice of India and the solicitor general lists horrifying tales of physical and sexual abuse unleashed by the owners and their aides in the tents. In a similar grievance letter, addressed to the same, Raghavan alleges that there is a tendency among the owners to set fire to the tents and destroy properties to claim insurance money.[130]

---

[125] A. V. Karim, 'Circus Kalakaranmarude Bhavi' [The future of circus artistes], *Circus Worker* 1, no. 1 (1980): 2.

[126] Balan, 'Circus Sovitenaattil', 27.

[127] Joseph Peter, 'Thallu Kondittilla Phalam!' [No use of beatings!], *Circus Worker* 1, no. 5 (August 1980): 5–7.

[128] Letter draft, Indian Circus Employees Union, Thalassery, n.d.

[129] Interview, Ravindran, Gemini Circus, Neyyattinkara, 12 July 2012.

[130] Letter addressed to the chief justice of India, private collection, K. V. Raghavan, n.d.

Owners of big circus companies are immensely rich and run many other businesses. While a circus company plays in major cities such as Bangalore or Calcutta, the income for a single day might go up to INR 25 lakhs, while the investment at the outset must have been a mere INR 25,000.[131] Prabhakaran's letter states, 'No circus in India has been begun with an investment of one lakh rupees by and large. All these were begun with temporary arrangements and with the partnership of acquaintances and friends.'[132]

State and Circus

Raghavan notes that there is no system to provide protection or insurance against accidents. He further adds that the state and central governments should come up with new plans and schemes to encourage circus workers.[133] Ajith Kumar—who met with an accident while performing, which resulted in total paralysis and ultimately was fatal—had difficulty getting his insurance amount as the company management had played a fraudulent game, says his wife who is also a retired circus artiste.[134] The *Kalakaumudi* reports Nani's wretched, paralysed life after her fall while performing the cycle trick.[135] Raghavan notes the deaths of child artistes, Vanaja, Anjali, and Anitha, and the jeep jumpers, Leela and Mala, of the Rayman Circus.[136] Champad describes three fatal accidents

[131] Interview, A. V. Karim, Cherakkara, 23 July 2010.

[132] Letter addressed to the chief justice of India; private collection, V. M. Prabhakaran.

[133] Raghavan, 'Circus Jeevanakkarude Durithanhal Annum Innum', 20.

[134] I met Ajith Kumar at his humble home in Thalassery. He fell down from the trapeze and got paralysed from neck down after a spinal code injury. He has been totally bedridden for the past 10 years. He got 80,000 rupees from the insurance company, but the provision for this compensatory payment was through the company management and they unfortunately withheld the payment for a long time, claiming that they had spent that much for the treatment. Interview, Ajith Kumar and Reeja, Kolassery, 2 May 2012.

[135] Surendran, 'Koodara Smaranakalude Thanalil' [In the shadow of memories about the tent], *Kalakaumudi* no. 280 (1981): 18.

[136] K. V. Raghavan, 'Kalayum Kalaaswadakarum' [Art and spectators], *Circus Worker* 1, no. 3 (June 1980): 30.

of Narayani, Rajaram, and Nani, and notes that there are too many reported accidents in the rings that cannot be listed in one go.[137] Balan writes on the accidents that happened in Kamala Circus alone that were fatal to four performers.[138] Ravindran told me that there would hardly be any acrobat who had not faced an accident in the ring and it completely depended on their luck.[139] K. V. Raghavan notes wryly that it becomes big news when film stars meet with minor accidents, but fatal accidents happen with circus artistes in the ring at the time of their performances, often resulting in death, but this hardly appears as news and the spectators seem to forget it easily.[140]

An editorial of the *Circus Worker* notes the plight of small circuses in the hands of ignorant officials: 'Both the State and Central governments have not taken into consideration the differences in the size of the circus companies or the financial condition of the proprietors or other such factors.' It further adds, 'In the eyes of our government the destitute circuses run by some families for daily bread in Kerala, Karnataka, Tamil Nadu, Andhra and Maharashtra and the huge industry called circus that flourish on the sweat of poor artistes owned by filthy rich people with cunning business acumen who lives in palatial bungalows are one and the same!'[141] Rajan Palayad notes that the state policy towards circuses, both small and big, is the same, resulting in a great dilemma for the small groups of entertainers.[142]

As noted earlier, *Mathrubhumi Illustrated Weekly* had published several articles on the circus in various countries during the 1950s and 1960s. These articles probably represent the hope that the newly formed democratic government will take hold of the circus industry. Bhaskara Panikker says in his article on the Soviet Circus, 'Russian circus had a similar drabness like our circus even after producing numerous wonderful performers. This was because the proprietors' eyes were on profit and the artistes were not getting reasonable wages'. He further

[137] Champad, *An Album of Indian Big Tops*, 80–5.
[138] Balan, *Circus*, 6–8.
[139] Interview, Ravindran.
[140] Raghavan, 'Kalayum Kalaaswadakarum', 28–30, 5.
[141] 'Editorial', *Circus Worker* 1, no. 2 (May 1980): 1.
[142] Rajan Palayad, 'Jeevithamenna Circus' [Life that is circus], *Circus Worker* 1, no. 11–12 (February–March 1981): 4

adds that the circus, after the Revolution, omitted all those deadly acts that put the artistes in danger and became one that respected human life.[143] Both Balan and Damodaran write that they were astounded to learn that many Russian performers were bachelor-degree holders. Damodaran opines, 'The lack of higher education remains a stumbling block in the way to a good future for these acrobats who are the best in their field. They are not able to accept offers from different parts of the world because of this lack'.[144] Kandambulli Balan, impressed by the relation between the Czechoslovakia and its circus team, informs the Malayali readers, 'The circus artistes get all state benefits such as bonus, pension, healthcare and health insurance. ... Every year the government arranges foreign performance tours for two to three circus companies. The members of these companies get around three hundred rupees tour fee monthly, along with their regular salary'.[145]

Padmanabhan argues that the state is being partial to circus while it gives honorary degrees and awards to experts in music, classical arts, and theatre. He asks, 'Is it because the kathakali performers and its patrons are upper castes that it is reputed? Is it because the circus artistes are low castes such as ironsmith, Thiyyas and fisher folk that it is treated with disrepute?'[146]

Rajnarayan Chandavarkar, who examines the social formation of working classes and the development of industrial capitalism in colonial India, observes,

> Historians who set out to investigate 'popular culture' or delineate 'working-class culture' have sometimes either written its economic and social context out of the account or simply taken it for granted. ... Conversely, assumptions about the cultural characteristics of the working classes at various stages who of development have often informed the analysis of their attitudes to work and politics. It is often taken for granted that casual workers primarily sought temporary employment, rural migrants

[143] Bhaskara Panikker, 'Soviet Circus', *Mathrubhumi Illustrated Weekly* 29, no. 52 (1952): 8.

[144] K. Damodaran, 'Keralathinoru Circus University' [A circus university for Kerala], *Mathrubhumi Illustrated Weekly*, 35, no. 19 (1957): 31.

[145] Kandambulli Balan, 'Czechoslovakian Circus', *Mathrubhumi Illustrated Weekly* 38, no. 8 (1960): 9.

[146] Padmanabhan, 'Sarkassukar Ayitha Jathikkar', 16.

were unsuited to factory discipline and early industrial workers were inherently volatile. ... These characterizations constituted the ideology of capitalists seeking a more firmly subordinated labour force and historians have often adopted them unwittingly.[147]

The formation of trade unions in the Indian circus should also be read within this context. But if we shift our focus for a moment to non-human labour in the circus rings, other interesting questions will emerge. Could the performance of animals be viewed as 'labour'? Are our theories of labour equipped enough to address subjects such as performing animals? As pointed out in the second chapter, Jason Hribal argues that 'animals are part of the working class' as 'animal rights movements are part of the working class movement, for their formations have always been linked', although he hardly mentions performing animals. But the challenge to labour history in addressing animal labour is three-fold, as he observes: firstly, to 'consider the role of animals in the development of capitalism', secondly, 'the basic assumption that one needs to be human to be a worker', and lastly, in question are 'the parameters currently applied to the sphere of the "working class".[148] We may also remember the telling query posed by the Kerala High Court in the circus animal ban case: 'If humans are entitled to fundamental rights, why not animals?'[149] With regard to disability rights, Kalpana Kannabiran has pointed out,

> The wisdom of the movement for disability rights has undoubtedly played a key, constitutive role in terms of revisiting the discourse on the labourscape. ... To the extent that the disability stand point shines the torch on 'real utopia', and redefines democratic egalitarian possibilities, the concern with disability is not limited to persons with disabilities, but proliferates from there to encompass resistance to all forms of discrimination and creates a different language for law and justice.[150]

[147] Rajnarayan Chandavarkar, *The Origins of Industrial Capitalism in India: Business Strategies and the Working Classes in Bombay, 1900–40* (Cambridge: Cambridge University Press, 1994), 16.

[148] Jason Hribal, '"Animals are Part of the Working Class": A Challenge to Labor History'. *Labor History* 44, no. 4 (2003): 436, 453.

[149] Judgment 2000.

[150] Kalpana Kannabiran, 'Who is a "Worker"? Problematising "Ability" in the Conceptualisation of Labour', *Indian Journal of Labour Economics* 57, no. 1 (2003): 86.

The study of 'labour' in the circus industry, I hope, will contribute to the history of labour in terms of a radically different understanding of human and non-human labour. In the case of non-human performers/ workers, the justice systems hardly take into consideration the economics of labour, nor have labour histories problematized non-human labour enough to redefine the concept of labour itself.

It would be interesting in this context to note the Uttarakhand High Court judgment by the division bench of Justice Rajiv Sharma and Justice Lok Pal Singh: 'The entire animal kingdom including avian and aquatic are declared as legal entities having a distinct persona with corresponding rights, duties and liabilities of a living person.'[151] In another judgment, a bench headed by Rajiv Sharma declared the rivers Ganga and Yamuna as juristic/legal persons/living entities having the status of a living person, although the Supreme Court stayed the High Court order later on.[152] It triggers thoughts on whether one really has to be a living person to possess legal rights, and also the duplicity with which these justice questions are dealt with.

From the thorny questions regarding labour of adults and animals, let us move on to another problematic terrain: child performers. The ban on the training and performance of children in 2011 by the apex court brings to the fore a lot of significant issues regarding the rights of children, notions of exploitative labour, and a history and culture of performative forms.

[151] Judgment dated 4 July 2018, *Narayan Dutt Bhatt* v *Union of India*, Writ Petition no. 43 of 2014.

[152] Judgment dated 20 March 2017, *Mohd. Salim* v *State of Uttarakhand and others*, Writ Petition no. 126 of 2014.

Coda

Children of a Lesser God

Two children's rights activists, Kailash Satyarthi from India and young Malala Yousafzai from Pakistan, shared the 2014 Nobel Peace Prize. This global recognition for Mr Kailash Satyarthi has an intimate connection with Indian circus. The peace prize winner has been waging a war, so to say, against circus companies in India for decades:

> Mr. Satyarthi was lying on the ground, bleeding profusely from the head, while a group of men converged on him with bats and iron rods. They worked for the Great Roman Circus, which was illegally employing teenagers trafficked from Nepal as dancing girls. Mr. Satyarthi, a Gandhian activist in simple white cotton tunic, had come to free them. (*The New York Times*, 10 October 2014)[1]

On 18 April 2011, the Supreme Court of India banned the employment and performance of children and adolescents below 18 years in Indian circus.[2] This was another fateful moment for Indian circus,

---

[1] Nisha P R, 'Jumping Devils: A Tale of Circus Bodies', *Perspectives in Indian Development*, Occasional Paper Series 55 (New Delhi: Nehru Memorial Museum and Library, 2015), 1–25.

[2] The Supreme Court ban on children below 14 in 2011 was based on various laws including the Child Labour (Prohibition and Regulation) Act, 1986; Employment of Children Act, 1938; The Children (Placing of Labour) Act, 1933; the Minimum Wages Act, 1976; the Bonded Labour System (Abolition) Act, 1976; Juvenile Justice (Care and Protection of Children) Act, 2000; and

like the ban on the training and performance of certain wild animals two decades earlier. Under Article 21A, the Supreme Court ordered the Government of India to issue suitable notifications prohibiting the employment of children in circuses within two months from the date of the judgment. The Bench also directed the government to conduct simultaneous raids in all circus companies to liberate children and check if their fundamental rights were being violated. It was on the petition filed by Kailash Satyarthi's non-governmental organization Bachpan Bachao Andolan (BBA) (Save the Childhood Movement) that the Supreme Court ban came into force. They argued that children in circuses underwent exploitative labour, sexual abuse, bondage, and servitude:

> The petition has been filed in public interest under Article 32 of the Constitution in the wake of serious violations and abuse of children who are forcefully detained in circuses, in many instances, without any access to their families under extreme inhuman conditions. There are instances of sexual abuse on a daily basis, physical abuse as well as emotional abuse. The children are deprived of basic needs of food and water.[3]

The petitioners further elaborated that they had appealed to all major circus company owners to stop 'trafficking, bondage, child labour and other violations of child rights' and held campaigns in front of many circuses. The petitioners proposed to notify the circus as a 'hazardous industry'. According to them, at least 500 girls were illegally employed in about 50 circuses across India. The instability in their life due to the 'nomadic existence' and the lack of formal education were other major criticisms against circus. Along with these are cramped spaces, inadequate food, erratic sleep timings, poor sanitation, absence of health care personnel, high risk factor of the acrobatics, paltry remuneration, contract bondage, and, above all, the daily routine in circuses hindering their all-round development. However, the rescued children were

---

the Right of Children to Free and Compulsory Education Act, 2009. The Child Labour (Prohibition and Regulation) Amendment Act 2016, no. 35 of 2016, substituted 'children' with 'adolescents' by renaming the Act itself as Child and Adolescent Labour (Prohibition and Regulation) Act, 1986, and raising the age limit to 18.

[3] Writ Petition (C) no. 51, 2006, *Bachpan Bachao Andolan* v *Union of India & Others* (hereafter, 'BBA Petition, 2006').

proposed to be kept in the care of protective homes unless their parents were willing to take them. Bhuvan Ribhu, national secretary of the BBA, said that many of them have returned home and they have taken in some of the children.[4] Jamie Skidmore, in his article written on child performers in Indian circuses, notes that BBA has been 'rescuing' child performers with the help of local authorities since 2003 and has ashrams known as Bal Mitra Gram (child friendly village) that have been opened in different locations in India with an aim to 'eliminate child labour'.[5] Some other NGOs, such as the Child Line India Foundation, have also stepped forward to take care of these children. The court instructed that Nepali children be handed over to the NGOs in Nepal. The Esther Benjamins Trust functioning in Nepal claims on its website,

> Our NGO rescues Nepalese children who have been trafficked or displaced into India—including many who were sold into Indian circuses and forced to work as performers. We offer refuge and rehabilitation to rescued children and young people (and sometimes also their siblings) who cannot be returned to their families for fear of being re-trafficked. Our refuges offer access to a full education and a range of vocational training opportunities.[6]

This indeed throws light on the fact that no proper rehabilitation has been planned. It is also noteworthy in this context that none of these children were offered placement in the Kerala Circus Academy, the only circus academy in India, which had been established the year before, in 2010.[7]

Interestingly, the Indian Circus Employees Union, which had joined hands with circus company owners in the case of the animal ban, shifted their allegiance in the case of children in the beginning of

[4] Interview, Bhuvan Ribhu, New Delhi, 12 November 2012.

[5] Jamie Skidmore, 'Defying Death: Children in the Indian Circus', in *Entertaining Children: The Participation of Youth in the Entertainment Industry*, eds Gillian Arrighi and Victor Emeljanow (New York: Palgrave Macmillan, 2014), 225–31.

[6] Available at https://www.unodc.org/ngo/showSingleDetailed.do?req_org_uid=22111, last accessed on 6 October 2014.

[7] Kerala Circus Academy came into being just seven months prior to the ban of children. The CEO of the Kerala Circus Academy said that he was unaware of the ban; interview, M. P. Velayudhan, Kannur, 16 June 2013.

the legal battle. Though later on, they changed their stand and filed a suit arguing for the need for training children in circuses.[8] In a letter addressed to the Chief Justice of India, a leader of the Indian Circus Employees Union, the late V. M. Prabhakaran, points out, '[N]owadays parents do not send their children to circus because it only ruins the future of the children. The sole beneficiaries are the circus owners. Neither the children nor their parents gain anything out of it.'[9]

The Supple Body

Children have always figured prominently in the history of physical training and culture in circuses. Items such as the 'highwire', 'boneless', 'seesaw acrobat', 'bamboo pole', and 'china plate' are almost exclusively performed by child performers. This is because circus acrobatics demand absolute balancing of the body and a child's body could master the skill easier and better. Moreover, circus trainers believe, just as *kalaripayatt* practitioners, that a child's body can be moulded in accordance with the requirement since it is more flexible and supple. A strict diet and strenuous training are fundamental parts of circus acrobatics training. The training would usually begin early in the morning and go on for about five hours. An outsider view could be totally different, as the BBA petition expresses: 'life of these children begins at dawn with training instructors' shouting abuses, merciless beatings and two biscuits and a cup of tea'.[10]

It would be interesting if we read this discourse of 'cruelty' along with some other physical cultures that are recognized as legitimate, essentially by being 'traditional' or 'modern'. Gymnastics training imparted to children in many countries such as China for gaining Olympic gold has been criticized as abusive and devastating. The auto-biography of the iconic action star Jackie Chan, who began his rigorous training at the age of 7 at the China Drama Academy where they were preparing children for the Peking Opera, describes how they were given just enough food to survive and underwent strict training that

[8] Interview, C. C. Ashok Kumar.

[9] A copy of this letter was addressed to Solicitor General Gopal Subrahmaniam (private collection, V. M. Prabhakaran).

[10] BBA Petition, 2006.

resulted in beatings for the slightest mistakes.[11] One can find tales of gruelling training sessions and 'cruel masters' in the reminiscences of many prominent kathakali performers which, of course, is accepted as a 'traditional' method for learning the art.[12] Same is the case with *kalaripayatt* or dance forms or gymnastics or athletics. Interestingly, many contemporary dance styles have incorporated circus exercises and performances. Another popular instance in recent times would be the television reality shows with child performers that often involve acrobatics. Circus acrobatics involves labour, art, and sport. When it comes to children, their rights and privileges can easily be violated. Hence, the state has to undertake measures that recognize the complexity of these performances and legitimize its training process.

The limitation of the framework of cruelty/liberation is strikingly apparent here. 'Childhood' cannot be treated as a romantic universal category. It has to be looked at in the context of regional economies and social inequalities that shape it. A child has often been viewed by various cultures as an epitome of innocence or a person-in-the-making. In his seminal work *Childhood in World History*, Peter N. Stearns observes that one knows more about the history of childhood in the West and in China than in the developments in Africa or India, and the imbalance remains frustrating. He further notes that building on eighteenth-century intellectual currents, a striking feature was the idealization of children as 'wondrous innocents, full of love and deserving to be loved in turn'. The 'modern model of childhood', he says, even when it 'began to be formulated in Western society, in the eighteenth and nineteenth centuries a quite different set of changes affected children in many other parts of the world', and that 'colonialism and slavery were not the only forces shaping childhood outside the West during the early modern period and the nineteenth century'.[13] Vijayalakshmi Balakrishnan, in her influential research on the history, memory, and identity of Indian childhoods,

[11] Jackie Chan and Jeff Yang, *I am Jackie Chan: My Life in Action* (New York: Ballantine Books, 1998), 26–40.

[12] For instance, see the autobiography of the great Kathakali artiste, Kalamandalam Krishnan Nair, *Ente Jeevitham Arangilum Aniyarayilum* [*My Life on Stage and Backstage*] (Kottayam: D. C. Books, 1991), 54–6.

[13] Peter N. Stearns, *Childhood in World History* (New York and London: Routledge, 2011), 79, 84, 91.

observes how the idea of 'child as a mini-adult' emerged from the situation of working children and their relationship with the Indian state.

> This idea was mooted by what in the beginning was a loose collective of trade union leaders working with migrant workers in the city of Bangalore. In their analysis, children work due to the grinding poverty in India, and at least in the foreseeable future, this situation is unlikely to change. Therefore, for the state it would be important to accept the reality of work in children's lives and devise ways and means to improve their quality of life. They proposed that child workers be treated as a legitimate part of the work force, and be given all the statutory protections available to adult workers, 'recognizing the child as a worker and conferring on him a right to unionize to improve his conditions of work and living'.[14]

We need to ask questions such as 'who is a child' and 'what does it mean to be a child in postcolonial geographies such as Asia, Africa, or the Caribbean'. Sectoral papers published by the Organization of African Unity (OAU) and the United Nations Children's Fund, as part of their OAU conference held in Senegal in 1992 on assistance to African children, notes,

> 80 million African children [who] live daily in circumstances so difficult that they must work for survival, often unprotected and frequently on city streets, who endure the storms of man-made and natural disasters, suffer abuse, exploitation, neglect, and adult abandonment; withstand the wounds of discrimination; and are extremely vulnerable to assault by drugs, delinquency and AIDS.[15]

UNICEF notes that over half of the world's out-of-school children, around 33 million of them, live in Africa, and by 2050, the number of African children under 18 will be one billion.[16] Most of our socio-legal

---

[14] Vijayalakshmi Balakrishnan, *Growing Up and Away: Narratives of Indian Childhoods, Memory, History and Identity* (New Delhi: Oxford University Press, 2011), 146.

[15] Organization of African Unity (OAU) and the United Nations Children's Fund (UNCF), *Africa's Children, Africa's Future: Background Sectoral Papers*, (New York and Addis Ababa: OAU and UNCF, 1992), 173.

[16] Available at https://www.unicef-irc.org/article/1864-knowledge-for-children-in-africa-2018-publications-catalogue-published.html 15 January 2019; https://data.unicef.org/wp-content/uploads/2015/12/Children-in-Africa-Brochure-Nov-23-HR_245.pdf, last accessed on 15 January 2019.

Image C.1   Child Acrobats of Galaxy Circus, circa 1960
Source: Private collection of K. K. Sreedharan.

discourses are centred on the binary of cruelty/emancipation. This naturally opens up some key aspects and enquiries regarding body, performance, dignity, livelihood, global economy, caste, and racism. In this context, we will also have to discuss uncomfortable questions not only about the trendy discourse on child trafficking but also the fuzzy borders in the face of livelihood and survival.

During my fieldwork, many circus artistes narrated to me their ill-treated childhoods where they had to undergo beatings and starving as part of their training. Sexual abuse is also not uncommon. There are also cases of fatal accidents. Most children came to circuses according to the agreements made between their parents and middlemen in exchange for the advance money they got. Some of them had to spend more years than the agreed period in the tents while some never returned. But we must bear in mind that these conditions lay bare the inequalities and violence of the world outside the tents. John Irving, author of *Son of Circus*, notes:

> The Indian circuses reflect an atavistic and compassionate life. ... Who are most of the acrobats? They are children, mostly girls; for many of them, the alternative to this life would have been begging (or starving) or prostitution. And what is the circus life for them? It is three performances a day, every day. To bed about midnight, up about six.[17]

Circus has definitely provided an alternate space and livelihood for many children, especially from the subaltern communities around the subcontinent. Over the past century, circus rings have witnessed the heroic transformation of many ordinary lives into great performers.

The Supreme Court, which banned children and adolescents from performing in circuses, had, however, instructed that the Nepali children be handed over to NGOs from Nepal. A striking fact is that one of these NGOs, The Esther Benjamins Trust (which has recently changed its name to Child Rescue Nepal), started a circus company with these children, called 'Circus Kathmandu'; one should say, a bizarre outcome of this ban. The trust, based in Germany, claims that '[i]n 2010 thirteen young Nepalese people who had been rescued from trafficking and the streets turned to contemporary circus to build their self-esteem and to chart a path out of stigmatism and poverty', and 'they are now in a position to make the free choice to use the circus skills they acquired as children, to enjoy an amazing international career'.[18] We shall discuss this idea of 'social circus' soon and the need to think through the global web of non-governmental capital, postcolonial states, and policy production in the Global South.

---

[17] Foreword to Mary Ellen Mark's Book *Indian Circus* (1993), available at http://www.maryellenmark.com/text/books/indian_circus/text001_icircus.html, last accessed on 25 August 2014.

[18] Please see http://www.circuskathmandu.com, last accessed on 11 January 2019; *http://www.ebtrust.org.uk/latest-news/circus-kathmandu-june-2014.aspx*, last accessed on 30 March 2015; https://www.childrescuenepal.org/, last accessed on 15 January 2019.

In Europe and North America, current circus ideas, such as 'noveau cirque' or the contemporary circus and 'social circus', have been on the move since the latter half of the twentieth century. The French term stands for new circus skills developed on a theme or a story, performed by trained artistes in an auditorium or theatre, unlike the traditional ring. At the same time, they try to retain traditional circus items, such as 'trapeze', 'juggling', aerial skills, and acrobatics, in the new aesthetic impact of lighting, music, and costume. These performances seldom have animals and children.[19] 'The traditional circus is based on the element of wonder, the modern circus on aesthetics. The former is objective, more of techniques, but our performance is more emotional, interactive and visionary,' says Lenaig Fanniere, a French circus artiste of 3X Rien company that toured India in 2014.[20] Pierre Cluzaud, another member, told me that he has been trained under a traditional circus artiste and uses that technique, but his performance is not rigid. For him, the 'new circus' is breaking the rules set by traditional circuses. The form is more inclusive, hence has elements of story, poetry, live and recorded bands, drama, acrobatics, juggling, and clowning.[21] Ernest Albrecht points out in the introduction of his book *The Contemporary Circus: Art of the Spectacular*,

> In 1974 Alexis Gruss and his *Cirque National a l'ancienne* reintroduced western audiences to the sanctity of the single ring and the possibilities of the circus as an art form. This is the circus that inspired both Paul Binder of the Big Apple Circus and Guy Caron of Cirque du Soleil, and it was the first to feature many of the elements that came to be the hallmarks of the contemporary circus.[22]

Popular and successful contemporary circuses, such as Cirque du Soleil, with high capital investment have 'normalized' circus into the

---

[19] 'Cirque du Soleil, founded in 1984', abandoned 'circus's historic use of animal performers and making its human ensemble the centerpiece of its productions'. Ernest Albrecht, *The Contemporary Circus: Art of the Spectacular* (Plymouth: Scarecrow, 2006), 78, x.

[20] Interview, Lenaig Fanniere, circus artiste, 3 X Rien, Thiruvananthapuram, 30 October 2014.

[21] Interview, Lenaig Fanniere and Pierre Cluzaud, Thiruvananthapuram, 30 October 2014.

[22] Albrecht, *The Contemporary Circus*, ix.

mainstream with an emphasis on acrobatics and gymnastics, with an aim of social development and emancipation. Cirque du Soleil had its debut visit to India in 2018 with several performances in Mumbai and Delhi. The troupe consisted of a cast and crew of 62 artistes of different nationalities, including two Indian acrobats.[23] While Indian companies still charge INR 100–300, the Cirque du Soleil ticket rates ranged between INR 2,000 to 12,500 and were exclusively sold online.

Transnational Lives

Circus historian Sreedharan Champad narrates Kannan's initiation into Keeleri's circus *kalari* thus: One day Keeleri heard a child's sobs while he was walking and when he looked up he saw child Kannan sitting on the high branch of a jackfruit tree. Tearfully the child told him that the fragrance of the ripe fruit led him there but now he was afraid to climb down. Keeleri smiled and asked him to jump into his hands, which he did. Child Kannan was taken straight to the circus *kalari*, and a glorious acrobatic career began at the age of 7.[24] In 1928, at the age of 22, Kannan left for Europe where he made a great mark.[25] The book *The Circus: 1870s to 1950s* has a 1933 poster of Hagenbeck-Wallace Circus, which mentions him as 'Bombayo, the Man from India in the most astounding midair somersaulting exploits ever witnessed'. The book notes in its caption, 'the remarkable Indian acrobat Kannan Bombayo became an international circus star for performing double somersaults on a bounding rope. The fact that he was Indian was a bonus that the Hagenbeck–Wallace circus didn't fail to enhance visually in this 1930s poster, which linked the show with the circus' exotic menagerie and its Indian elephants.'[26] It was Betram W. Mill, owner of Betram Mill's Circus, who had introduced him as 'Kannan Bombayo'. He toured the

---

[23] Available at https://www.indiatoday.in/lifestyle/what-s-hot/story/cirque-du-soleil-comes-to-mumbai-and-delhi-with-the-world-premiere-of-bazzar-1320244-2018-08-22, last accessed on 14 January 2018.

[24] Champad, *An Album of Indian Big Top*, 30.

[25] Also see A. Sreedhara Menon, *Cultural Heritage of Kerala* (Kottayam: D. C. Books, 2008), 130.

[26] Noel Daniel, *The Circus, 1870s–1950s* (Los Angeles: Taschen, 2008), 131.

United States of America with Ringling Bros. and Barnum & Bailey Circus and such was his clout that he performed solo in their central ring with a weekly salary of 400 dollars.[27] Murkoth Ramunny, the chronicler of Malabar, notes,

> [H]e married in Italy, the European girl who had been his friend. … In the course of his engagements he played at the Olympia and toured America with the Barnum and Bailey's combined show. Rulers of many countries like His Majesty, the King of Britain, Herr Hitler and Signor Mussolini bestowed medals on him as marks of their favour. Altogether Kannan had 405 medals.[28]

Kannan Bombayo's encounter with Adolf Hitler in Berlin is legendary among the circus community in Malabar. It is said that after watching Kannan's spectacular performance of double back somersaults on a simple slack rope in mid-air in his popular item known as 'rope dance', Hitler exclaimed with his mouth agape, 'Jumping devil of India!'[29] This was definitely a remarkable moment that should be read along with the feat of Jesse Owens in Berlin Olympics—two dark bodies demolishing the Fuhrer's myth of Aryan supremacy.

That Kannan Bombayo died in a ship sailing through the Mediterranean Sea poignantly underscores the point of movement that we are discussing. Race and colour antagonisms were exacerbated by this movement to 'elsewhere'. The long and complicated history of transnational movement in this itinerant industry is yet to find a place in social science research. There were many other men and women such as Kannan who found livelihood and identity across borders with this physical-performative form. But these lives, regrettably and significantly, do not figure in any historical narratives of Malabar or Kerala.

British Library's vast collections contain files with details of European circus artistes in India, Indian acrobats travelling to Europe, and their

---

[27] Champad, *An Album of Indian Big Top*, 32.

[28] Murkoth Ramunny, 'The Jumping Devil of India: Circus Artiste Who Created Sensation Abroad', in *Malabar Mahotsav 1993 Souvenir* (ed. M. G. S. Narayanan) (1993): 161–4.

[29] There are different versions of this tale where Hitler checked the shoe soles of Kannan, or the 'jumping devil' reference was given to Kannan as an autograph and so on.

passport information with photographs in the early twentieth century. The file dated 11 June 1885 notes the distressed condition of Indians in France: 'a troupe of 26 acrobats, ten of whom stated to be British Indians, have been abandoned by the Director of a Circus which was at Perpignan', the south of France.[30] A murderous attack committed on 'a Mr Bean, member of a circus company' beyond the 'Peshawar frontier' is mentioned in the Indian Office Records (IOR).[31] The letter of I. Brine, engineer and merchant, narrates the story of his missing brother who was travelling with a circus:

> Some time ago a Brother of mine went away to South Africa ... stayed there with Cooks Travelling Circus. From Africa, they went to India since which time we have not heard from him, the date of his last letter is December 10th and place he was there at was Cashmere in India. We are under the impression that he has tried to get back to Africa.[32]

Another story speaks of the destitute condition of 'Jamal Chotobai, ... an Indian juggler, who, with his wife and family, were stranded at Biarritz'.[33] I found in the IOR a dozen passports of Indian acrobats, sometimes with their family members, who travelled to Europe. The duplicate passport issued by the Empire of India to Mr Ramjee Rao Kaudoji has details of the place and year of his birth as Madras 1913, and his profession is entered as 'acrobat'. The passport issued on 25 February 1935 also includes the passport number, national status, a distinguishing mark, and a photograph.[34] There are detailed communications between the viceroy and governor general of India, Linlithgow, and superior governing officials of Sind, Simla, and Bombay on introducing a travelling circus for 'stimulating public interest to the

[30] *Indian Office Records* (hereafter, 'IOR') /L/PJ/6/155, File no. 1045, 11 June 1885.

[31] Letter from undersecretary to Government of India, Foreign Department, to secretary to Government of Punjab, 20 April 1829, *IOR*/L/PS/6/555, Coll 89, October 1867–February 1868.

[32] Letter from I. Brine to Colonial Office, London, dated 14 April 1896, *IOR*/L/PJ/6/418/, File 656.

[33] Letter from Arthur L. Rowley, H. M. Consul to Bordeaux, to H. M. Consul–General at Marseilles, 25 February 1915, *IOR*/L/PJ/6/1361, F1100.

[34] Duplicate passport, IOR/L/PJ/11/4/333: 1935.

war'.[35] There are some harrowing accounts of Indian circus troupes caught in the calamities of the world war, only to return to India starving and suffering. But not all tales are traumatic ones. For instance, a small double-pole circus such as Rugmabai, that pitched its tent in Burma, lost everything during the Second World War, and the owner and Lady Sandow, to whom the circus owes its name, returned on an elephant's back to India. This is a story that circulates in the memories of some circus artistes in Thalassery.[36] In the late 1940s and throughout the next decade, Kamala Three Ring Circus, which was touted as the largest circus company in Asia and the second largest in the world, had spectacularly successful tours in Ceylon, Malaya, Hong Kong, Macau, Philippines, Siam, Borneo, Burma, and also Pakistan. Gunnel Cederlof mentions that in the 1880s a group of Nilgiri Toda were contracted for a circus in order 'to show them as "ethnological rarities" in Europe, Australia and North America, and came to be known as the "Travelled Toda"', reminding one of the Wild West shows, world's fairs, and 'human zoos' where Africans and Native Americans were exhibited.[37] A news item from *MM* (1913) describes the racism faced by a Malayali artiste in Sumatra. The report ridicules the fact that the artiste who worked in a white man's company was not allowed to perform, much to the consternation of the owner, while the animals were allowed to. All these point to the exoticizing of non-white bodies and the race/colour hatred the artistes might have faced in 'alien' lands.

Gloria Vandervielen, a well-known artiste and item dancer in Indian circus, is settled in Thalassery with the Malayali family of her brother, Minni, for the past 40 years, though without an Indian citizenship. All of Gloria's sisters and brothers worked in Indian circuses all their lives till they retired. She remembered that her father introduced ladies volleyball in Great Bombay Circus and many a new cycling tricks and

[35] For instance, letter from the private secretary to Viceroy and Governor General of India Linlithgow to the private secretary to the secretary of state of Simla, dated 30 June 1941, *IOR/L/PJ/7/4676*.

[36] Interview, Sreedharan, Janaki, Ravindran.

[37] Gunnel Cederlof, 'The Toda Tiger: Debates on Custom, Utility, and Rights in Nature, South India 1820–43', in *Ecological Nationalisms: Nature, Livelihoods, and Identities in South Asia*, eds Gunnel Cederlof and K. Sivaramakrishnan (Delhi: Permanent Black, 2005), 70.

comic acts in the circus arena. She narrates the transnational story of her life thus:

> My circus life started with my father and mother, who had their own circus that was started in China. My mother's family was not of a circus background, they were Armenians. They wanted to go out of Iraq, where they had their own house. There was some trouble between the Germans and the Arabs. They sealed off all the property and her great-grandfather was killed. Thus, my mother's family migrated to America and settled down in Boston. My mother was given to a circus family when the War broke out; all her four or five siblings were separated. As a young girl, she learnt balancing trapeze and ladder acts. She married my Dad in Jerusalem. His family was based in Belgium. That was the time when circuses regularly visited India. My whole family was here, they died here, my grandfather died in Belgaum. I was born in the British Harminston's Circus in China on 16 November 1935. My sister, Rosena, was born in Singapore Malay; my eldest sister in Persia; and elder brother, George, in Calcutta.[38]

The whole terrain is interspersed with war, race, religion, gender, body, labour, livelihood, gaze, and spectatorship. There were acrobatic and dance items, such as 'butterfly dance', 'sailor dance', 'Egyptian dance and serpentine dance', and 'china plate', which were exclusively performed by artistes from abroad. Some of the items were aimed at sexuality. Gloria's life throws light on the poor 'whites' who were migrating across continents to find a livelihood in the entertainment industries of the Global South. Her life would immediately remind one of the popular 'vampire' dancer of Bollywood's yesteryears, Helen—the alien voluptuous white body, as opposed to the familial, domesticated Indian womanhood.

Newspaper collections of the Australian National University Library show that many Indian acrobats, both human and non-human, were participating in Australian circuses.[39] George from North America has a different story to tell. George's father and his father's brothers were working in the British estates in the early twentieth century before they joined the circuses of India. George, who is in his 70s now, returned to America and settled there just 15 years ago. He came to Gemini Circus

---

[38] Interview, Gloria Vandervielen, Thalassery, 5 December 2012.

[39] *Morwell Advertiser* (19 February 1932); *Daily news* (26 February 1919 and 28 December 1938); *Examiner* (30 December 1948); *Argus* (26 January 1939).

a few years ago to meet his old colleagues. George, an expert in cycling acts, was popular in the Indian rings in his younger days.[40] Likewise, many of Indian artistes who went to Malay and Singapore in the 1950s along with Kamala Three Ring Circus have been settled there for many years.

Circus Schools

There have been some notable attempts to establish circus schools, and efforts have also been made to revive the circus *kalari*s in by the second half of the twentieth century. The most noteworthy of these attempts were of K. Damodaran, owner of Kamala Circus, and Kallan Gopalan, owner of Rayman Circus. It is worth mentioning here that Professor Ramamurthi had tried to establish an institute for physical training at Ellur in Andhra Pradesh a couple of decades earlier (*Mathrubhumi*, 8 July 1924).

Damodaran wanted to build a circus college and a hostel at Kathirur.[41] His daughter, Kamala, said that Damodaran had kept aside acres of land in Kathirur, Thalassery, for his school and imagined it to be a centre for circus acrobatics, though this plan remained unfulfilled.[42] Interestingly, *King Pole* magazine, published from London, reports:

> At the moment there is project afoot to establish a regular Circus Academy at KADIRUR to which the Indian Government is donating the land. In such an institution young people could be taught in a sound manner far removed from the harsh methods employed to-day. Child performers would also be regulated and more enthusiastic support from the different social backgrounds would be forthcoming.[43]

In 1957, Damodaran wrote an article in *Mathrubhumi Illustrated Weekly*, titled 'Keralathinoru Circus University' (A Circus University for Kerala). He visualizes the university giving both academic and acrobatic education to circus people who will excel over the European circus artistes, who have both academic degrees and physical excellence:

---

[40] Interview, Ravindran and Sukumaran.
[41] Kallidumbil, 'Kalaripayattum Circussum', 195–209.
[42] Interview, Kamala.
[43] 'Circus in India', *King Pole* 2, no. 15 (1959): 22.

'As the student advances in her academic education to get a university degree, she should also be advancing in her training practices till she attains a means of livelihood by being proficient in at least one of the acrobatics.'[44] He imagines an animal trainer learned in zoology. While he visited the Russian circus troupe, he was impressed by the well-mannered artistes and amazed to know that they were all university graduates. He mentions that the circus artistes here are mostly from poor families and since they are not educated, these proficient artistes have lost opportunities abroad. He compellingly argues that the union government has been promoting music, drama, and cinema, while it was not even ready to admit that circus is an art. This is the very reason for the crisis in Indian circus. He pins hopes on the newly formed state of Kerala. He has no doubts that Kerala is the best place for establishing the university as Indian circus is mostly in the hands of Malayalis.

Years later, in the *Big Top* magazine, mouthpiece of the Indian Circus Federation, Damodaran claims that the venture is underway and reiterates the point that he 'had started a training centre in Tellicherry in Kerala, a few years ago. The centre is working in a modest way. To raise it to the status of a college giving all-round education along with circus training and to enable the college to admit large number of students, more finance is required'. Since the union government had yet to show interest in his project, Damodaran requests the 'munificent people of this country including artistes and art lovers' to liberally donate to the 'Circus College Fund' and 'help the Indian Circus to have a full-fledged training centre of its own'.[45]

In early 1950s, K. Gopalan established a physical training centre of circus acrobatics in the garden guest house of Raghojirao Bhonsle in Sakkardara, Nagpur, Maharashtra. It also included a zoo, foreseeing a lucrative future in the existing animal trade: 'From India so many animals are being exported abroad that brings dollars in good deal. If tamed and trained animals could be exported, it would fetch even more.'[46] The report, with photographs, notes that such a circus training institute for humans and animals would be the first of its kind in Asia,

---

[44] Damodaran 'Keralathinoru Circus University', 32.

[45] K. Damodaran, 'Appeal for Fund', *Big Top* 1, no. 1 (1965), 33.

[46] 'Circus Vidhyabyasa Kendram' [Circus Training Institute], *Mathrubhumi Illustrated Weekly* 30, no. 34 (1952): 19–21.

and such training schools account for the success of Western circuses. In a situation when circus is weakening day by day, the attempt is pertinent and needful. It is interesting that the apprehension about circus as a perishing art is evident in these pieces written half a century ago when circus in India had been thriving.

In 1957, Kandambulli Balan also wrote compellingly about the need for a circus college, putting forward a significant suggestion to include *kalaripayatt* and circus in the curriculum of the kathakali school, Kerala Kalamandalam, which was in its formative stages.[47] We must bear in mind here that the state of Kerala, which came into being in November 1956 incorporating Malabar, Kochi, and Travancore provinces, was also being imagined at the time. This imagining of a homogenous 'Malayali' nation had been and still is a contentious process. Balan's proposal of placing circus, a 'modern' vocation and livelihood of mostly subaltern communities, especially women, along with kathakali and *kalaripayatt*, predominantly upper-caste Hindu 'traditional' forms, therefore, has telling sociopolitical connotations. It is interesting to note that in 1958, Vallathol, renowned poet and the founder of Kalamandalam, was felicitated in a grand reception at Gemini Circus, in which about 5,000 people participated. The circus owner made a contribution to the Kalamandalam fund.[48] These probably throw light on the desire of the circus community for circus to become part of an elite institution such as the Kalamandalam.

Since circus was at its best in the USSR and the Soviet model had been the vogue during the first decades of our new nation state (not to mention that the first government in Kerala was communist), both Balan and M. V. Shankaran, owner of Gemini Circus, keenly speak about collaborations with Moscow. Balan states that if a circus college with modern technologies is established in India, it would definitely be in Kerala and that the cultural department of the Soviet government has promised help for all the initial functioning, including sending a teacher.[49] M. V. Shankaran led a group of selected artistes to the

[47] Kandambulli Balan, 'Keralavum Circussum' [Kerala and Circus], *Mathrubhumi Illustrated Weekly* 34, no. 51 (1957): 22.

[48] Kandambulli Balan, 'Mahakavi Circussil' [Great Poet in Circus], *Mathrubhumi Illustrated Weekly* 36, no. 5 (1958), 33–7.

[49] Balan, 'Circus Soviet Naattil', 22.

International Circus Festival in the USSR in 1964. Radha Kannan, who was one of the performers in the troupe, has photographs of this visit, including one with the famous astronaut, Yuri Gagarin.[50] He writes in the *Big Top* immediately after Gemini's Russian tour that the curriculum in the Moscow academy is prepared by experts and experienced circus people. He pities the absence of circus schools in India, and adds, 'I was told that if the Government of India make necessary arrangements and requests, the USSR Government was prepared to give admission to Indian students to this school'. He concludes by saying that 'the immediate establishment of a circus academy or circus school was the point I stressed' when he met Prime Minister Jawaharlal Nehru.[51] It should be noted here that the Russian artistes had wide admiration among the circus artistes in Thalassery. Sukumaran, a retired artiste and trainer, still keeps a tattered book written in Russian on acrobatics with photographs of Russian artistes. One may remember that in the disastrous magnum opus of Raj Kapoor, *Mera Naam Joker* (1970), which was shot in Gemini Circus, the protagonist Raju falls in love with a Russian trapeze artiste, Marina.

As diplomatic relationship improved between India and the Soviet Union during the 1950s, along with science, technology, space missions, bilateral trade, Communist ideals, and Soviet literatures, circus ideas also seem to have been circulated. Katherine Foshko notes, 'The Indo-Soviet Cultural Society, founded in 1952 as a successor to the Friends of the Soviet Union Society created by Nehru in 1941 promoted awareness of Russian and Indian cultures through regular "Months of Friendship"'. She further adds, 'More than a thousand branches of the Society existed in both countries in its heyday, leading to vigorous cultural exchanges. ... These rich cultural links continued into the 1970s and 1980s.'[52] The *New York Times* (14 December 1975) reports, 'Permanent circuses perform year round in 61 Soviet cities, and 15 other circuses travel constantly around the country. Talent is drawn from a

[50] Interview, Radha Kannan.

[51] M. V. Shankar, 'Circus in USSR: Impressions of my Russian Tour', *Big Top* 1, no. 1 (October 1965): 20–4.

[52] Foshko Katherine, 'Re-energising the India–Russia Relationship: Opportunities and Challenges for the 21st Century', Gateway House Research Paper no. 3, Indian Council on Global Relations, September 2011, 24.

nationwide reservoir of 2,640 fulltime professional performers who are shifted from city to city.' The report adds that in the Soviet Circus and Variety Art School in Moscow, half of the time is spent in learning circus subjects while the other half on normal school curriculum. The report notes that 'many of the children come from circus families, something the Soviet authorities encourage strongly in an effort to maintain the deep roots of the circus tradition', and that 'every child in the acrobatic program is required to take classical ballet'. The performers are 'very highly paid'—'$185 a month'—in general and the best performers are paid by the performance up to $1200, 'plus 30 percent extra if they work in Siberia'. 'But in Russia circus is more than an entertainment'; another report of the same newspaper (11 September 1988) notes: 'Lenin thought enough of the circus as a potent social institution to nationalize it in 1919', that 'in the pre-Revolutionary years [when] circus was a medium for political expression'. This, the report states, is no longer so and circus acts draw mostly from folk legends, Russian proverbs, or patriotic ideals. An ironical version of history would be the case of the Chinese acrobats who were a major presence in Indian circuses, but left the country after the 1962 Sino-Indian war, never to return.

However, the first time there was any fruitful move from a government to initiate something on these lines had been a project under the Sports Authority of India's (SAI's) Thalassery centre in 1992 to train the children of circus people in sports and gymnastics. But since 2000, the authorities have stopped admitting these children.[53] While SAI claims that they were not getting applications from the children of circus people, the circus community alleges that the seats allocated to their children were handed out to 'well-offs' by the officials.[54] So, the decision of the Kerala government to establish a circus academy in Thalassery was seen as a constructive move by many who had spent their prime time in rings and tents.

Kerala Circus Academy

The Kerala Circus Academy was inaugurated on 2 August 2010 and started functioning in a rented building at Chirakkuni. (There is glaring

[53] Interview, Arun Kumar, SAI, Thalassery, 23 June 2013.
[54] Interview, Suniti.

irony in the fact that this building had been the home of the representational form often blamed for the impending 'death' of the Indian circus industry; it was a cinema theatre.) By 2016, the academy ceased functioning altogether. A news report states that 'no student from the state has shown interest in joining the institution'.[55]

'The primary purpose was to select ten children from various circus companies and include another ten from the locality. In the Malayalam dailies applications for admission were called for. Eleven applications were received and six people appeared for interview in May 2011. But nobody joined. Like this twice applications were called for with almost no response,' says Velayudhan, the CEO of the academy.[56] Nevertheless, there still are six girls and four boys from different parts of India and Nepal. While four of them are from Tamil Nadu, another four are from the east, Assam and Bengal, and one each from Bihar and Nepal. Raghavan, the trainer, said, 'After turning into fourteen these children would go back to Gemini Circus as artistes.'[57] In effect, all these 10 children belong to companies under a single owner and they will return to the same after finishing their training.

After their early morning training, the children go to Dharmadam Basic Upper Primary School, a government-aided school with Malayalam as the medium of instruction. The only logic behind these children, who speak different languages, being taught in Malayalam seems to be that they are going to work in Malayali companies. This obviously limits their chances and opportunities in a wider world.

---

[55] 'Circus Academy: Doing a Blindfolded Tightrope Walk', *The New Indian Express* (5 March 2013); There were reports on the issue in Malayalam as well, for instance, 'Kerala Circus Academy Thakarchayilekku' [Kerala Circus Academy on the Verge of Ruin], *Mathrubhumi* (16 June 2013).

[56] Velayudhan further adds,

In October, when the new collector came in, a meeting was organized. As per the suggestions from the locality, I suggested that, as in the sports training centres, if the training is done during evening and morning schedule, there is a chance that students of localities join. This suggestion was passed by the managing committee. Two applications were received from the locality. They left the academy after five-six days. Interview, Velayudhan.

[57] Interview, Raghavan, Kerala Circus Academy, Kannur, 18 June 2013.

The syllabus submitted by the curriculum committee (almost a replica of the managing committee) stipulates the training time as '6 AM to 8 AM' and '4.30 PM to 7 PM'. Training is given in 'Floor exercises (Boys & Girls)', 'Vaulting Table (Boys & Girls)', 'Beam (Girls)', 'Parallel Bars (Boys)', 'Uneven Bars (Girls)', 'High Bars (Boys)', 'Rings (Boys)', and 'Pommel Horse'. Under the title 'Jobs and Entertainment', it adds 'clowning (make up) and jokes and entertainment'. The syllabus carries under 'Specialization (optional)', 'Tent Preparation, different types of circus event, dress making, music activities, food preparation, jobs and entertainment (jokers), light and sound, animal circus, etc'.[58] Since no instruments and equipment are provided, the three trainers instruct them in these ground exercises. 'A list of instruments was prepared but

Image C.2   Children in Kerala Circus Academy, 2012
Source: Author.

[58] Separate exercises are given to advanced standards under these titles (From the syllabus submitted to the Managing Committee and later on to the government, dated 3 May 2011).

it was not sent to the government. Only a hook for the *slanting wire* was made available,' said Raghavan.[59]

Apart from the three trainers, the two cooks at the school were also retired circus artistes. A call for application by the Collectorate, Kannur, titled 'Wanted Circus Personnel', specified the qualifications of the 'Administrator—No. of Post 1' as 'A pass from the Gymnastics Institute or Technical Institute of Gymnastics', and experience as '10–15 years of Administrative experience in a reputed circus company'; and 'Chief Trainer—No. of Post 3' should have as qualification a 'basic training certificate from the Circus Federation' and 'five years training experience in a reputed circus company'.[60] The monthly salary of the trainers was INR 6,000 and the cooks' was INR 5,000. The CEO drew INR 15,000 monthly.[61] It should be noted here that while the jobs of cooks and trainers were given to circus artistes, high-level posts were taken by political party leaders and retired government officials. In March 2012, INR 1 crore was released from the district collectorate treasury, of which INR 50 lakh was spent.[62] The monthly expenditure of the academy was INR 1 lakh.[63]

At Kundoormala, Thalassery, 10 acres of land was considered as a site for constructing a permanent infrastructure for the circus academy. In the last meeting held at Thiruvananthapuram, it was suggested by the then sports minister, Ganesh Kumar, that the circus academy may function along with gymnastics and *kalaripayatt* in the proposed sports complex at Mundayad, Kannur, itself.[64] Other suggestions, such as whether it

[59] Interview, Raghavan.

[60] Application titled 'Wanted Circus Professionals', Collectorate, Kannur, M6.45315/08(1), dated 6 May 2009.

[61] It should be noted here that the present CEO is a retired bureaucrat and does not have any of the qualifications for the administrative post stipulated in the notification.

[62] Initially, INR 25 lakh was released, and it is mentioned in the note for the meeting at the Sports Council, Trivandrum, dated 5 September 2008 that this amount will not be sufficient, so other funds from the MP and MLA funds should be utilized apart from those collected from the circus companies and self-governing establishments. (Note for the meeting at the Sports Council, Trivandrum, dated 5 September 2008.)

[63] Interview, M. P. Velayudhan.

[64] *Mathrubhumi*, 16 June 2013; interview, M. P. Velayudhan.

could again be accommodated with SAI, had also come up. A significant proposal came from the chairman of Kerala Sangeet Natak Academi, Soorya Krishnamurthi. He assured that all the current benefits granted during the period to drama artistes by the Academi, such as pension, insurance, medical treatment, and training places, could be made available to circus artistes too. The chairman also proposed to attach the circus academy with the Sangeet Natak Academi and develop it. But nothing came out of these plans since there was pressure from both the cultural and sports ministries, says Krishnamurthi. He added, 'Sports ministry asserted that circus comes under sports and they are entitled for any move concerning it. But they don't move and plus circus is not a *sport*, it's an *art*.'[65]

This opens up the crucial problem of treating circus *as* a sport, which renders invisible its complexities as a performative form with multiple layers.[66] As in the foreign circus academies, students should have the opportunity to get professional training in band music, textile design, acrobatics, dance, tent technology, and programme management. As Roland Barthes notes, '[I]n fact wrestling is an open-air spectacle, for what makes the circus or the arena what they are, is not the sky … it is the drenching and vertical quality of the flood of light'.[67]

Circus in India today is by no means a region-specific art. 'The government of India should think of setting up a school to teach circus art, preferably to be located in New Delhi, where boys and girls from all over India may be recruited and trained to become first grade circus stars, who may be in great demand throughout the world,' envisions an anonymous author in *Big Top*.[68] Over the past 150 years, it has become a transnational enterprise. So, instead of perceiving it as a physical training institute, the central government should take it up at the 'national' level, as in the case of the National School of Drama as an advanced centre for performance and physical cultures.

[65] Interview, Soorya Krishnamurthi, Thiruvananthapuram, 6 October 2013.

[66] Arun Kumar told me that there are circus items that involve gymnastic exercises. But they are not the same; interview, Arun Kumar.

[67] Roland Barthes, *Mythologies* (New York: Farrar, Straus and Giroux, 1972), 15.

[68] Anon. 'Circus in India: Its Problems, Solutions', *Big Top* 1, no. 1 (1965): 10.

Permanent circus theatres of Russia, Britain, and United States of America successfully host circuses during different seasons. Having such theatres here, at least in metro cities, could set up a new model. The state can also give support to cooperative circus companies in its small-scale industry schemes. What I have gathered from my fieldwork is that a majority of circus artistes and labourers do not want to send their children to circus companies because they want them to get educated and have a better future. Another recurring complaint is regarding the exploitative and dangerous labour conditions. The government could arrange for the recruitment of students from its circus academies and professional companies for jobs and internships in other circus companies around the world under proper legal contracts.[69] This would not only help this performative form to sustain but also help to stamp out the stigma around it, for which the state and the society have substantially contributed.

There is a general perception that circus in India is a dying industry. Approximately 20 circuses faced closure in the years following the ban of children. There were more than 200 circuses five decades ago, a number which is now less than 10, says the owner of Great Bombay Circus, Dilip Nath.[70] Many major traditional circus companies around the world have been closing shop for good in recent times; for instance, the five-ring Ringling Bros. and Barnum & Bailey Circus in the United States of America, after 146 years in show business, and Gemini Circus in India, which has a history of seven long decades.[71] The unsympathetic attitude of governments and administrative bodies as well as the legal

---

[69] An SAI official said that most children of the circus people admitted in the SAI have won national level medals while some have won international games. 'Cultural exchange programs can take them across the national boundaries'; interview, Dinesh, SAI, Thalassery, 24 June 2013.

[70] Interview, Dilip Nath.

[71] It should be noted that an estimate of the daily collection of Gemini Circus in October 2014—which could accommodate around 3000 spectators at a time—at the camp in Mysore was approximately INR 5 lakhs. It collected approximately 30 lakhs running houseful for five consecutive holidays. Yet, the company shut down after three years (interview, Ravindran). In a season, a company would perform every month of the year except the three-day breaks during camp shifting and one to two days because of heavy rain. Some of the Kerala

proscriptions on the training and performance of animals and children are often cited by the circus community as reasons for this downfall. During my fieldwork in India, the only point on which the circus managements and workers agreed was about the 'anti-circus' outlook of the administrative bodies; for instance, public grounds. Many of the grounds that once used to host circus tents are now inaccessible to them. Nowadays in most major cities, circus has to set shop in grounds in the outliers of the city, without sufficient facilities. Workers and managers shared the sentiment that even those companies that were doing really well have been shutting down or changing drastically into smaller tents and troupes.

Any entertainment industry that wants to stay alive has to keep changing according to the demands, challenges, and possibilities of the times. The import of European, American, Australian, and also African performers by Indian circus companies, showcasing them as the 'main attraction', is a good instance of such an attitude. Performers from Nepal and the erstwhile Soviet bloc, such as Uzbekistan and Armenia, had a major presence in Indian circus companies in the past couple of decades. The gradual retreat of Malayali acrobats, who had dominated the rings for a long time, in search for other, better vocations in the oil-rich Persian Gulf countries from the early 1970s, known as the 'Gulf Boom', had brought about this momentous change. The flow of Nepali performers (mainly from Hetauda), who dominated the ring in the more recent past, has lessened considerably since the overthrow of the monarchy in Nepal and the establishment of a democratic republic in 2008. Most of these foreign acrobats who work in Indian circuses as guest artistes hail from economically backward regions, such as Bangladesh, Vietnam, Mexico, Baluchistan, Uzbekistan, Armenia, and Mongolia. It is noteworthy that their pay also differs with the country of their origin, rather than with the complexity of the item performed.

---

companies make sure that they camp at Kollam and Kannur every year, since these two towns always give good collections (more than one crore for a camp) with the least expenditure. These big circuses visit at least two major cities, such as Chennai or Bombay, every year. In small cities, where the ticket rates differ, some of the big companies could collect about three lakhs for a day (interview, Devadas, Trivandrum, 2 September 2018).

This phenomenon leads us to other livelihood questions related to global economy and labour migration across boundaries. African performers have become a significant presence in the contemporary context. In order to locate this dramatic shift between the historic past and the present, my ongoing project explores the conditions within postcolonial states, both in the Indian subcontinent and the African continent, that facilitated this current movement of performers from East Africa.

Bibliography

Archival Sources

Kozhikode Regional Archives

Proceedings of the Board of Revenue (R-Dis files), 1860–1920
Tellicherry Sub-Collector's Office Records, List-I & II, 1857–1939
Madras Records, 1816

Indian Office Records, 1885–1941

Kerala State Archives, Thiruvananthapuram

Cover Files, Napier Museum, 1857–1940
Confidential Files, National Museum, 1913–45

National Archives, Delhi

Proceedings of Home Department (Education, Judicial), 1850–1920

Census Reports

Census of India, 1901, 1961, 1971
Imperial Census, 1881, vol. I & II
Census of the Bombay Presidency, 1872
Census of Malabar, 1871
Census Handbook of Malabar, 1951

Newspapers

Argus, 1903, 1939
Bombay Chronicle, 1913, 1914
Chandrika, 2001
Daily News, 1904, 1919, 1938
Examiner, 1948
Gippsland Times, 1922
Indian Express, 2012, 2013
Kerala Kaumudi, 1978
Lakeland Ledger, 1981
Malayala Manorama, 1901, 1903, 1905, 1908, 1909, 1910, 1911
Morwell Advertiser, 1932
Mathrubhumi, 1923, 1924, 1934, 2009, 2013
Mitavadi, 1913, 1914, 1915, 1916, 1917, 1918, 1919
New York Times, 1975, 1981, 1988, 2014
Queanbeyan Age, 1909
Sydney Morning Herald, 1912
The Hindu 1963, 2012
New Indian Express, 2013
Times of India, 1926, 1979, 2012

Interviews

Abu S., former curator and superintendent of Natural History Museum, Thiruvananthapuram Zoo, 19 May 2010
Ali Aktar, ring boy, Royal Circus, 12 May 2008
Ajitha, retired circus artiste, Melur, 12 March 2006
Ajith Kumar, retired circus artiste, Kolassery, 2 May 2012
Arun Kumar, gymnastics instructor, SAI, Thalassery, 23 June 2013
Ashok Kumar C. C., president of the Indian Circus Employees Union, Thalassery, 17 February 2011, 21 June 2011, 15 October 2012, and 30 January 2014
Ashok Shankar, partner of Gemini, Jumbo, and Royal Circuses and former president of the Indian Circus Federation, New Delhi, 18 January 2013
Babu, circus artiste, Royal Circus, 22 May 2007
Babu, circus artiste, Jumbo Circus, 16 July 2009
Babu, ringmaster, Gemini Circus, 19 June 2012
(Late) Bhaskaran, retired circus artiste and instructor, Thalassery, 18 July 2007
Bhagwantrao D. More, Mumbai, 27 December 2012
Bhayyaji, mess supervisor, Gemini Circus, 23 June 2012

Bhuwan Ribhu, Bachpan Bachao Andolan activist, New Delhi, 12 November 2012 and 25 August 2013

Charles Chandra, retired zoo doctor, Thiruvananthapuram Zoo, 16 May 2010

Daisy, Stephen's wife, Pallur, 12 December 2010

Dayanandan, president of the Circus Labour Union, Thalassery, 29 May 2008 and 12 February 2012

Devadas, manager of the Jumbo Circus, Trivandrum, 2 September 2018

Digpal Singh, bandmaster, Royal Circus, 17 May 2008

Dileep, bandmaster, Royal Circus, 23 May 2008

Dilipnath, owner of the Great Bombay Circus, New Delhi, 19 December 2012 and (telephonic interview) 3 January 2013

Dilip, owner, Rambo Circus, Pune, 22 December 2012

Dinesh, accounts officer, SAI, Thalassery, 24 June 2013

Edward Williams, retired circus manager and grandson of Keeleri Kunhikannan, Chirakkara, 26 March 2010, 30 December 2011, 12 December 2013, and 19 January 2014

George, tent master, Royal Circus, 29 and 30 May 2008

Gloria Vandervielen, retired circus artiste, Thalassery, 5 December 2012

Gopal Yadav, tent master, Gemini Circus, Kottayam, 23 June 2009

Govindan, retired circus artiste, Thalassery, 25 January 2011

Harish, electrician, Royal Circus, 12 June 2008

Jake Rendle-Worthington, London, 22 June 2016

J. F. Stephen, retired circus manager, Pallur, 12 December 2010

Kalicharan, manager, Galaxy Circus, 18 March 2007

Kamala, circus artiste, Thalayi, 24 September 2010

Kamala, daughter of Damodaran (Kamala Circus), Seidarpalli, 30 July 2012

Karim A. V., retired circus artiste and union leader, Cherakkara, 28 September 2012 and 23 July 2010

Kareem, announcer, Galaxy Circus, Thalassery, 23 March 2007

Kausu, retired circus artiste, Melur, 28 August 2007

Krishna Iyer V. R., former judge of the Supreme Court of India and minister in the 1957 ministry in Kerala, 22 July 2013

Kumaran, retired circus artiste, Kannur, 12 March 2009

Kunhiraman, retired circus artiste, Melur, 24 January 2009

Kunnukuzhi S. Mani, writer, Thiruvananthapuram, 18 July 2014

Leela, retired circus artiste, Thiruvangad, 17 January 2012

Lenaig Fanniere, 3 X Rien, Thiruvananthapuram, 30 October 2014

Madhu, circus manager, Jumbo Circus, 12 April 2009

Mohandas, circus manager, Jumbo Circus, 14 April 2009

Moreswar, retired animal trainer and performer, Melur, 5 June 2006

Mukundan, retired circus artiste and nephew of Damodaran (Kamala Circus), Saitharpally, 23 September 2012

Muraleedharan K. G., *kalaripayatt* practitioner, CVN Kalari, Kottayam, 7 March 2014

(Late) Murkoth Ramunny, former administrator, Dharmadam, 31 January 2009

Narayanan, tent master, Royal Circus, Kannur, 9 June 2008

(Late) N. P. Narayanan, retired circus artiste, Chirakkuni, 19, 22, and 25 May 2008 and 9 July 2009

Nazeer, Royal Circus, 13 June 2008

Parasuram Mali, retired animal trainer and former owner of Parasuram Lion Circus, Tasgaon, 25 December 2012 and 6 May 2013

Pierre Cluzaud, artiste and partner, 3 X Rien, Thiruvananthapuram, 30 October 2014

(Late) Prabhakaran, retired circus artiste and union leader, Payyoli, 3 February 2009 and 13 May 2010

Prema, retired circus artiste, Chirakkuni, 23 October 2006

Pushpa, retired circus artiste, Melur, 14 July 2006

Radha Kannan, retired circus artiste, Banglore, 17–19 July 2012, 29 April 2013, and 7 October 2013

(Late) Raghavan K. V., first president of the Indian Circus Employees Union, Thalassery, 11 and 14 March 2010

Raghavan, retired circus artiste and instructor at the Kerala Circus Academy, 18 June 2013

Rajamma, retired circus artiste, Thiruvangad, 17 January 2012

Rajan, retired circus artiste, Thalassery, 8 June 2008

Rajendra Deval, grandson of Bandopant Deval, Miraj, 24 January 2013

Rajan, retired circus artiste, Muzhappilanhad, 17 September 2009

Rajan, generator operator, Gemini Circus, 19 July 2012

Raman, retired circus artiste, Melur, 29 March 2008

Ramachandran C. M., former accountant, Indian Circus Federation, New Delhi, 12 February 2010; Thalassery, 25 June 2011 and 30 December 2012

Ramanathan, retired circus artiste and instructor at the Kerala Circus Academy, Thalassery, 18 June 2013

Ravindran E., circus instructor and union leader, Kathirur, 3 March 2011, 16, 19, and 22 September 2011, and 7 March 2012; Gemini Circus, Neyyattinkara, 12 July 2012

Reeja, retired circus artiste, Kolassery, 28 February 2011

Sadasivapillai, chief superintendent, Thiruvananthapuram Zoo, 18 May 2010

Sahadevan, circus manager, Jumbo Circus, 12 April 2009

Sajeevan, 'street circus' performer, Thalassery, 13 January 2010

Salman, artiste, Jumbo Circus, 29 April 2007

Sankaran, owner of Gemini, Jumbo, and Royal Circuses, Kannur, 29 October 2012

Santhosh, *kalaripayatt* practitioner, CVN Kalari, Thiruvanhad, Thalassery, 14 February 2009

Sathyanarayanan, *kalaripayatt* practitioner, CVN Kalari, Thiruvananthapuram, 12 November 2014

Shivaprasad, ticket in-charge, Royal Circus, 18 May 2008

Shobha, circus artiste, Gemini Circus, 19 June 2012

Sivadasan, *kalaripayatt* practitioner, CVN Kalari, Thiruvanhad, Thalassery, 14 February 2009

Soorya Krishnamurthi, chairman of the Kerala Sangeet Natak Academi, Thiruvananthapuram, 6 October 2013

Sreedharan, retired circus artiste and instructor, Andalur, 17 September 2006, 24 March 2008; Thalassery, 19 February 2007; Muzhikkara, 2 January 2009; Galaxy Circus, Thalassery, 14 March 2009

Sreedharan K. K., retired circus artiste and former owner of the 'Great Gemini Circus', Meethale Peedika, 10 May 2008 and 30 February 2011

Sreedharan Champad, retired circus artiste, writer and historian, Pathayakunnu, 6 November 2006

Sujit Dilip, partner, Rambo Circus, Pune, 13 December 2011

Sukumaran K. K., retired circus artiste, Kolassery, 12 November 2012

Sulu, retired circus artiste, Thiruvangad, 17 January 2012

Suniti, retired circus artiste, Elayidathu Mukku, 9 February 2012 and 14 May 2012

T. H. P. Chentharassery, author, Thiruvananthapuram, 15 July 2014

Umesh, ring boy, Royal Circus, 12 May 2008

Vamakshi, neighbour of M. K. Raman, Chirakkara, 21 January 2009

Vanaja, retired circus artiste, Melur, 23 May 2008

Vasantha, retired circus artiste, Melur, 29 May 2008

Velayudhan M. P., CEO of the Kerala Circus Academy, Kannur, 16 June 2013

Velayudhan, tailor, Rajkamal Circus, 12 May 2010

Viswanathan, retired circus artiste, Thalassery, 30 August 2007

Wilson, animal trainer, Jumbo Circus, 22 April 2007

Yesoda Bai, curator at the Tirupati Zoological Park, 28 August 2014

Periodicals and Journals

'Aanakal Colomb Mrugasalayil' [Elephants in the Colombo Zoo]. *Mathrubhumi Illustrated Weekly* 31, no. 51 (1954): 24.

'Aana Nenchil' [Elephant on the Chest]. *Mathrubhumi Illustrated Weekly* 33, no. 47 (1956): 31.

Alter, Joseph S. 'The Body of One Color: Indian Wrestling, the Indian State, and Utopian Somatics'. *Cultural Anthropology* 8, no. 1 (1993): 49–72.

Ananthan, Kambil. 'Pracheena Acharanahalum Viswasanhalum' [Ancient Observations and Beliefs], In *Gnanodayayogam Sathabdi Charithra Smaranika 2005*, edited by Champadan Vijayan. Thalassery: Sree Gnanodaya Yogam Centinary Committee for History Preparation, October 2005, 75–91.

'Avar Swathanthryathilekk!' [Towards Freedom!]. *Circus Worker* 1, no. 1 (April 1980).

Balachandran. 'Viswavijnanam 2000 Chodyangalil' [Global Knowledge in 2000 Questions]. *Janayugam* 37 (1968): 16.

Balakrishnan, K. 'Malabaarilekku oru Ethinottam' [A Peep into Malabar]. *Kaumudi Weekly*, Malayalam Era 1131 Midhunam 4–Karkidakam 15 (7 issues). Reprinted in *Kaumudi Special Edition*, (July–September) (2009 [1955]): 18–35.

Balan, Kandambulli. 'Abhyasikalude Kuude' [With the Acrobats]. *Mathrubhumi Illustrated Weekly* 33, no. 9 (1955): 9–17.

———. 'Circus Indiayil' [Circus in India]. *Mathrubhumi Illustrated Weekly* 32, no. 45 (1956/7): 67–73.

———. 'Circus Soviet Naattil' [Circus in Soviet Land]. *Mathrubhumi Illustrated Weekly*, 34, no. 49 (1957): 20–7.

———. 'Soviet Circus Indiayil' [Soviet Circus in India]. *Mathrubhumi Illustrated Weekly* 34, no. 51 (1957): 19–23, 30–3.

———. 'Keralavum Circussum' [Kerala and Circus]. *Mathrubhumi Illustrated Weekly* 34, no. 51 (1957): 19–22, 28.

———. 'Mahakavi Circussil' [Great Poet in Circus]. *Mathrubhumi Illustrated Weekly* 36, no. 5 (1958): 33–7.

———. 'Czechoslovakian Circus'. *Mathrubhumi Illustrated Weekly* 38, no. 8 (1960): 6–12.

———. 'Maharashtrathil ninnu Malayalathilekk' [From Maharashtra to Malayalam]. *Circus Worker* 1, no. 1 (1980).

Balan, Vyloppilli. 'Dhomthar Damoo Dhotre [Strong Damoo Dhotre]'. *Mathrubhumi Illustrated Weekly* 31, no. 16 (1953): 18–24.

Bhaskarappanikker. 'Soviet Circus'. *Mathrubhumi Illustrated Weekly* 29, no. 52 (1952): 8–10.

Brandon-Jones, Christine. 'Edward Blyth, Charles Darwin and the Animal Trade in the Nineteenth Century India and Britain'. *Journal of the History of Biology* 30, no. 3 (1997): 145–78.

Burgess, Hovey. 'The Classification of Circus Techniques'. *The Drama Review* 18, no. 1 (1974): 65–70.

Champad, Sreedharan. 'Circussinte Eettillam' [The Birth Place of Circus]. In *Smrithichitra: Thalassery Vidyabhyasa Jilla 2004–5*, edited by Raju

Kaattupanam. Thalassery: Vidyarangam and Subject Council of Thalassery Educational District, 2005, pp. 149–53.

Chandrasekharan, U. 'Bharath Circus'. *Mathrubhumi Illustrated Weekly* 44, no. 28 (1966): 22–6.

Chatterjee, Manini. '1930: Turning Point in the Participation of Women in the Freedom Struggle'. *Social Scientist* 29 (July–August 2001): 39–47.

Chirakkal, T. Balakrishnan Nair. 'Keralathile Kayikabhyasakala' [Physical Art of Kerala]. *Mathrubhumi Illustrated Weekly*, 34, no. 33 (1956): 71–4.

Chowdhury, Indira. 'Speaking of the Past: Perspectives on Oral History'. *Economic and Political Weekly* 49, no. 30 (2014): 39–42.

'Circus in India'. *King Pole* 2, no. 15 (1959): 21–2.

'Circus in India: Its Problems and Solutions'. *Big Top* 1, no. 1 (1965): 9–11.

'Circussukarkku Orakhilendia Sanghatana' [An All India Association for Circus People]. *Mathrubhumi Illustrated Weekly* 31, no. 48 (1954): 16.

'Circus Vidyabhyasa Kendram' [Circus Training Centre]. *Mathrubhumi Illustrated Weekly* 30, no. 34 (1952): 19–21.

Damodaran, K. 'Keralathinoru Circus University' [A Circus University for Kerala]. *Mathrubhumi Illustrated Weekly* 35, no. 19 (1957): 31–3.

———. 'Vedic Origin of Circus', *Big Top* 1, no. 1 (1965): 5–7.

———. 'Appeal for Fund'. *Big Top* 1, no. 1 (1965): 33.

'Editorial'. *Big Top* 1, no. 1 (1965): 3–4.

'Editorial'. *Circus Worker* 1, no. 2 (1980): 1–2.

'Editorial'. *Circus Worker* 1, no. 3 (1980): 1–2.

Foshko, Katherine. 'Re-energising the India–Russia Relationship: Opportunities and Challenges for the 21st Century'. Gateway House Research Paper no. 3, Indian Council on Global Relations, September 2011.

Ghosh, Amitav. 'Of Fanas and Forecastles: The Indian Ocean and Some Lost Languages of the Age of Sail'. *Economic and Political Weekly* 43, no. 25 (2008): 56–63.

'Gorilla Circussil' [Gorilla in Circus]. *Mathrubhumi Illustrated Weekly* 45, no. 50 (1968): 29–32.

Gopalan, Teacher Keezhanthi. 'M K Raman'. *Mathrubhumi Illustrated Weekly* 29, no. 52 (1960): 22, 27.

'Grand Fairy Circus'. *Mathrubhumi Illustrated Weekly* 34, no. 11 (1956): 20.

Haraway, Donna. 'Teddy Bear Patriarchy: Taxidermy in the Garden of Eden, New York City, 1908–36'. *Social Text* 11 (1984–5): 20–64.

Hribal, Jaison. '"Animals are Part of the Working Class": A Challenge to Labor History'. *Labor History* 44, no. 4 (2003): 435–53.

Hughes, Stephen P. 'The Pre-Phalke Era in South India: Reflections on the Formation of Film Audiences in Madras'. *South Indian Studies* 2 (July–December 1996): 161–204.

'Indian Circus Federation: Annual Meeting'. *Big Top* 1, no. 1 (1965): 33.

'Indira'. *Mathrubhumi Illustrated Weekly* 35, no. 35 (1957): 20.

Kallidumbil, Sasikumar. 'Kalaripayattum Circussum' [*Kalaripayatt* and Circus]. In *Gnanodayayogam Sathabdi Charithra Smaranika 2005*, edited by Champadan Vijayan. Thalassery: Sree Gnanodaya Yogam Centinary Committee for History Preparation, October, 2005, pp. 195–209.

Kannabiran, Kalpana. 'Who is a "Worker"? Problematising "Ability" in the Conceptualisation of Labour'. *The Indian Journal of Labour Economics* 57, no. 1 (2014).

Karim, A. V. 'Circus Kalakaranmarude Bhavi' [The Future of Circus Artistes]. *Circus Worker* 1, no. 1 (1980): 2.

Kimbell, Lucy. 'Object Strikes Back: An Interview with Graham Harman', *Design and Culture* 5, no. 1 (2013): 103–117.

Krishnan, M. 'The Wild Life (Protection) Act, 1972: A Critical Appraisal'. *Economic and Political Weekly* 8, no. 11 (1973): 564–6.

Kumaran, Murkoth. 'Oru Apoorna Athmakatha' [An Unfinished Autobiography]. *Kaumudi: Murkoth Kumaran Special Edition*, (January–March) (2009 [1937]): 4–14.

Kunhappa, Murkoth. 'Circus: Malayalikalude Sambhavana' [Circus: Contribution of Malayalis]. *Mathrubhumi Illustrated Weekly* 51, no. 28 (1951): 34–6.

———. 'Circussabhyasam' [Circus Acrobatics]. *Mathrubhumi Illustrated Weekly* 26, no. 34 (1958): 14–16, 46.

———. 'Circussilude Arogya Sambadanam' [Gaining Health through Circus]. *Circus Worker* 1, no. 3 (1980): 22–4.

———. 'Circus in Malabar: Keeleri Kunhikannan Teacher'. In *Malabar Mahotsav 1993 Souvenir*, edited by M. G. S. Narayanan, 1993, pp. 122–131.

———. 'Thiyyarude Charithram: Oru Vihaga Veekshanam' [History of Thiyyas: An Elaborate Perspective]. In *Gnanodayayogam Sathabdi Charithra Smaranika 2005*, edited by Champadan Vijayan. Thalassery: Sree Gnanodaya Yogam Centinary Committee for History Preparation, 2005, pp. 102–114.

Lakshmanan, V. 'Kusthi Annum Innum' [Kushti Today and Yesterday]. *Janayugam Weekly* 10, no. 35 (1967): 20–3.

Latour, Bruno. 'On Interobjectivity'. *Mind, Culture and Activity* 3, no. 4 (1996).

Maan, Barua. 'Between Gods and Demons'. *Seminar* 651 (November, 2013): 75–9.

McDonald, Ian. 'Hindu Nationalism, Cultural Spaces and Bodily Practices in India'. *American Behavioural Scientist* 46 (July 2003): 1563–76.

'Malabarinnu Weight Lifting Sanghatana Venam' [Malabar Needs a Weight Lifting Organization]. *Mathrubhumi Illustrated Weekly* 30, no. 5 (1952): 24.

Mangalatt, Raghavan. 'Thalassery'. *Mathrubhumi Illustrated Weekly* 38, no. 25 (1960): 31–6.

Mitra, Sarbajit. 'Bengali Babus on the Flying Trapeze: Circus and Body Culture in Colonial Bengal'. Paper presented at the international conference on 'Physical Cultures: Bengal and Beyond', Jadavpur University, Kolkata, 21–2 February 2014.

Mushtaq. 'Calicut Athletic Club'. *Mathrubhumi Illustrated Weekly* 33, no. 32 (1955): 34.

Narayanan, S. 'Prof. Keeleri Kunhikannan'. *Circus Worker* 1, no. 4 (July 1980): 5, 8.

———. 'Survey of Circus in India'. *Circus Worker* 1, no. 5 (August 1980): 12–13, 15.

Natesh, Rishi G. 'Kalamozhiyunna Kalaripayatt' [Kalaripayatt in Decline]. *Kalakaumudi Weekly* 387 (February 1983): 26–9.

Nikhil. 'V M Raman'. *Circus Worker* 1, no. 4 (July 1980): 27–8.

Nirmala, Kodepudi. 'Circussukari' [Circus Girl]. *Kerala Kavitha Silver Jubilee Issue* (January 1993): 68.

'Nirmathakkal Sanghatikkunnu' [Producers Unite]. *Mathrubhumi Illustrated Weekly* 46, no. 32 (1968): 43.

Nisha P R. 'Vishamam Kondum, Ishtam Kondum: Stree Circus Kalakarikalude Athmakathanangal' [Out of Misery, Out of Love: Autobiographical Narrations of Women Circus Artistes]. *Pachakuthira* 2, no. 10 (2006): 5–7.

———. 'Jeevitham Kondoru Reality Show' [A Reality Show with Life]. *Mathrubhumi Illustrated Weekly* 86, no. 9 (2008): 22–6.

———. 'Jumbo Minorities'. *Conservation and Society* 8, no. 2 (2010): 151–2.

———. 'Performing Bodies, Physical Cultures: Looking at the Circus Kalaris in Malabar'. *Social Science Probings* 22, no. 1 (June 2010): 69–91.

———. 'India Circus Images'. *The Circus Historical Society Newsletter* 4, no. 3 (June 2013): 3–4.

———. 'A Tight Rope Walk: Chronicle of a Circus Trade Union'. *Social Scientist* 42, no. 3–4 (March–April 2014): 91–103.

———. 'Ban and Benevolence: Circus, Animals and Indian State'. *Indian Economic and Social History Review* 54, no. 2 (2017): 239–66.

———. 'The Circus Man Who Knew Too Much'. *Economic and Political Weekly* 52, no. 34 (2017): 18–19.

Padmanabhan, Thalayi. 'Sarkassukar Ayitha Jathikkar' [Circus Workers Untouchable Caste]. *Circus Worker* 1, no. 4 (July 1980): 15–16.

Paikkatt, Sreedharan. 'Sri: M K Raman Teacher'. *Circus Worker* 1, no. 2 (1980): 14–17, 20.

———. 'Miss Gloria'. *Circus Worker* 1, no. 3 (1980): 6.

Pandian, M. S. S. 'Gendered Negotiations: Hunting and Colonialism in Late 19th Century Nilgiris'. *Contributions to Indian Sociology* 29, no. 1–2 (January–December 1995): 239–63.

Panikkar, K. N. 'Indigenous Medicine and Cultural Hegemony: A Study of the Revitalization Movement in Keralam'. *Studies in History* 8, no. 2 (August 1992): 283–308.

Parameswaran, Venkulam. 'Sthreekalum Yogabhyasavum' [Women and Yoga Exercises]. *Mathrubhumi Illustrated Weekly* 35, no. 14 (1957): 35–6.

Peter, Joseph. 'Thallu Kondittilla Phalam!' [No Use of Beatings!]. *Circus Worker* 1, no. 5 (August 1980): 5–7.

Phillips, Anne, and Taylor Barbara. 'Sex and Skill: Notes towards a Feminist Economics'. *Feminist Review* no. 6 (1980): 79–88.

Photograph. *Mathrubhumi Illustrated Weekly* 35, no. 16 (1957): 13.

Pierre, Nora. 'Between Memory and History: *Les Lieux de Memoire*'. Translated by Marc Roudebush. *Representations* 26, no. 7 (1989): 7–24.

Pothuval, R. V. 'Keralathile Kalari' [Kalari in Kerala]. *M N Nair Masika* 3, no. 2 (September–October 1937): 102–6.

Radhakrishna, Meena. 'Civil Society's Uncivil Acts: Dancing Bear and Starving Kalandar'. *Economic and Political Weekly* 42, no. 42 (October 2007): 1–7.

Raghavan, K. V. 'Indiayile Thozhil Niyamanhalum Circus Thozhilalikalum' [Labour Laws in India and the Circus Workers]. *Circus Worker* 1, no. 2 (May 1980): 22–3.

———. 'Circus Jeevanakkarude Durithanhal Annum Innum' [Problems of Circus Workers: Yesterday and Today]. *Circus Worker* 1, no. 11–12 (February–March 1981): 18–20.

———. 'Kalayum Kalaaswadakarum' [Art and Spectators]. *Circus Worker* l, no. 3 (June 1980): 28–30.

Raghavan, Thayath. 'Kalakeralathinte Romancham' [The Thrill of Kerala Art Scene]. *Circus Worker* 1, no. 3 (1980): 7–12.

Rajan, Palayad. 'Jeevithamenna Circus' [Life that is Circus]. *Circus Worker* 1, no. 11–12 (February–March 1981): 4–5.

Ramachandran, Nedunhanda. 'Circus Koodarathil' [In the Circus Tent]. *Janayugam Weekly* 44, no. 12 (June 1969): 20–4.

Ramani, Thalassery. 'Circussile Ring Boyikal' [Ring Boys in the Circus]. *Circus Worker* 1, no. 5 (August 1980): 14–17.

———. 'Circus Kalakarikalekkurich Oralpam' [A Little about Circus Women Artistes]. *Circus Worker* 1, no. 3 (August 1980): 27–8.

Rosselli, John. 'The Self-Image of Effeteness: Physical Education and Nationalism in Nineteenth-Century Bengal'. *Past & Present* 86 (February 1980): 121–48.

Shankar, M. V. 'Circus in USSR: Impressions of my Russian Tour'. *Big Top* 1, no. 1 (October 1965): 20–4.

Sivasundaram, Sujit. 'Trading Knowledge: The East India Company's Elephants in India and Britain'. *The Historical Journal* 48, no. 1 (2005): 27–63.

Sreejith, K. 'Leisure in Colonial Malabar'. *Exploring History: A Journal of Indian and Asian History* 3–4, no. 1–2 (January–June 2013): 1–19.

Sreeraman, V. K. 'Kandambulli Balan'. *Bhashaposhini* (September 2014): 43–6.

Stephen, J. F. 'Maattuvin Chattangale' [Change the Rules]. *Circus Worker* 1, no. 1 (April 1980).

———. 'Indian Circus Employees Union: Uthbhavavum Pravarthana Panthavum' [Indian Circus Employees Union: Origin and Functions]. *Circus Worker* Annual Issue (1981): 136–7, 139.

Surendran. 'Koodara Smaranakalude Thanalil' [In the Shade of Tent Memories]. *Kalakaumudi* no. 280 (4 January 1981): 15–21.

———. 'Thambil Maranam Vithacha Theenaambukal' [The Fire Flames Which Sow Death in the Tent]. *Kalakaumudi* no. 287 (22 February 1981): 4–6.

Swart, Sandra. '"The World the Horses Made": A South African Case Study of Writing Animals into Social History'. *International Review of Social History* no. 55 (August 2010): 241–63.

Talwar, Amrita. 'Go Home Teddy'. *Outlook*, 30 October 2006, pp. 48–50.

'Union News'. *Circus Worker* 1, no. 1 (July 1980):

Vasudevan, K. 'Sree Subrahmanya Buva: A *Yoga* Expert'. *Mathrubhumi Illustrated Weekly* 31, no. 11 (May 1953): 18–23, 38.

Watt, Carey. 'The Meaning and Legacy of Physical Culturist Eugene Sandow's Visit to India in 1904–5'. Paper presented at the international conference on 'Physical Cultures: Bengal and Beyond', Jadavpur University, Kolkata, 21–2 February 2014.

Werner, Rammert. 'Where the Action Is: Distributed Agency between Humans, Machines, and Programs'. Technical University Technology Studies Working Papers, TUTS-WP-4-2008.

Published and Unpublished Books Works

Achuthanunni, C. *Bharam Vahikkunna Kuunanmarum Circusssukaran Rajavum* [The Little People who Bear the Load and the Circus King]. Kottayam: Vidyarthimithram Book Depot, 1963.

Albrecht, Ernest. *The Contemporary Circus: Art of the Spectacular*. Plymouth: Scarecrow, 2006.

Alter, Joseph S. *The Wrestler's Body: Identity and Ideology in North India*. Chicago: Chicago University Press, 1992.

———. *Yoga in Modern India: The Body between Science and Philosophy*. New Jeresy: Princeton, 2004.

Anderson, Kay. 'Animals, Science and Spectacle in the City'. In *Animal Geographies: Place, Politics, and Identity in the Nature–Culture Borderlands*, edited by Jennifer Wolch and Jody Emel. London and New York: Verso, 1998.

Ansari, M. T. 'In the Interstices of India: Islam and the Processes of Narration'. Doctoral dissertation, Central Institute of English and Foreign Languages, Hyderabad, 2002.

Arnold, David. *The New Cambridge History of India: Science, Technology and Medicine III: Science, Technology and Medicine in Colonial India*. Cambridge: Cambridge University Press, 2004.

Assael, Brenda. *The Circus and Respectable Society in Victorian Britain*. Doctoral dissertation, University of Toronto, Canada, 1998.

Balachandran, G. *Globalising Labour? Indian Seafarers and the World Shipping; C. 1870–45*. New Delhi: Oxford University Press, 2012.

Balakrishnan, P. *Kalaripayatt: The Ancient Martial Art of Kerala*. Trivandrum: CVN Kalari, 1995.

Balakrishnan, Vijayalakshmi. *Growing Up and Away: Narratives of Indian Childhoods, Memory, History and Identity*. New Delhi: Oxford University Press, 2011.

Barthes, Roland. *Mythologies*. New York: Farrar, Straus and Giroux, 1972.

Baston, Kim. 'Circus Music: The Eye of the Ear'. In *The Routledge Circus Studies Reader*, edited by Peta Tait and Katie Lavers. London and New York: Routledge, 2016.

Basu, Abanindra Krishna. *Bangalir Sarkus* [*Bengali Circuses*]. Calcutta: Publicity Studio, 1936.

Bhaskaran, Theodore S. *Trade Unionism in South Indian Film Industry*. Working Paper 36. Noida: V. V. Giri National Labour Institute, 2002.

Bhaskaranunni, P. *Keralam Irupatham Noottandinte Aaarambhathil* [*Kerala at the Beginning of Twentieth Century*]. Thrissur: Kerala Sahitya Academy, 2000.

Bouissac, Paul. *Circus and Culture: A Semiotic Approach*. Bloomington: Indiana University Press, 1976.

Brereton, Bridget. 2001. 'Gendered Testimony: Autobiographies, Diaries and Letters by Women as Sources for Caribbean History'. In *Slavery, Freedom and Gender: The Dynamics of Carribean Society*, edited by Brian L. Moore, Carl Campbell, and Bryan Patrick. Jamaica: University of West Indies Press, 2001.

Bryant, Levi. *The Democracy of Objects*. Ann Arbor: Open Humanities Press, 2011.

Butalia, Urvashi. *The Other Side of Silence: Voices from the Partition of India*. New Delhi: Viking, 1998.

Carmeli, Yoram. *Family and Economics in an English Circus: 1975–79*. Doctoral cissertation, University of London, 1985.

Chakrabarty, Dipesh. *Rethinking Working Class History: Bengal, 1890–40*. New Jersey: Princeton University Press, 2000.

———. *Provincializing Europe: Postcolonial Thought and Historical Difference*. New Delhi: Oxford University Press, 2001.

Chambers, Paul. *Jumbo: The Greatest Elephant in the World*. London: Andre Deutsch, 2007.

Champad, Sreedharan. *Circusinte Lokam* [*The World of Circus*]. Kozhikode: Mathrubhumi, 2008.

———. *An Album of Indian Big Tops*. Houston: Strategic Books, 2013.

Champad, Sreedharan, and Suresh V. K. *Thamb Paranja Jeevitham* [*Life Told by Tent*]. Kottayam: DC Books, 2012.

Chan, Jackie, and Yang Jeff. *I am Jackie Chan: My Life in Action*. New York: Ballantine Books, 1998.

Chandavarkar, Rajnarayan. *The Origins of Industrial Capitalism in India Business Strategies and the Working Classes in Bombay, 1900–40*. Cambridge: Cambridge University Press, 1994.

Chari, A. S. R. *Memoirs of an Unrepentant Communist*. Bombay: Orient Longman, 1975.

Chaturvedi, Vinayak. 'Vinayak and Me: Hindutva and the Politics of Naming'. In *The Indian Postcolonial: A Critical Reader*, edited by Elleke Boehmer and Rosinka Chaudhuri. New York: Routledge, 2011.

Chelambra, C. M. Musthafa Haji. *Mappilah Khalasi Kadha Parayunnu* [*Mappilah Khalasi Telling the Tale*]. Kozhikode: Pratheeksha Books, 2011.

Chentharassery, T. H. P. *Ayyankali*. Thiruvananthapuram: Prabhath, 2009.

Chirakkal, T. Sreedharan Nair. *Kalaripayatt: Complete Guide to Kerala's Ancient Martial Art*. Chennai: Westland, 2007.

Chitrabhanu, Vaikom. *Magikkinte Lokam* [*The World of Magic*]. Kottayam: NBS, 1974.

Chungath, Rajan. *Aana Manushyante Aathmakatha: Dr K. Radhakrishna Kamailude Jeevitham* [*The Autobiography of the Elephant Man: The Life of Dr K. Radhakrishna Kaimal*]. Kozhikode: Mathrubhumi Books, 2015.

Cowie, Helen. *Exhibiting Animals in Nineteenth Century Britain: Empathy, Education, Entertainment*. London: Palgrave, 2014.

Damodaran, Nettoor P. *Anubhavachurulukal* [*Folds of Memory*]. Kottayam: NBS, 1987.

Daniel, Noel. *The Circus, 1870s–1950s*. Los Angeles: Taschen, 2008.

Davis, Janet M. *The Circus Age: Culture & Society Under the American Big Top*. Chapel Hill: University of North Carolina Press, 2002.

———. *The Gospel of Kindness: Animal Welfare and the Making of Modern America*. New York: Oxford University Press, 2016.

Deval, Bandopant. *Circus Barobal Chaleez* [*Along with Circus for Forty Years*]. Mumbai: Majestic, 1982.

De Vere, Allen James. *Swahili Origins: Swahili Culture and the Shungwaya Phenomenon*. Nairobi: East African Educational Publishers, 1993.

Dhotre, Damoo. *The Wild Animal Man*. Boston and Toronto: Little, Brown and Company, 1961.

Divyabhanusinh. *The End of a Trail: The Cheetah in India*. New Delhi: Oxford University Press, 1999.

Dvinsky, Emmanuel. *Durov and His Performing Animals*. Moscow: Foreign Languages Publishing House, 1960.

Fawcett, F. *Nayars of Malabar*. Madras: Government Press, 1915.

Gangadharan, Thikkurissi. *Puthariyankam*. Thiruvananthapuram: The State Language Institute, 1984.

Gebel-Williams, Gunther, and Toni Reinhold. *Untamed: The Autobiography of the Circus's Greatest Animal Trainer*. New York: Williams Murrow and Company, 1991.

Guha, Ramachandra. *The States of Indian Cricket: Anecdotal Histories*. New Delhi: Permanent Black, 2005.

Guha, Ranajit. *Elementary Aspects of Peasant Insurgency in Colonial India*. New Delhi: Oxford University Press, 1999.

Harman, Graham. *Towards Speculative Realism*. Washington: Zero Books, 2010.

Hediger. H. *The Psychology and Behaviour of Animals in Zoos and Circuses*. New York: Dover, 1962.

Henderson, J. Y. *Circus Doctor*. Boston: Little, Brown and Company, 1951.

Hunter, W. W. *The Indian Empire: Its People, History and Products, 1886*. New Delhi and Chennai: AES, 2009.

Innes, C. A. *Malabar Gazetteer-Vol. I and II*. Thiruvananthapuram: Kerala Gazetteers Department, 1997 [1908].

International Encyclopedia of Dance, Vol. 2. New York: Oxford University Press, 1998.

International Tiger Studbook. Leipzig: Zoologischer Garten Leipzig, 2002.

Irving, John. *A Son of the Circus*. New York: Ballentine Books, 1994.

Isaac, Thomas, Richard W. Franke, and Pyaralal Raghavan. *Democracy at Work in an Indian Industrial Cooperative: The Story of Kerala Dinesh Beedi*. London and Ithaca: Cornell University Press, 1998.

Iyer, L. K. Ananthakrishna. *The Mysore Tribes and Castes, Vol. III*. Mysore: Mysore University Press, 1930.

Jack, Dana C., and Anderson Kathryn. 'Learning to Listen: Interview Techniques and Analyses'. In *The Oral History Reader*, edited by Robert Perks and Alistair Thompson, 157–71. London and New York: Routledge, 1998.

Jamie, Skidmore. 'Defying Death: Children in the Indian Circus'. In *Entertaining Children: The Participation of Youth in the Entertainment Industry*, edited by Gillian Arrighi and Victor Emeljanow, 219–33. New York: Palgrave Macmillan, 2014.

Jamieson, David, and Davidson Sandy. *The Love of the Circus*. London: Octopus, 1980.

John, N. G. *Cinemayum Njanum: 70 Varshangal [Cinema and Me: 70 Years]*. Kottayam: DC Books, 2012.

Johny, K. J., and Venugopal C. *Cinemayude Kalpadukal [Footsteps of Cinema]*. Thrissur: Current Books, 2009.

Kaliyadan, Ratheesh, ed. *Circus: Reports on Circus*. Thalassery: Government Girls' H.S.S., Thalassery, 2010.

Kandambulli, Balan. *Circus*. Kottayam: NBS, 1961.

Karlekar, S. S. *Circusichya Jagaat* [*The World of Circus*]. Mumbai: Majestic, 1961.

Karlekar, S. S. *Grand Circus*. Mumbai: Majestic, 1964.

Karunakara, Menon Pannikkotta. *Dakshinendyayile Jaathikal* [*Castes in South India*]. Calicut: Vidya Vilasam, 1915.

Khamkar, Subhash P. *Entertainment Tax in Maharashtra State: Its Economic Impact and Analysis*. Maharashtra: University of Mumbai, 2000.

Kiley-Worthington, Marthe. *Animals in Circuses and Zoos: Chiron's World?* Essex: Little Eco-Farms, 1990.

Krishnan, Nair Kalamandalam. *Ente Jeevitham Arangilum Aniyarayilum* [*My Life on Stage and Backstage*]. Kottayam: DC Books, 1991.

Krishnapillai, Thoppil. *Ezhayiram Raavukal* [*Seven Thousand Nights*]. Kottayam: Current Books, 1996.

Kumar, Udaya. 'Self, Body and Inner Sense: Some Reflections on Sree Narayana Guru and Kumaran Asan'. In *The Indian Postcolonial*, edited by Elleke Boehmer and Rosinka Chaudhari, 214–37. London and New York: Routledge, 2011.

Kunhappa, C. H. *Smaranakal Maatram* [*Memories Only*]. Thrissur: Current Books, 2000.

Kurup, K. K. N. *Samooham, Charithram, Samskaram* [*Society, History, Culture*]. Kozhikode: Poorna Publications, 1990.

Kwint, Marius. 'Circus and Nature in Late Georgian England'. In *Histories of Leisure*, edited by Rudy Koshar, 45–60. New York: Oxford University Press, 2002.

Lane, Margaret Stuart. *The Big Book of Animal Stories*. London: Oxford University Press, 1928.

Latour, Bruno. *We Have Never Been Modern*. Cambridge: Harvard University Press, 1993.

Llosa, Mario Vargas. *The War of the End of the World*. London: Faber and Faber, 2004.

Madhavan, M. *Social Reform Movements in Malabar*. PhD Dissertation, University of Calicut, Kerala, 2010.

Madhavan, Harilal. *Home to Market: Responses of Ayurvedic and Unani Formularies Production from 1830s to 1920s*. Working Paper 408, Centre for Development Studies, Trivandrum, 2008.

Mani, S. Kunnukuzhi, and Anirudhan P. S. *Mahthama Ayyankali*. Kottayam: DC Books, 2013.

Mathew, Bina, ed. *Balarama Digest*. Kottayam: MM, 2005.

Mathew, Rosmin. *Kalaripayattu: Ankathattum Rangavediyum* [*Kalaripayatt: Combat Space and Performing Stage*]. Thiruvananthapuram: The State Language Institute, 2009.

Mayer, Charles. *Trapping Wild Animals in Malay Jungle*. New York: Duffield.

Menon, Dilip M. *Caste, Nationalism and Communism in South India: Malabar, 1900–1948.* Cambridge: Cambridge University Press, 1994.

Menon, Sreedhara A. *Kerala District Gazeteers: Canannore.* Trivandrum: Government Press, 1972.

Military Department, USA. *Tent Pitching.* Washington: Military Department, 1956.

Morgenstern, Erin. *The Night Circus.* London: Harvill Secker, 2011.

Mukherjee, Hrishikesh. *Censorship of Films.* Pune: Board of Extra-Mural Studies, University of Pune, 1982.

Muthiah S. *A Madras Miscellany.* Chennai: East West, 2011.

Nair, Sreehari. *Gemini Shankaran & the Legacy of Indian Circus.* Thalassery: Gayathri Designs and Promotions, 2013.

Namboodiripad, E. M. S. *History, Society and Land Relation.* New Delhi: Left Word, 2010.

Nance, Susan. *Entertaining Elephants: Animal Agency and the Business of the American Circus.* Baltimore: Johns Hopkins University Press, 2013.

Organization of African Unity and the United Nations Children's Fund. *Africa's Children, Africa's Future: Background Sectoral Papers.* New York and Addis Ababa: OAU and UNCF, 1992.

Padmanabhapillai, G. Sreekanteswaram. *Sabdataravali.* Kottayam: NBS, 1983 [1923].

Pillai, A. K. B. *The Culture of Social Stratification/Sexism: The Nayars.* Massachusetts: Copley, 1987.

Pillai, M. S. Koothattukulam. *Mrigasalayil [In the Zoo], Vol. I.* Kottayam: NBS, 1962.

———. *Mrigasalayil [In the Zoo], Vol. II.* Kottayam. NBS, 1963.

Pillai, N. Parameswara. *Coffee Housinte Katha [The Story of Coffee House].* Thrissur: Current Books, 2005.

Pillai, N. N. *Njan [Me].* Kottayam: Current Books, 2012.

Plumb, Christopher. *Exotic Animals in Eighteenth-Century Britain.* PhD dissertation, University of Manchester, U.K., 2010.

Prakash, Gyan. *Mumbai Fables,* Delhi: Harper Collins, 2010.

Rajendrababu, K. *Nammude Museum [Our Museum].* Trivandrum: Directorate of Public Relations, 1978.

Rama, Warrier N. V. *Njangalude Kunjettan [Our Brother].* Kottayam: Current Books, 2000.

Ramachandran, Nair G. Pattom. *Thiruvananthapuratthinte Ithihasam [The Legend of Thiruvananthapuram].* Thiruvananthapuram: Sahityavedi, 1996.

Rammohan, K. T. *Tales of Rice: Kuttanad, Southwest India.* Thiruvananthapuram: Centre for Development Studies, 2006.

Ramanan, Mohan. *Nineteenth Century Indian English Prose: A Selection.* New Delhi: Sahitya Akademi, 2004.

Rangarajan, Mahesh. *India's Wildlife History: An Introduction*. Delhi: Permanent Black, 2001.

Rangarajan, Mahesh. 'Region's Honour, Nation's Pride: Gir's Lions on the Cusp of History'. In *The Lions of India*, edited by Divyabhanusinh, 252–61. Delhi: Black Kite, 2008.

Rangarajan, Mahesh, Ajay Desai, R. Sukumar, P. S. Easa, Vivek Menon, S. Vincent, Suparna Ganguly, B. K. Talukdar, Brijendra Singh, Divya Mudappa, Sushant Chowdhary, and A. N. Prasad. *Gajah: Securing the Future of Elephants in India: The Report of the Elephant Task Force*. New Delhi: Ministry of Environment and Forests, 2010.

Robinson, Philip T. *Life at the Zoo: Behind the Scenes with Animal Doctors*. New York: Columbia University Press, 2004.

S., Sanjeev. 'On Castes, Malayalams and Translations'. *Translation in Asia: Theories, Histories, Practices*, edited by Ronit Ricci and Jan van der Putten. Oxon and New York: Routledge, 2014.

Sankaran, Gemini, and Thaha Madayi. *Malakkam Mariyunna Jeevitham* [*Somersaulting Life*]. Kottayam: DC Books, 2012.

Sankaran, Namboodiripad Kanippayyur. *Ente Smaranakal II* [*My Reminiscences*]. Kunnamkulam: Panchangam, 2005.

Saramago, Jose. *The Elephant's Journey*. London: Harvill Secker, 2010.

Sasidharan, P. K. 'Kalarippayatt: Performance Paradigm as Aesthetics and Politics of Invisibility'. In *Performers and Their Arts: Folk, Popular and Classical Genre in a Changing India*, edited by Simon C. Charlesley and Laxmi Narayan Kadekar, 164–80. New Delhi: Routledge, 2006.

Scigliano, Eric. *Love, War and Circuses: The Age-Old Relationship between Elephants and Humans*. Boston and New York: Houghton and Mifflin, 2002.

Scott, James. *The Art of Not Being Governed: An Anarchic History of Upland Southeast Asia*. New Haven: Yale University Press, 2009.

Seizer, Susan. *Stigmas of the Tamil Stage: An Ethnography of Special Drama Artists in South India*. Durham: Duke University Press, 2005.

Sharma, Jyotirmaya. *Terrifying Vision: M S Golwalker, the RSS and India*. New Delhi: Penguin/Viking, 2007.

Shirolker, Shyamala. *Circus! Circus!* Pune: Sri Iswaryaganesh Publications, 2004.

Singer, Peter, ed. *In Defense of Animals*. New York: Harper and Row, 1986.

Sinha, Mrinalini. *Colonial Masculinity: The Manly Englishman and the Effeminate Bengali in the Late Nineteenth Century*. New York: Manchester University Press, 1995.

Sivadasamenon, M. P. *Malabarile Shikar* [*Hunting in Malabar*]. Palghat: Udaya Publications, 1959.

Sorcar, P. C. *History of Magic*. Calcutta: Indrajal, 1970.

Spencer, Moore. *From Magazines to Twitter Memes: The Visual Methods of Animal Activist Social Movements 1860–2018*. Canada: Queens University, 2018.

Sriraman, V. K. 'Nayattinu Poya Narayanan Nambuthiri'. In *Pumulli Aaram Thamburan* [The Sixth Lord of Pumulli], edited by V. K. Sriraman, 90–4. Kozhikode: Mathrubhumi, 2013.

Stearns, Peter N. *Childhood in World History*. New York and London: Routledge, 2011.

Sunandan, Kizhakke Nedumpally. *Ways of Knowing: Asaris, Nampoothiris and Colonialists in Twentieth Century Malabar, India*. PhD dissertation, Emory University, Atlanta, 2012.

Tait, Peta. *Wild and Dangerous Performances: Animals, Emotions, Circus*. London: Palgrave Macmillan, 2011.

Tait, Peta, and Katie Lavers, eds. *The Routledge Circus Studies Reader*. London and New York: Routledge, 2016.

Thani, Lokesh. *Skills and Tactics: Gymnastics*. Delhi: Sports Publications, 1999.

The New Encyclopedia Britannica, Vol. 16. Chicago: Encyclopedia Britannica, 1998.

Thikkodian. *Arangu Kanatha Nadan* [*Actor Who Had Never Been on the Stage*]. Kottayam: DC Books, 2008.

Thomas, Keith. *Man and the Natural World: Changing Attitudes in England 1500–1800*. Harmondsworth: Penguin Books, 1983.

Thompson, Paul. 'The Voice of the Past: Oral History'. In *The Oral History Reader*, edited by Robert Perks and Alistair Thompson. London and New York: Routledge, 1998.

Trautman, Thomas R. 'Towards a Deep History of Mahouts'. In *Conflict, Negotiation and Coexistence: Rethinking Human–Elephant Relations in South Asia*, edited by Piers Locke and Jane Buckingham, 47–74. New Delhi: Oxford University Press, 2016.

Varghese, Joyiamma. *Problems of Retired Circus Artists in Thalassery*. MA dissertation, Calicut University, Kerala, 1992.

Varghese, Molly. *Dynamics of Trade Unionism in Kerala with View to Find Gandhian Alternative to the Industrial Problems in Kerala*. PhD dissertation, Mahatma Gandhi University, Kerala, 2000.

Varma, Surendra, Sujata S. R., Suparna Ganguly, and Shiela Rao. *Captive Elephants in Circuses: A Scientific Investigation of the Population Status, Management and Welfare Significance*. Bangalore: Compassion Unlimited Plus Action, 2008.

Vasudevagurukkal, E. P. Kadathuruthi. *Kalaripayatt: Keralathinte Thanathu Ayodhanakala* [*Kalaripayatt: The Original Martial Art of Kerala*]. Kottayam: DC Books, 2000.

Vasudevan, Nair M. T. *Ramaneeyam Oru Kalam* [*Beautiful Times*]. Thiruvananthapuram: Maluben, 1998.

Veeraraghavan, D. *The Making of the Madras Working Class*. New Delhi: Left Word, 2013.

Velu, Pillai T. K. *The Travancore State Manual, Vol. IV*. Trivandrum: Government of Travancore, 1940.

Venkatachalapathy, A. R. *In Those Days There Was No Coffee: Writings in Cultural History*. New Delhi: Yoda Press, 2006.

Vijayakumar, K. *Kalaripayatt: Keralathinte Sakthiyum Soundaryavum* [*Kalaripayatt: Strength and Beauty of Kerala*]. Trivandrum: Department of Cultural Publications, 2000.

Vijayan, M. N. *Nammude Sahityam Nammude Samooham* [*Our Literature, Our Society*] *1901–2000, Vol. 2* . Thrissur: Kerala Sahithya Academy, 2000.

Vijayaraghavan, K. 'Kalaripayattinte Eettillam' [The Birth Place of Kalaripayatt]. In *Malabar: Paithrukavum Prathapavum*, edited by P. B. Salim, N. P. Hafiz Muhammed, and M. C. Vasishtt, 517–19. Kozhikode: Mathrubhumi, 2011.

Vijayaraghavan, K. C., and Jayasree K. M. *Sree Lokanarkavu*. Vadakara: Malabar Devaswam Board, 2011.

Visscher, Jacob Canter. *Letters from Malabar*. Madras: Adelphi Press, 1862.

Walimbe, Praveen Prabhakar. *The World of Circus*. Pune: Tanaya-Esha, 2003.

Williams, Jean. *Themes for Educational Gymnastics*. London: Lepus, 1974.

Zarrilli, Philip B. *When Body Becomes All Eyes: Paradigms, Discourses, Practices of Power in Kalaripayattu, a South Indian Martial Art*. New Delhi: Oxford University Press, 1998.

Internet Sources

'1981 Bangalore Circus Fire'. *Wikipedia.org*, 23 November 2012. Available at http://en.wikipedia.org/wiki/1981_Bangalore_circus_fire. Accessed on 23 November 2012.

'Advisory Body Seeks Ban on All Circus Animals, 2013'. *Indian Express*. Available at http://www.indianexpress.com/news/advisory-body-seeks-ban-on-all-circus-animals/1163341/. Accesed on 18 November 2013.

'Alasdair Cochrane: Making Animal Rights Inclusive'. *Columbia University Press Blog*, 2013. Available at http://www.cupblog.org/?p=8131#more-8131. Accessed on 5 August 2014.

'American Circus Lingo'. *Goodmagic.com*, 2008. Available at http://www.good-magic.com/ carny/c_a.htm. Accessed on 10 June 2014.

'American Federation of Labor–Congress of Industrial Organizations (AFL-CIO)'. *Britannica.com*, 2013. Available at http://www.britannica.com/EBchecked/topic/19681/American-Federation-of-Labor-Congress-of-Industrial-Organizations-AFL-CIO. Accessed on 1 December 2013.

'Animals in Entertainment'. *Adinternational.org*, 2010. Available at http://www.adinternational.org/animals_in_entertainment/go.php?id=212&ssi=10. Accessed on 30 July 2014.

'Animals Rescued, Circuses Banned, India'. *Divine.org*, 2001. Available at http://www.indiadivine.org/content/topic/1928663-animals-rescued-circuses-banned/. Accessed on 30 July 2012.

Banerjee, Santanu. 'Death Stalks Last of The Tigon Species'. *Indian Express*, 1998. Available at http://expressindia.indianexpress.com/ie/daily/19980708/18950374.html. Accessed on 17 September 2014.

'Bolivia Bans all Circus Animals'. *The Guardian*, 2009. Available at http://www.theguardian.com/ world/2009/jul/31/bolivia-bans-circus-animals. Accessed on 23 March 2012.

'Central Zoo Authority, Rescue and Rehabilitation'. *Central Zoo Authority*, 2013. Available at http://www.cza.nic.in/rescue.html.Accessed on 12 January 2013.

Chakraborty, Tabas. 'Circus Ends, Nightmare Begins for Animals'. *Telegraph India*, 2001. Available at http://www.telegraphindia.com/1010725/front_pa.htm. Accessed on 29 July 2014.

Champad, Sreedharan. 'History of Circus'. *The Big Top*. Author's blog, 2009. Available at http://sreedharanchampad.blogspot.in/search?q=home. Accessed on 20 November 2012.

'Children in Africa: Key Statistics on Child Survival, Protection and Development'. *Unicef.org*, 2015. Available at https://data.unicef.org/wp-content/uploads/2015/12/Children-in-Africa-Brochure-Nov-23-HR_245.pdf. Accessed on 15 January 2019.

'Child Rescue Nepal'. *Childrescuenepal.org*, 2018. Available at https://www.childrescuenepal.org/. Accessed on 15 January 2019.

Choorakkody, Kalari Sangham. Author's blog, 2008. Available at http://choorakkodykalari.com/ kalari2.html. Accessed on 23 March 2014.

'Circus Employees in Mexico City Protest over Animal Ban'. *BBC*, 2014. Available at https://www.bbc.com/news/world-latin-america-27788291. Accessed on 28 November 2018.

'CircusFit: FUNdamentals of Fitness'. *Circusfit.com*, 2005. Available at http://www.circusfit.com. Accessed on 23 December 2013.

'Circus History Message & Discussion Board'. *Circus Historical Society*, 2003. Available at http://www.circushistory.org/Query/Query06g.htm. Accessed on 2 February 2014.

'Circus Kathmandu: Nepal's First and Only Contemporary Circus'. *Circuskathmandu.com*, 2018. Available at *http://www.circuskathmandu.com*. Accessed on 11 January 2018.

'Circus poster: Full Grown Living Tiger. Available at https://www.bl.uk/collection-items/circus-poster-full-grown-living-tiger. Accessed on 22 September 2014.

'Cirque du Soleil comes to India with the world premiere of Bazzar'. *India Today*, 2018. Available at https://www.indiatoday.in/lifestyle/what-s-hot/story/cirque-du-soleil-comes-to-mumbai-and-delhi-with-the-world-premiere-of-bazzar-1320244-2018-08-22. Accessed on 14 January 2018.

'Cirque School in Hollywood'. Available at http://content.time.com/time/photogallery/0,29307,2108216_2337801,00.html. Accessed 7 March 2014.

Cochrane, Alasdair. 'Animal Welfare vs. Animal Rights: A False Dichotomy'. *Centre for Animals and Social Justice*, 2013. Available at http://www.casj.org.uk/blogs-archive/animal-welfare-vs-animal-rights-false-dichotomy/. Accessed on 5 August 2014.

'Donovan, D. G., and R. K. Puri. 'Learning from Traditional Knowledge of Non-timber Forest Products: Penan Benalui and the Autecology of *Aquilaria* in Indonesian Borneo'. *Ecology and Society* 9, no. 3 (2004). Available at http://www.ecologyandsociety.org/vol9/iss3/art3. Accessed on 18 October 2014.

'Counter Punch'. 1996. Available at http://www.counterpunch.org/2011/01/18/a-message-from-tatiana. Accessed on 16 September 2014.

'Discovering Literature: Romantics and Victorians, The British Library'. Available at http://www.bl.uk/romantics-and-victorians/search?q. Accessed on 22 September 2014.

'Drill'. Encyclopedia Britannica. Available at https://www.britannica.com/topic/drill-military. Accessed on 11 March 2014.

'Ek Choti Si Love Story…'. *Deccan Herald*, 2012. Available at http://www.deccanherald.com/content/ 243568/F. Accessed on 16 November 2013.

'Equity'. Available at https://www.equity.org.uk/about-us/. Accessed on 1 December 2013.

'Esther Benjamin Trust'. 2014. Available at http://www.ebtrust.org.uk/latest-news/circus-kathmandu-june-2014.aspx. Accessed on 30 March 2015.

'Foreword to Mary Ellen Mark's Book *Indian Circus*'. 1993. Available at http://www.maryellenmark.com/text/books/indian_circus/text001_icircus.html. Accessed on 25 August 2014.

Goldberg, Karen. 'The Hartford Circus Fire of 1944, The Concord Review'. 1990. Available at http://www.tcr.org/tcr/essays/Web_Hartford.pdf. Accessed on 23 November 2012.

'Hindustani in the 21st Century'. *Britannica.com*, 2018. Available at https://www.britannica.com/topic/Hindustani-language. Accessed on 1 December 2018.

'History of Zoos'. *Central Zoo Authority*, 2013. Available at http://www.cza.nic.in/history.html. Accessed on 30 September 2014.

Hofmeyr, Isabel. 'Object-orient Reading: The View from the Custom House'. 2018. Hofmeyr, 2018. Available at https://wiser.wits.ac.za/content/object-oriented-reading-view-ustoms-house-13048.pdf. Accessed on 28 November 2018.

'Hornberg, Alf. 'Artefacts, Agency and Global Magic: How Amazonian "Ontologies" Can Illuminate Human- Object Relations in Industrialized Modernity'. Available at hornborg_artefacts-agency-and-global-magic.pdf. Accessed on 28 November 2018.

'Human Zoos: When Real People Were Exhibits'. *BBC*, 2011. Available at http://www.bbc.co.uk/news/magazine-16295827. Accessed 28 September 2013.

'Indian Circuses Struggle to Adapt after Court Bans'. *Big Story*, 2013. Available at http://bigstory.ap.org/article/indian-circuses-struggle-adapt-after-court-bans-0. Accessed on 29 November 2013.

Iossa, G., C. D. Soulsbury, and S. Harris. 'Are Wild Animals Suited to a Travelling Circus Life?' *Save Zoo Elephants*, 2009. Available at http://www.savezooelephants.com/pdf/WILD%20ANIMALS%20IN%20CIRCUS.pdf. Accessed on 22 December 2012.

'Kalaripayatt'. 2002. Available at http://www.kalaripayattu.org/aboutus.htm. Accessed on 23 March 2014.

'Kerala State Tourism Department'. *Historic Thalassery*, 2012. Available at http://www.keralatourism.org/kerala-article/212/historic-thalassery.php. Accessed on 14 November 2012.

'Knowledge for Children in Africa: 2018 Publications Catalogue'. *Unicef-irc.org*, 2018. Available at https://www.unicef-irc.org/article/1864-knowledge-for-children-in-africa-2018-publications-catalogue-published.html. Accessed on 15 January 2019.

'Mexico Bans Wild Animals in Circuses—But There's No Place for Them to Go'. *PRI.org*, 2015. Available at https://www.pri.org/stories/2015-07-02/mexico-bans-wild-animals-circuses-theres-no-place-them-go. Accessed on 28 November 2018.

'Mexico Circus Ban "Will Leave Thousands of Tigers, Elephants and Camels Homeless"'. *International Business Times*, 2015. Available at https://www.ibtimes.co.uk/mexico-circus-ban-will-leave-thousands-tigers-elephants-camels-homeless-1492365. Accessed on 28 November 2018.

'Mexico Deadline to Ban Circus Animals Looms but Doubt Shrouds Creatures' Fate'. *The Guardian*, 2015. Available at https://www.theguardian.com/world/2015/mar/27/mexico-deadline-ban-circus-animals-looms. Accessed on 28 November 2018.

'Ministry of Social Justice and Empowerment Notification'. 2001. Available at http://envfor.nic.in/legis/awbi/awbi19.html. Accessed on 30 July 2013.

Mishra, Garima. 'Show and Tell'. *Indian Express*, 2013. Available at http://indianexpress.com/article/news-archive/web/show-and-tell-7/. Accessed on 16 October 2014.

'Mysterious Blaze Kills 186 in 1944 Connecticut Circus Horror?' *New York Daily News*, 2014. Available at http://www.nydailynews.com/news/justice-story/3-rings-death-1944-conn-circus-horror-article-1.1599269. Accessed on 25 June 2014.

Nanda, Meera. 'Not as Old as you Think'. *Open the Magazine*, 2011. Available at http://www.openthemagazine.com/article/living/not-as-old-as-you-think. Accessed on 22 December 2013.

Nisha P R 'Folding the Tent: Kerala Circus Academy'. *Economic and Political Weekly*, 11 January 2014, Web Exclusive. Available at http://www.epw.in/web-exclusives/folding-tent-kerala-circus-academy.html. Accessed on 12 January 2014.

'North Central Railway'. 2010. Available at http://www.ncr.indianrailways.gov.in/view_section.jsp?lang=0&id=0,1,283,363,682. Accessed on 10 September 2012.

Nussbaum, Martha C. 'The Moral Status of Animals'. 2006. Available at http://3quarksdaily.blogs.com/3quarksdaily/2006/02/martha_c_nussba.html. Accessed on 21 March 2012.

Oppili, P. '25 Endangered Animals Rescued From Circus'. *The Hindu*, 2002. Available at http://www.thehindu.com/thehindu/2002/03/15/stories/2002031507140300.htm. Last accessed on 23 March 2014.

Pandit, Mimasha. 'Circus, Performance, and Building of National "Self"'. *Inclusive: A Journal of Kolkata Centre for Contemporary Studies*, 2013. Available at http://theinclusive.org/feeling-national-swadeshi-circus-performance-and-building-of-national-%E2%80%98self%E2%80%99. Accessed on 23 December 2013.

Prakash, Gyan. 'Circus Animals: Ordeal Ends for a Better Deal'. *Times of India*, 2001. Available at http://timesofindia.indiatimes.com/city/patna/Circus-animals-Ordeal-ends-for-a-better-deal/articleshow/1320569066.cms. Accessed on 29 July 2014.

Rickett, Charles. *The Boswells: The Story of a South African Circus*. Circus Federation, 2003. Available at http://www.circusfederation.org/uploads/circus_culture/about/southafrica_boswells.pdf. Accessed on 19 November 2012.

'Shut Down All Zoo and Circuses in India—Sukanya Kadyan'. *Change.org*, 2009. Available at https://www.change.org/en-IN/petitions/shut-down-all-zoo-and-circuses-in-india-sukanya-kadyan. Accessed on 29 September 2014.

'Sole Survivor: World's Last Tigon Waits for Death at Calcutta Zoo'. *India Today*, 1998. Available at http://indiatoday.intoday.in/story/worlds-last-tigon-waits-for-death-at-calcutta-zoo/1/265829.html. Accessed on 17 September 2014.

'Sri Lanka Gifts Anacondas to Thiruvananthapuram Zoo'. *The Hindu*, 2014. Available at http://www.thehindu.com/sci-tech/energy-and-environment/sri-lanka-gifts-anacondas-to-thiruvananthapuram-zoo/article5893355.ece. Accessed on 22 September 2014.

'Stop Circus Suffering'. *Animal Defenders International*, December, 2014. Available at http://www.stopcircussuffering.com/news/latin-america/mexico-bans-wild-animals-circuses/. Accessed on 28 November 2018.

'Swahili Language'. Encyclopedia Britannica, 2018. Available at https://www.britannica.com/topic/Swahili-language. Accessed on 1 December 2018.

Term 'drill'. Encyclopedia Britannica. Available at http://www.britannica.com/EBchecked/topic/171618/drill. Accessed on 11 March 2014.

Term 'Circus'. *Circus Historical Society: Circus History Message & Discussion Board*, 2006. Available at http://www.circushistory.org/Query/Query06g.htm. Accessed on 18 November 2013.

'The Development of Circus Acts'. Victoria and Albert Museum, 2014. Available at http://www.vam.ac.uk/content/articles/d/development-of-circus-acts/. Accessed on 3 August 2014.

'The Easter Benjamins Memorial Foundation'. 2014. Available at https://www.unodc.org/ngo/showSingleDetailed.do?req_org_uid=22111. Accessed on 6 October 2014.

'"The Greatest Show on Earth" Going, Going, Gone'. *Labor Tribune*, 2017. Available at https://labortribune.com/the-greatest-show-on-earth-going-going-gone/. Accessed on 9 December 2018.

'The Library: Functional Yoga'. 2006. Available at http://derekosborn.account-support.com/thelibrary/id53.html. Accessed on 19 November 2013.

Thomas, Rosie. 'Still MAGIC: An Aladdin's Cave of 1950s B-Movie Fantasy'. *Tasveer Ghar: A Digital Archive of South Asian Popular Visual Culture*, 2010. Available at http://tasveerghar.net/cmsdesk/essay/103/index.html. Accessed on 12 January 2011.

'Variety at Night is Good for You'. Available at http://www.nationaltheatreofvariety.org/variety.pdf. Accessed on 1 December 2013.

Legal Documents and Case Files

Amended Writ Petition, O.P. No. 155 of 1999.

Animal Welfare Board of India, Ministry of Environment, Forests and Climate Change, Reprot [*sic*] on Inspection of Captive Elephants Used in Thrissur Pooram 2016, dated 23 April 2016.

Argument Notes, O.P. No. 2636 of 1999, *M. A. Sasidharan and others* v *Union of India and Another*.

Central Government Orders Prohibiting Sale of Animals by Zoos, G.O. No. 3-52/87/WL-1, Department of Environment, Forest and Wildlife, Government of India. Dated 28 October 1987. *The Wildlife Protection Act 1972*. 2008, 144–5.

Circular No.9-9/97-AWD, Animal Welfare Division, Ministry of Social Justice & Empowerment, Government of India, dated 23 June 2000.

G.O. dated 15 May 1980 (M.S.) No. 201/80/G.A.D, G O (M S) No. 134/2009, Department of Education, Youth and Sports, Thiruvananthapuram, dated 18 June 2009.

Judgment dated 6 June 2000, *N.R. Nair and Others* v *Union of India*, Original Petition No. 155 of 1999.

Judgment dated 20 March 2017, *Mohd. Salim* v *State of Uttarakhand and others*, Writ Petition No. 126 of 2014.

Judgment dated 4 July 2018, *Narayan Dutt Bhatt* v *Union of India*, Writ Petition No. 43 of 2014.

Minutes, 39th General Meeting of Animal Welfare Board of India, Chennai, 23 August 2013.

Notification no. F 26-7/91 PWL-I, dated 2 March 1991.

Notification File no. 9-9/97-A. W., dated 14 September 1998.

Original Petition No. 155 of 1999, *N. R. Nair and others* v *Union of India and Another*.

Report of the Committee constituted by the Ministry of Environment and Forests, Government of India, to review the ban on exhibition and training of performing animals, CWP 890/91.

Special Leave Petition (Civil) of 2000 in the matter of O.P. No. 155 of 1999 R.

The Wild Life (Protection) Act, 1972 (53 of 1972). Subs. by Act 16 of 2003, section 3 (w.e.f. 1 March 2003).

Writ Petition (C) No. 51, 2006, *Bachpan Bachao Andolan* v *Union of India & Others*.

Index

About the Author

Nisha P R received her doctorate from the University of Delhi, India. Her research was on the social history of circus and circus performances in twentieth-century south India. Her monograph *The Jumping Devils: A Tale of Circus Bodies* has been published in the Nehru Memorial Museum and Library Occasional Paper Series. Her writings have appeared, amongst others, in *Indian Economic and Social History Review, Economic and Political Weekly, Conservation and Society, Indian Journal of Gender Studies,* and *Social Science Probings.* She has been awarded the Swedish South Asia Studies Network fellowship in Lund University, Sweden, Charles Wallace India Trust Research Grant, UK, Indian Council of Historical Research Junior Research Fellowship, New Delhi, the Papiya Ghosh Memorial Trust PhD Fellowship from the Centre for Studies in Social Sciences, Kolkata, India, and Writing Fellowship from the Johannesburg Institute for Advanced Study, South Africa. She has curated 'Indian Circus: A Photo Exhibition' in at the Nehru Memorial Museum and Library in 2013 (18–24 January) and organized an international conference, *Circus Histories and Theories* (21–2 June 2018), at the Centre for Indian Studies in Africa, University of the Witwatersrand, South Africa, where she has been a Social Science Research Council Transregional Research Fellow.